AFRICOBRA

AFRIC

WADSWORTH
A. JARRELL

EXPERIMENTAL ART TOWARD
A SCHOOL OF THOUGHT

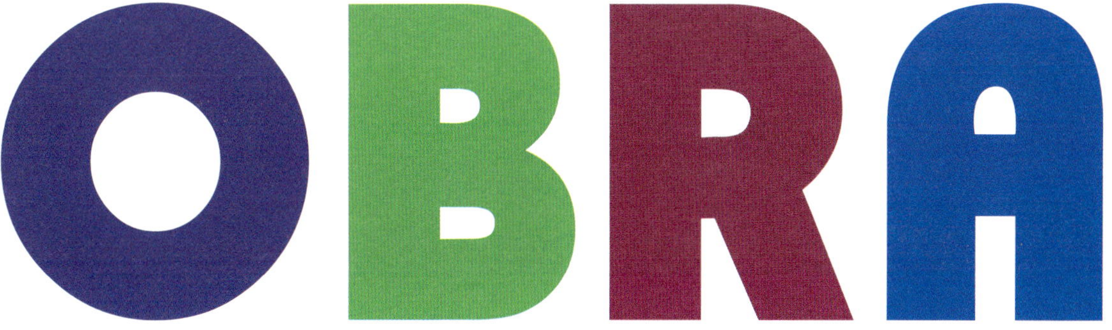

Duke University Press   Durham and London   2020

With a foreword by Richard Allen May III

Designed by Courtney Leigh Baker in Scala, Avenir, and
handdrawn type based on Bauhaus. Typeset by BW&A Books.

Library of Congress Cataloging-in-Publication Data
Names: Jarrell, Wadsworth, [date] author.
Title: AFRICOBRA : experimental art toward a school of thought /
Wadsworth Jarrell ; with a foreword by Richard Allen Mays.
Description: Durham : Duke University Press, 2020. |
Includes bibliographical references and index.
Identifiers: LCCN 2019032731 (print) | LCCN 2019032732 (ebook)
ISBN 9781478000426 (hardcover)
ISBN 9781478000563 (paperback)
ISBN 9781478002246 (ebook)
Subjects: LCSH: AFRICOBRA (Group of artists) | Black Arts movement—
Illinois—Chicago. | Ethnicity in art. | Art—Political aspects—
United States—History—20th century.
Classification: LCC N6538.N5 J37 2020 (print) | LCC N6538.N5 (ebook) |
DDC 704.9/42—dc23
LC record available at https://lccn.loc.gov/2019032731
LC ebook record available at https://lccn.loc.gov/2019032732

Cover art: *Black Prince*, 1971. Acrylic on canvas, 64 × 44 inches.
© Wadsworth Jarrell. Courtesy of the artist and Mr. and Mrs. Munson
and Christina Steed.

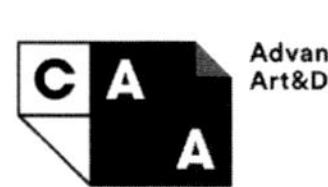

Publication of this book
has been aided by a
grant from the Wyeth
Foundation for American
Art Publication Fund of
CAA.

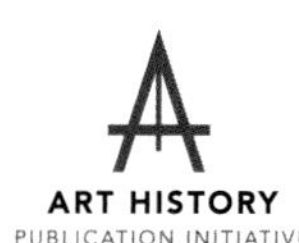

This book is made possible
by a collaborative grant
from the Andrew W. Mellon
Foundation.

To my wife, Jae, and our children, Wadsworth Jr., Jennifer, and Roslyn, who have added extra dimensions to my life.

To the AFRICOBRA artists—a very special innovative collective of righteous revolutionary image makers. And to the memory of visionary founding member Jeff R. Donaldson, 1932–2004, whose revolutionary ideas made this book a possibility.

A special dedication to the memory of my father and mother, Solomon and Tabitha Jarrell, who did not live to see important exhibitions in Chicago early in my career, including a 1961 exhibition at the Hyde Park Art Center.

MY PEOPLE

The night is beautiful

So the faces of my people.

The stars are beautiful,

So the eyes of my people.

Beautiful, also, is the sun

Beautiful, also, are the souls of my people.

Langston Hughes

Jeff R. Donaldson.

Did you hear me? I said, Jeff Richardson Donaldson!

He was a bad boy. Yes he was.

Say, what did he do?

He was awake while others were asleep.

INFLUENCED BY, AND CADENCE AND SOME WORDS BORROWED
FROM, THE POEM "BOOM BOOM," BY THE LATE POET

Gilbert Hines   RIP, MY FRIEND

1

2

3

4

5

6

7

8

9

10

Contents

AFRICOBRA PRINCIPLES AND PHILOSOPHY

COOL ADE COLOR a variegation of bright, intense colors with sensibility and harmony. This principle is parallel, derivative, and grounded in the name for the bright array of colorful clothes worn by African Americans in the sixties, described as Cool Ade colors. Further, it extends to clothing worn by Black people everywhere: South Side Chicago, Harlem, Philadelphia, Detroit, Los Angeles, Port-au-Prince, Darkar, Lagos—anywhere Black people exist.

FRONTAL IMAGES images inspired by the awesome images of African sculpture, which presents strength, directness, and dignity.

OPEN COLOR integration of subject and background to an extent where, in some instances, both become synonymous and form a synthesis stressing freedom.

POSITIVE IMAGES images committed to humanism inspired by Black people and their experiences; images dedicated to the enlightened dignity of Black people by accentuating the positive; and art that reflects and relates to African people, with which African people can identify.

ARBITRARY USE OF LIGHT AND LINE lost and found line that displays sensitivity regarding weight, broken line, and continuity, implemented to accent and delineate specific areas of finesse; reverse direction of light employed to reject the theory of a single light source from one direction.

WRITTEN STATEMENTS direct, unequivocal statements written on the picture plane and incorporated in the composition to clarify the concept; art that is imbued with a specificity of sophistication that speaks to African people and carries messages with the visual impact of a billboard—poster art.

VISIBILITY clarity of form and line based on the interesting irregularity one senses in a freely drawn circle or in an organic object; the feeling for movement, growth, changes, and human touch.

FREE SYMMETRY the syncopated rhythm pertinent to African dance, walk, and song; repetition with change, as in the African American–created blues.

PROGRAMMATIC art that teaches, preaches, and embraces concepts that offer positive and feasible solutions to our collective problems—local, national, and international.

SHINE exhibiting exemplary skills and vision in a profession; performing or executing an extraordinary feat—to shine, turn around, throw down. Also, taken literally, "shine" refers to a luster emblematic of Black lifestyles, as related to spit-shined shoes, shiny cars, glossy hairstyles, and plastic-covered furniture.

EXPRESSIVE AWESOMENESS art that does not appeal to serenity but is primarily concerned with the eternally sublime rather than ephemeral beauty; art that moves the emotions and appeals to the senses—art for the people.

MIMESIS AT MIDPOINT a composition that marks the spot where the real and the unreal, the objective and the nonobjective, the plus and the minus meet. That is a place—a living space, between absolute realism and pure abstraction—where the ambiguity of the art flirts between both genres.

HORROR VACUI a Latin phrase connoting fear of space: filling up the void of negative space by making use of the entire space of the picture plane.

movement (1) the act or process of moving; (2) a series of organized activities working toward an objective. *—Merriam-Webster's Dictionary and Thesaurus*

In 2002, I met Wadsworth Jarrell for the first time by phone. At a local library, his rendition of Malcolm X, *Black Prince*, graced the cover of an early issue of *American Visions* magazine. Reading about Jarrell inspired me to call him to learn more about his art and about AFRICOBRA. I left a message on his voicemail at his New York studio. To my surprise, he returned the call. Thirteen subsequent years filled with countless conversations, formal introductions to AFRICOBRA founding members and current members, and numerous interviews facilitated by Jarrell resulted in my delivering presentations on AFRICOBRA in college classrooms and at academic conferences. Jarrell is truly a revolutionary. Moreover, he has a visceral story to share about one of the most important events in art history—the AFRICOBRA art movement.

In *AFRICOBRA: Experimental Art toward a School of Thought,* Jarrell poignantly discusses the founding members' transformation from individual visual artists, formally trained at prominent academic institutions, to Black artists intentionally gathering and forming a collective, seeking to make an aesthetic difference within the context of the civil rights and Black power movements. It is similar to the metamorphosis of Malcolm Little to Malcolm X, Cassius Clay to Muhammad Ali, and Stokely Carmichael to Kwame Ture. Living through such turbulent times inspires change.

In a similar manner, Jarrell's text takes readers directly to the discussions and art critiques that transformed COBRA (Coalition of Black Revolutionary Artists) into the African Commune of Bad Relevant Artists. Thus, the school of AFRICOBRA was born. Most importantly, this collective included three female members, who fully participated as equals in critiques and in art exhibitions. These artists were founding members Jae Jarrell and Barbara Jones-Hogu, as well as Carolyn Lawrence, who joined COBRA in 1969.

Similar to how the blues was about more than just making music, AFRICOBRA was about far more than simply making art. For example, during the civil rights movement, television portrayed the violent and inhumane atrocities perpetrated by European Americans on African Americans peacefully protesting for their human rights as citizens. AFRICOBRA's art powerfully shouted messages of resistance, solutions, and cultural pride that were African inspired and executed with technical excellence. Jarrell's text, like an art gallery tour, brings readers face to face with such works as *Rise and Take Control*, *Unite*, and *Stop Genocide*, by Barbara Jones-Hogu; *Ebony Family*, *Revolutionary Suit*, *Urban Wall Suit*, and *Brothers Surrounding Sis*, by Jae Jarrell; *Black Prince*, *Revolutionary*, and *Liberation Soldiers*, by Wadsworth Jarrell; *Uphold Your Men* and *Black People, Get Some Land*, by Carolyn Lawrence; *God Bless the Child That's Got His Own* and *Here Comes the Judge*, by Jeff Donaldson; *Egyptian Solar* and *Cool Ade Icicles*, by Napoleon Jones-Henderson; *Towards Identity* and *Uhuru*, by Nelson Stevens; *Wake Up, Say It Loud* and *I Am Somebody*, by Gerald Williams; *Liberation*, by Howard Mallory; and *A Revolution Begins with One Black Family*, by Frank Smith.

Of significance, when Jarrell tells the story of the great *Wall of Respect* mural for the people, he discusses the formation, purpose, and role of OBAC (Organization of Black American Culture), allowing readers to understand how artists are galvanized toward playing an active role in the civil rights and Black power movements. Moreover, being a member of OBAC as well as an artist who participated in creating the mural gives Jarrell impeccable credibility to truly own, discuss, and pass on such history to future generations.

In the chapter titled "Recruitment," Jarrell demonstrates how vital the preservation and dissemination of African American visual art history is. Jeff Donaldson was the architect of CONFABA (Conference on the Functional

Aspects of Black Art), which brought together many Black art historians, important Black artists, and Black history students at Northwestern University in May 1970. Jarrell's description of the conference arguably shows that such a meeting was ahead of its time. It remains the template for future African American art conferences.

AFRICOBRA: *Experimental Art toward a School of Thought* is a remarkable text that in African American vernacular "throws down" and "keeps it real with soul." Ultimately, with his unique griot voice, Jarrell paints a history that is unapologetically Black about an art movement that used the creative tool as a weapon of change.

I am indebted to a great many people who made this book possible, to whom I would like to express my sincere appreciation. Extremely important to the inception of this book are the AFRICOBRA founding members, Jae Jarrell, Gerald Williams, and Barbara Jones-Hogu, to whom I pitched the idea of an AFRICOBRA member—someone from the inside—writing our story, which they all agreed on, consenting to taped interviews. I am also indebted to the AFRICOBRA members Napoleon Jones-Henderson, Nelson Stevens, Carolyn Lawrence, Sherman Beck, Omar Lama, Howard Mallory, and Frank Smith for consenting to taped interviews, which I relied on heavily. Importantly, I want to express my sincere gratitude posthumously to founding member Jeff Donaldson for his immeasurable and insightful contributions.

An enormous amount of appreciation is due Richard Allen May III and Michael D. Harris for undertaking the tremendous responsibility of editing this book. I am appreciative of their astute stewardship of my manuscript, offering pertinent suggestions that fine tuned, shaped, and guided this manuscript to a finished product. Many thanks to Edmund Barry Gaither for his Postscript, which contributes important and expansive knowledge regarding the Black arts movement and 1960s artistic fermentation.

I owe an enormous amount of appreciation to Ken Wissoker, editor at Duke University Press, for his interest in my manuscript; even in its raw stages, he saw historical value in it. I also want to thank Olivia Polk, Jade Brooks, Elizabeth Ault, Bonnie Perkel, and the entire editorial staff at Duke

University Press. I want to express my sincere thanks to many other people: Jameela Donaldson, for allowing me to use her father's in-depth material regarding CONFABA (Conference on Functional Aspects of Black Art); Cherilyn Wright, for consenting to a taped interview and for supplying me with pertinent written material about CONFABA; Useni Eugene Perkins; Haki Madhubuti; Teri Hines, for permission to use portions of a poem by her husband, Gilbert Hines; and the Gwendolyn Brooks Foundation, for allowing its poems to appear in this book. Thanks to Bridget Riley for permitting me to use her image in this book, and thanks to photographers Bobby Sengstacke, Roy Lewis, Gerald Williams, and David Lusenhop for furnishing their impeccable photographs. Thanks to Robert Paige for his input and for introducing Cool Ade color (AFRICOBRA's first principle), and a special thanks to Jae for her patience with me and for her invaluable knowledge and input, which were tremendously important to this book. Last but not least, I sincerely want to thank Jeffreen Hayes, scholar, Threewalls executive director, and curator, for her interest in the AFRICOBRA collective; for curating AFRICOBRA: *Messages to the People*, which was on view at the Miami Contemporary Museum of Art, North Miami, November 27, 2018–April 7, 2019; and more recently, for curating AFRICOBRA: *Nation Time*, which was selected as an official Collateral Event of the 58th international art exhibition La Biennale di Venezia, May 11–November 24, 2019, in Venice, Italy.

INTRODUCTION

One of the most enduring and significant manifestations of the Black Arts Movement of the sixties was the creation of AFRICOBRA with its compelling ideology.
—Larry Neal, "AFRICOBRA/FARAFINDUGU"

As a new consciousness, the search during the '60s and '70s was to identify the international dimensions of the rationalization of Africanism in art. Artists began to find aesthetic principles forged from the Black value system and rooted in spiritual ties to Africa. This new ideology became the basis for the Black Arts Movement, and no other group expressed more eloquently the ideas of this new doctrine than AFRICOBRA. —Eddie Granderson, "A Shared Ideology"

This book details a pro-Black revolutionary art movement formed at the pinnacle of the civil rights, Black power, and Black arts movements. This is the first comprehensive report to describe the initial structure, conversations, art, exhibitions, and philosophical constructs of AFRICOBRA (African Commune of Bad Relevant Artists), written by a founding member and archivist for the collective, a painter and photographer, who contributed significant groundbreaking iconography defining an African American aesthetic as well as recording AFRICOBRA's history in photographs. In writing this book, I have a distinct advantage over art historians, whose information is secondary, relying on what has been written by other art historians—which may or may not be accurate—and with them, imposing their personal views on what the artists' intentions were by interpreting the meaning of shapes and form in the artists' works.

AFRICOBRA: *Experimental Art Toward a School of Thought* chronicles a small collective of African American artists (figure 1.1) striving to create a visual language that represented an African American aesthetic rooted in the culture of the gritty Black neighborhoods of Chicago and, beyond that, is significantly embedded in African aesthetics. In this book, the terms Black and African American are used frequently. The word Black refers only to skin complexion, while African American implies origin. Everyone in the United States of America—and in the world—descended from a country of origin, while Black people in America descended from the continent of Africa. History has attested to our direct and unequivocal origins, because of slave traders plundering African countries and indiscriminately capturing African people to be brought back to the Western world as slaves.

AFRICOBRA: *Experimental Art Toward a School of Thought* has two interlocking components: the story of the creation of a pro-Black artists' movement and an account of the artistic and political ferment that took place in Chicago in the sixties and seventies.

1.1

Photograph by Ann. *AFRICOBRA Group Photo with Neighborhood Children*, 1970.

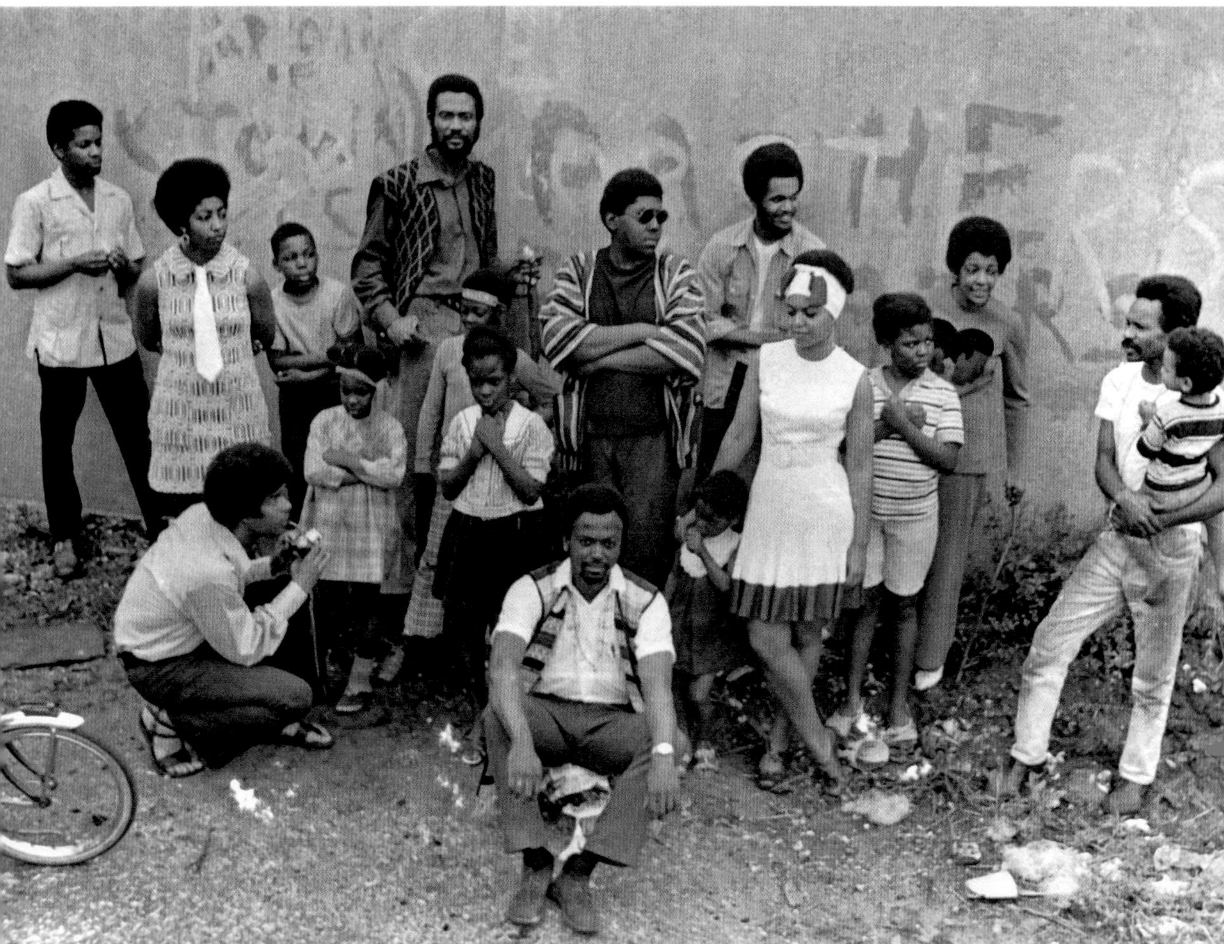

African American artists making art without concern for the opinions of white institutions and white critics was long overdue. The sixties presented such a time for Black artists to step up and, with experimental art, instigate a rethinking of the canon of art by introducing a new language that addressed African American people and their heritage and culture. It was extremely important to create a visual language that related to and spoke to Black people in the context of significant compact compositions—art responses to horror vacui, similar to congested urban Black neighborhoods imbued with vivid colors and with musical energy embodying familiar rhythms flowing through them.

The importance of creating a new aesthetic lies in its ownership—Black ownership, where in the past only whites, basically white males, claimed ownership of inventive artistic endeavors. Additionally, African Americans create their own artistic language so that generations of young African American artists have a storehouse of knowledge, a library, of new visual information to be proud of and relate to as influential in their progress and growth. It is important to create something that is our own, that hasn't been copied, reinterpreted, and co-opted by mainstream American society.

In 1968 in Chicago at wj Studios and Gallery, located at 1521 East 61st Street (the home and studios of Wadsworth and Jae Jarrell), cobra (Coalition of Black Revolutionary Artists) was founded. Founding members were Jeff Donaldson, a painter; Jae Jarrell, a fashion designer; Wadsworth Jarrell, a painter and photographer; Barbara Jones, a printmaker; and Gerald Williams, a painter. This small collective of artists formed to address the pressing, significant concerns about a Black aesthetic and ownership of art. wj Studios was located in the heart of a Black neighborhood, and we wanted our art to reflect that environment, while also moving beyond local environs to national and international arenas. Collectively, cobra formed to purposely create art that embodied an aesthetic, a substance in terms of meaningful content with a political agenda, rather than creating art that is accidental or an optical trick like trompe l'oeil or optical art (op art), which is grounded in methods of graphic and meticulously rendered dizzying curvilinear lines and morays that fool the eye (see, for example, the fields of vibrating lines in figure 1.2, created by the English-born master perceptual abstractionist and foremost exponent of op art Bridget Riley).

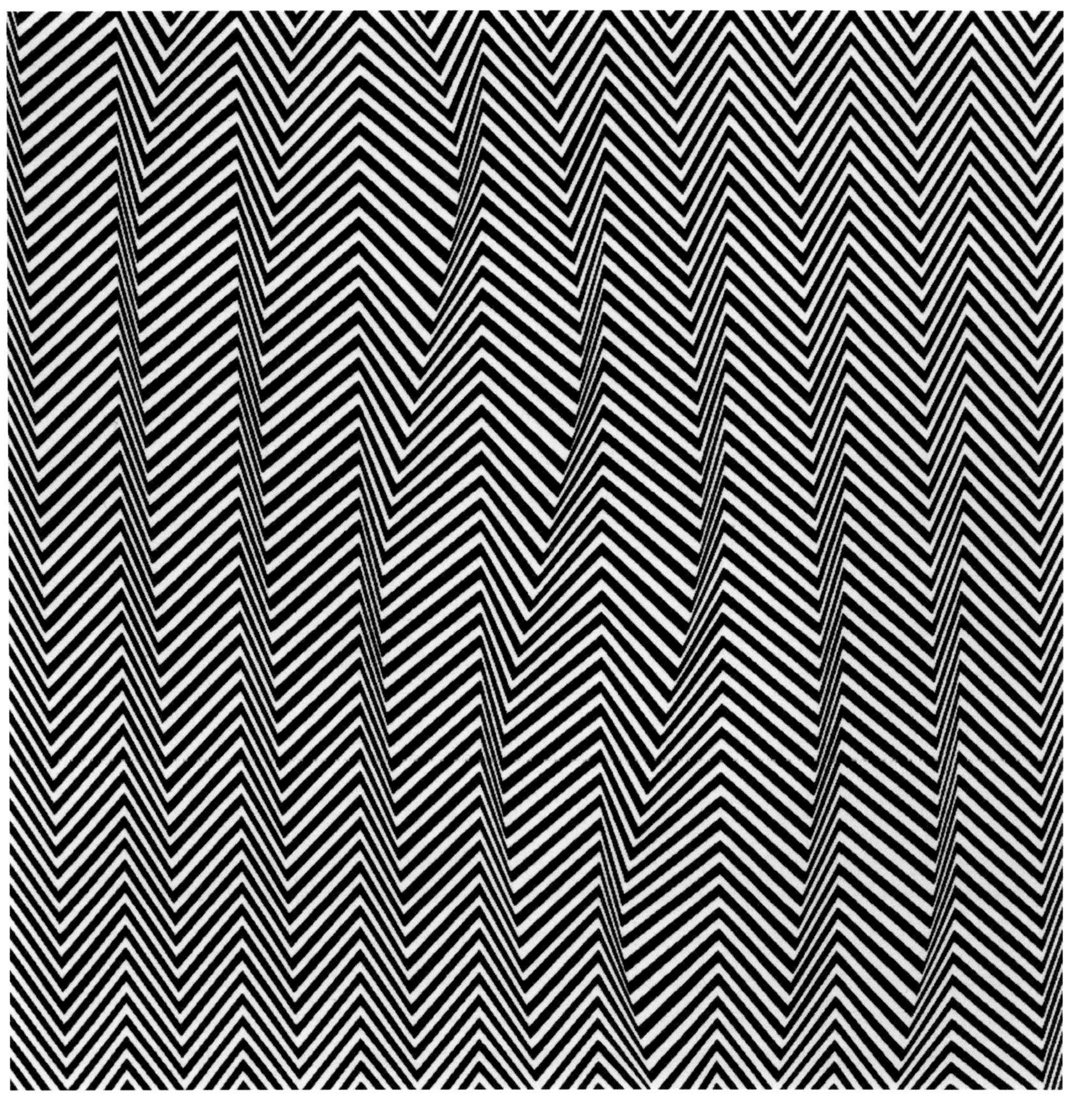

COBRA artists claimed our turf, following the advice of Booker T. Washington to "cast down your bucket where you are."[1] COBRA did just that and aspired to advance our precepts of art beyond what the Harlem Renaissance artists had achieved; we sought to create a mecca—a bastion of fresh creativity that would arguably be the paradigm for a Black aesthetic, similar to what jazz musicians accomplished with their music but independently controlled. We explored ideas of developing an identifiable approach to choice of colors, imaging, and experimental methods of application: the use of collage,

I.2

Bridget Riley, *Descending*, 1966. Emulsion on hard board, 36 × 36 inches. Courtesy of Alan Cristea Gallery, London, UK.

patterns, intuitive space, and form constructed of letters and words. By developing principles as components of a philosophy, such as open color, free symmetry, and writing on the plane, our full-spaced and extended compositions were reminiscent of avant-garde music—particularly an Ornette Coleman solo.

In 1970 in Chicago, a colleague of mine, William Gay, teaching in the Woodlawn Experimental Schools Project, visited my Chicago studio. He was impressed with a large unfinished painting, remarking, "When I look at this painting, it is saying, B-B-B-B; it is constructed basically of the letter B. You guys in COBRA are miles ahead of other artists. You guys' style remind me of music, especially be-bop, the music of Charlie Parker and Dizzy Gillespie. In New York in 1942, Bird and Diz hit the block with be-bop; other musicians didn't know what they were playing."[2]

Europeans and Euro-Americans created their own definition of what art is by appealing to absurdity with conceptual ideas and creating institutions (museums and galleries) that they protected like fortresses, barricading themselves behind a cadre of intellectual writers. Artists chosen to exhibit in the institutions were their own kind—mostly white men and occasionally a few white women and other ethnic groups, such as African American artists whose works were not seriously grounded in ethnicity unless the art was negatively demeaning their own. But museum directors and art gallery owners and white critics bestowed the highest honors and accolades on white men. It wasn't important whether white male artists' works were skillfully crafted, or whether their ideas were trite or stolen from another culture; they were considered the art gods, the Supermen, Batmen, and Captain Americas of art. White male artists are claimed to be the architects of the breakthrough between European and American aesthetics for having created their own genre, known as abstract expressionism. Since African Americans had harnessed the medium of music, "fine art is the last bastion for Europeans and Euro-Americans."[3]

Although Harlem Renaissance artists made a strong, credible request, with remarkable art in every imaginable style, to be accepted and viewed as American artists, only a few achieved "critical acclaim," and not as mainstream American artists. With the creation of COBRA, we were Black revolutionary artists who rejected the notion of being "sanctioned" by the establishment and exhibiting our art in white-owned museums and galleries. Instead, we defined and chartered our own direction, and we chose museums and galleries and other venues owned or operated by African Americans.

COBRA's ideology regarding art representing our people was congruent with and advocated what the scholar, poet, author, and politician Aimé Fernand David Césaire said in a 1956 speech in Paris: "We find ourselves today in a cultural chaos. And this is our role: to liberate the forces which, alone, can organize from this chaos a new synthesis which will be the reconciliation—*et depassement*—of the old and the new. We are here to proclaim the right of our people to speak, to let our people—black people, make their entrance on the great stage of history."[4] COBRA set out to present Black people elegantly on the stage of history as described by Césaire. We presented skillfully crafted, beautiful, positive, and compelling images of people who looked like us. To quote the author Nubia Kai's 1979 essay for the catalog AFRICOBRA: *The First Twenty Years*, "To AFRICOBRA members and their African fore-bearers, technique and content are not separate, disparate elements, but mutually symbiotic components of good art. The formula for them was simple: you can't convey a message to your audience if it is not said well."[5] To advance AFRICOBRA history forward, in a 2010 interview in Chicago with TV Land and NOLA Film Production, founding member Barbara Jones-Hogu and Napoleon Jones-Henderson (who joined in 1969) echoed those same sentiments. Barbara said, "We were not concerned whether the critics and art dealers were critiquing us or not. We were really focusing on communicating visually with the viewer, and the viewer we were looking at looked like us."[6] Napoleon added, "We were not concerned about the art world. We were addressing our people." In 2007, in my interview of founding member Jae Jarrell in her New York studio, she said, "We shook a raised clenched fist at mainstream America—like in your face. We were making art of our choice without concern for the powers to be."[7]

Metaphorically speaking, COBRA artists were visual bell ringers announcing that African life did *not* begin with slavery in America. We informed that Black people's existence eclipsed world civilization as the precursor race, as the origin of civilization, an advanced group of people who developed highly sophisticated cultures that were influential and copied worldwide. Such cultures existed in dynasties in Ghana, Mali, Zulu Kingdom in South Africa, Egypt, Benin, and Ife. Other important civilized kingdoms were in the Nubian Dynasty, the Great Zimbabwe empire, the Kingdom of Mapungubwe, and Timbuktu. In the book *Afrocentricity*, scholar Molefi Kete Asante states, "Among ancient civilizations Africans gave the world Ethiopia, Nubia, Egypt, Cush, Axum, Ghana, Mali and Songhay. These ancient civilizations are responsible for medicine, science, the concept of monarchies and divine-kingships, and Almighty God."[8]

But Black people who were born as slaves invested immeasurably in America. Whether Black people were considered citizens of this country—and a referendum from Congress, even to this day, is required to sustain voting rights—Black people, African American people, are natural-born American citizens and have ownership in America, because it was built on the backs of our free labor. In the book *Nobody Knows My Name*, James Baldwin asserts, "It may have been the popular impulse to keep us at the bottom of the perpetually shifting and bewildered populace; but we were, on the other hand, almost personally indispensable to each of them, simply because, without us, they could never have been certain, in such a confusion, where the bottom was; and nothing, in any case, could take away our title to the land which we, too, had purchased with our blood."[9]

I would argue that reparations are owed all African Americans because of more than three hundred years of forced free labor for companies who profited from our labor. Other ethnic groups whose lives were impeded and whose rights were taken away, and who were forced to live and work for free in deplorable conditions in concentration camps, such as the Japanese in the United States and Jews in Germany, were paid reparations by US and German governments, and by companies, such as Volkswagen, that indulged in forced free labor.

We knew that art alone could not change what had happened, or what was still happening in the lives of Black people, but we could affect, cerebrally, our future journey by informing. COBRA proposed to revolutionize art by presenting compositionally solid, informative, and conceptually revolutionary art that comprised African American communities, with us having ownership of our own ideas. It was important for us to name ourselves and to name our art, "poster art." We named ourselves and named our art so that others would not name us and categorize our art by naming it. For COBRA, it was politically, historically, and spiritually essential to disallow our collective being circumscribed by someone else, namely, art critics (the art police). The day COBRA acquiesced to others' definition of us, to quote an old southern expression, "It would be too wet to plow."

Naming is extremely important. It necessarily provides identity links to one's ancestry—who you are and where you came from. It is no accident that names on products are the guarantee of quality and the primary selling factor. Naming ourselves was unprecedented for artists, whose names were usually someone else's idea, namely, art critics, such as New York's Clement Greenberg, Harold Rosenberg, and Leo Steinberg—the Kings of Cultureburg, as Tom Wolfe called the three critics in his 1975 book *The Painted Word*—and Robert Coats, the critic who coined the term abstract expressionism. Additionally, the name impressionist was affixed to the style of a group of nineteenth-century artists in Paris by art critic Louis Leroy, in an article in the Parisian newspaper *Le Charivari*. English-born art critic Lawrence Alloway coined the name pop art. The name Harlem Renaissance for artists working and living in Harlem between 1920 and 1930 was not the choice of

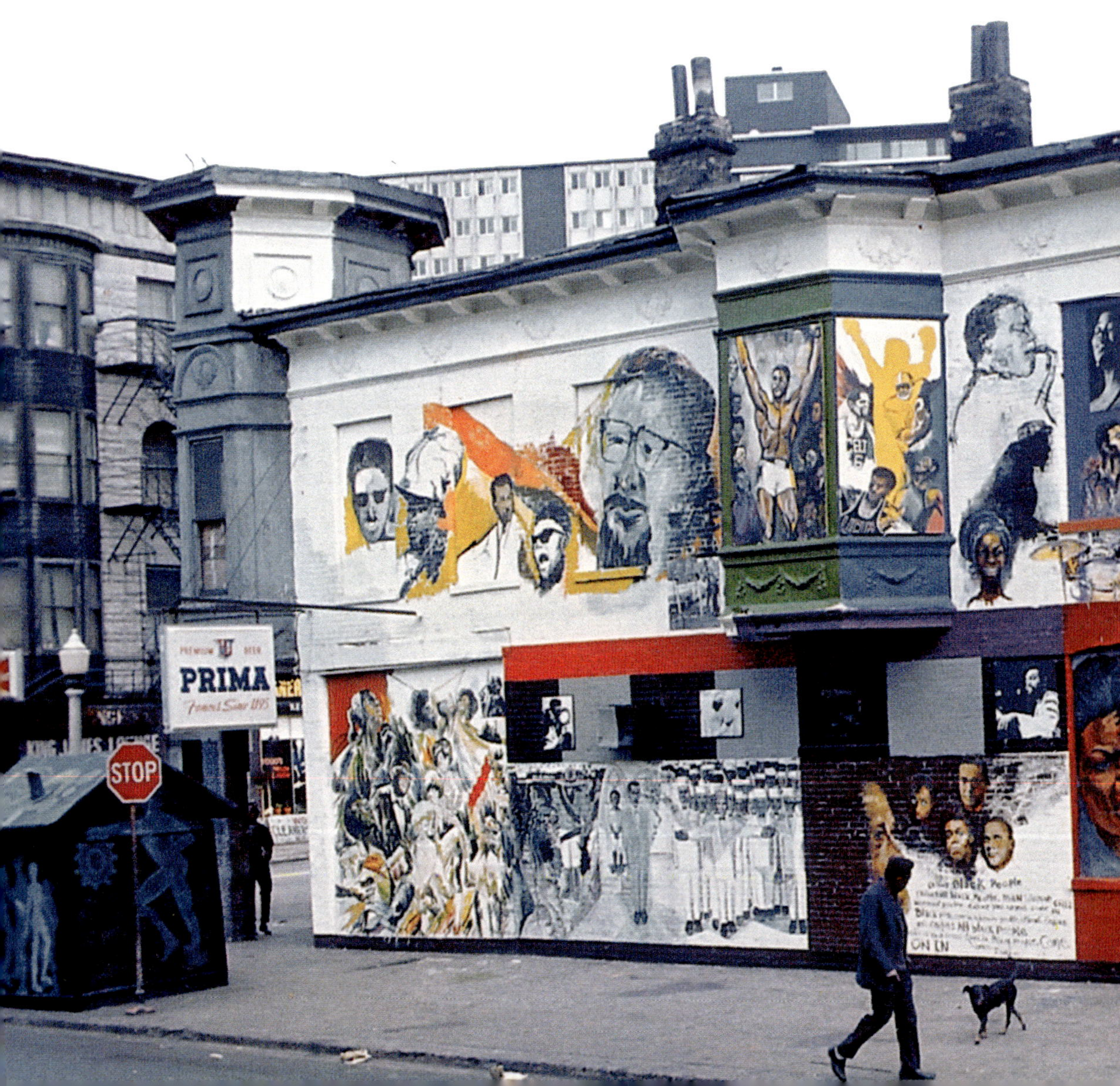

the artists themselves. The term was later ascribed to the cultural, social, and artistic outburst that took place in Harlem. During the time, it was known as the New Negro movement, named after the anthology by Alain Locke.

The mention of art critics always reminds me of two occurrences. Citing the incidents in reverse order, in 1980, when I was a professor at the University of Georgia in Athens, teaching drawing and painting, I was invited to be on a panel for a doctoral student's dissertation encompassing mural painting. Primarily, I was invited because I was an artist who worked on the *Wall of Respect* and because two students and I had recently completed a huge mural (31 × 61 feet), entitled *Ascension*, on an outside wall of the Athens Community Center. There was a discussion about the mural *Ascension* led by Professor Edmund Feldman, who taught art criticism. He said, "When [an] artist finishes a work of art, it's out of his hands, he has nothing to say about it,

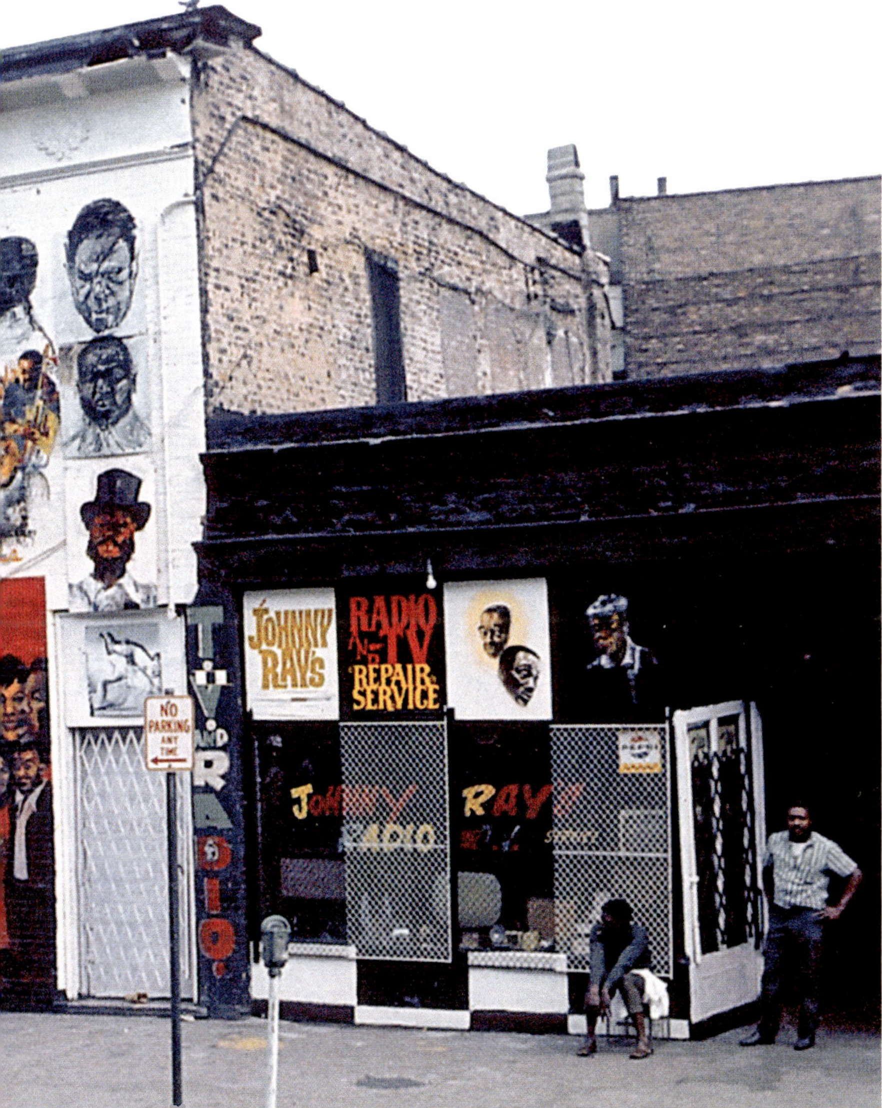

I.3

Multiple artists, *Wall of Respect*, Chicago, 1967. Photograph by Robert Sengstacke.

because it is our baby then. It is then left up to the art critic to articulate what the artist is attempting to say."[10] I perceived his remarks as pompous and condescending. I said, "It seems to me that an art critic's position is questionable and is held in limbo until an artist makes a work of art and exhibits it. If an artist never makes art and exhibits it, art critics are out of a job."[11] In 1956 in a color class at the School of the Art Institute of Chicago, the instructor, Professor William Cowans, described the art critic as "a one leg person teaching people how to run track."[12] Lisa Farrington notes in her book *African-American Art: A Visual and Cultural History*, "Primary source documents stand in stark contrast to secondary sources, which alter, adulterate, extract from, expand on, or in some way modify the primary source. This gives the visual arts a distinct advantage over the written word, because art, by nature, is almost always a primary source, existing principally in its original form."[13]

In Chicago in the sixties, the phrase "Black is Beautiful" was emblazoned on billboards, train overpasses, walls of buildings, and COBRA's art as a reminder that Black people are beautiful just as they are. The repeated phrase was visceral. As a result, Black people emerged comfortable and proud of beautiful Black-self: with kinky-curly natural hair styled into Afros, full lips (without Botox injections), wide noses, firm protruding buttocks, and speech patterns that were considered by some not to be proper English. English is a second language for African people because our ancestors came unwillingly by force to America, speaking fluently in various African languages: Yoruba, Swahili, Twi, Nubian, Arabic, Hausa, Igbo, Fulani, Berber, Amharic, Somali, and others.

The new arrivals in America from multiple African countries learned English from indentured servants (freed prisoners owing debts) and from poorly educated people who had escaped Europe to settle in America and who were fortunate enough to own or be overseers of Black slaves. Their command of the English language was questionable compared with the better class of properly speaking Europeans who remained in Europe. In other words, the early American settlers spoke in dialects of the uneducated, with Londoners speaking Cockney, the French speaking Gaulish, and the Spanish and Portuguese speaking in various dialects. The English language taught to Africans was also lexically influenced by a Gaelic substratum. With that mix of dialects and broken English being spoken, and with Africans speaking in their own languages and dialects, it is remarkable that the new arrivals from

Africa and their offspring mastered any form of communication, let alone proper English.

Nonetheless, the captured, shackled Africans brought culture to America: visual art (which was primarily suppressed by slave owners), music, dance, song, poetry, blacksmithery, religion, indigenous rituals and customs of kingship practiced in several African countries, and a host of eloquent, inventive expressions embodying theatrical qualities. Today, the dominant expressions heard and seen in American society—in movies, advertisements, bars, sporting and political events, and everyday activities—were created by African people. The expressions are the soul of American culture. Rock 'n' roll is heavily influenced by and "borrows" tenets from African American–created blues, and pop singers—all nationalities—are influenced by Black gospel music. Notably, this cultural influence extends to Black athletes, who were the first to celebrate with high fives; chest, high body, and fist bumping; and spiking the football after scoring.

Nothing has the hidden implications, the liquidity, and the raw poetic theatrical presence as the phrases espoused by Black southern "country-hick bumpkins," barely literate sharecropper farm boys, whom I vividly remember in the 1930s and 1940s coming to town in Athens, Georgia, on Saturdays, some riding in mule-driven wagons, dressed in brand new bib overalls, spit-shined Stacy Adams shoes, and Big Apple caps, with the bills cocked to the side or turned backward (five decades ahead of the hip-hop revolution), vying for casual sexual relationships with women:

> "Hey, baby. I'm not the doctor, but I'm the doctor's son.
> I'll be your doctor till the doctor comes—what I say? Hey
>   now, what I say?"

> "Hey, Shuga, come heah and let daddy bitecha."

> "If that's yo woman, you better pin her to yo side, 'cause,
> if she flag my train ums sho-gon let 'er ride."

> "Looka heah, baby, two suns can't shine in one world.
> Two boys can't go with one girl—well, hush my mouth."

> "Say, pretty, I'm not talkin'bout the saw and the saw dust,
> I'm talkin'bout baby shon'nuf. Um huh—what you say."

What concluded COBRA's philosophical constructs were the aggressive artistic and explosive political activities occurring in Black Chicago in the sixties. Murry N. DePillars, an artist, scholar, and educator who joined AFRI-COBRA in 1980, described in the book *Wadsworth Jarrell: Artist as Revolutionary* the culture and lifestyle that COBRA advocated: "Black, urban Chicago—its emerging traditions, combined with those of southern cities and towns[—] formed the fertile soil for the blossoming of a cultural dynamic. Therefore, art that emerged from Black culture should be based on a syntax that is encoded yet understandable to Black people. Such art becomes—historically and metaphorically speaking—the geographical shadow of Black people."[14]

AFRICOBRA sought entry into the encoded lifestyle of Black folk—the secret area addressed by DePillars. Artist, scholar, historian, and member of AFRICOBRA Michael D. Harris, in an essay for the online catalog *AFRICOBRA Now: An Aesthetic Reflection*, cited Elizabeth Alexander's concept of the Black interior: "Black life and creativity behind the public face of stereotype and limited imagination: the Black Interior is a metaphysical space beyond the Black public everyday toward power and wild imagination that Black people ourselves know we possess but need to be reminded of."[15] When DePillars described an art of Black people that should be based on an encoded syntax, he might have been speaking of the composite of inventive and coined expressions and styles created by Black people: the way we dress, sing, and dance, and the way we talk and walk—hip talk and hip walk.

In the 1920s through the 1940s, there was a language in Harlem based on a familiar cultural syntax devised by African American musicians and other "hip" Black folks who spoke in encoded language, a lexicon created to be understood only by Black people. That synthesis included such terms as soul brother and sister, soul music and soul food, coppin' me some pecks, serious boardin', and layin' on a scarf. Additional expressions were layin' in the cut in the crib (or the pad), coppin' some happenin', mackin' the game, jumpin' clean in pressed vines or threads, sharp as a tack, sharp as a mosquito's peter, ready as a radio, pepper head, pepper top, wheelin' around in boss shorts, get down, I'm down with that, funk, pee-funk, and funky music. In addition, in the 1920s through the 1940s, Black folks devised expressions like What's happenin', baby? What's shakin', dude? Hey cheen, what's on the limb for the lizard? Black folks also made use of and coined words to metaphorically mean something other than the original meaning, like hip, hipster, hip-cat, hip-kitty from Kansas City, square from Delaware, lame from Maine, dig, mellow, rappin', jive, cool, bread, scopin', turn on, and turn me on to some happenings, in phrases like Are you hip to that? Can you dig it? That's cool. He's a cool cat. She's a cool chick. Hand communication consisted of slapping palms—gimme some skin, Jack; gimme some skin, Jim. Current Black athletes along with other hip Black folks have transformed the encoded hand communications into aforementioned celebratory high fives and chest, high body, and fist bumping. As inconsequential as it might sound, Black athletes' and current Black folks' creative transformation of 1920s–1940s encoded hand communication and African American coined expressions have been copied and co-opted into everyday American culture. Those expressions, lifestyles, and attitudes were what AFRICOBRA aspired to capture in our art.

Another area in the lives of Black folks was occultism, or spirituality, which AFRICOBRA was interested in as well. This is an area beyond Christianity that metaphysically addresses the order and balance of circumstances: happiness, misfortune, wealth, health, life, and death. For instance, mythology asserts that a banshee—a female spirit believed to possess prophetic power—wails incessantly outside a home to announce that a death will soon occur in the family. Important in African American folklore and believed as truth is that anyone born with a veil (a caul) covering his or her face is special. It is believed that such a person is vested with the magical power of clairvoyance and can see spirits, predict future occurrences, and communicate with dead ancestors.

Spiritual practices such as these originated in African cultures. The theories and practices have been transformed in Haitian, Trinidadian, Bahamian, and southern American mythology, especially in Black communities in the low country of Georgia (the Gullah Sea Islands), in South Carolina, and in Louisiana (down behind the sun).

It is an accepted reality among many Black folks that magical powers are practiced for trickery—for control, by casting a spell tricking someone. In the song "I Don't Know," by Willie Mabon, that fact is revealed:

You sprinkle Goofer Dust all around my bed,
You'll wake up one morning and find your own-self dead.[16]

In "Hoochie Coochie Man," Muddy Waters sang:

I got a black cat bone, I got a mojo too,

I got High John the Conqueror Root,

I'm gonna mess with you.[17]

Trinidadian folklore was revealed in the 1976 art exhibition in Washington, DC, titled *Douens*, by the consummate Trinidadian artist LeRoy Clarke, as well as in David Brizan's text for the exhibition catalog: "Douens are spirits of premature babies who die before religious rites are performed and who linger perennially in a dismal twilight."[18] In a lecture, LeRoy Clarke described douens as the dust of dead babies.

I will not reveal every experience of my upbringing in southern African American culture in the thirties, forties, and fifties. Some things do not need to be said. In a film of Muddy Waters traveling with his band, he advised his musicians: "There are some secrets you need to keep in your pocket."[19]

I grew up in a Black southern culture where conjure men and women's obtrusive presence in communities was respected—mostly out of fear. They proposed to foretell occurrences and cure all kinds of illnesses, especially those directly related to falling victim to somebody's trick (somebody laid down a potion, and the victim walked over it). They advertised themselves by word of mouth as "doctors" who were capable of removing a spell cast by, perhaps, a jealous lover out of anger or revenge. Some of their dwellings were marked with colored bottles and jugs and painted rocks, as well as symbolic items, such as rusty horseshoes, animal bones, dead petrified cocks, and a rabbit's foot. For instance, in April 1982 in Athens, Georgia, attorney Janice Thurman (now Janice Mathews) told me about visiting a potential client, the folk artist Dilmus Hall, whose front yard was inundated with his sculpture and painted artifacts. On a fence hung a single human shoe framed in a wooden box. She said, "When I pulled up in front of his house and saw all of those symbolic things, I was afraid to go inside."[20]

I hope that this book is valuable in teaching African American and American art history. Additionally, my hope is that it reaches an audience of other disciplines and people at large who do not have any knowledge of art. Readers will probably discover that I am not your garden-variety academic writer. I taught photography and drawing and painting at Howard University in Washington, DC, for six years (1971–77), painting for one semester at Spelman College in Atlanta (1985), and drawing and painting for ten years at the

University of Georgia (1978–88). Primarily, I am a painter, sculptor, print-maker, and photographer. I have lived for many years in several major cities, north and south: Chicago, Boston, Washington, DC, Atlanta, and New York City. At present, I live in Cleveland, Ohio. I have also traveled to other countries: Africa, England, Italy, the Caribbean (Martinique and the Bahamas), the Netherlands (Amsterdam and Rotterdam), Japan, Korea, Denmark, and Sweden.

I consider myself to be an aficionado of great Black music: gospel, blues, and jazz. My memory is clear on the history of urban and country Black functions and cultural events in the thirties through the sixties. Those memories include fieldworkers' rhythmic songs, where the lead singer sings the first lines and is answered by a chorus, similar to what Baptist preachers experience from their congregations: "Preach the word, Reverend. Yes, say it—say it. Tell it. Talk about it. Lawd have mercy, and amen amen." Additionally, I retain memories of itinerant harmonica (mouth harp) and guitar players; hog-killing day (when the weather turned cold enough); cotton and pea picking; log-burning fireplaces; shallow-surface well diggers employing the sledgehammer-and-shaker method; blacksmiths; school and church gatherings featuring competitive gospel quartets; plays; recitals; emotionally charged solos sung at funerals; house rent parties; picnics and barbeques; after-hours juke joints; Saturday night fish fries; and other practices and secrets in African American life. Those memories are etched in my brain as if they happened yesterday, which gives me a good sense of African American culture, history, and lifestyles.

Expressions, Methods, and Influence

AFRICOBRA's experimentation encompassed various approaches, methods, and materials. Our methods and influence went beyond our members and was visible in the work of American mainstream and African American artists, as well as in the work of artists in other countries. In addition, AFRICOBRA's influence was circumfluent in the work of Washington, DC, artists, including faculty and students at Howard University. Most notable and readily recognizable AFRICOBRA influences in other artists' work was a confluence of style: African-influenced patterns and motifs; inventive patch-work and appliqué; tie-dye; collaged items such as aluminum foil, rickrack (zigzagged cloth ribbon), and cowrie shells; and highly intense colors (aka Cool Ade colors), and graffiti-inspired writing on the plane.

In 1979, the scholar Kenneth Rodgers wrote an essay entitled "The AFRI-COBRA Collective" for the exhibition catalog AFRICOBRA/*Fromaje*: "Not only did AFRICOBRA pave the way for other Afro-American artists to follow, but they laid the cornerstone for a stylistic expression unparalleled in the annals of American history."[21] Thurlow Evans Tibbs Jr., then director of the Evans-Tibbs Collection in Washington, DC, wrote in an essay for the same exhibition:

I think people in the Washington, DC, area did not take AFRICOBRA very seriously in its beginnings, and that was a mistake. It is an important and original art movement in the black and in the American art community. Its impact on American design was as significant as that of Abstract Expressionism in the 1950s, which, though little appreciated at that time, has now become a major artistic movement. In time, this too will be the case with AFRICOBRA. AFRICOBRA has affected every facet of design, including textile making, fashion and household design. The aesthetics espoused by AFRICOBRA is now the most popular visual material today. The work of today's Pop Graffittists was done by AFRICOBRA 20 years ago; it had far reaching impact on every element of design. In retrospect, it will be seen as an original American idiom that drew on African tradition, and like jazz, should be recognized as a national treasure.[22]

In 1971, Edward Spriggs, then director of the Studio Museum in Harlem, wrote an essay titled "AFRICOBRA: Intermediarily" for the AFRICOBRA II exhibition catalog:

This is the second year of the AFRICOBRA at the Studio Museum in Harlem. They are here for the second time because we believe that they represent one of the most dynamic combinations of thought, talent, and commitment that we know of in the visual arts during this era of the "*Black Aesthetic*" in America.

AFRICOBRA is a Chicago-based cooperative group that—from their perspective as African Americans—is going about the righteous business of identifying and making use of the style and rhythm qualities, both the apparent and actual, that finds expression in the lives of black people everywhere. We see in AFRICOBRA's concepts and philosophy the emergence of an honestly real-world and people-oriented body of creations.

For them the Black Aesthetic is not only a possibility, but is in continuous evolution in the lives of people of African ancestry. It functions daily in their every mode of expression. We also believe that they are in the fore of those common characteristics shared by what is generally accepted as Black music and Black poetry.

So whatever you take the AFRICAN COMMUNE OF BAD RELEVANT ARTISTS' work to be, they are not to be considered simply as images of heroes, of sorrow, or anybody's notion of protest. Consider AFRICOBRA's images to be arti/factors of rhythms. Bridges. Progressions across zones of feeling/thot. Yesterday. Tomorrow. Bloods memory. Shines/sounds like our own life/ritual celebration.

They see "art" as a movement in-the-round completing an[d] complementing our bas-relief existence. AFRICOBRA's image/rhythms are about busting open the Moslem–western-art idea that exist in the plastic landscape of our minds. The "zombie" in us they want released. The inner shavings of our lives, AFRICOBRA wants to spread upon earth surface and sky. They want to replenish our mind/soul/vision/ generations.

AFRICOBRA, Intermediarily. The African Commune of Bad Relevant Artists. We dig their spirit as a family of image-makers making diversity in their unity. And they say, still more is possible. And they want you to have some.[23]

1

BLACK IN CHICAGO

If white people were treated like Black people are being treated, this country would have hell to pay. —Bill Borin on the Detroit Riots

On February 1, 1953, I moved to Chicago, the most racially segregated major city in the United States. A reminder of how pandemic segregation and racism are in Chicago is the 1919 race riot. During that "red summer," between July 27 and August 3, thirty-eight people died, and more than five hundred were injured. The riot started when a young African American boy, who was swimming at the 27th Street Beach (designated for Black people), drifted to the 29th Street Beach (which was exclusively for whites). When he realized that he had reached the beach for whites, he was out of wind, so he attempted to come ashore and was immediately stoned by white bathers. The boy swam back into the water and drowned.

I moved to Chicago fresh out of the military—to be specific, right out of combat in North Korea. I thought that living in Chicago, as opposed to living in the South, would offer me a greater amount of freedom in employment and a better choice of schools and places to live. In the 1940s as a teenager, I had visited Chicago, living with my older siblings, a brother and two sisters, for an entire summer. Their apartment was in a Black neighborhood at 33rd Street and Wabash Avenue. At that time, and as a youngster, I did not know how racially segregated Chicago was.

After being discharged from the army and entering civilian life, strains of the war lingered within me—the sounds of persistent machine gun fire and exploding mortar and artillery rounds. Sounds as simple as a backfire from an automobile, or a plane passing overhead, would send me sprawling to the ground, ducking for cover. Using the ground for protection was a survival tactic taught to soldiers in basic training. Soldiers were constantly reminded to "hug the ground and stay alive." That condition of anxiety lasted approximately one year, but edginess and quick ill-temper and impatience lasted longer. The long lines in the military—for the mess hall, to receive supplies (summer and winter clothing and equipment, such as field mess gear, bedding, combat boots, canteens, backpacks, helmets, and rifles)—only taught me impatience. The phrase "hurry up and wait" was a popular expression among soldiers. It came from the insistence by noncommissioned officers and squad leaders for soldiers to hurry and form lines.

I served in the US Army as a cannoneer in a heavy field artillery company (155 mm howitzers) that was foundational support to infantry divisions closer to the front line of battle. I had been drafted into the army in February 1951, at the age of twenty-one, and served twenty-four months (the required duration of service for draftees at that time). The economy in the country was relatively stable. In Chicago, jobs were easily obtained by low- and high-skilled workers in manufacturing, the steel industry, the slaughterhouse and meat packing companies, automobile assembly plants, paint-making companies, the building industry, government and city services, and the vast printing and retail industry.

Chicago at that time was alive with entertainment: nightclubs, taverns, and movie theaters featuring stellar jazz and blues musicians. A few notable jazz clubs on the South and North Sides and downtown (the Loop) were the Crown Propeller, Club DeLisa, Ritz Lounge, Club Relax, the Strand Bar (which later became McKees Disc-Jockey Club), the Capitol Lounge, the Beehives, Mr. Henry's, the Cotton Club, the Blue Note, Cadillac Bob's, Robert's Show Lounge, Knob Hill, and Club Evergreen.

In addition, I witnessed extraordinary music and dance performances at movie theaters: the Regal, the Tivoli, the Chicago, and the Rialto Theater (Minsky's World Famous Burlesque), which featured such musicians and performers as the Count Basie Band, Dizzy Gillespie Big Band, Sammy Davis Jr. with the Will Mastin Trio, and the exciting and talented Larry Steele Dancers.

Others included Louis Armstrong's Combo, the famous burlesque dancer Sally Rand, and the Paris Revue, featuring the fabulous Josephine Baker.

Chicago has been labeled "The Blues City," mainly because the Delta musicians brought with them their music and southern culture. They performed in such blues clubs as the 708 Club, the Checkerboard Lounge, Pepper's Lounge, Silvio's Lounge, Theresa's Lounge, and others not as well known. Occasionally, I visited the 708 Club, the Checkerboard, and Pepper's and Theresa's Lounges in the fifties and early sixties, witnessing amazing performances by blues greats like Muddy Waters, Little Walter, Magic Sam, Little Johnny Taylor, Buddy Guy, Junior Wells, and Jimmy Reed. This was a decade before the British musicians copied their music and introduced African American musicians to a white audience. Music saturated the air, and on every block there was a tavern or club featuring live music.

This entire situation was new and exciting to me because I was not too long out of Athens, Georgia. The caliber of employment and music, theater, and dance performances in Chicago did not exist in Athens, which had no steel industry, no manufacturing to speak of, no legitimate theater, no music scene, nor substantive career-oriented positions of any kind—except for teaching—especially not for Black people, unless they owned their own businesses. Most jazz and blues music, at that time labeled "race music," was only heard in juke joints and on radio. Occasionally, in the 1940s, my high school buddy and I would go to a record shop and check out records and listen to them in booths. We listened to bebop musicians Dizzy Gillespie, with Joe Carroll scatting; Charlie Parker; Miles Davis; Art Blakey; Fats Navarro; Thelonious Monk; Max Roach; and Tadd Dameron.

Regional bands from Atlanta occasionally came to Athens to perform for dances, including the Billy Wright Band, and truthfully, a few of them were proficient musicians but not on the professional level of creative improvisation as those I saw in Chicago. The music scene in Chicago was overwhelmingly infectious, and it would become instrumental in defining characteristics of content and form in my art: rhythm, colors, and the improvisational raw soul.

I came to Chicago and brought with me my raw artistic skills. As far back as I can remember, my only desire was to become a visual artist. After all my siblings left home for college, the military, and employment in northern states, and later after the passing of my father, my mother and I had long

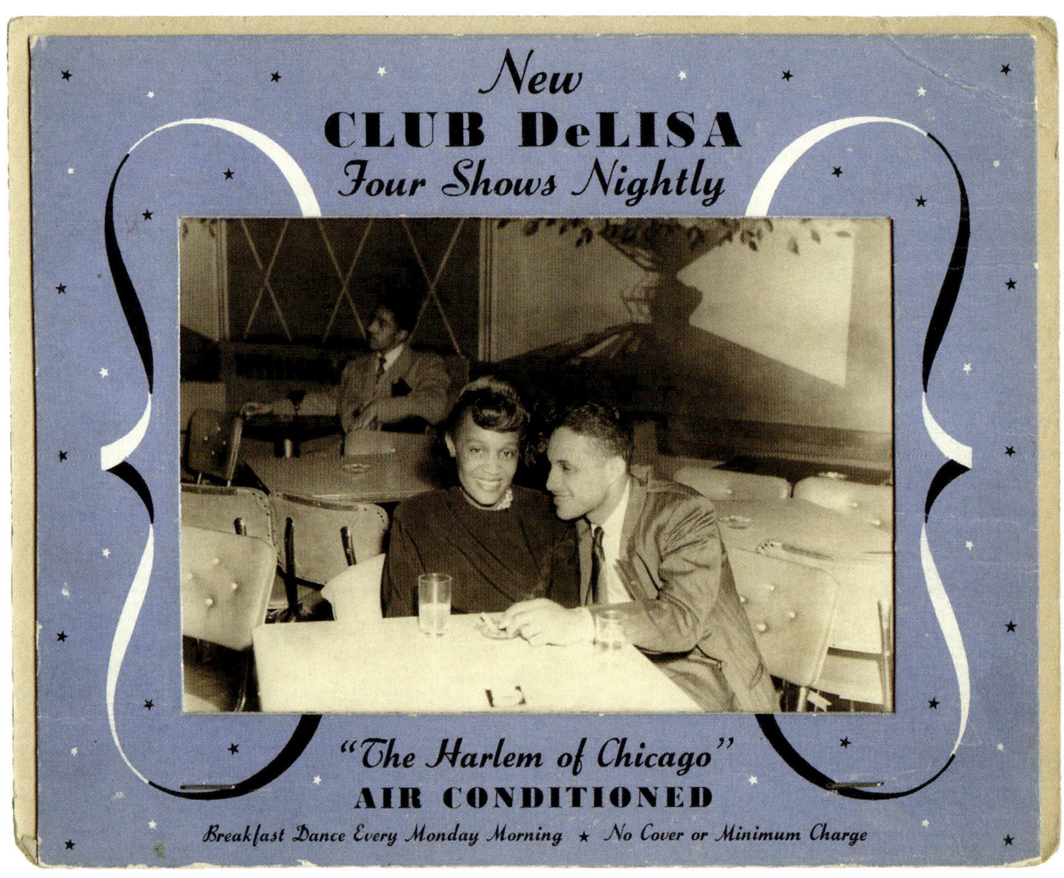

Photographer unknown. *Club DeLisa*, Chicago, 1948. Nellie Jarrell (*left*) and unknown man.

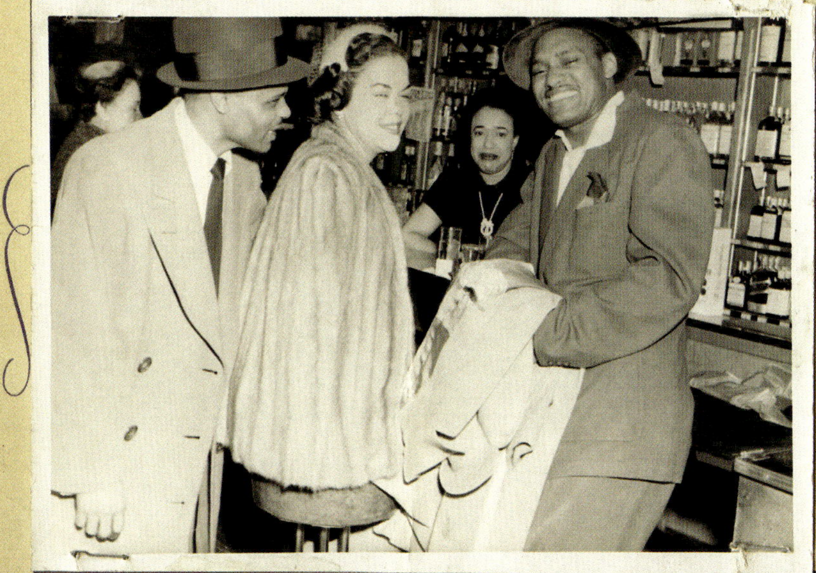

1.2

Photograph by Judson Jarrell. *Club Evergreen*, Chicago, 1954. Solliston Jarrell (*left*) with unknown women and man.

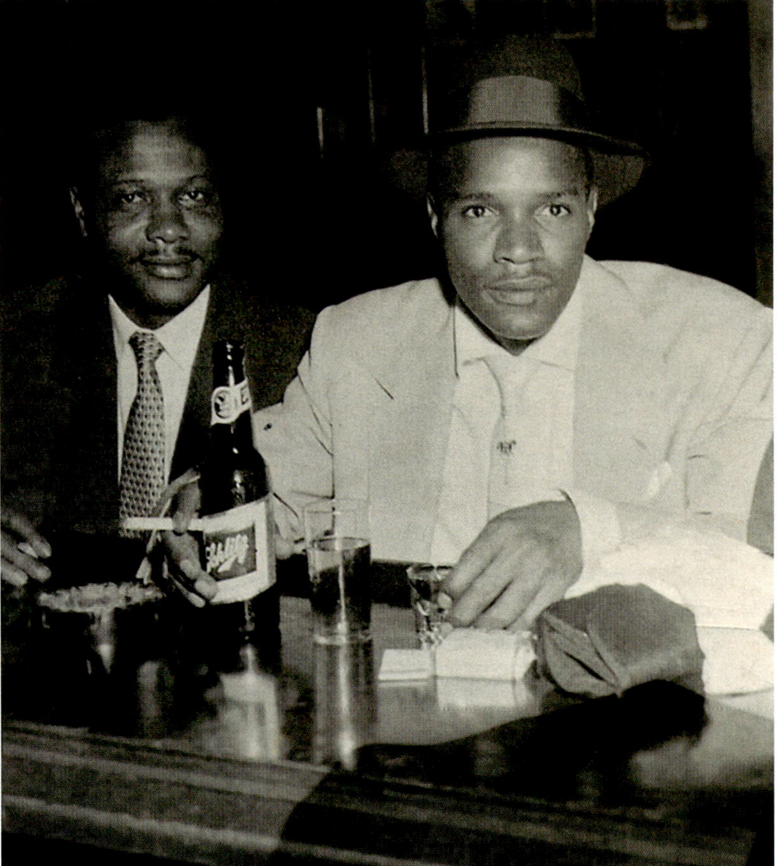

Photograph by Judson Jarrell. *Club Relax*, Chicago, 1954. Solliston (*left*) and Wadsworth Jarrell.

fireside discussions about my becoming an artist. I drew the latest cars and copied characters from the Sunday funnies, which morphed into creating comic strips populated with my own characters. In grammar school, my teachers also encouraged me to attend an art school. I sketched portraits in pencil and experimented with watercolor depicting landscapes. The colors were made from plants and vegetables with a boiling process—beets for red, onions for yellow, and indigo plants for blue. In high school, I became the illustrator of sporting events for the school paper, and I was the official company artist in the US Army from 1951 to 1953.

After being discharged from the army and moving to Chicago, my first exposure to formal art classes began in the evening program at Ray Vogue School of Art from 1953 to 1954. From 1954 to 1958, I attended the School of the Art Institute of Chicago, and that was my first encounter with a museum school and great world art. It is difficult for me to put into words what that experience was like, seeing master works of art on display every day. I had not seen any art in Athens, even though the Georgia Museum of Art had existed on the campus of the University of Georgia since 1945. It opened to the public in 1948, but because of segregation, African Americans were not allowed to visit.

Shortly after my move to Chicago, I discovered that the city contained ethnically segregated neighborhoods, including German, Jewish, Polish, African American, Italian, Mexican, Puerto Rican, Irish, Asian, Bohemian, and Lithuanian. The division of neighborhoods created the perception of small towns within a larger city. I also found out that the same racism as in Georgia existed in Chicago. For instance, there were places that Black people could not enter. The Trianon Ballroom, at 62nd Street and Cottage Grove Avenue, was one, even though it was located in a Black neighborhood.

White-only establishments were prevalent and part of the fabric of the segregated South. I and other migrant Black folks assumed that the industrialized North would be different. The difference I found between North and South was that racism in the North was subtle. By contrast, Georgia and the remainder of the South were not as hypocritical as the North. Their racist rules and customs were imperiously visible. Southerners had signs everywhere: "White Only," "White" and "Colored" drinking fountains, "Colored Entrance," "White Ladies" restroom, and "Colored Women's" restroom. White women were heralded as ladies. In southern antebellum society, the signs clearly implied that Black females could never reach the status of lady-ship, so they were called women.

Additionally, southern African Americans, including me, discovered in Chicago that we were called niggers—exactly what we were called down South. When I lived in the South, African Americans responded to that epithet by referring to whites, especially poor whites, as crackers, pecks, rednecks, and poor white trash. That label was extended to the more affluent whites as well. We called them crackers and rednecks with money. My aunt Obelia, who came from Ohio to live with my family in the 1940s, referred to whites as hunkies and bohunks. Our rationale was to not be disarmed or defined by name calling.

My brother-in-law Leonard F. Johnson, a bright, talented portrait artist, said that the late C. B. King Sr., the astute, dynamic civil rights attorney of Albany, Georgia, who was also my brother-in-law, said to him in the 1970s: "There are only two kinds of people in America—niggers and crackers, and ironically, neither name [has] anything to do with race."[1] C. B. was implying that racial slurs do not define people, even though in America, everything is viewed in black and white.

The former executive director of the Chicago Urban League Edwin Berry addressed the city's racism and segregation in the book *The Boss*: "Chicago is the most residentially segregated city in the United States, where a Negro dare not to step outside of the environs of his race."[2] Deliberately or accidentally entering ethnic neighborhoods posed great danger for African Americans or anyone ethnically out of place. In the Mexican neighborhood on the Northwest Side, on Chicago Avenue at Wood Street, there was street gang activity. A pair of sneakers dangled high in the air on telephone lines was a stern warning to interloper gang members and other ethnic outsiders. The explanation was symbolic, but it contained a powerful message. My daughters, Jennifer and Roslyn, said that when they lived in that neighborhood while students at the School of the Art Institute of Chicago, they were told what the sneakers represented by gang affiliates who controlled the neighborhood: "The last guy we caught over here that didn't belong, we beat the hell out of him, and here is his sneakers to prove it."[3]

As a young man who served "his country" fighting to defend "democracy," I rationally assumed dividends would be, at best, equal opportunities. But I was mistaken. In 1953, living in Chicago taught me a powerful lesson. I learned that being a Black man anywhere in America meant facing inequality based solely on the color of one's skin. That was my baptism into reality. It became obvious to me that regardless of which state I lived in, bigotry would follow me like a shadow. I perceived the reality check as racist, terse, and riveting. It also became clear to me that the true voice of white Americans in Chicago was "screaming" the words: "Welcome to 'Up North.' Welcome back home to America, Black boy!" The scholar Molefi Kete Asante echoed similar sentiments in his book *Afrocentricity*: "The United States emerged from the second European World War indebted to its African citizens who had fought bravely to defend democracy. But instead of reaping the accrued interest from the debt, African American men and women were denied at home the very democracy they defended abroad."[4]

The ethnically segregated city of Chicago, home of brutally cold winters and sweltering hot summers, with putrid odors from the stockyards and glue factories, is where masses of African Americans migrated to from the South. "Hog Butcher for the World, Tool Maker, Stacker of wheat, Player with Railroads and the Nation's Freight Handler: Stormy, husky, brawling, City of the Big Shoulders."[5] We migrated to Chicago for employment, but there was an additional reason: a measure of less overt discrimination. The poet, playwright, music critic, and scholar Amiri Baraka stated in his book *Blues People*, "Not every Negro left the South to get a better job, some left so they could find a greater degree of freedom, and some so they could walk the streets after 10 PM (many southern towns having ordinances against night rambling nigras)."[6]

Sharecroppers, as well as sons and daughters of sharecroppers, discovered that ordinary folk, such as postal and factory workers, bartenders, nightclub bathroom attendants, Pullman porters, taxi drivers, and bootblacks could prosper in Chicago. A phrase often repeated among Chicagoans was "If you can make it in Chicago, you can make it anywhere." The upside in Chicago was that Black folks became owners of apartment buildings and single-dwelling homes, as well as entrepreneurs with successful businesses, such as automobile dealerships, an ice cream manufacturing company, manufacturers and purveyors of meat, and cosmetic companies. Additionally, African Americans realized their professional dreams as magazine and book publishers, real estate brokers, doctors, athletes, musicians, stockbrokers, registered nurses, attorneys, judges, artists, scientists, architects, butchers, disc jockeys, television and radio news commentators, educators, photographers, designers, writers, actors, playwrights, dancers, fashion designers, electricians, carpenters, contractors, politicians, and journalists. A large percentage of the influx of southerners to Chicago from the twenties to the sixties had never owned practically anything. Since the twenties, more real property and businesses have been owned by African Americans in Chicago than in any other city in the United States.

In 1955, events engendered African American collective resistance to blatantly racist and unjust laws. That collectivism was primarily realized and sustained by the successful Montgomery, Alabama, bus boycott, which happened when Martin Luther King Jr. was elected to head the protest campaign against the policy of racial segregation on public transportation. Yet, collective resistance and Black consciousness en masse did not spread north until the early sixties. A large number of Black folk "up North," especially younger people who were born and grew up in northern states, assumed that it was a polemic situation in the South, rather than systemic.

The year 1955 was also when the "wolf-whistle murder" made headlines in Black publications: the *Chicago Defender*, the *Pittsburgh Courier*, and Johnson Publishing's *Ebony* and *Jet* magazines. The story broke about a fourteen-year-old Chicago Black boy, Emmett Till, who had been murdered by white men in Money, Mississippi, for whistling at a white woman, according to media reporting. The white woman, along with her husband (who in a 1956 interview in *Look* magazine admitted that he and his brother had committed the crime), owned a rural store mainly supported by African American clientele.

This tragic story was disturbing, and Till's murder was an incredibly barbaric act. It shocked me along with other conscious people of the world. Rational people of all races wondered how an egregious crime of this magnitude could occur and be tolerated on American soil, with the criminals going unpunished. As a former resident of segregated Georgia, I found it quite understandable. I remember aggression such as that, but mostly vicariously through stories told to me by older Black folks, except for one incident, which I remember vividly. In 1946, when I was in high school at Union Baptist Institute, a story published in the Athens and Atlanta newspapers described a wanton lynching: two Black men and their wives had been bound to trees and shot to death near Monroe, Georgia. Not one of the white men involved was ever held responsible. Barbaric aggression such as this caused me to be vigilant, especially as a young person living in the South. Whether they were random or planned crimes, incidents such as these were always in the back of my mind, because it was imminently possible that at any moment, it could happen to me while walking alone on those lonely, dark country roads in Georgia.

Nevertheless, this horrible crime did not encourage any Black students at the School of the Art Institute to make art that encompassed social commentary. I and other Black students at the Art Institute made art judged solely by European standards. Our influences and the artists we revered were the impressionists, postimpressionists, the fauves, and the cubists: Henri de Toulouse-Lautrec, Claude Monet, Paul Cézanne, Vincent Van Gogh, Henri Matisse, Maurice Utrillo, Marc Chagall, Amedeo Modigliani, André Derain,

Georges Braque, Constantin Brâncuşi, and Pablo Picasso. We did not realize that the latter five artists were imitators of African art.

My reason, and possibly other Black students' reason, for not attempting to pursue social commentary in art was because the School of the Art Institute's curriculum was composed of European methods and aesthetics. Faculty members were predominantly former residents of Europe who reinforced the European ideology. There were no examples for Black students to follow, and there was no mention of African or African American art. Those subjects never entered any conversations or critiques. Consequently, my knowledge of African art and aesthetics was literally zero. My knowledge of Africa was largely influenced by newspaper comic illustrations and the movies. At that time, I did not know that Africa was a continent; I thought it was a country.

To move ahead five decades, founding AFRICOBRA artist Gerald Williams said in a 2005 interview that at that time, he had virtually the same knowledge about Africa as I had: "Most Black people in America were limited to news clips, sparse pages in history books, and Hollywood's rendition of African history. (Tarzan movies depicting savages and cannibals parading naked through the jungle with bones in their noses, afraid of their shadow, while Tarzan, who killed alligators with a single small knife, was the brave one)."[7]

In all honesty, I did not have the facilities or the vision of art-making principles to guide creative ways of applying color, nor cogent knowledge of how to construct a composition. I was a beginner learning the craft and guided by the established curriculum of art history, life drawing, design, life painting, and paintings of stoic still-life arrangements. I am speaking of the 1950s, when Black consciousness, in terms of making art, did not exist in my mind. Mine was locked into what was taught to me, that art bore no ethnic, political, or gender derivatives. My mind was cluttered with European artists, and naïvely I was fascinated by their unstable lifestyles. My head was also filled with European writers. At Wilson Junior College, the books assigned for my literature class included such authors as Jean-Paul Sartre, Franz Kafka, Albert Camus, Søren Kierkegaard, Jean Genet, and the existentialist author Fyodor Dostoevsky. Through those books I was made aware of communist ideology.

By contrast, in the 1940s at Union Baptist Institute in Athens, Georgia, a private school independent of the Georgia school system, "Negro history" classes, now labeled Black studies, exposed me to African American writers such as Countee Cullen, Langston Hughes, Claude McKay, Paul Laurence Dunbar, James Weldon Johnson, W. E. B. Du Bois, Zora Neale Hurston, Ralph Ellison, Richard Wright, Ann Petry, and Chester B. Himes. Still, I had not read anything about African American artists. Through personal study and research, I became aware of master Black artists who formerly worked and lived in Chicago: Archibald Motley, with his ethnic scenes of Black entertainment life; Charles White's powerfully rendered images; and Eldzier Cortor, who painted elongated images steeped in African aesthetics. Unfortunately, these Black artists were no longer in Chicago. I read that Motley—whom I never met—maintained a home part time there and part time in Mexico. I was also aware of his brother, Willard, a writer who also lived in Mexico, from his novel *Knock on Any Door*.

After meeting the painter Fred Jones, I observed the same African influence in his work as in Cortor's. I also discovered through Jones that in the 1940s, he and Cortor attended the School of the Art Institute of Chicago at the same time and collaborated on exhibitions. Those accomplished Black artists introduced me to a world of power and imaginative stylization. Today I am grateful for that.

After graduating from the School of the Art Institute of Chicago, my first paintings were of myriad street scenes depicting African American and other ethnic neighborhoods. It would be a few years later, after civil rights demonstrations and riots, along with the explosive cultural climate of the sixties, before the idea fully crystallized in my mind of what my concerns about art should be. In the midsixties, I became liberated. That changed me as a man and as an artist, prompting me to become "a revolutionary."

The change in my ideas about making art were motivated by major racial and politically charged events, such as Emmett Till's senseless murder and Martin Luther King Jr.'s aggressive activities, including leading the bus boycott in Montgomery, Alabama, and his visit to Chicago. In 1966, Dr. King brought his nonviolent movement to Gage Park and Marquette Park to protest Chicago's segregation in employment and in housing. Additionally, I was impressed with seeing how the Black Muslims organized into a body of pride and independence. A major inspiration that drove my rationale and decisions in art making was prompted by the assassination of Malcolm X. Many thought that he engendered the Black arts movement and viewed him as a Black prince. In Malcolm's eulogy by Ossie Davis in New York, he was

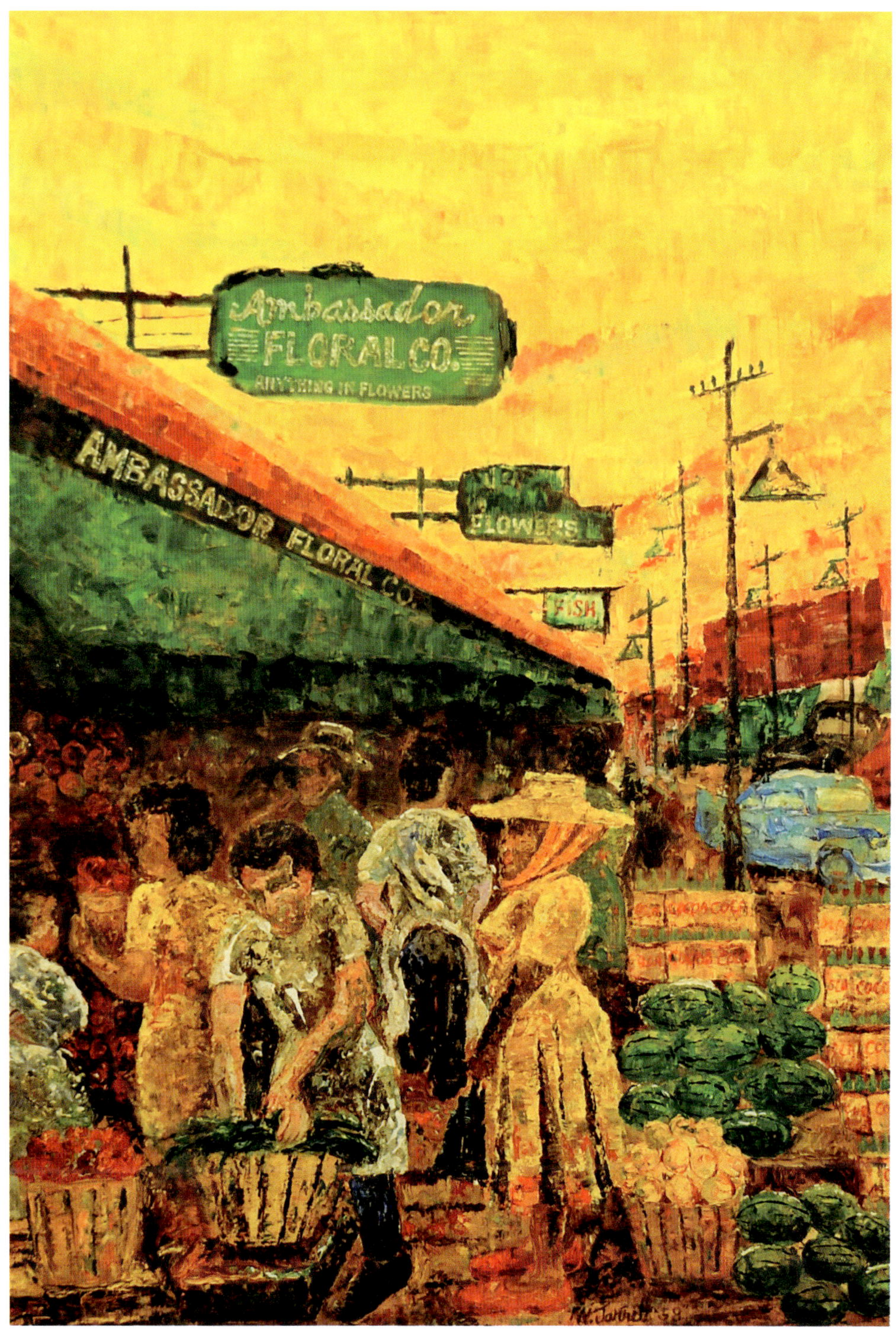

Ambassador
FLORAL CO.
ANYTHING IN FLOWERS
AMBASSADOR FLORAL CO.
FLOWERS
FISH

enshrined as such. To paraphrase Davis, "Harlem has come to bid farewell to one of its brightest hopes, extinguished now, and gone from us forever. . . . If you knew him, you would know why we must honor him. . . . Malcolm was our manhood, our living Black manhood. And we will know him then for what he was and is—a prince, our own Black shining prince."[8]

Many racial incidents in Chicago, in the South, and in the military caused me to become a revolutionary. Those combined circumstances heavily influenced what my art would reflect. Another occurrence that influenced my art making was a protest march through the Bridgeport community in Chicago led by comedian and activist Dick Gregory. It was amazing to witness on television the resistance and defiance displayed by white residents of that neighborhood: "The second night the marchers showed up, the neighborhood mob grew to almost a thousand. The marchers were showered with eggs and tomatoes, firecrackers and rocks. Women came out of their houses to turn on lawn sprinkle[r]s, soaking the marchers as they walked by."[9]

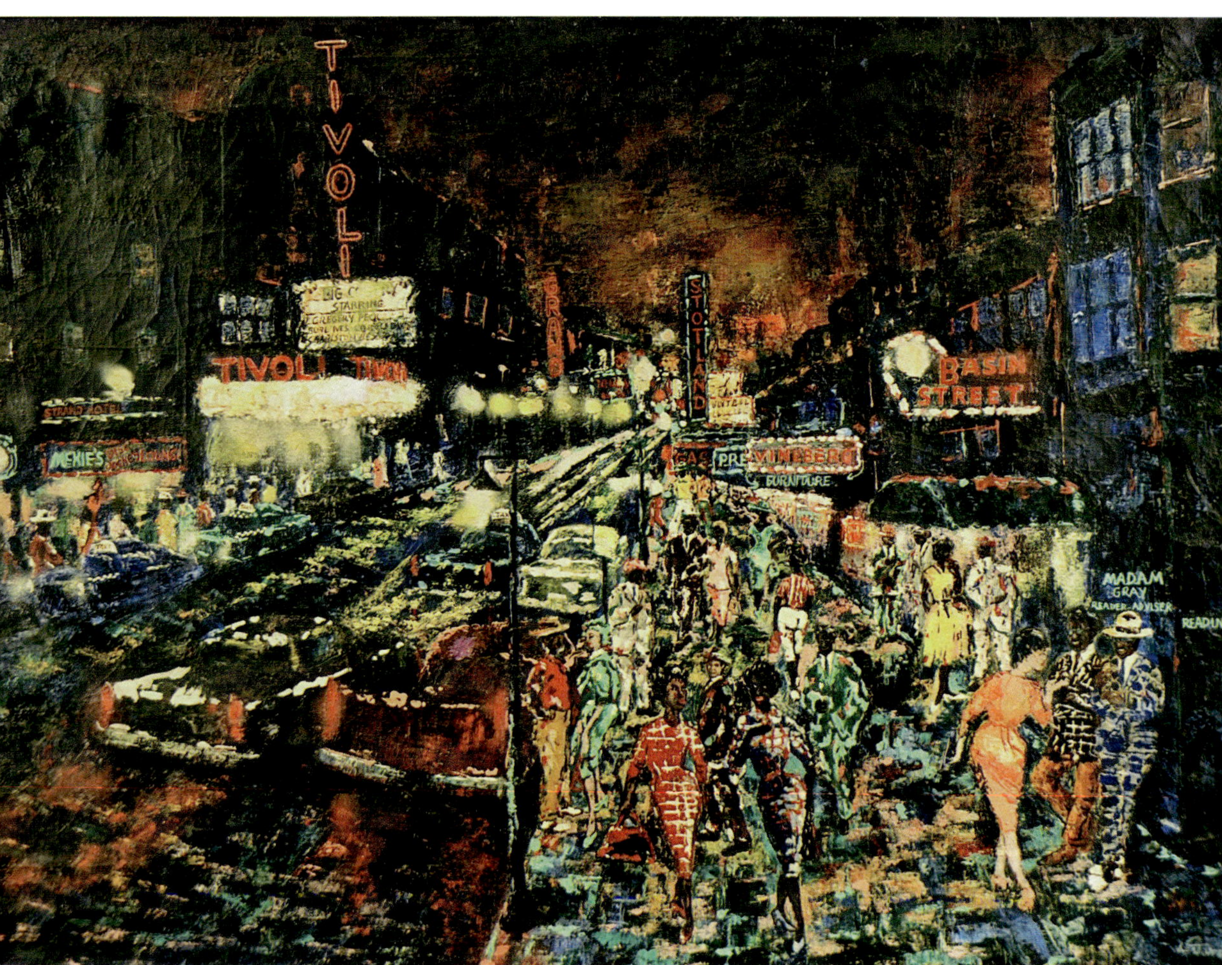

1.5

Wadsworth Jarrell, *Neon Row*, 1958. Oil on canvas, 29.5 × 42 inches. Collection of the artist.

Also affecting my art-making decisions were the protest marches and boycotts led by the Reverend Jesse Jackson, then national director of Operation Breadbasket, whose target was white businesses located in Black communities. Operation Breadbasket's rationale was that white businesses in Black communities should share the profit by hiring people who lived in those communities—not just rank-and-file workers but Black people in upper management. Reverend Jackson targeted five businesses in the dairy industry as well as supermarket chains, namely, Jewel Tea and Red Rooster. The boycotts were successful. On August 8, 1966, the *Chicago Daily News* reported: "Campaign here nets Negroes 224 new jobs in Chicago's dairy industry." The effectiveness of the boycotts impressed me.

In 1966, Martin Luther King Jr.'s protest march inspired me to make *Sign of the Times*, my first painting to include social commentary. In the center of the painting is a portrait of Dr. King, with civil rights marchers on one side carrying signs decrying unjust conditions for African Americans. The other side shows white youths living a life of leisure and indifference. Their indulgence consists of partying while attempting to learn steps in the latest African American–created dances: the twist, the watusi, the monkey, the bird, the jerk, the shake, and the boogaloo. I wholeheartedly agree with poet, scholar, and publisher Haki Madhubuti: "I was glad to leave the fifties but did not realize how the sixties would change me, my people and America."[10]

The divide between Black and white in Chicago was not resolved around the negotiating table. The unresolved racial issues revolving around open housing, employment, the political structure, and school and community concerns caused Chicago to become a powder keg awaiting the lighting of the fuses. Within this tense situation, dictator-style leadership maintained the status quo by ignoring warnings of complete anarchy, which only prompted the fuses to be lit. Riots erupted on Chicago's West and South Sides. The same happened in Newark, New Jersey, and in Detroit, Michigan. Television and newspaper reports vilified African Americans for burning down their own neighborhoods. The reports came from white announcers and journalists who had *not walked one block* in the shoes of a Black person.

On July 26, 1967, during the Detroit riots, a white friend of mine, Bill Borin, visited WJ Studios and Gallery. We were watching television, and he became emotionally upset and raised his voice: "If white people were treated like Black people are being treated, this country would have hell to pay. If you think burning a few buildings and looting stores are something, man, you haven't seen nothing. We would tear up this whole damn country. If we couldn't be free, nobody could."[11]

Shortly after Borin made that statement, on July 30, 1967, another white friend, the art collector Martin Goldsholl, who lived in a western suburb, was visiting my studio and expressed similar views: "I've been watching on television all of the unrest and turbulence that is happening. Why don't they give them what they want? All they are asking for is equal rights like other American human beings have. If this were white people, we wouldn't sit still five minutes for this kind of behavior. We would collect the rent—I mean, not just burn buildings in Black neighborhoods, I am speaking of burning down the entire country."[12] As Bill and Martin imparted about the treatment of Black people in the United States, the retaliation to overt discrimination pales in comparison to how white people would react if they experienced the same blatantly unjust and inhumane treatment.

In 1968, on the West Side of Chicago, after the assassination on April 4 of Martin Luther King Jr., there were forty-eight hours of rioting.

The riot left two miles of Lawndale, on West Madison and on 16th Street, resembling a war zone. Once again, television and newspaper reports by white journalists condemned the turbulence as an excuse for Black people to loot. The brilliant poet and playwright Useni Eugene Perkins responded with a powerful poem in the book *West Wall*, accompanied by photographs by Roy Lewis, the talented visionary photographer of the 1960s civil rights movement. Lewis illustrated the book with photographs depicting the 16th Street neighborhood and used them in his *West Wall mural*. Useni wrote:

Symbols of liberation,
Rejoicing to form a third world Anthem,
They (whites) say there ain't no culture on
the turf of West Sixteen Street only dirty
Storefronts/Vice Lords/Cobras . . . and relics
of riot torn buildings destroyed by niggers
who only wanted to be seen on t.v. (in living color).
And be listed in the obituary column of The BLACK
DISPATCH (as victims of riot control mercenaries).[13]

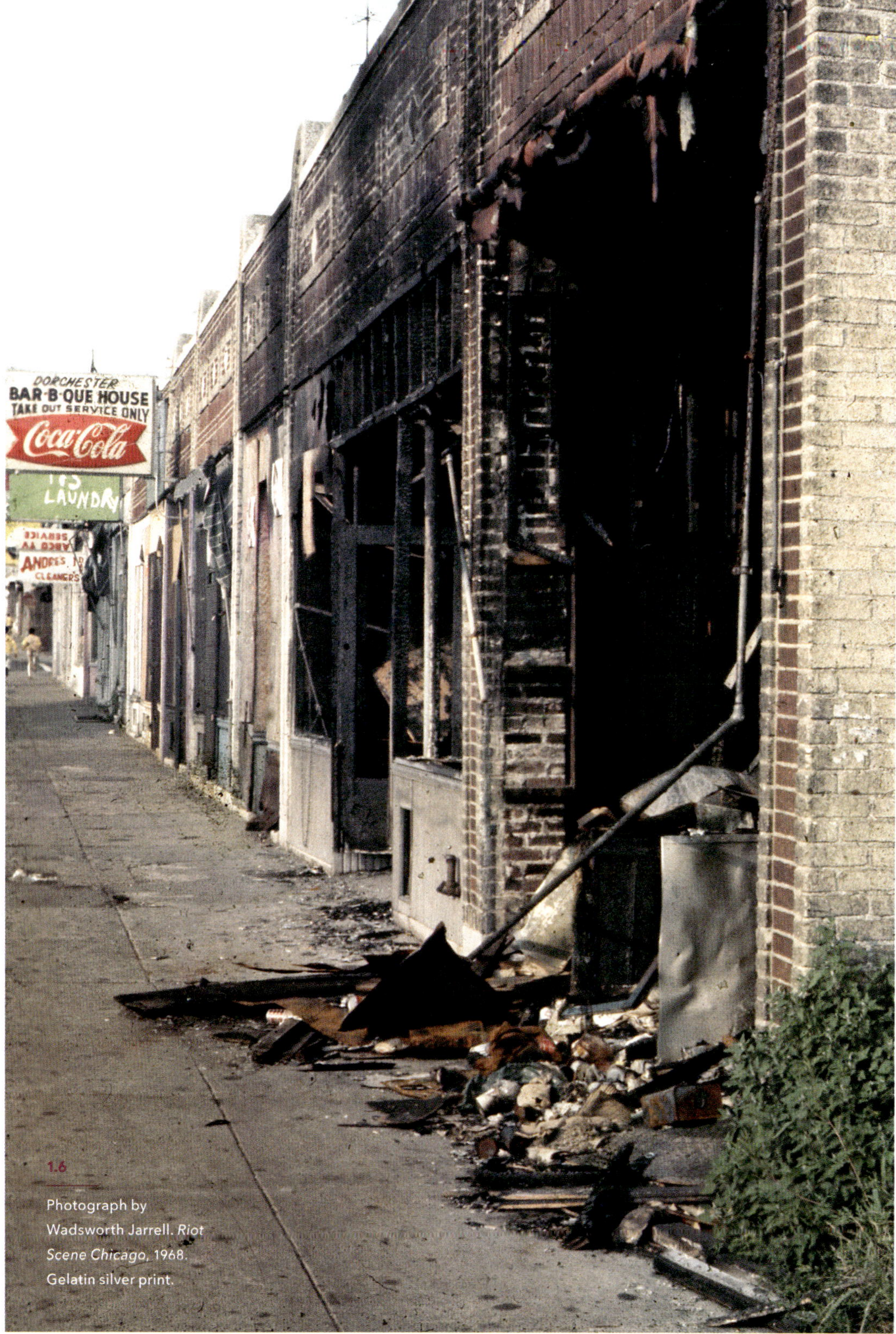

1.6

Photograph by
Wadsworth Jarrell. *Riot
Scene Chicago*, 1968.
Gelatin silver print.

During this era of unrest in Chicago, in the sixties and seventies, fist pumping and soapbox speeches calling for "whitey's" demise were frequent occurrences in Black neighborhoods. The speeches, in some instances, revealed their plan of attack. Some older and wiser African Americans advised against that. In July 1967, secrecy was the theme of a speech made by artist, designer, art collector, and gallery owner William McBride. His emotional speech was made before an audience of Jae Jarrell, Norman Parish, me, and Haki Madhubuti, who were there promoting his new book, *Think Black*. Jae, Norman, and I were visiting galleries on 31st Street, in the block between Calumet Avenue and South Parkway (now King Drive). In that single block were 353 East Gallery, owned by Jose Williams, Alfred Tyler, Howard Mallory, and Bill and Mary Daniels; McBride's Gallery; an antique shop owned by the artist William Carter; and a studio owned by photographer Frank Shepard. McBride said: "If you profess to be a Black revolutionary and intend to do harm to someone, you don't tell them what you are going to do, or what choice of weapon you are going to use. Brothers seem to take pride in exposing their plan to 'whitey' by telling him: 'In This Hand I Have a Rock.' When you tell him that, he's prepared and waiting for you."[14] McBride's speech referenced boastful rhetoric as heard in the signifying that emanates from Black communities. Among African Americans, signifying perhaps dates back to slavery, when distinctions existed between "house Negro" and "field Negro," light skin and dark skin, and "good hair" opposed to nappy hair. Signifying has similar rhetorical characteristics to joning, peacocking, rappin', and playing the dozens. It is also known as crackin' on each other. Additionally, signifying has been reincarnated in hip-hop music, which is void of musical instruments and composed basically of profane, hollow, and repetitive boastful lyrics demeaning their own. Hip-hop performers are not musicians; they are poets and dancers.

Chicago in the sixties and seventies was a hotbed of creative fermentation. In 1961, the inventive atmosphere brought the founding of Ebony Museum of Negro History by Charles and Margaret Burroughs, later renamed the Museum of Negro History and Art and, in 1968, the DuSable Museum of African American History. In 1963, the Darlene Blackburn Dance Troupe was founded. In 1965, the Association for the Advancement of Creative Musicians (AACM) was founded by Muhal Richard Abrams, Steve McCall, Jodie Christian, and Phil Cohran. In 1967, the Organization of Black American

Culture (OBAC) was founded, and the OBAC Writers and Visual Arts Workshops produced the *Wall of Respect* mural as a visual component of a multidisciplinary group project. In 1968, the Kuumba Theater was founded by Val Gray Ward, and in the same year, five visual artists formed AFRICOBRA (African Commune of Bad Relevant Artists). In 1976, Eta Creative Arts Foundation opened, with Abena Joan Brown as director.

Bolstering the creative climate in 1960s Chicago was the opening of several African American–owned galleries, including those that exclusively exhibited African American artists: A'fam Gallery, owned by Jose Williams and Alfred Tyler; the Irene Clark Gallery; Dorothy Dunn Gallery; the Osun Gallery, owned by Yaounde Olu; the Rodger Wilson Gallery; Lakeside Gallery, owned by Barry Plotkin; Zeno Gallery; and WJ Studios and Gallery.

In addition, several specialized galleries exhibited handmade jewelry, African cloth and clothing inspired by African garments, and African-inspired personal grooming items. The creativity at that time was basically engendered by, and in the matrix of, the Black revolution—which was the civil rights, Pan African, and Black power movements. This interconnected explosion of creativity earned Chicago the title of, in the words of Jeff Donaldson, the "Mecca of Black Art." The visual component of the Black arts movement was born in Chicago in 1967 (the *Wall of Respect*), and in 2020, it still inserts itself with a viable presence and a formidable impact on the Chicago history of the Black Arts movement, and in American and African American communities across the nation and the world. Investigating the revolutionary rhetoric and social critique that continue in nationalist discourse remains an important method for artists into the twenty-first century, because it continues to have a discernible effect on African American culture well beyond the Black arts era.[15]

In an essay written for *Time* magazine, Henry Louis Gates Jr. argues that "the idea of a Black American renaissance has a long and curious history." Gates discusses the 1901 writings of distinguished Black critic and poet William Stanley Braithwaite, in which he describes the beginning of a "Negroid Renaissance." In addition, Gates's essay sheds light on the Harlem Renaissance, referring to Alain Locke and other writers and artists of that time as part of the Second Renaissance. Gates then mentions the Black arts movement of the sixties: "The third renaissance was the Black Arts Movement, which extended from the mid-'60s to the early '70s. . . . Erected on a shifting foundation of revolutionary politics, this 'renaissance' was the most short-lived of all. By 1975, with the Black Arts movement dead, Black culture seemed to be undergoing a profound identity crisis."[16]

I would argue that the Black arts movement was not dead by 1975; actually, the fruits of the movement still exist in 2020 because of what transpired, and what was birthed, in the sixties and seventies—such as standard philosophies created by poets and writers, visual artists, and musicians, as well as the founding of significant arts and cultural organizations. Several of those organizations and institutions are still relevant fifty plus years later as cultural icons in Black communities. In addition, a significant amount of art produced during that era is in the permanent collections of major museums and other important institutions that curate current significant art exhibitions.

Those cultural institutions founded in the sixties and seventies that still exist include, to cite a few, National Black Theater in Harlem, founded by Barbara Ann Teer; the Black Repertory Theater, founded in 1976 in St. Louis; The OBAC Writers Workshop—one of the longest existing writers' workshops in history—founded by a group of writers and poets in Chicago in 1967; the DuSable Museum of African American History in Chicago, founded in 1961 and renamed in 1968; the African American Museum in Philadelphia; the African American Museum in Los Angeles; the African American Museum in Dallas, founded in 1974; and the National Center of Afro-American Artists, founded by Elma Lewis in 1970 in Boston, to parallel her Elma Lewis School of Fine Arts.

Musicians, art collectives, poets, and book publishers that got started in the sixties are still producing relevant music concerts, publishing poetry and giving readings, and exhibiting art at neighborhood and major institutions, including the AACM collective, the AFRICOBRA collective, and the Weusi Artist Collective. Poets like Angela Jackson who published with Third World Press, which is now the largest African American press in the world.

And finally, the first proposal, written by sociologist, activist, and author Nathan Hare, in 1968 for the Department of Black Studies at San Francisco State University, is well-known and relevant today in major white colleges and universities, where Black scholars are heads of Black studies programs. It is ironic that negative criticism is heaped on a movement of the era that made positive and long-lasting progress. Significantly, if it were not for the sixties civil rights, Black power, and Black arts movements, Black people would still be referred to as colored and as Negroes, and there would *not* be Black studies programs in major white universities. As scholar and historian Lerone Bennett Jr. notes, "It is fashionable nowadays to deride the movement and heap scorn on the militants who pushed America across a critical threshold. But this is misleading of history. For the movement of the sixties and seventies was Black America's finest hour and one of the finest hours in the history of the Republic."[17]

During the era of the civil rights, Black power, and Black arts movements, it was the militants—including assertive cutting-edge artists—who broke new ground that politicians, civic leaders, and academic intellectuals advanced to claim. Artists of that era were primary sources of and precipitated what would become—and still are—topics of many art historians' lectures and books articulating the Black aesthetic. As artist, scholar, and educator Floyd Coleman said in a lecture, "The art and culture of the 1960s is arguably the most productive and artistically inventive period in the history of African-descended people in North America."[18]

The Black Arts movement is not dead—there has not been a funeral—because of the vibrant artist collectives and cultural organizations that were established in the sixties and seventies and continue to thrive, inspire, and influence. The eulogy and epitaph have yet to be read or written. The Black arts movement is indeed alive and kicking—high and forceful in 2020, and for years to come—with the impact of a disobedient, contrary Georgia mule.

2

GENESIS

In August 1963 at an art fair in Chicago, Jeff Donaldson made passionate and engaging remarks about revolutionary art. He spoke to the small collection of artists who were anxiously seeking customers at the art fair. Jeff's comments were a mixture of substance and his usual humor: "Man, I can't kill nothing and won't nothing die. We should stop showing in all these art fairs and being concerned about selling art. We need to get together as a group—a Negro collective—and make art of our choice, Black art, that's not for sale. Our aim should be about developing a new language created out of sharing a common aesthetic creed."[1]

Jeff was announcing to the world that a cultural revolution was imminent, and it would comprise Black people in Black communities. His remarks seemed rational and not difficult to understand and achieve. His idea was important and attainable, given that it was the first decade of introspection into African American values and African culture. Additionally, it was the decade when Black people began to purge the years of willingly accepting European aesthetic values as the standard-bearer for art.

For too long in art schools, Black artists had studied and digested the history of white artists worldwide but found nothing in the curriculum that taught the history of African American artists or African art. In all reality, Jeff's proposal for creating Black art and a Black aesthetic as a new visual language through a group of Black artists was a fresh thought—a revolutionary thought. His statement was perhaps a page taken out of Frantz Fanon's book *The Wretched of the Earth*, with inspiration taken from the Black Muslim's self-reliance philosophy.[2]

The art fair was held at the 55th Street Shopping Center, which consisted of a few retail stores anchored by the CO-OP Food Market. The Hyde Park neighborhood where the art fair was held was a bedroom community of University of Chicago professors and many affluent and intellectual residents. It was a scenario that artists thought had the ingredients for great sales.[3] The organizer of the art fair was Margaret Burroughs—the art matriarch of Chicago. She displayed her work and extended invitations to a few other artists, namely, Jeff Donaldson, Rosie Dotson, Clifford Fox, Fred Jones, Clifford Lee, Norman Parish, and me. Many Black artists wrestled with the idea of what role art should play in the civil rights movement, or whether art should enter the political arena at all. Jeff articulated the significance of creating art with African people as subjects. He said, "Man, you know we could devise hip ways to present Black people. We will show them in their elegant Blackness, creating new ideas and always staying ahead of the pack."

My response was "I can dig it. We need to make art that shows the dignity of Negroes whatever scene they are in. Our art should exclude paintings that I often see in art fairs of big-eyed Black children sitting on the curb with tears streaming from both eyes. What the hell are they crying about? What are those artists trying to say?"

Jeff laughed. "Hey man, those cats are only interested in money. They are attempting to come up with something they think is salable, you know, make a fast buck."

"Yeah, I know. I am interested in selling my art also, but at least I am attempting to create what I call good art, you know, art that says something and is well crafted."[4]

The discussion turned to finding the perfect fit of proficient artists who were interested in forming a collective. There were few sales except for spontaneous pastel portraits created by Clifford Fox. The fair turned out to be more of a social gathering. At this time, most Black artists considered attaching "Black" to their art as a third rail that would possibly produce grounds for rejection from mainstream galleries and museum exhibitions. The majority of art exhibited in the art fairs at the time contained very little "Black ethnicity." Most artists displayed art that could be categorized as "sterile," "tame," or "castrated," designed mostly to attract wealthy white customers. The artists were overly sensitive about exhibiting works containing Black subject matter, more so than the white customers, who believed they were not aware or did not care about one's ethnicity.

At that stage of my career, with influence from study at the School of the Art Institute, I had neither taken courses in African art history, nor visited the continent of Africa, so naturally my influences came from the study of European art history. Jeff was more informed than other artists about Africa. His knowledge about the continent and its culture came from his study of African art history, his visit to Africa, and his part ownership of a shop in Hyde Park, Sticks and Stones, that featured African artifacts and sculpture. Jeff established a reputation as a game changer, a forceful orator, who possessed skills in organizing people.

He succeeded by intimidation, cajoling, and diplomacy. He could influence and change hard-core minds who otherwise would not have joined any organization, even if it were as innocent as the Boy Scouts. His articulation of ideas concerning a Negro art movement made it seem like the right thing to do. In September 2004, Norman Parish, owner of Parish Gallery in Washington, DC, described Jeff's effect on people: "Jeff's influence was so widespread that it seeped into others, even some by osmosis, whether they admitted or even recognized it."[5]

Jeff's oratorical acumen, keen knowledge of world art, vast vocabulary, and take-no-prisoners approach established him as an astute and intimidating force to be reckoned with. In March 2007 in Baltimore, I interviewed two AFRICOBRA members, Frank Smith and Nelson Stevens, about Jeff. Nelson said, "I had ideas that I presented in meetings, but Jeff, that brother, would always beat me down. His ideas always seemed better. Jeff was the 'Head of the Spear.'"[6] Frank saw Jeff's influence as more tyrannical but also related a positive personal experience: "Jeff was not only influential; he was a dictator. There is a guy I know who nicknamed Jeff Idi Amin. But Jeff had a penchant for educating people and bringing them into the educational process. If it was not for him, I never would have taught at the college level."[7]

The exhibition at the art fair had its value because it was the first time Jeff and I discussed forming an artists' collective, and it was where I discovered what would become WJ Studios. Fred Jones told me of an artist's studio available in the rear of the building he lived in. He was very excited, explaining the

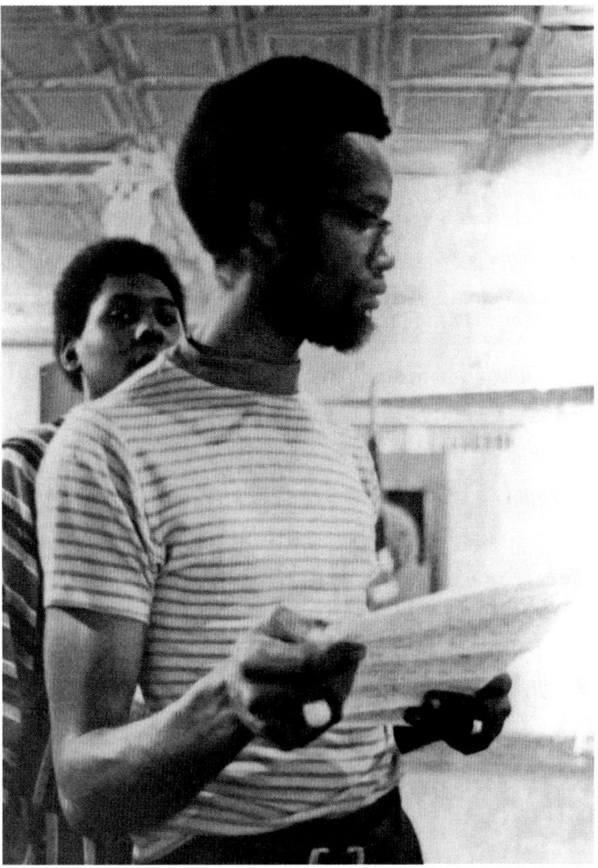

2.1

Photograph by Wadsworth Jarrell. *Ed Spriggs and Omar Lama at the Studio Museum in Harlem,* 1970. Gelatin silver print.

interior of the studio. "Man, I am talking about a real studio with sky lights and tall ceilings. One of the studios is as wide as this mall space out here."[8]

I was successful in attaining it at a reasonable cost and excited about the potential and the aura the studio presented. Four years later, I opened a gallery space and changed the name to wj Studios and Gallery, which became a viable showplace. In the foreword for the book *Wadsworth Jarrell: The Artist as Revolutionary*, artist and scholar Murry DePillars wrote:

> The Jarrells' home in Chicago was also the site of wj Studios and Gallery. wj's became the place to go. In addition to its exhibitions of works of art, including Jae's designs, wj's became the site for black poets to read their works and musicians to perform. The names of the artists having an association with wj's, ring out like gold coins: Muhal

Richard Abrams, Steve McCall, Anthony Braxton, Johari Amini, Haki Madhubuti, Carolyn Rodgers, Jeff Donaldson, Barbara Jones-Hogu, Carolyn Lawrence, Napoleon Jones-Henderson, and the list go on.[9]

Second Wind: Invasion of a Northern Suburb

The affluent suburb of Winnetka, Illinois, is sixteen miles north of Chicago. In the sixties, the population was 98 percent white and 2 percent African American. Winnetka was free of overcrowded neighborhoods and schools, a subway system, and congested streets filled with pedestrians; the small population of African Americans presented little chance for a racial uprising. Some of the wealthiest families that owned businesses in Chicago resided there. Like many suburbs surrounding Chicago, Winnetka held annual art fairs. The suburbanites strolled past artists' displays pushing babies in strollers, eating ice cream and hot dogs, and staring unabashedly at African American artists. The sight of African Americans in a capacity other than servitude seemed to amaze them. Jeff observed a related circumstance when he decided to have a drink of water from a leather-covered bottle. He came to visit Norman and me at our displays and announced, "Man, I was taking a swig of water from my jug, and a crowd of white people gathered to watch me. What the hell was that about? You should have heard what that old hunkie man asked me. He asked if I went to school for art, or did I just pick it up? I told him that I am a few hours short of getting my PhD in art. Man, you should have seen the look on his face. He grabbed the arm of the boy with him, 'Come on, you can't trust any of them.'"[10]

Norman and I were amused but skeptical of what really happened between Jeff and the old man. We knew that he was a master weaver of tales, and when he repeated them, he often embellished. Shortly after he left to return to his display, Norman turned to me laughing. "You know if he tells us that story again, it's going to be different."

I laughed. "You know Jeff is a great storyteller. He told me his grandfather was over seven feet tall, and he would go into the woods in Arkansas and catch bears with his bare hands. He also told me another story about visiting his brother in Chicago when he was an adolescent. 'When I first came to Chicago as a teenager, I was crossing 47th Street, and when the cars were approaching, I broke into a run. My friend who had been in Chicago a month

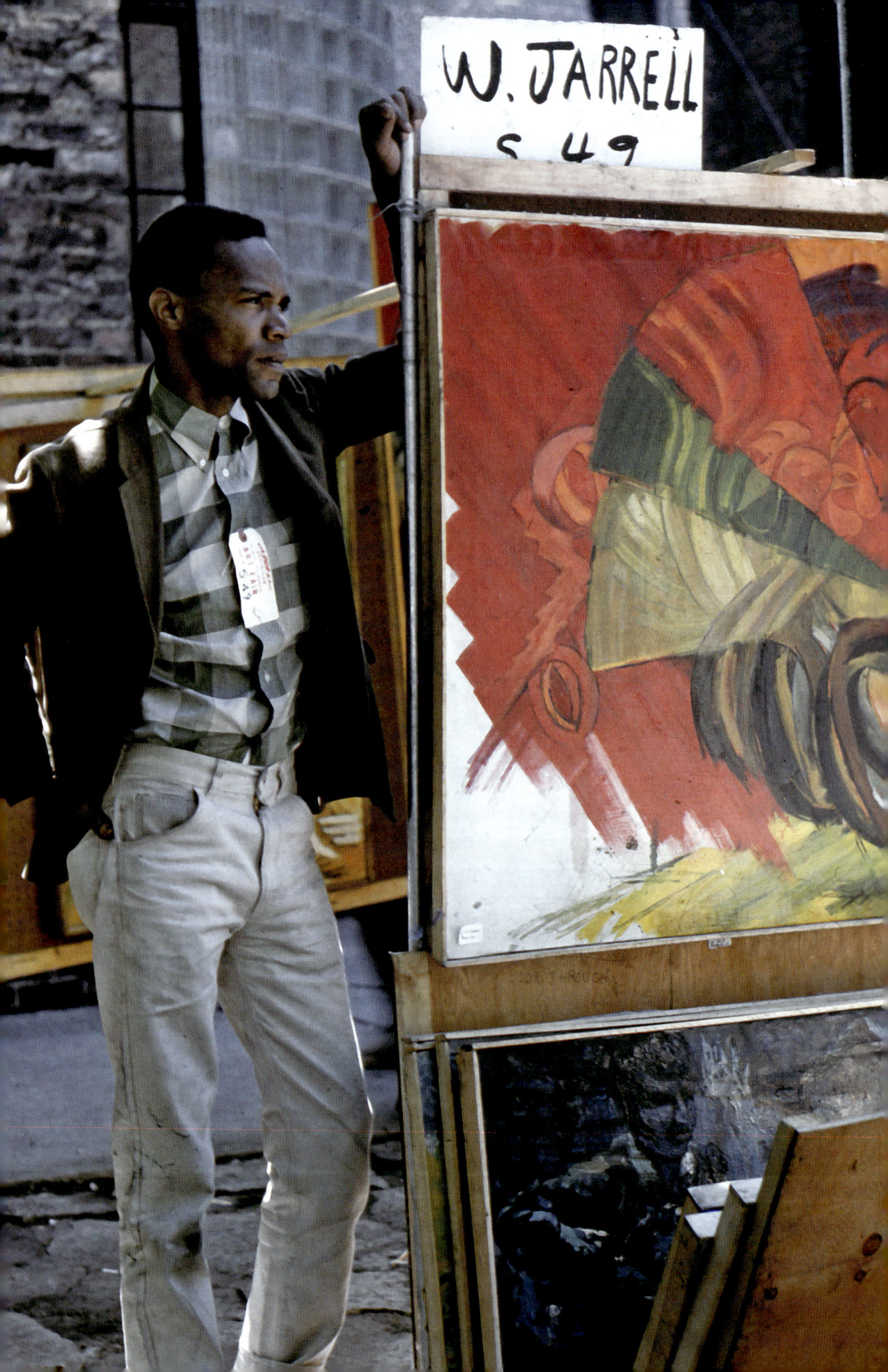
W. JARRELL
S 49

or two before me said, "Don't run. The hip thing to do is take short steps and move your arms real fast back and forth as if you are running.'"[11]

A well-meaning potential customer approached my display and expressed her admiration for my work. She proceeded to praise my talent and said she thought that my work was the best and most exciting in the show.

I smiled and retorted, "I doubt that, because there are other artists in this fair that have excellent work, and some of it is better than mine." I asked the question that concerned every artist in the art fair. "Why isn't anyone buying? I understand that Winnetka is the wealthiest suburb in the Chicago area."

She laughed. "Yes, that is what everyone claims. But by the time the mortgages on the homes, and the notes on the three cars parked in the driveways are paid, there isn't any cash left for anything else."[12] The lady asked if I would be interested in exhibiting my work in her home before a captive audience. Of course I agreed, but in my mind, I could not forget the statement she had made about the residents' income. Unfortunately, the exhibition never materialized. With very little interest shown by the suburbanites in purchasing our art and nothing else significant to do, we again discussed the subject of producing Black art.

"I am serious about pursuing the idea of forming a Negro art collective, and creating what we will label Black art," Jeff continued. "All we need for starters is a small nucleus of proficient artists, and we can produce some dynamite art that will blow the roof off everything."

I offered some suggestions. "Jeff, you know your work and mine includes jazz musicians, so what we will have to do is create a new way of expression. And through our expressions, we will demonstrate that Black jazz musicians, brothers and sisters, are the creators of that art form."

"Hey, you got that right. If someone doesn't emphasize that point, then all we will have left is the popular notion created by hunkies, that Paul Whiteman is the king of jazz, and we know what that is."

I laughed. "Yeah, white propaganda. I suppose musicians like Duke, Pops, the Hawk, Prez, Diz, Bird, Sonny, Ray, Monk, Miles, and Trane are minor players. At least, that is the way everything is presented through propaganda promoted by the media. I remember growing up in Georgia in the forties watching the newsreels shown at the movies—practically all of the jazz musicians were white. Occasionally showcased was a Black woman like Lena

Photographer unknown. *Wadsworth Jarrell at Art Fair*, Old Town, Chicago, 1965.

Horne leaning against a tree singing 'Stormy Weather,' or Maxine Sullivan, dressed as a maid sporting a head rag, looking up from her washtub singing the same song. That's like the joke I've heard often in Black communities, where a Black person is hired to do an important job, like a professor at a white university, a news commentator at a television station, or a lawyer at a white law firm. The boss tells him or her, 'While walking around, tie a broom to your ass so you can also be sweeping the floor.'"

Jeff became animated. "That's what I'm talking about. These hunkies have done a number on us and on their own people as well. With our art, we are going to have to turn all this jive around. Now, why in the hell would two accomplished singers like Lena and Maxine have to dress up as servants in order to sing in movies? That's nothing but pure racism."[13]

At the close of the art fair, artists began the arduous task of dismantling displays and loading them and their art inside or on top of vehicles. Jeff looked over the fairgrounds and yelled, "You can't buy anything now. I have packed up all of my jive. You had your chance!" He started to enter his car, then stepped out and yelled again, "YOU HAD YOUR CHANCE!"

We left the wealthy suburb at sunset, heading back to the city. There were no more serious discussions between Jeff and me about forming a Negro artist collective until 1968, after the formation of the Organization of Black American Culture and the erection of the *Wall of Respect*.

3

THE WALL OF RESPECT

And to understand that era, one has to visualize it against the rhythms of the Spirituals and Freedom Songs and the vision of artists who took art out of art galleries and splashed it on the walls of buildings. —Lerone Bennett Jr., introduction to *Tradition and Conflict*

In June 1967, a group of African American artists in Chicago embarked on a project that would include community participation. We visualized an outdoor mural in an African American neighborhood portraying Black folks in significant, relatable roles, inspiring cultural pride. The mural was named the *Wall of Respect*, and it would be the first of its kind executed by African American artists. Scholar, artist, AFRICOBRA member, and art historian Michael D. Harris attests to the relevance of a community mural:

> Most murals prior to the *Wall of Respect* had been executed on interior walls. They were created in black institutional spaces, and many were designed by iconic artists such as Aaron Douglas, Charles White, Charles Alston, Hale Woodruff and John Biggers. An interior mural theoretically is not openly available to everyone. With the *Wall of Respect*, murals began to be staged outdoors in community, rather than institutional settings. When a mural is painted in and for a community, it has moved into vernacular space and popular culture.[1]

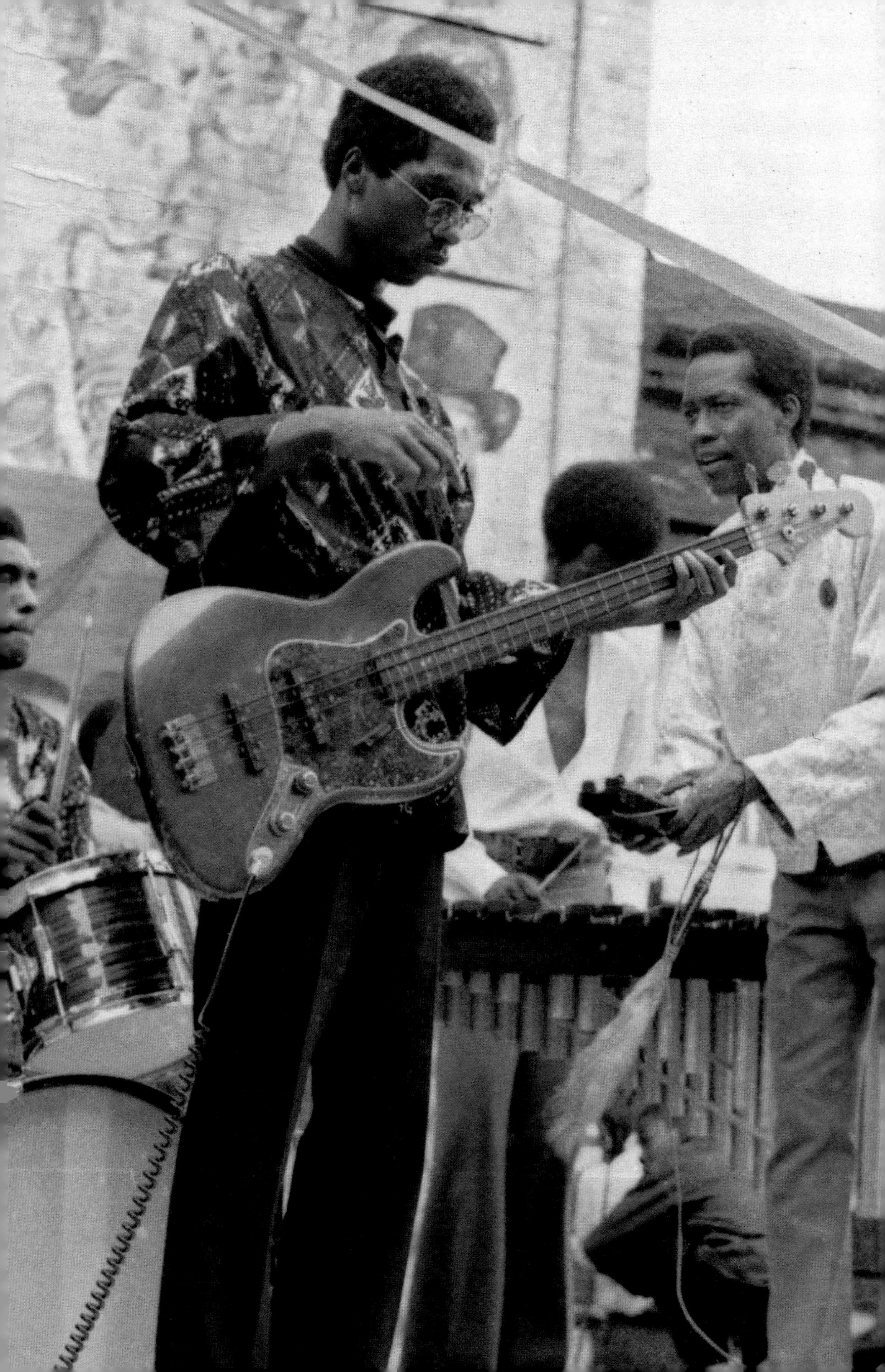

The intriguing idea of creating an artistic project in Chicago at the peak of the American phenomenon labeled the "Black revolution" was extremely important. The mural was in concert with the civil rights, Black power, and Black nationalist movements, depicting Black iconic figures in politics, sports, music, religion, dance, literature, and theater. In 1960s Chicago and other urban communities, the country witnessed a revolt of Black revolutionaries focused on changing the rules of how politics was done and on viewing art from another perspective. The term "revolution" was affixed to the Black struggle by the Last Poets, a New York group of African American poets and musicians. They were pioneers of the rap genre and influential in the emergence of hip-hop. The poets addressed the civil rights movement in their spoken word-rap tune "When the Revolution Comes." In the seventies, musician Gil Scott-Heron, who was considered by some to be the godfather of hip-hop, referenced the movement in a song. In 1970, he recorded the album *Pieces of a Man*, in which a poem-song repetitiously stated, "The Black Revolution Will Not Be Televised." In 1971, *Ebony* magazine published a third volume of the *Ebony Pictorial History of Black America* with the term in its title: *Civil Rights Movement to Black Revolution*.[2]

Demonstrations demanding equality for African Americans flashed across television screens in kaleidoscopic motion, with images jockeying for position. The images were of protest marchers, police officers and National Guardsmen in riot gear, and dead or wounded and handcuffed rioters, which grabbed the front pages of major newspapers and magazines. The skylines were aflame in Watts, Newark, Detroit, and other cities. No one expressed it more eloquently than scholar, author, historian, and senior editor of *Ebony* magazine Lerone Bennett Jr. He wrote in his introduction to the exhibition catalog *Tradition and Conflict*:

> During and after demonstrations, they discussed art, consumed, and made art a possession of all people and the expression of their deepest hopes and desires. Surging through the streets, clashing with police, scattering, regrouping, clutching at rumors, chanting rhythmic slogans, singing, screaming, crying, testifying . . . the insurgents were transformed by the fire of battle into an awesome power. In Watts and Detroit and Newark and Birmingham, they danced on a flaming world and made poetry out of their anguish and hopes.[3]

3.1

Photograph by Wadsworth Jarrell. *Unknown Guitar Player and Phil Cohran on Frankiphone, Wall of Respect*, 1967. Gelatin silver print.

"Freedom, Now," "Revolution," "Black is Beautiful," "Black Power," and "I'm Black and I'm Proud" became watchwords, and they permeated the air in Black neighborhoods and business districts, as well as on the airwaves. The fight for equality was unfolding, violently, moment by moment, in the streets of cities and towns, and in the nonviolent movement led by Martin Luther King Jr., the Student Nonviolent Coordinating Committee (SNCC), and by other principal people in the civil rights movement who organized demonstrations within polling places to register Black voters, where whites reluctantly complied. In Chicago, the climate was volatile among African Americans. There were protest marches on city hall, one led by Dr. King, demanding an audience with Mayor Richard Daley to discuss discrimination in housing and employment, police brutality, and the need to appoint more African American representation, such as precinct captains in Black neighborhoods. The sixties were a time when art made by African Americans had pertinent meaning that reflected the era. Creating beautiful poems for poetry's sake, making art of serene cityscapes and landscapes, and creating meaningless nonobjective works for the sake of art were no longer significant to us. For Black artists, this tumultuous era demanded relevance in art, works that advocated self-esteem, praise, culture and heritage, and resistance to the establishment's one-sided racist policies.

A diverse group of educators, poets, writers, scholars, and a visual artist formed OBAC (Organization of Black American Culture), pronounced o-bah-si, which derives from the Yoruba word *oba*, for king or ruler. All kings in Yoruba culture are known as obas. The *oyo oba* carries the title *alaafin*—man of the palace.

The founders of OBAC were writer, scholar, and editor of *Black World* Hoyt Fuller; sociologist Abdul Alkalimat; poet Conrad Kent Rivers; university professors Donald H. Smith, Ann E. Smith, and George Ricks; scientist Joseph R. Simpson; scholar, art historian, and visual artist Jeff Donaldson; pubisher Bennett Johnson; playwright and actor Val Gray Ward; and attorney Duke McNeil. The visual art component of OBAC included designer Sylvia Abernathy and photographers Billy Abernathy, Darryl Cowherd, Roy Lewis, and Bobby Sengstacke. The painters were Edward Christmas, Jeff Donaldson, Elliott Hunter, Barbara Jones, Carolyn Lawrence, Norman Parish, Myrna Weaver, Bill Walker, and me.

OBAC embraced Black nationalism, which was similar to, but broader in

scope than, what took place in New York City in 1965. In New York, two poets, Amiri Baraka and Larry Neal, were credited with starting the Black arts
movement with the founding of the Black Repertory Theater. The Black arts
movement in New York differed from the Black arts movement in Chicago.
New York did not include visual artists and scholars of other disciplines,
which limited their movement to writers, poets, and actors.

Jeff was director of the visual component of OBAC. In June 1967, he ini-
tiated the first meeting, held at an empty store in Harper Court (a complex
of restaurants and art-related shops in Hyde Park, now demolished). The
meeting stressed the idea of a Black artists' workshop advocating the creation of Black art. Jeff, as moderator, was asked by someone in the audience,
"What is Black art?" His answer was concise: "Any art that we produce in our
workshop will be Black art." The first meeting was an introduction to recruit
artists who were interested in working as a collaborative.

Two weeks later, the next scheduled meeting was held at artist Myrna
Weaver's studio and gallery at 73rd Street and Stony Island Avenue. Artists
were asked to bring one example of their work. A large crowd gathered in her
gallery. People were everywhere, sitting in chairs, on the floor, and standing
around the walls. The room was full of creative energy and expectation. I
brought a medium-size oil painting of a horse race. Starting in the sixties, I
experimented with "action paintings," which translated dynamic movement.
Horse racing fascinated me, and it was a perfect fit into my theory of movement, so I visited Arlington Park and Hawthorne Racetracks, capturing the
action in sketchbooks. The painting that I brought to the meeting did not
reveal any link to African American ethnicity. It was semi-abstract or highly
stylized with white jockeys astride the horses. (That period was prior to my
research of African Americans in thoroughbred racing.) The painting was
in the genre of abstract expressionists, with ample color and large flowing
brushstrokes, simulating motion.

What stands out vividly in my mind from the meeting at Myrna Weaver's
gallery was my introduction to the talented and opinionated photographer
Billy Abernathy. His persona projected confidence as a highly skilled professional and simultaneously as an ordinary "regular guy." His entire aura
exuded streetwise knowledge and hipness, because his speech was laced
with slang. Abernathy presented two razor-sharp black-and-white photographs of nude African American women photographed from a low angle.

The photographs were so well rendered that pores in the women's skin were visible.

OBAC's early meetings did not produce concrete ideas about direction. Yet, the number of African American artists drawn to the meeting clearly demonstrated interest in the possibility of artists working collaboratively. By the third meeting, in June 1967, one week later, at Myrna's studio and gallery, we began making progress. Bill Walker presented a brilliant idea of what our mission could be, and exactly where it could take place. Bill said, "I have permission from the tavern owner to paint a mural on a building at

Wadsworth Jarrell, *Win and Place*, 1966. Oil on canvas, 20 × 24 inches. Collection of the artist.

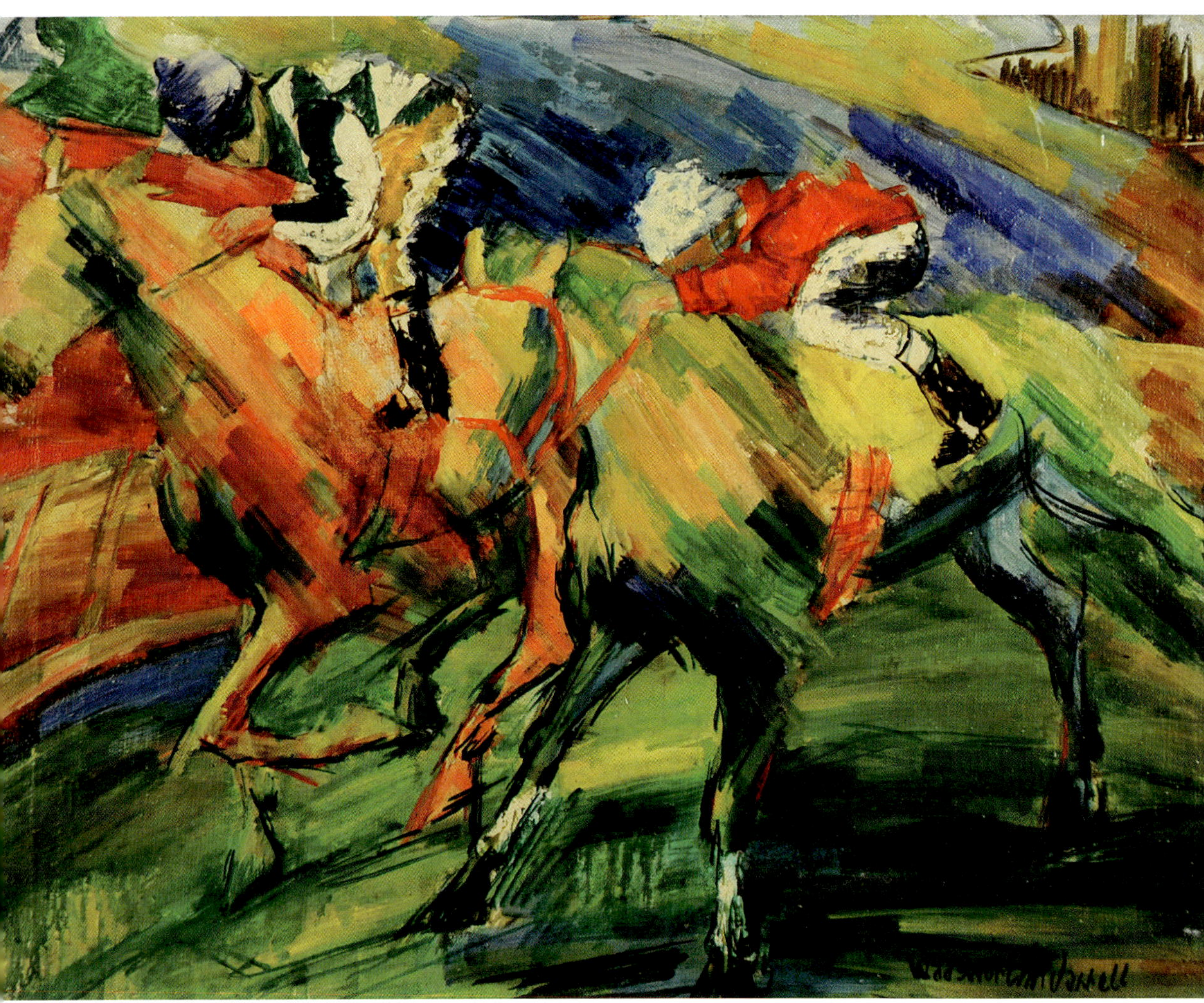

43rd Street and Langley Avenue. He is not the owner of the building, but nevertheless, I am committed to painting a mural on that building, and you all are welcome to join me."

The entire project was Bill Walker's call, because he negotiated permission to paint on the building and was totally responsible for the space where the *Wall of Respect* would be erected. This was major progress. We had arrived at the point of moving beyond meetings and discussions. It was an opportunity to bring our ideas to fruition. We piled into cars and headed down to 43rd and Langley. The neighborhood was run down. The tenement building we went to see was typical of buildings in Chicago, with retail stores on the first floor and residential tenants above. The building was located in the part of town known as the Black Belt and Bronzeville. It was two stories, boarded up with sheets of plywood on the top floor, with a tavern and a radio and television repair shop on the ground floor. Street gang graffiti was scrolled across the lower level. The Black Stone Rangers turf extended from Woodlawn into the Forestville neighborhood, with their graffiti written on walls, buildings, and overpasses. The Stones marked their turf by announcing to interlopers in bold square block letters:

BEWARE! THIS IS BPS TERRITORY

BLACK P. STONE NATION

In spray paint in smaller letters, they scribbled:

GESTAPO MOBSTERS. LIL MOBSTERS. GANGSTER FBI

THE STONES RUN IT UP IN HERE.

The OBAC artists knew that this was Black Stone Ranger territory, and we immediately understood that the gang's members were a forceful element in the neighborhood. It was imperative that we have their stamp of approval. We knew that all our efforts painting a mural on a building in their territory could easily be covered over with their graffiti if we did not recognize their presence. We could have been run out of the neighborhood. One factor perhaps worked in our favor regarding gang members in the neighborhood. Bill Walker was known in that community as an artist and as a mural painter. Still, on a Saturday early in July 1967, we arrived at the wall to begin our project without consulting anyone in the neighborhood except the tavern owner. Money was pooled for house paint (outdoor) that artists would use to paint images; for scaffolding that was needed to reach the second level; and for the man from the neighborhood who was hired to prime the wall white and erect the scaffolding. That project consumed the remainder of the day.

An essay by Gregory Foster-Rice, who was working on his PhD at Northwestern University in Evanston, Illinois, entitled "The Artistic Evolution of the *Wall of Respect*" covers the duration of the mural painting (1967–71). The overall essay is well written and contains important history, but descriptions of some of the original members who worked on the *Wall* and of some activities are questionable, and I disagree with his characterization. As a member of OBAC and as an artist who attended all OBAC meetings and participated in all decision making and the mural's erection, I very clearly saw and heard

3.3

Photograph by Gerald Williams. *Gang Graffiti*, Chicago, 1971. Gelatin silver print.

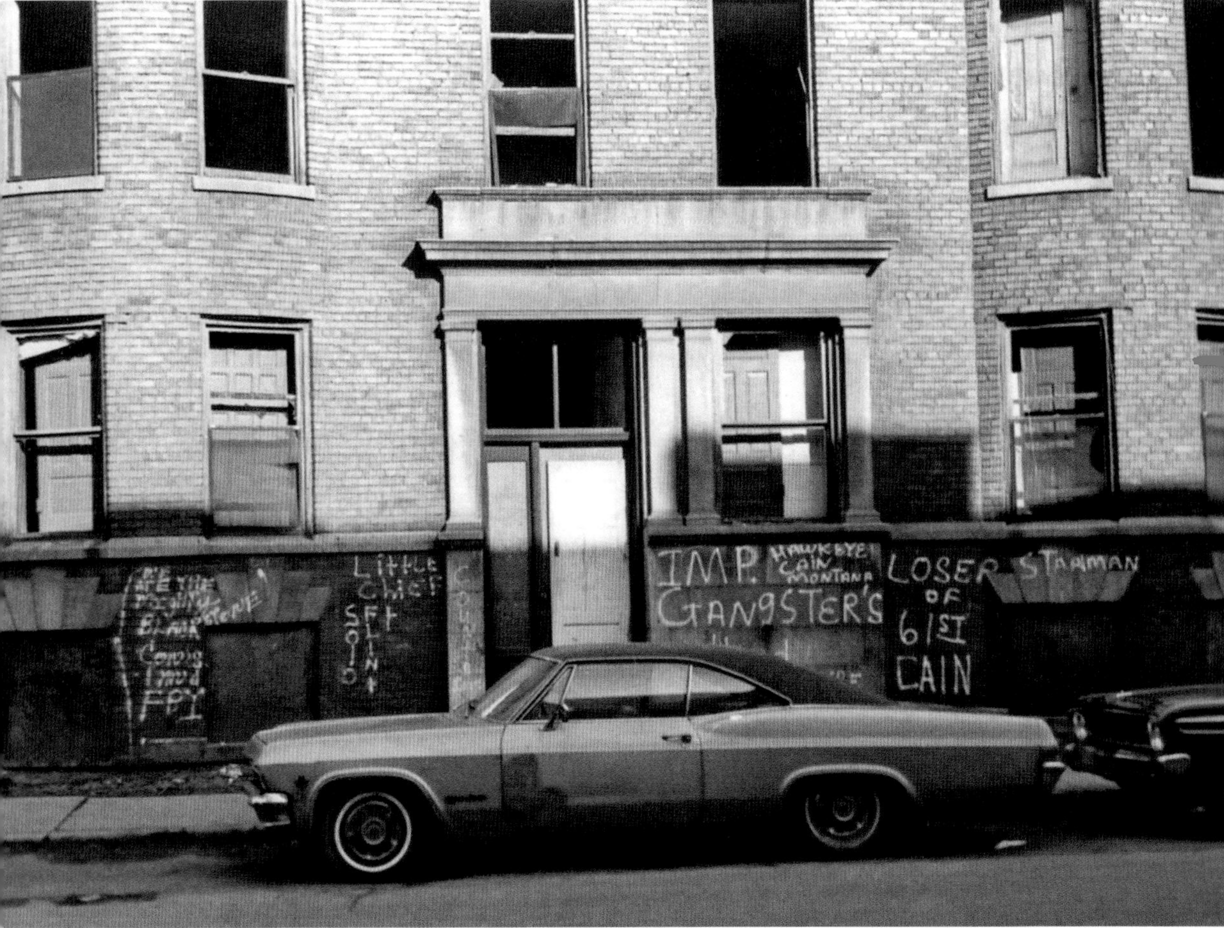

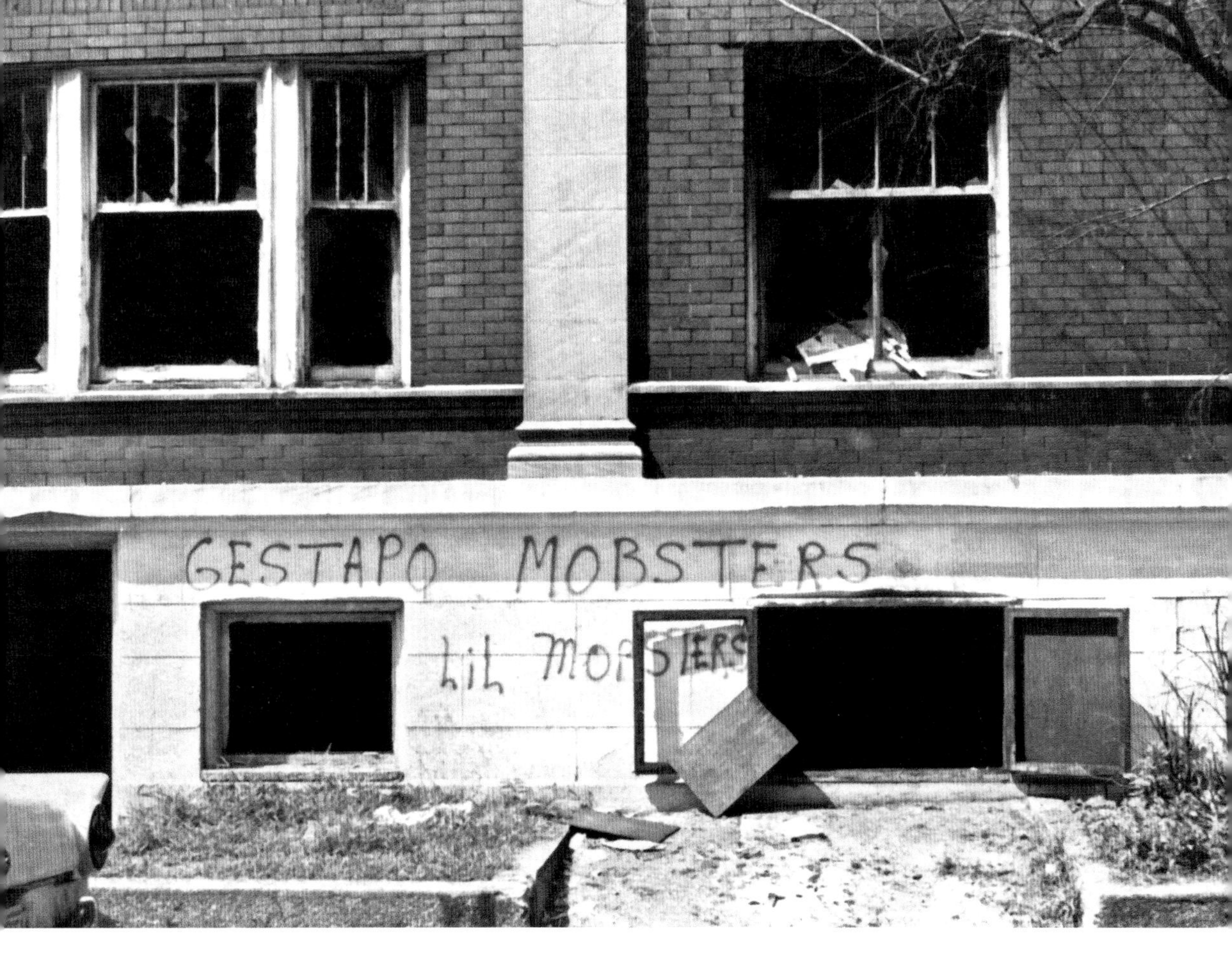

everything that transpired. The OBAC artists were all professional artists, with no student involvement, with perhaps the exception of Sylvia Abernathy, who attended Illinois Institute of Technology. In a written statement Norman Parish sent to me in September 2008, he clearly stated: "I was seven years out of art school." He also said, "The committee of OBAC artists chose the images that would go in each section without input from the community where the mural was painted."[4] Yet Foster-Rice claims in his essay, "The OBAC artists wanted to create a unified visual statement of the Visual Arts Workshop, so instead of allowing community members to contribute directly to the *Wall*, they drew up a list of figures that was modified and approved

3.4

Photograph by Wadsworth Jarrell. *Gang Graffiti*, Chicago, 1970. Gelatin silver print.

by the community. For instance, former gang member turned community activist, Herbert Colbert, insisted that the more militant Stokely Carmichael, rather than Martin Luther King, be included on the *Wall*."[5]

I totally disagree with both statements, because they are so untethered from the decisions and policies set forth by the OBAC artists. Foster-Rice is not completely at fault here; his essay is obviously based in part on interviews with principal OBAC members. But it seems to me that memories have faded for some members, and certain ones enjoy telling tall tales by embellishing. The *Wall of Respect* was created in and for a community, but the embellishment about community input and approval of the art is excessive. From the beginning, the mural was a community project without the approval of images by the community.

In 1998, Jeff Donaldson wrote a report on the *Wall of Respect* that made basically the same claim as Foster-Rice, that the Forestville community aided in deciding what and who would be placed on the *Wall of Respect*, and again, I disagree.[6] My reason for pointing out the questionable statements of Foster-Rice and Donaldson is to set the record straight. History is made. It remains constant and never changes—and *never* is it interpreted. Additionally, if this report goes uncontested without proper corrections, or without voicing an insider's view, what is untrue becomes the true history. If the OBAC artists had allowed the community in Forestville to participate in the selection process of who would be on the *Wall*, resolution would have been impossible. The OBAC artists were making a bold statement by consciously showcasing important, well-known African Americans, some who stood for causes and had a history of fighting for those causes. It was not about choosing "anybody," such as someone's friend or relative from the neighborhood, to be placed on the *Wall*.

While working on the *Wall,* however, I did agree with two women from the neighborhood who suggested replacing my sketch of the female singing group the Supremes with the Marvelettes, Motown Records' first female act. But concurring with the women's suggestion was not a group decision to change what we all had already chosen. It was my personal call. I thought, in the final analysis, that the Marvelettes had more history than the Supremes. What I do know, and what I observed, was that no other artists changed from the original images chosen by the OBAC committee at Myrna's studio and gallery.

We were ecstatic to find a physical space where we could execute our ideas. At that time, we had no idea that our mural would make history as the precursor of the mural movement in North America. Additionally, we did not know that our mural would be the *model* that started the visual component of the Black arts movement. We agreed that this structure was perfect for our project.

A few artists followed the neon Prima Beer sign in the window and entered the tavern to have a cold beer and to meet the owner. OBAC artists had attended meetings since June. It was now July, and it was time for us to present art with social commentary parallel to the civil rights movement. We wanted to speak to Black people, and we wanted to show that Chicago artists could shout out to the world that, as the Chicago-based blues musician Muddy Waters sang in "Hoochi Coochi Man," "Everybody knows I'm here."

Within the next few days, a meeting was held at Myrna's studio and gallery, and we began organizing. The conversation shifted to what titles should be assigned to each section and which individuals would occupy the spaces. After much intense debate and testimony, we chose the titles Statesmen, Sports, Jazz, Rhythm and Blues, Religion, Literature, and Theater. Sylvia designed the 31 × 60-foot space by breaking it up into seven sections, with color bands separating each. She also suggested which sections would include limited and full-spectrum colors. The debate continued about who would occupy each space. We as the OBAC committee chose high-profile figures to highlight in the chosen titled spaces, individuals who embodied strength, embraced Black political consciousness, and who were fervently vocal.

- For the Statesmen section, we chose Adam Clayton Powell Jr., H. Rap Brown (Jamil Abdullah Al-Amin), Stokely Carmichael (Kwame Ture), Marcus Garvey, and Malcolm X (Malik El Hajj Shabazz). Roy Lewis contributed a photograph of the dedication of Malcolm X Park.
- The Sports section contains Wilt Chamberlain, Lew Alcindor (Kareem Abdul-Jabbar), Muhammad Ali (Cassius Clay), Bill Russell, and Jim Brown.
- The Jazz section includes Miles Davis, Nina Simone, Max Roach, Ornette Coleman, Thelonious Monk, Charlie Parker, Charles

Mingus, Sonny Rollins, Eric Dolphy, Art Blakey, John Coltrane, and a photograph of Sarah Vaughn by Billy Abernathy.
- The Rhythm and Blues section is composed of Billie Holiday, Dinah Washington, Aretha Franklin, James Brown, Ray Charles, Muddy Waters, Oscar Brown Jr., the Marvelettes, Stevie Wonder, Smokey Robinson and the Miracles, and a photograph of Stevie Wonder by Billy Abernathy.
- In the Religion section are Elijah Muhammad, Albert Cleage, Nat Turner, and a photograph of Elijah Muhammad's granddaughter by Bobby Sengstacke.
- Chosen for the Theater section were Ossie Davis, Ruby Dee, James Earl Jones, Diana Sands, Sidney Poitier, Claudia McNeil, Cicely Tyson, Robert Hooks, and a photograph of dancer Darlene Blackburn by Roy Lewis.
- The Literature section displays W. E. B. Du Bois, James Baldwin, Gwendolyn Brooks, John O. Killens, Lerone Bennett Jr., and a photograph of Amiri Baraka by Darryl Cowherd.

Leaders labeled soft were omitted—including Martin Luther King Jr., Roy Wilkins, Whitney Moore Young Jr., Louis Armstrong, who was labeled an "uncle tom"—as were musicians and literary people who had crossed over, or "gone south," into intimate relationships with whites. In the sixties, Black people who were avid defenders of Black causes—Black power and Black Nationalism—while married to whites were stereotyped as talking Black while sleeping white.

In June 1967, at Myrna Weaver's studio and gallery, when we were choosing individuals who would occupy the spaces, I suggested including Lou Rawls and Joe Williams in the Rhythm and Blues section, because of their dynamic gift to sing the blues. Billy Abernathy disagreed. He said, "Lou Rawls is married to a fat white woman. No, not Joe Williams either; he'll hug a white woman in a minute. I saw him a few months ago out at Army and Lou's Restaurant all hugged up with a white woman."

Other important names left out of the Rhythm and Blues section, though they could not all compositionally fit into a ten-by-twelve-foot space anyway, were B. B. King, Jackie Wilson, Joe Turner, Jimmy Rushing, Bobby Bland, Jimmy Witherspoon, Howlin' Wolf, Buddy Guy, and Junior Wells. Those stalwarts of music—those blues shouters—clearly put the world on notice that their cries, hot licks, and sensuous moans steeped in gospel music were the face of the blues from Kansas City to the Mississippi Delta to Chicago.

In hindsight, in my opinion, we were mistaken in considering people's private lives. A few highly regarded individuals among our choices were intimate with whites or married to them. We never followed through on the excuse that we would replace them as soon as we found a better choice. There was no possible replacement for such a dynamic figure as Amiri Baraka, who had been married to a white Jewish woman. Besides, Baraka was the centerpiece of Edward Christmas's mural section on Literature, which featured Cowherd's large photograph of Baraka and extracts from his powerful poem "sos."

It was not a problem for me to separate the personal activities of entertainers and high-profile people, such as who they drank, ate, or slept with. They were chosen, I assumed, because of their political stance and their important contribution to the arts. It was also a terrible mistake not to include Louis Armstrong and Duke Ellington in the Jazz section. They were two of the greatest musicians to enter the field of music, in vernacular, "two of the baddest dudes." Ellington was one of the greatest American composers, if not the greatest, and Armstrong, with his inventive horn technique and improvised singing style, influenced every important trumpet and cornet player and scat singer who came later.

Sylvia Abernathy asked who wanted to paint what section and hands went up to claim the sections of their choice. Jeff Donaldson chose Jazz, Myrna Weaver chose Sports, Edward Christmas chose Literature, Norman Parish chose Statesmen, Barbara Jones chose Theater, and I chose Rhythm and Blues. Billy Abernathy objected to my choice by asserting, "Bill Walker should have that section, because he understands musicians and included them in several of his paintings."

Abernathy's assertion was unfounded because he was uninformed that several artists, newspaper articles, and directors of art fairs and art galleries had stated that my paintings reflected the color, tempo, emotional aspects, and compositional explosiveness of music. My reply to him was "Musicians are my meat—that's what I do." Bill was familiar with my paintings. We had known each other since the fifties, during my tenure as a student at the School of the Art Institute of Chicago. He had observed and respected

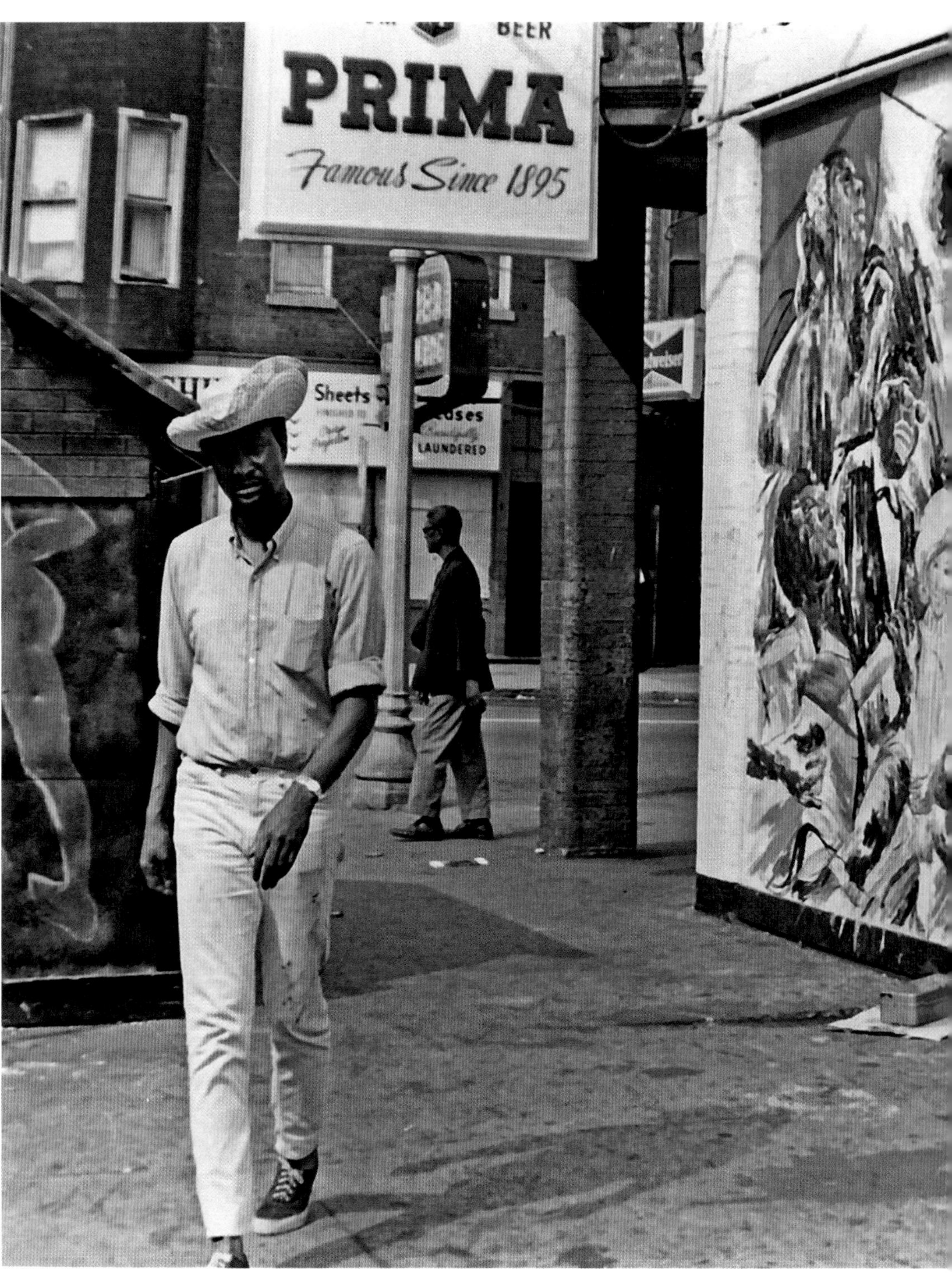
BEER
PRIMA
Famous Since 1895
Sheets
LAUNDERED

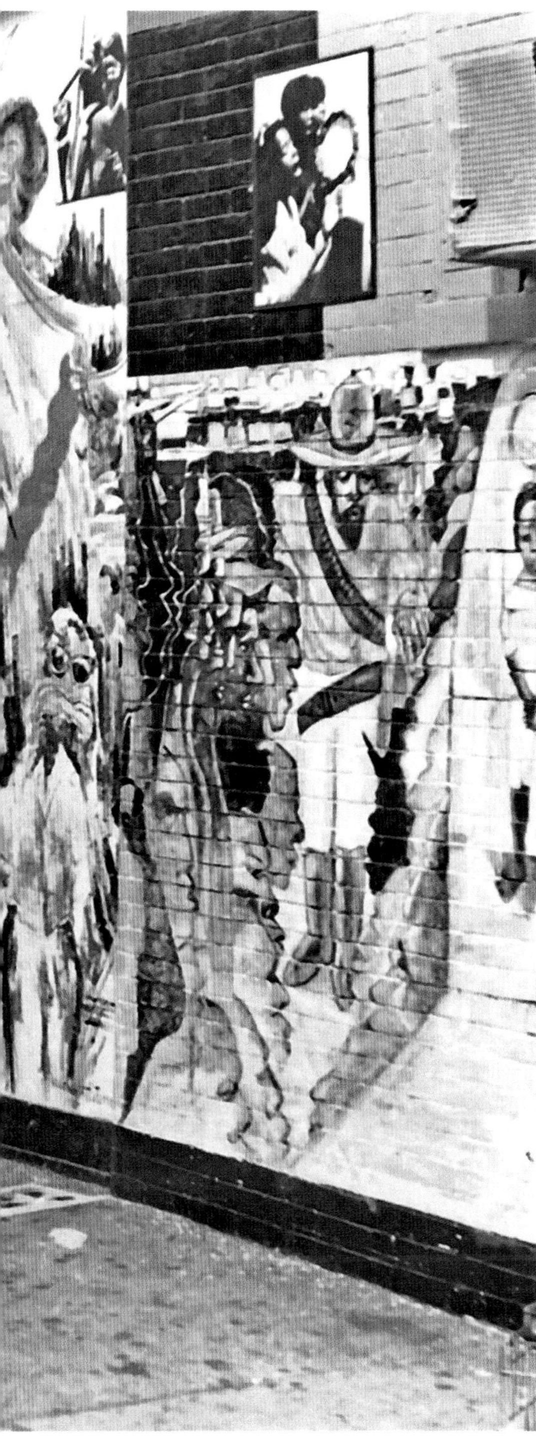

Photograph by Roy Lewis. *Jeff Donaldson at the* Wall of Respect, Chicago, 1967. Gelatin silver print.

my paintings of street scenes, horse racing, and nightclubs and musicians, which was my forte.

The first time I met Bill was in 1956 at a party in a Hyde Park apartment, hosted by Lucile Cunningham, who later became his wife. Other people at the party attended the School of the Art Institute: students, a few artist models, and local artists from around the city. An altercation ensued between a commercial artist named Gentry and me that almost resulted in a fight, but Bill and I immediately developed an affinity. He intervened and explained that Gentry was a masochist who loved getting whipped. Bill nicknamed me The Preacher because of my speech delivery, which reminded him of a Baptist preacher. Bill was diplomatic, and he avoided confrontation by saying, "I will take the Religion section."

After the selection of people for each section, we concluded all meetings. A few days later we arrived at the *Wall* with drawings. I made a maquette of my section, fashioned after the composition of a previous painting, *Hootenany*, so that it would guide me through organization of the oversized painting. I photographically enlarged my sketches and Norman's to actual size at the advertising studio where I was employed. This made it easier to achieve a likeness as well as correct proportions. I used an old technique that entailed rubbing charcoal on the backs of drawings to transfer them to the *Wall*. Norman used a more sophisticated method known as "pounce pattern"—associated with sign writers—to transfer his sketches to the *Wall*.

Painting on the *Wall* was difficult because of the rough brick surface. Using flat house paint was also difficult, especially blending it. That prompted me to return to my studio and retrieve my reliable oil paints. After two weeks of progress into the mural, another section was added. Dance was assigned to the artist Carolyn Lawrence, who painted dancers on the newsstand directly in front of the Rhythm and Blues section, near the curb of the street. That was my first time meeting the painter Elliott Hunter, who came by in a floppy straw hat, driving an old convertible Austin-Healy. Jeff asked Elliott to collaborate with him on his section, and he complied.

Our goal was to finish the mural by the third week in August and have a celebration to dedicate it to the community. Jae and I had been married two months, and we had made reservations to celebrate our honeymoon in the Bahamas the last two weeks in August. Therefore, working overtime to meet the deadline was my only option. It entailed weeknights, using spotlights, as well as painting on Saturdays and Sundays. As a result, my section was completed second; Myrna's Sports section was first.

Jae came by on a weekend to visit while I was working on the Rhythm and Blues section, and the initial wash on the musician Muddy Waters ran down, streaking his image. A couple nearby frowned and said to Jae, "It's a shame the paint ran down, ruining his image." Jae said, "He doesn't care; he likes it—that's part of his painting."

Shortly after we started working on the *Wall*, Myrna asked me if her help was needed and offered to paint the flat areas in my section. I declined her offer because my composition had one small flat area. Bill and Myrna became concerned whether the Rhythm and Blues section would be completed before my departure to the Bahamas. They suggested that if I were unable to finish my section before departing, they would finish it for me. My reply was firm: "My section will be finished, and if anyone painted on it, they would have to answer to me on my return, and there would be consequences."

Each artist used their knowledge to approach how they would arrive at completion. All images were painted directly on the *Wall* except in the Literature, Sports, and Jazz sections. In the Literature section, Edward Christmas painted one image, W. E. B. Du Bois, and collaged the remainder with enlarged black-and-white photographs. Elliott Hunter and Myrna Weaver painted on wood panels that were later mounted in the Jazz and Sports sections.

In the early stages of the mural, we noticed a few white men in suits mingling in the crowd, but near the end, they had increased in numbers. There were rumors, propelled by Jeff Donaldson, that we were being watched by the FBI as part of COINTELPRO (Counterintelligence Program), and there was a possibility that they had infiltrated our ranks. To me, it seemed trivial and inconceivable to believe that law enforcement, especially the FBI, would be concerned with a group of artists painting a mural on a tenement building in the ghetto.

During that era of turmoil, unsubstantiated rumors were magnified and assumed as absolute truth. But many rumors were justified and proved credible according to an FBI informant's confession. In 2005 on the television program *Like It Is*, hosted by the late Gil Noble, a Black man named Darthard

Perry, a.k.a. Ed Riggs, Bill Perry, and Othello, sat boldly in front of a television audience of millions and admitted his role as an undercover informant for the FBI. He articulated the primary goal of the agency by revealing classified data known only to insiders:

> The bureau infiltrated African American organizations such as music, visual art groups and theater, caused disruption and destruction that managed to shut some of them down. The bureau created "Black desks," which stored information used to infiltrate Black groups, social unrest, and revolutionary groups. They had files that let them know every magazine and book read by Blacks, as well as music they listen to. The FBI made in-depth studies of Black cultural groups, comedians, and used that information against them. I infiltrated an African American theater group in Los Angeles, Black Writers Workshop, which was destroyed by fire. I know, because I did the arson by using two kerosene cans, a bottle of Purex, gasoline, and a highway flare.[7]

In October 2011, on the television documentary film titled *Outlaw Gangsters*, the legality of COINTELPRO's operation came into question. The program profiled several underworld characters: Carlos Marcello of New Orleans; Mickey Cohen and Benjamin "Bugsy" Siegel of Los Angeles; Frank Lucas and Bumpy Johnson of Harlem, New York; and FBI director J. Edgar Hoover—creator of COINTELPRO. Speaking on the program were several prominent politicians and people in law enforcement who declared Hoover's COINTELPRO operation illegal. It was classified in the same category as underworld figures in the documentary.

Despite the presence of undercover detectives and rumors of infiltrators, there was a tremendous amount of excitement among the huge crowd from all over the city who came to view the *Wall* and see OBAC artists at work. During a Chicago interview of AFRICOBRA artist Carolyn Lawrence in 2010, she commented on the atmosphere surrounding the *Wall of Respect* while in progress: "That *Wall* had so much energy. When I was out there, I felt like that was all that was going on, because of the artists working, and the community responding to what was being done."[8]

In November and December 2008, I contacted Barbara Jones-Hogu and Bill Walker, both of Chicago, and Norman Parish, of Washington, DC, and asked them to write a statement expressing their thoughts about their personal experience of excitement and interaction with community, as well as the presence of law enforcement personnel, while working on the *Wall of Respect*. Barbara wrote:

> I was concerned about making facial expressions realistic. The figures were larger than I had painted faces and pictures before, so it was hard to see how I was progressing until I stepped away from the images. I felt more empowerment than joy. It was something I wanted to do, depicting our heroes and sheroes was a way of doing it. My imagery at that time personally was more political and dealt with racism as a whole, rather than identifying real people. So I was humbled dealing with subject matter. People came to talk to me and help me when I was painting, and the fact that they kept the Wall safe. No marks, lettering, or statements were painted on it. That was a clear statement of the community honoring what we were doing. I believe that they were proud of the Wall. I did not notice the plainclothes policemen as much as I noticed the men with guns who were on the roof of the building across the street from the *Wall*. That astounded me. Until this day, I do not know what they thought we were going to do, start a revolution in our neighborhood with art as the backdrop.[9]

Norman Parish recalled:

> The *Wall of Respect* was one of the most exhilarating experiences I have ever had. I was seven years out of art school, and this project gave me an opportunity to participate in an art event, which was to my surprise, the beginning of worldwide similar murals.
>
> We were providing art for the community to experience, and also give a format to express support for the Civil Rights Movement. The Committee of OABC artists chose all images that would go in each section without input from the community where the mural was painted. The Wall was a symbol of black pride at 43rd and Langley for the South Side Chicago community and a meeting place for activists.
>
> William Walker, who whitewashed my section on the *Wall*, stated in an article in a Chicago newspaper twenty-five years later, "I believe the mural was strong in its original form." It was pure nonsense[;] it was the worst thing you could ever do to an artist in no uncertain terms.[10]

Bill Walker wrote: "I did believe and strongly hoped that our paintings would be significant, not only to that neighborhood, but to the entire city of Chicago. As I look back today to 1967, it served as an inspiration to many—young and old. While working, I felt moved and privileged to have the opportunity to be part of the OBAC group."[11]

I had the opportunity to see Bill once in a while after the mural was finished. He visited my studio a few times, but the last time I saw him was in February 1971, during a snowstorm. My son, Wadsworth Jr. (whom Bill affectionately called Fats), and I had stopped by the Chicago Museum of Contemporary Art on Ohio Street, where Bill was working on a mural in the basement. He said that the mural would later become part of an exhibition there at the museum.

In late August 1967, on a Sunday afternoon, excitement continued to mount about the *Wall of Respect*. The Rhythm and Blues section was close to completion. While descending a stepladder, my foot almost made contact with the foot of a large square-shouldered white man who fit the profile of a police officer. Dressed in a suit and tie, he was clean shaven, with his hair crew cut. Billy Abernathy, who was standing next to the man, grinned and, referring to me in his hip hesitant style of delivery, said, "Man, you got it. This dude here can paint his ass off." A roar of laughter came from the crowd, and the man who resembled a police officer laughed also. That particular Sunday night, the Rhythm and Blues section was completed, and the next day, Jae and I left for Nassau.

The first week in September 1967 was my first time to see the *Wall of Respect* after completion and dedication to the community. Norman picked me up at my studio shortly after I arrived back in Chicago. He was excited to show me the mural. We both experienced shock, disappointment, and anger, because his entire section of the Statesmen had been covered over with white paint. It was replaced with a single small realistic portrait of Malcolm X (when he was Detroit Red, a street hustler). The small painting was by an artist who hadn't worked on the original Wall, and we didn't know who he was or from whence he came. Later, we discovered his name was Edaw (Eugene Wade). We did not rest with the evil deed, so we confronted Myrna Weaver. There were rumors that she was the culprit in the erasure of Norman's section, but we received only double talk and accusations of others from her. We confronted Jeff and asked why Norman's section had been erased. Jeff decried the blatant act and explained that he was not involved in the erasure, and that he had confronted Bill and asked why he painted over Norman's section. Jeff said that Bill's reply was "I did it because I did not think his section was finished—it wasn't up to par."

Jeff said that he asked, "What is par?"

In my opinion, Norman Parish's painting, evocatively depicting the statesmen, was superior in concept and in execution, more so than the array of paintings that followed in that section. His was congruent with the total concept of the *Wall of Respect*. More importantly, the erasure of Norman's section removed the only section on the *Wall of Respect* that explicitly comprised several political images: the congressman Adam Clayton Powell Jr., Stokely Carmichael, H. Rap Brown of SNCC, and Marcus Garvey, the architect of the Universal Negro Improvement Association (UNIA) Back to Africa movement.

Later, the realistic painting of Malcolm X that had replaced Norman's Statesmen's section was augmented with small paintings of Carmichael and Rap Brown as well as a large raised fist, with a background of streaked brush strokes. The painting that Norman had executed included powerful political men. Imagine his painting being replaced with only two small renderings of political figures and a raised clenched fist. I said to Norman, "In order for that fist to replace what you painted on the Wall, it must be powerful—like High John the Conqueror."

Fifty-three years later, I still regret missing the dedication ceremonies of the *Wall of Respect*, but I heard that it was a grand affair. "The Mighty Black Wall," coined by the poet Haki Madhubuti, was now completed, and it was a tremendous success in terms of artists reaching our goals. The OBAC artists had completed a phenomenal project beyond our expectations. We also shared with the community, and with the Chicago population at large, day-to-day experiences of artists working on the *Wall* from start to finish, and they were the richer for it.

Independent writer Burleigh Hines wrote an article for the *Chicago Daily News* entitled "Mural in the Ghetto." He mentioned in his article the location of the mural and the fact that it represented and addressed the civil rights movement. He also mentioned names of heroic images on the *Wall*. He described the mural as a paint-in, a happening, if you will, with connotations of Black militancy. Being white, he perceived it as militant because of the powerful Black images. He viewed it through the lens of a white man. Hines wrote, "The artists are reluctant to speak about the wall." OBAC artists had discussed, and everyone had agreed, that as individuals, no artist would sign their spaces or give interviews. Although one artist did make a statement: "We don't give a damn if Mayor Daley ever sees it."[12]

Jeff Donaldson and Lerone Bennett Jr. commented on the magnetic power and the spectacular celebratory closing ceremony of the *Wall of Respect*. Jeff wrote,

> Curiosity seekers, uneasy tourists, art lovers and political activists of every stripe, congregated daily and in ever increasing numbers. Musicians played as the work proceeded. Writers recited their work. Dancers danced, singers sang, and the air was charged with camaraderie and pioneering confidence. Before the Wall was finished on August 24, 1967, it already had become a shrine to Black creativity, dubbed the "Great Wall of Respect" by writer John Oliver Killens, a rallying point for revolutionary rhetoric and calls to action, and a national symbol of the heroic Black struggle for liberation.[13]

Lerone Bennett Jr. wrote, "One of my most vivid memories of that period, to cite a personal experience, is of the dedication of the *Wall of Respect* on the South Side of Chicago. Never, so long as I live, will I forget the challenge and, yes, the exhilaration of speaking to a rebellious crowd ringed with policemen."[14]

Shortly after the erection of the *Wall of Respect*, OBAC artists disbanded. The artists had joined only to work collaboratively on that one project. The physical and psychological benefits that the *Wall of Respect* provided for the community were recognizable images of Black people and a permanent outdoor art exhibition. The *Wall* also enlightened a proud community, which was gratified to be singled out as special enough to receive such a momentous gift of larger-than-life-size images in tableaux of beautiful colors. People in the community were not only afforded an opportunity to witness artists at work, but experienced communal participation by offering comments and suggestions. With these factors, the mural reached people on a personal level, and gave them a feeling of partnering with the artists. The entire atmosphere shared with the neighborhood brought about high regard for the mural. The project was conceived and erected as a bold statement and for the personal satisfaction of the obac artists. More significantly, it was created for the people in the Forestville community. The creation of the mural showcased a group of brave, talented artists who took bold measures in turbulent times, under the watchful surveillance of armed police officers and suspected infiltration of fbi informants.

The concept and execution of the mural collectively represented an agent for change, a prototype, a shining beacon, giant footprints, and possibilities for others to contemplate or follow. The *Wall of Respect* (demolished in 1971) still possesses importance in the twenty-first century because it was the genesis of urban community outdoor murals in North America and the visual voice of the struggle for equality in Chicago and across the nation.

Norman Parish told me about the enthusiastic crowd that gathered on August 27, 1967, to partake in the celebration, to witness the dedication of the mural to the community, and to hear the reading of poignant poems composed especially for the *Wall of Respect* by Gwendolyn Brooks and Haki Madhubuti.

THE WALL

Gwendolyn Brooks

A drumdrumdrum.
Humble we come.
South of success and east of gloss and glass are
Sandals;
flowercloth;
grave hoops of wood or gold, pendant
from black ears, brown ears, reddish-brown
and ivory ears.

black boy-men.
Black
Boy-men on roofs fists out "Black Power!" Val
a little black stampede
in African images of brass and flowerswirl,
fist out "Black Power!"—tightens pretty eyes.
leans back on mothercountry and is tract,
is treatise through her perfect and tight teeth.

Women in wool hair chant their poetry.
Phil Cohran gives us messages and music
made of developed bone and polished and honed
cult.

It is the Hour of tribe and of vibration,
the day—long Hour. It is the Hour
of ringing, rouse, of ferment-festival.

On Forty-third and Langley
black furnaces resent ancient
legislatures
of ploy and scruple and practical gelatin.
They keep the fever in
fondle the fever.

All
worship the Wall.
I mount the rattling wood. Walter
says, "She is good." Says, "She
our Sister is." In front of me
hundreds of faces, red-brown, brown, black, ivory,
yield me hot trust, their yea and their
Announcement
that they are ready to rile the high-flung ground.
Behind me. Paint.

Heroes.
No child has defiled
the Heroes of this Wall this serious Appointment
this still Wing
this Scald this Flute this heavy Light this Hinge.

An emphasis in paroled.
the old decapitations are revised,
the dispossessions beakless.

And we sing.[15]

Don L. Lee (Haki Madhubuti)

sending their negro
toms into the ghetto
at all hours of the day
(disguised as black people)
to dig
the wall, (the weapon)
the mighty black wall (we chase them out—kill if
necessary)

whi-te people can't stand
the wall,
killed their eyes (they cry)
black beauty hurts them—
they thought black beauty was a horse—
stupid muthafuckas, they run from
the mighty black wall
brothers & sisters screaming
"picasso ain't got shit on us.
send him back to art school."

we got black artists
who paint black art
the mighty black wall
negros from south shore &
hyde park coming to check out
a black creation
black art, of the people,
for the people,
art for people's sake
black people
the mighty black wall

black photographers
who take black pictures

can you dig it?
blackburn
le roi,
muslim sisters,
black and gray it's hip

they deal, black photographers deal blackness for
the mighty black wall
black artists paint
du bois / garvey / gwen brooks
stokely / rap / james brown
baldwin / killens / muhammad ali
alcindor / blackness / revolution
our heroes, we pick them, for the wall
the mighty black wall / about our business blackness
can you dig it?
If you can't you ain't black / some other color
negro maybe?

the wall the mighty black wall

"ain't the muthafucka layen there?"[16]

4

THE INCEPTION

The year 1968 was unusually turbulent. The Vietnam War was in full progress. In Chicago on February 15, the brilliant harmonica (mouth harp) player Marion "Little Walter" Jacobs died from head wounds received in a street fight. On April 4, Martin Luther King Jr. was assassinated in Memphis, Tennessee, and riots erupted in more than one hundred cities. Additionally, on June 5 in Los Angeles, Robert F. Kennedy was assassinated. In Oakland, California, on July 15 began the trial of Huey P. Newton, cofounder and minister of defense of the Black Panther Party. He was tried and convicted of manslaughter in the death of police officer John Frey and sentenced to two to five years in prison. And of positive significance, in June of that year, five Chicago artists—Jeff Donaldson, Jae Jarrell, Barbara Jones, Gerald Williams, and I—gathered at the wj Studios and Gallery at 1521 East 61st Street to explore the feasibility of starting a revolutionary art movement. With a group of artists, we thought that our goal had a better chance of being attainable than as individuals, and our work would have a larger impact on our audience.

The studios where we had the meeting were rich in history, dating back to the nineteenth century. After I moved in and renamed it wj Studios and Gallery, artist Bacia Gordon revealed to me that she had purchased the property, which contained a frame house and studios, from the University of Chicago. Additionally, she said the studios had been built especially for the sculptor Charles Mulligan (1866–1916), who used the studios to execute a monumental piece of sculpture to be exhibited in a pavilion at the Columbian

Exposition at the Chicago World's Fair of 1893. The studios were two blocks away from the site of the Columbian Exposition, at 60th Street, the Parkway Plaisance, 59th Street, and Stony Island Avenue at Jackson Park. As a painter, I was impressed with what I was told about the studios and made inquiries and attempted research on the location but to no avail. A friend, Rebecca Zorach, a former art history professor at the University of Chicago and now the Mary Jane Crowe Professor of Art History at Northwestern University, sent me her research on the studios. It was important and revealing:

Memo: to Ray E Brown cc Winston E. Kennedy Com. & Real Est. Off. Edward A. Maser

In re: James E McBurney house and studio, 1521 E. 61st St. I want to call your attention to the McBurney studio and house now on the market, the house, on the South side of 61st Street, is of no particular interest but the studio is quite unique. Built for the then prominent sculptor Mulligan, with Louis Sullivan as architectural consultant, it was designed in emulation of Parisian studios and, with the exception of Taff's Midway Studios, was regarded as the finest studio in Chicago. After seeing it, I can believe the report.

For most of this century it was used by the muralist and portrait painter James E. McBurney, and has been maintained unchanged since his death in 1955 by Mrs. McBurney, now it is for sale, and while the immediate neighborhood is deplorable, a radical renewal of the area from 60th to 61st Streets, between the Illinois Central and Stony Island, would make the studio and its location near Jackson Park quite desirable. On the north side of 61st Street, at 1516 I believe, is the residence occupied for many years by Lorado Taff. The studio is rich in association with such figures as Opie Reid, and Clarence Darrow.[1]

When I moved into the studios in 1963, there had been no occupants for eight years, and Mulligan's plaster maquette for his Columbia Exposition sculpture was still there. As a matter of fact, when I moved out of the studios in 1971, I left it there. The model was square, four faced, with a dome top, measuring approximately thirty-six inches wide and forty inches high, with figures circling the model representing people of different nationalities around the world.

The historical background of the studios was of great significance, with Mulligan having them built while working as an important sculptor at that time, and with McBurney, an important muralist and portrait painter, occupying them for several years. With the founding of the COBRA/AFRICOBRA collective there, I believe the studios increased in historical importance.

The building consisted of two studios with exposed brick walls and concrete floors—one thirty by thirty feet, the other fifteen by thirty feet, both two stories high. A wall with an open arch door separated the studios. The skylights were panes of frosted glass reinforced with chicken wire, nineteen inches wide and ninety-six inches long. A floor was constructed in the smaller studio to create two floors, and a kitchen and half-bath were partitioned downstairs. A bedroom upstairs had its own bathroom. Gordon said that the painter James McBurney, who took possession after the sculptor Mulligan left, made the revisions in the studio. The smaller studio had a parking space for my 1960 Ford, and later for my Vette (1964 Corvette Sting Ray).

Bacia Gordon used the spaces to set up a small artists' colony. Curt Frankenstein, a painter, rented the large studio, where he worked and taught painting classes once a week. Mulligan's and later McBurney's frame house in the front was now home to Fred Jones and Bernard Goss, both painters. After Frankenstein left, a medical doctor who dabbled in oils took possession of his studio. He moved out after marrying an Israeli woman and moving to Israel. Gerald Williams, a painter, and Robert Paige, a fabric designer, came to rent the space as well.

In June 1964, I met Jae (Elaine A. Johnson), and later that year we began dating. At that time, she owned a boutique for women in Hyde Park, Jae of Hyde Park, located at Blackstone Avenue and 51st Street, where she designed and crafted the inventory on her clothing racks. Together we remodeled my studio, gained access to both studios after Williams and Paige moved out, and opened galleries in both spaces. Shortly after renovations were completed on the studio, Jae and I presented a two-person exhibition entitled *A Look at '67*, and her father and stepmother, Roscoe and Amanda Johnson, came from Cleveland, Ohio, to the opening. Jae and I were married on June 2, 1967.

The first meeting of artists at WJ Studios and Gallery was in June 1968, a few weeks after the conference *Arts and the Inner City*, which was held at Columbia College in Chicago. This conference drew the ire of some Chicago Black visual artists because they were not invited and felt disrespected. Jeff Donaldson, along with visual artists, photographers, musicians, and a designer, hastily formed a group entitled COBRA (Coalition of Black

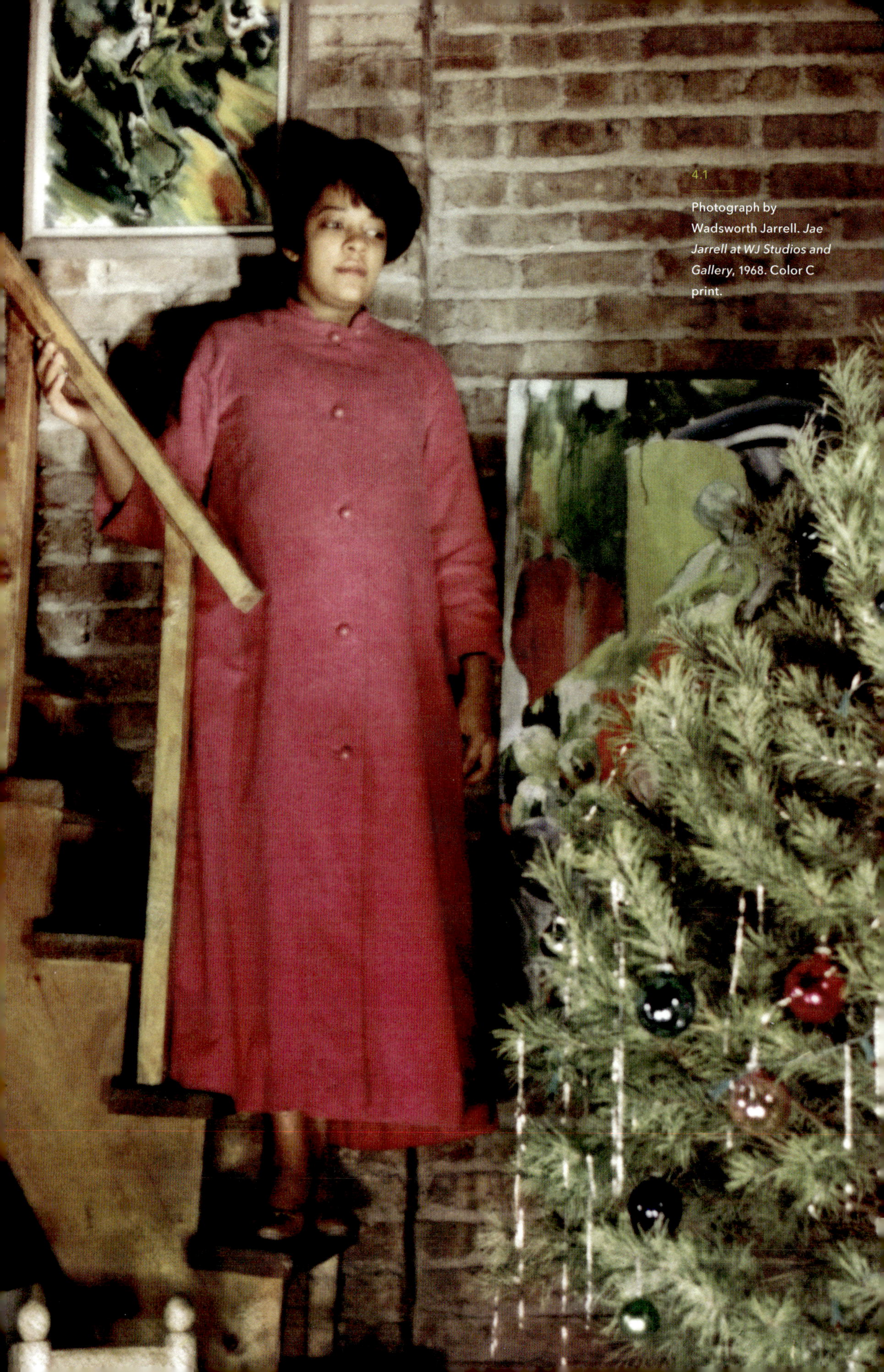

Photograph by Wadsworth Jarrell. *Jae Jarrell at WJ Studios and Gallery*, 1968. Color C print.

Revolutionary Artists) to protest the fact that they were overlooked. Jeff was the spokesman for COBRA, and he told us (artists at the meeting) that he had presented a strong argument. He said,

> The committee for the conference invited all of these people, mostly writers, who didn't know a damn thing about visual art. They invited people like John O. Killens, Amiri Baraka, Lerone Bennett Jr., Don Lee, Gerald McWorter, Robert Macbeth, James Sherman from the Writer's Workshop in Watts, Colin Carew from DC, Saul Bellows, And the only

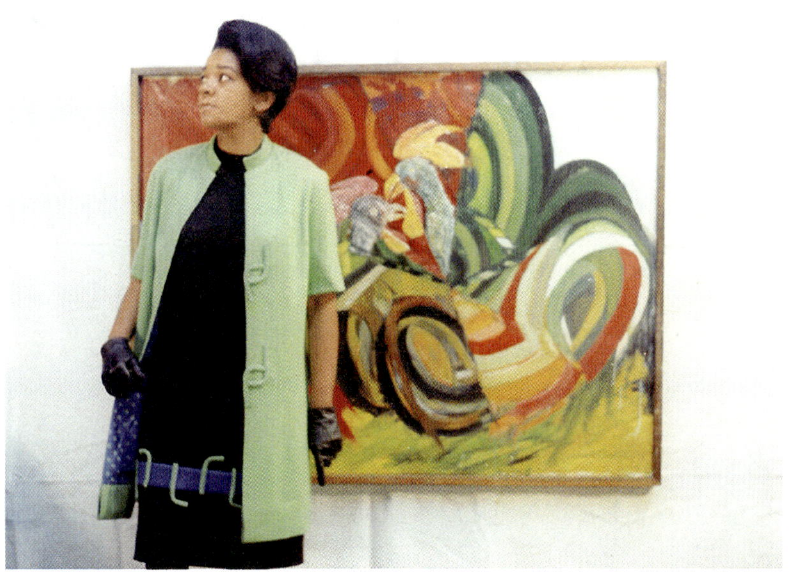

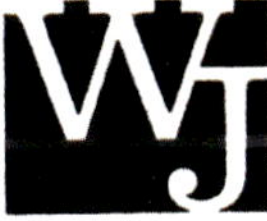

4.2

Photo by Wadsworth Jarrell. Jae Jarrell on brochure for Wadsworth and Jae's two-person exhibition *A Look at '67*, Chicago, 1967. Color C print.

two people that knew anything about visual art was Margaret Burroughs, and a Mexican dude Luis Valdez, director of an art program in California.

The local artist Harry Bouras, who taught at Columbia College, chaired the meeting. Our COBRA group had folks in it like Muhal, Bob Paige, Sylvia, and Billy Abernathy. We walked into that conference and busted it up. We killed it. I read the eulogy when I declared the conference illegal and immoral. That persuaded all of the Black people at the conference to form a Black caucus. In the end they sided with COBRA.[2]

The *Chicago Daily* newspaper had an extensive article about the conference, including images of the COBRA group and overlapping line drawings of Jeff speaking in different positions. "We read about the meeting in the *Daily News*," Jae told him, "and we saved the illustrations in the paper for you."

"That conference showed you just how white people try to take over Black affairs, and pick and choose who they think should be at the conference," Jeff responded. "Of course, invited would be a bunch of intellectual white people."

Jeff, Jae, Barbara, Gerald, and I had gathered at WJ Studios and Gallery to talk about creating a movement in art that included only African American artists and that reflected an African American aesthetic rooted in common art-making principles, with a political perspective. We discussed ideas of envisioning art that embodied emotional essentials and compelling expressions to fortify pride, vivacity, and collective consciousness in African American people. Also, we discussed art that would include encoded messages and high-energized colors that would act as a liberator of minds—Black minds. The conversation in the meeting centered on us producing art that contained strong Black images, combined with statements written on the art, advocating what Black people should do about oppression. We thought that plain written statements were extremely important to a people who had been tyrannized in America all their lives. Therefore, positive images would uplift our people's spirit.

As a group of artists trained in Western art procedures, we knew that we had to unlearn certain aspects of our teaching and expand the boundaries to a non-Western approach. We envisaged having art exhibitions that would be similar to the dynamic of musical compositions. Such a context has everyone acting as an individual in an orchestra, but with an ear for the total arrangement, working in harmony within the whole. Our vision referenced music, especially jazz, where the rhythm section plays the tempo, and each instrumentalist is free to create spontaneously. Each presents solos over the top of the rhythm section while remaining within the same key and concept of the arrangement.

We knew that visual artists working collectively presented a more complex challenge than musicians doing the same. Musicians often work from a beginning or a fragmented composition, which is the melody or the theme, whether it is written, hummed, or sung. With visual artists working in collaboration, theme and certain colors might be chosen, but each specific version is expressed differently. As a result, the art may or may not have the congruency and fluidity of a music score. We wished to pursue a similar egalitarian concept embraced by musicians such as Sun Ra, Ornette Coleman, the AACM, and Albert Ayler. We realized that a group of visual artists would have to learn how to work together to develop a common philosophy and to produce work with the exact same intensity. This factor had to be recognized even though the hue range might vary.

Three of the artists attending the first meeting at WJ Studios and Gallery had worked on the *Wall of Respect*: Jeff Donaldson, Barbara Jones, and me. The *Wall* project was successful, but we were not content. We imagined other possibilities we could achieve. Being products of individualism, as most visual artists are, this approach was new for us. In AFRICOBRA: *The First Twenty Years*, the brilliant author Nubia Kai wrote, "Being a conduit of African cultural transmission and a visible earmark of its invincibility, AFRICOBRA successfully challenged Western concepts of art, like Black musicians had always done, by simply playing their own tune. They contradicted the Western notion that the visual artist is rabidly individualistic and works better in an isolated environment."[3] As for the *Wall of Respect*, we were just an enthusiastic group of artists expressing views in our own style through a group project.

In June 1968, at the meeting at WJ Studios and Gallery, we spread art along the walls of the studio and took turns expressing criticism, exploring each work to find a thread of ethnicity and commonality. We realized that all the work displayed individuality but also similarities because of our cultural familiarity with subject matter and content. The work had no large flat areas of inactivity. The picture planes were broken up into lines and shapes, making the work very active.

Jeff chose one of my oil paintings, *Saturday*. It was a cityscape depicting people in my neighborhood on a Saturday afternoon, gathered on the front porch of an apartment building. It was a typical scene in some Black neighborhoods, where communal gatherings on porches or steps occurred, especially on weekends. He pointed out my use of brilliant colors and complimented the design and my application of paint.

Jeff pointed at my painting. "Look at this painting. Jarrell's ideas are different. In the past his paintings made use of deep space. Every one consisted of brush strokes diagonally on the canvas. Look, he has abandoned that concept, which is European, and is now painting horizontal and vertical. That is an African concept."

"I like the colors he uses," Barbara said. "He captured the essence of people in this neighborhood, and also made them beautiful."

"Yeah," Jae added. "I commented to him about that earlier concerning the colorful clothes on the people, especially the doo-rags the brothers are wearing."

I laughed. "The colorful doo-rags fascinated me. I see young brothers wearing them up on 63rd Street and in other neighborhoods. I felt like I couldn't make a painting of a gathering in the hood without including them. When I lived on 49th and Drexel, the landlord's teenage son played guitar in a doo-wop band. Although his hair was not processed—it was cut short, but he wore an assortment of colorful doo-rags. I asked him why did he wear them? He replied, "I gotta keep my doo together.""

"So, they were more of a style?" Gerald asked.

"Yeah, the brothers always make profound statements in dress that others mimic."

Jeff presented a strong watercolor painting entitled *Man*, an image of a Black man and woman, the man with one tightly clenched fist. Both figures exude confidence and have expressive eyes that stare straight at the viewer.

My critique was complimentary: "This is an impressive painting. It is stylized for the viewer to concentrate mostly on the areas you want them to. Here, you include subtlety with bold areas, and sometimes the subtle areas are almost lost." LeRoy Neiman once said to his class at the School of the Art Institute of Chicago, "It is what you leave out of a painting that determines its success." Interestingly enough, Jeff's painting made use of open color before it was introduced as a cobra principle.

"Yes, it is impressive how you emphasized their heads and hands and a portion of the man's shirt," Jae added.

Barbara moved her hands in circular motions: "I Love those afros and the concentrated color, especially around the shoulders and head of the woman."

"It is interesting how you fade part of the images into the background, and add broken line for emphasis," Gerald noted.

Jeff went over to the painting, pointing with one hand. "That is the nature of the medium. I manipulate it to show subtle areas juxtaposed against bold. I included pen and ink broken active lines—thick and thin—to keep rhythm flowing through the painting. I tried to make the man and woman appear strong. The man's fist is clenched to show that he is her protector, you know, a warrior."

Jae presented a multicolored patchwork garment—a dress revealing that her vision presaged creations in the "quilt-oriented craze" that came much later. The color hue ranged from hot pink and red to warm magenta. Jae explained, "This garment is constructed of pieces of material that might be considered scraps. Although they might appear as scraps of material, the pieces are joined together to present an elegant garment, which is my idea of a theme of Rags to Riches."

"No," Jeff interjected. "Rich Rags."

"Okay, Rich Rags. I like that too."

Barbara commented, "The construction of the garment reminds me of quilts. I really like the idea and the colors."

"I am not a quilt maker," Jae responded. "That never entered my mind, but I do know patchwork. It is something I learned as a youngster. I have been making garments since I was in high school."

Gerald observed the garment. "The area where the patchwork is concentrated reminds me of a gathering of people, like a summit. That area also is the focal point of the piece."

"Yeah," I agreed, "that area contains a lot of tension, not necessarily tightness, but busy, as if some kind of activities are happening, like Gerald indicated."

Barbara's work consisted of two silkscreen prints entirely of social commentary. Her work uniquely addressed, in a direct way, racial intolerance in America and the resolve of Black people, with highly stylized inscriptions of words and statements written directly on the screen prints. The prints were entitled *Your Brother's Keeper* and *High Priestess*. Barbara noted, "In my work I am addressing oppression and racism that's occurring at present. I am using symbols and words to express my feelings. Lettering is something I incorporated in my art when I was in high school."

I noticed an obvious symbol in the print *Your Brother's Keeper* and asked, "I couldn't help but notice the symbol of the swastika in the middle of the print. Is that in reference to Jews in the holocaust?"

"No," Barbara retorted. "The Nazis made the symbol infamous murdering people—a symbol of death—but the symbol has been around for centuries, and its original meaning has been distorted. This symbol originally and historically means good, strength, and power. In my work, my focus is to exert power and strength of Black people."

"Composing lettering in your work adds to the strength of the piece," Jae added.

Jeff advised: "You have the idea, but you have to be careful your work isn't interpreted as protest art, you know, art that points out atrocities committed against Black people. I'm not saying that yours fit that mold because you are implying that Black people must unite in order to be stronger. But be careful and don't walk that fine line. We need to create our own language, one that relates to Black people, and one that they can dig. Like most art we see created in this era only points in that direction—listen, these hunkies already know what they have done to us without us having to show that in our art. Some of the art created by Black artists, they think that they are saying something profound by applying the color black, or painting a canvas completely black. Hell, that's a weak statement, almost like an afterthought, where Black people are only mentioned in passing. I'm talking about making art that kicks ass and aggressively state what Black people ought to be doing by offering solutions."

I nodded in agreement. "I can dig what you mean by Black artists, who think they are saying something profound by depicting Black people picking cotton, and Black women resembling washer women carrying large loads on their heads, or splashing black or red paint on a canvas. To them, red represents suffering and blood."

"Yeah," Jae added, "Black people's blood. They are describing in the most negative way an atrocity that happened where a Black person got taken out."

"One thing our work should not be about or include is glorifying so-called Black memorabilia," I said. "You know, images like Uncle Remus, Aunt

Jemima, and grinning Black people eating watermelons or voraciously devouring chicken legs."

"Yeah, Jarrell is right," Jeff agreed. "All those images and all of the implications implied were created by white people for their pleasure."

"You got that right." Jae laughed. "The sole purpose of all of that Black memorabilia is to degrade Black people. It projects Black people as inferior, witless, unattractive, and shows us happily assuming those inferior roles. That trash is to let Black people know their place."

Jeff added, "Those artists are naively attempting to put a positive spin on something negative. What I see is both Black artists and Black collectors of that kitsch are ignorant and willing perpetrators of a sick and hateful idea."

"And you know," I interjected, "Black folk who collect that trash, or dreck, as my friend Martin Goldsholl calls it, are duped into thinking it is our history and that it has a value."

Barbara noted, "Our work should be positive and free of subjugation."

Gerald gestured toward Barbara. "Barbara is right, our work should be inspirational and not incorporate those Sambo/mammy images."

I responded, "Black artists who make a career out of including so-called Black memorabilia in their work are worse enemies and do more damage to the race than white people. Look at all of the attention given Aunt Jemima in Black artist's artwork, and she ain't even *real*. Hey, to bring it closer to home, look at Murry's drawing where he has Aunt Jemima popping out of a cereal box to beat someone into submission with a spatula that's probably bought at the five and dime store."

Gerald laughed. "I have seen some paintings of her armed with baseball bats and all kinds of automatic weapons."

"Or like Jeff's painting of Aunt Jemima attempting to defend herself with only her bare fist," I said laughing. "Jeff has her pitted against a state trooper who is brandishing a billy club."

Jeff retorted. "Hey man, in mine, that sister has her fist balled up getting ready to knock that trooper out."

"Yeah but," Jae laughed, "the trooper has a club and a gun."

"We should stick to positive scenes," Barbara suggested. "Let white people have their created racist characters. Our work should not promote them."

Gerald Williams, the youngest person at our first meeting, a student or recently out of school, had few if any professional exhibitions of record. By sharing the same building that housed our studios, I had witnessed his work. From my bedroom windows, I could see him working downstairs in his studio. His work clearly was that of a beginner. Most of it consisted of countless academic figural impressions and landscapes. He did not have a focus. He was all over the place, and at that time he was working in oils. Gerald presented a painting of a street vendor entitled *Peanut Lady*. It was obvious that he was struggling to learn the craft and searching for a personal approach— an identifiable style. After his tenure in AFRICOBRA, he developed into a very good and inventive artist. Gerald explained, "I am attempting to capture activities and something relative to our community. I found this subject interesting. This lady is a fixture near the El on 63rd and Cottage selling peanuts. So, I tried to capture her in that environment."

The lady vendor was familiar to me also. I inserted, "Yes, I have seen her. It is a surprise that I haven't made a painting of her. I used to carry a sketchpad around town, on 63rd, 47th, and on Maxwell Streets, making sketches of people of interest. One time I was down on Maxwell Street making a drawing of a bootblack who seemed to disapprove. I heard him say to his buddy standing nearby. 'He can draw me but he better not show it.'"

"What did you say to that?" Jeff asked.

"I didn't say anything to him. I wasn't worried about him. If he had started something, I was prepared to defend myself."

Jeff asked, "It was like don't start nothing there won't be nothing?"

"No," I retorted, "it was more like, don't start no rootin' and tootin', there won't be no cuttin' and shootin'."

"You know," Jeff laughed, "Jarrell is always looking for ways to say something profound."

I laughed. "Speaking of profound, in the army we were standing reveille at six in the morning when the first sergeant and a soldier exchanged words. The soldier told the sergeant he would kick his ass. The sergeant said: 'If you kick me, you will make a track and a dot the rest of your life.'"

Jae and Barbara made comments critiquing Gerald's painting. The critiques in the beginning were more complimentary than critical but would later become sincere. This would be a test of our egos. We expressed a willingness to work as a collective, realizing its uniqueness and multifaceted characteristics, given each artist's background and education. All of us had studied at the School of the Art Institute of Chicago in some form, or had attended the same institution for advanced studies. Jeff and Barbara had attended the Illinois Institute of Technology and Design. Jeff and I had roots in the South—Arkansas and Georgia. Barbara and Gerald were products of Chicago, and Jae was born in Cleveland, Ohio. With all our experiences and with parents of varied professions, and as mature artists, we brought an enormous amount of talent and expertise to the table.

Our experiences emboldened our ideas and resolve as artists because of our formal educational backgrounds in art and our professional exhibition endeavors. Additionally, we were products of strong family structures. All of us had family members we thought of as role models.

The meeting was casual. We were in the studio sipping coffee, eating cookies and cheese and crackers, and brainstorming for approximately five hours. We indulged in discussions about a direction to pursue, including methods of execution that would easily encompass a political viewpoint, and that would emblematically define us as a new group. During breaks and to sustain the creative energy in the room, various jazz and blues music on long-play records churned from my fifteen-inch Electro-Voice speakers.

We decided to focus on two important ideas that would later become components of our philosophy—intuitive space and definition. We unanimously agreed that we should abandon abstract or semiabstract approaches and direct our efforts toward realism. This was decided because realistic impressions would be a simple avenue to convey our compositions.

Jeff said emphatically, "We need to start from zero, abandon our present techniques and ideas, and with realism, create brand new ideas. Also, realism is something our people can dig on directly."

It is not that our collective questioned the intelligence of Black people to comprehend abstraction, because we knew they listened to the innovative music of jazz musicians such as Eric Dolphy, Ornette Coleman, and John Coltrane. These musicians' work is extremely abstract, and there are few if any complaints about their music being misunderstood. Importantly, we imagined that strongly rendered and defined images would be more "seeable," as described by Jeff. We knew that anything we created was going to be unique and original.

"You know" Jeff observed, "our work is already realistic—mine, Barbara's, Gerald's, Jarrell's, especially this street scene painting here, but we don't expect Jae as a fashion designer to produce images on her work."

Jae replied, "I want to include images on my designs too. I want to paint and appliqué images on my designs so my work will be comparable with the rest of the work."

"You know how to paint?" Jeff asked.

"You bet I do," Jae responded. "At the institute, I was in drawing and painting and design classes."

The question was then asked, What are we going to call ourselves?

Jeff responded, "We can take on the name COBRA (Coalition of Black Revolutionary Artists)." We adopted the name and became the Coalition of Black Revolutionary Artists.

The question was next raised about the European group COBRA (Copenhagen, Brussels, and Amsterdam). Would we be conceived as influenced by the COBRA group, or perhaps adopting their name? The acronym was the same, but the actual words and styles of the work took on an entirely different meaning. And significantly, they were white, and we were Black. Being Black in America is difficult or literally impossible for any other ethnic group to comprehend. To understand our experiences in America, as the expression goes, "you had to be there," or you had to have lived it. In America, our forefathers experienced brutal, extreme racism, and those experiences of bigotry were in part transformed in us. We surmised absolutely that our cause encompassed a greater significance than theirs, because theirs was only about the art and our group was about something more than just the art.

Jae asked if the name COBRA was in any way related to the snake.

"Well, it could be," Jeff explained. "The idea I had in mind, not only was to create what we will label Black Art, but also to have a COBRA School of Art. I envision a building with one gigantic room, Jarrell and Gerald teaching painting in two corners, and Barbara teaching printmaking in another corner, Jae teaching fashion design in a corner, and me teaching African and African American History and painting theory in one corner. With a situation like that, we could interchange ideas, you know, like a communal and revolutionary way of educating our people."

Jae asked, "What about the snake. How does COBRA relate to the snake?"

Jeff pondered a moment. "Well, I can see it now, a steeple on top of the COBRA school of art building with a COBRA snake wrapped around it." He twirled his fingers in a circle to indicate a coiled snake. "One thing is of extreme importance if we are going to break free of European aesthetics: we need to find our personal voice that collectively speaks in one voice—a group of people saying the same thing at the same time. That entails creating our own language that is related to and includes values of Black people. I am not talking about copying African masks and sculptures like the cubist artists and some artists in New York and other cities did."

Barbara suggested, "Maybe we should create art that relate to the civil rights movement, the protest marches, and other activist activities."

Jeff contemplated for a moment. "Could be, but nothing related to the nonviolent movement; that is not what we should be about. We subscribe to what Malcolm advocates: if someone attacks you by hitting you over the head with a stick, you retaliate by breaking one of their legs."

I offered my opinion. "Our contribution to the civil rights movement should be with our art. I was walking to the store last week and a white guy was in the neighborhood—right out there on 61st Street—attempting to recruit people to join the nonviolent movement for demonstrations. I said to him that the organization would not want me, because I am not nonviolent. If someone strikes me or I am spat upon, I would respond with all the force I can muster up. And I explained to him that I am an artist and that my contribution to the movement will be with my art."

"That's right," Jae added. "We are not going to sit on stools at lunch counters trying to integrate Woolworth. Whatever we do should be with our art."

"Yeah," Gerald agreed. "That's a trip trying to integrate those kind of places. You have to be a different kind of person to allow someone to blow smoke in your face and push you off stools to the floor."

"You are right there, man," Jeff inserted. "If that happened to me, I would get up and wipe the floor with him."

Barbara pointed out, "They are trained and tested for all those kinds of things before they let you participate in demonstrations."

"Yes," I inserted. "I was made aware of that by David Evans when he was a student at Tennessee State University. He was part of the group that attempted to integrate a five and dime store lunch count in Nashville. His account revealed white guys would get on each side of a Black person and blow smoke in his face. He also said that a white guy came up behind him and pulled him off the stool, causing him to fall flat on the floor. I asked him what did he do? He said that he arose and got back on the stool. He said that women were advised not to participate, but they insisted, prompting white guys to put their hands in their blouses, fondling their breasts. I told him if that had been me, I could not have sat still for that. I would have tried my best to stomp on one of those dudes and cave his chest in."

Jeff offered an interesting suggestion. "What COBRA will do is make positive remarks to Black people. Our art will compliment our people by letting them know how beautiful they are, and we will remind them to respond to violence by retaliating with every fiber in their bodies. We will use our art as a weapon."

"Jeff's right," I responded. "The art we make has to be beyond what we see in exhibitions."

"What do you mean?" Gerald asked.

"Our art has to be beyond the category of mediocre. In this society we live in, mediocrity is accepted as a virtue."

"We ain't in this society," Jeff retorted.

"Yeah but," I responded, "we coexist in this plastic decadent society. All that is required is to be as good as some other artist. I was told that by LeRoy Neiman and the Chicago illustrator Ballantine. They both said that inventiveness is not required to become a good illustrator or a good fine artist. They said as long as you are as good as some other artists, not better than, you can be successful. We have to have confidence in what we do, instead of seeking approval from the art world. We can't wait for the golden fairy to pee on us."

Jeff waved a hand toward the art around the wall. "Whatever art we make will be better than the jive we see in most museums and galleries."

As a group, we decided to refrain from conventional procedures, where Robert's Rules governed the structure of meetings with the majority votes carrying the motion or idea put forth. Any proposal introduced in a COBRA meeting had to be agreed on unanimously before it became part of our philosophy. We also decided that no members would hold office like president and vice president. We only chose a secretary to record functions of meetings and a treasurer to handle money we received from exhibition fees and later from sales of silkscreen prints. We did not require members to pay dues. We thought that those European practices would define us as an "art club" instead of what we were: a revolutionary artists' collective whose goal was to bring about a change in art by creating a Black aesthetic.

A VISUAL ART PROPOSAL

In September 1968, Jeff Donaldson returned to Chicago from his summer teaching position in Mississippi. He was completing his PhD at Northwestern University in Evanston, Illinois. Being an instructor of African American history at the university motivated him to explore a theory with visual art as the theme. He envisioned raising the consciousness level of African Americans. With his proposal, "Exploring a Black Aesthetic—A Visual Art Proposal," he sought financial assistance for the idea, and it was distributed among COBRA members for feedback. Members were skeptical, however, of the document's potential ramifications.

Two artists, Phil Salters, a painter, and Robert Paige, a fabric designer, were invited to attend the meeting as prospective members. The proposal stated Jeff's desires and his rationale for funding a group of Black artists, who subscribed to experimentation and sought to create a Black aesthetic. Portions of Jeff's proposal, including the title and his introduction, outlined essential elements germane to African Americans. Additionally, his proposal explained the amount of financial support needed—$100,000, for ten artists to work on creating experimental art for one year. The amount proposed was for art materials and equipment, salaries for the artists, and miscellaneous expenses.

In the introduction statement, Jeff wrote:

The essential attributes of any environment are that of producing its own myths, of shaping the past according to its own needs and, more importantly, of ordering its present and directing its future. This statement encapsulates the rationale for the slogans which is abound in the black community that extols, proclaim and glorify the richness and depth of black culture such as, "Black is Beautiful," "self-determination," "Soul," and above all, "Black Power."[1]

Later in the proposal, Jeff wrote:

Black artists who rely on their craft for subsistence are somewhat controlled and directed by the dictates and tastes of "mainstream" aesthetics. As a consequence, the art produced by Black people, especially that art which has been found "acceptable," that is, art which has found its way into galleries, museums and collections in America, has been, in most cases, either "universal" (another way of saying in the European-American tradition, or "exotic"). In other words, art produced by Black artists that are reflective of the total Black Experience that reflects the uniqueness of the Black Sensibility, have been rarely "acceptable or saleable."[2]

The proposal resulted in critical dialogue among members. We suggested that the idea could be a future endeavor, because acquiring a grant for a pro-Black group of artists could have consequences contrary to our beliefs. There was always a possibility of grant givers seeking to have control and exercising their authority to castrate the content of the art. Independence was germane to the COBRA philosophy, and if we acquiesced to the demands of granting foundations, achieving our goal of defining a Black aesthetic could be limited. We were not willing to allow that possibility. As revolutionaries, our motivation was inventive experimentation and self-reliance.

In support of opposition to applying for grants, Gerald argued that no one bestowed gifts on anyone without expecting reciprocation. He spoke about the amount of the grant: "That is a relatively small amount for ten people, which is $7,000 for each artist. That amount I suppose is to sustain each artist and cover expenses for a year."

"That's not a whole lot of money," Jeff responded, "but a person can survive off that amount, which is equivalent to, or more than, what teachers in Chicago are paid before taxes. But remember, materials and supplies will be provided."

Jae asked Jeff, "What will the materials and supplies and equipment be?"

"Paint, brushes, painting knives, canvas and stretchers, paper, pencils, charcoal and anything else we think we should have."

"My needs will be an assortment of fabrics and sewing supplies. I have enough equipment except maybe some cutting tools."

Jeff explained, "The grant will cover all of our needs. Twenty-four grand ought to be enough for all of our requirements."

Barbara's suggestion was in favor of financial assistance. "I am for applying for a grant. We need seed money to get us off the ground, and we are talking about reproducing prints from our work; we will need money for that."

Jeff cleared his throat. "I outlined in the proposal that we are talking about quality reproductions, not like the black-and-white prints that we see these cats peddling on the streets. I am talking about prints the size of our work, but not the size of those big-ass paintings of Jarrell's."

I found humor in Jeff's description of my work. I said, "We should carefully consider whether or not we should pursue financial support. What will happen if we are refused?"

Jeff laughed. "You know, Jarrell's got a point. If we apply for a grant and we are refused, that would be like getting naked in front of someone and get rejected."[3]

We decided unanimously to postpone or scrap the idea of a grant and find an independent way to generate funds. The conversation changed to critiquing African, American, and European aesthetics. We discussed the Picasso sculpture at Daley Plaza in downtown Chicago. We contextualized the sculpture as being obviously influenced by an African mask and constructed using African artistic procedures. The Picasso sculpture exhibited two similar shapes on opposite sides of the work, and most European artists' work has symmetry. But this one was clearly rendered differently. This procedure, as well as the distortion of proportions, was purely African in concept. African art includes repetition with change. That repetition with change procedure also applies to African American blues.

We indulged in analytical discussions of exhibitions in mainstream museums and artist Jim Dine, who painted men's bathrobes minus the human form. Discussions in the meeting included color-field artist Gene Davis, who had been pictured in a magazine applying paint to the canvas by sweeping it on with a broom. COBRA artists said that the effects derived from the broom process resembled a bolt of fabric, but the art was lacking in imagination compared to commercial fabric designers and printing companies. Fabric-weaving and printing companies, like Burlington Mills in North Carolina, and rug companies, like Georgia Carpet Industries in Dalton, Georgia, employ artists to create their designs, which are later mass produced.

In the early sixties, I had my first visit to New York City's museums and galleries. Seeing the art in those places resulted in my feelings concerning mainstream contemporary art. My thoughts were "If the art on display represented the definition of what art is, I did not desire to be part of that insipid scene because my mind is in a different place." I told COBRA members about the article in *Art News* covering a New York gallery exhibition where the entire show was a nude white woman sitting in a bathtub filled with champagne, which the audience drank from. When the woman exited the bathtub, that was the end of the show.

Phil Salters said that he had witnessed an equally absurd event as a student at the School of the Art Institute of Chicago. He said, "I saw the strangest example of an art performance by two white guys presenting their senior exit show. They were in a space set up to resemble a boxing ring, with ropes and a referee. The guys dressed up as roosters, with fake metal claws attached to their hands, assimilating fighting cocks. They circled each other in the ring, clawing at each other's groin, suggesting the gouging out of the opponent's testicles."

Jeff laughed, shaking his head. "In some cases, mainstream artists—especially males—search for statements that will elicit reactions of shock from viewers. And you know, art critics and dealers praise them as brilliant rising stars in the art world. Those artists are exhibited in major museums and galleries around the world, but that lame mode of art is castrated and rings hollow. When white males decide to present what they consider a profound statement, they often resort to taking off their clothes, exposing their genitals."

Years later, in 1993, the art critic for the *Atlanta Journal/Atlanta Constitution*, Catherine Fox, wrote a review of the exhibition *20 Artists 20 Years*, held at Nexus Contemporary Art Center in Atlanta, Georgia. Her review was in concordance with Jeff's assertion: "Although 'Robbed Text,' Alan Sondheim's video, is more visually appealing than previous work, it certainly echoes it:

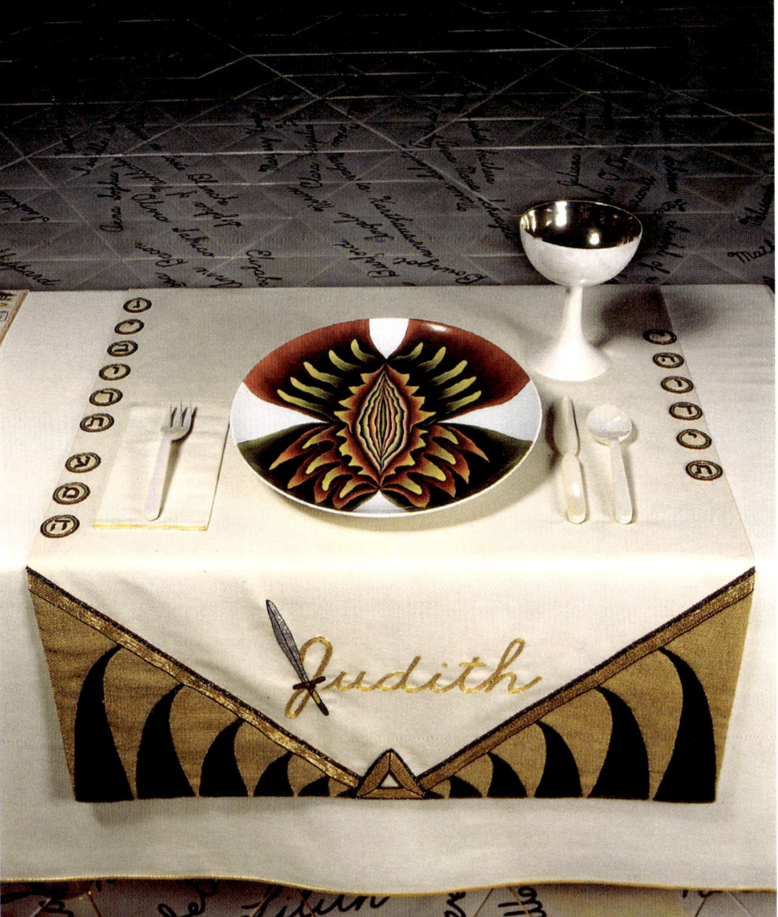

5.1

Detail, Judy Chicago,
The Dinner Party, 1974–79.
Ceramic, porcelain,
textile, 576 × 576 inches.
© 2019 Judy Chicago /
Artists Rights Society
(ARS), New York. Brooklyn
Museum, Gift of the
Elizabeth A. Sackler
Foundation, 2002.10.
Photograph courtesy
of Donald Woodman,
Albuquerque, New
Mexico, 2013.

it's another version of the artist contemplating his genitals. . . . It's hard to take seriously an artist who invokes theory and politics to validate what seems basically a desire to remove his clothes."[4]

Jae offered commentary about the opposite gender. "Don't forget about white females. The most profound statement that they seem to muster up is about eroticism and their vaginas."

Jae's criticism of white female's art included the high-profile artist Judy Chicago. In 1974–79, an installation by Chicago entitled *Dinner Party* was exhibited at the Brooklyn Museum of Art, in Brooklyn, New York, and is now part of the museum's permanent collection. The impressive installation is vast, engaging, skillfully composed, and occupying its own room. The triangular installation is a table displaying place settings (dinner plates, drinking glasses, and silverware), with napkins and some of the plates fashioned as female genitalia. Even though the exhibition concentrates solely on female genitalia, Chicago's exhibit is brilliance with originality, with drawings on walls outside the installation room referencing her ethnicity.

Bob Paige's remarks about white mainstream artists were equally critical. "Well, you know that's a white concept of art—that's Euro-American thinking. And you know their ideas when it comes to art are contrary to any other culture in the world."

I joined in the criticism. "I think artists who make art that exposes themselves is more of a trend, but also, it indicates that something is missing. Probably what is missing is the absence of vision—not having anything significant to say. What I am saying, anybody can masturbate in public."

Barbara interjected, "Black artists should be concerned with creating art that's significant and art that relates and communicates to people, our people."

Gerald added, "White artists have exhausted the amount of thievery they are able to glean from other cultures. Artists like Picasso, Braque, Paul Klee, Modigliani, Brâncuşi, Juan Gris, Jean Metzinger, Delaunay, Fernand Léger, and others have stolen everything that they could from African art. Now, all that is left for contemporary white artists are their inventions, which is the equivalence of trash art." (A few museums and galleries in New York have presented exhibitions of artists who use trash, or rubbish, as subject matter.)

Jeff addressed white America's portrayal of African American people: "They get their kicks by portraying Black people as cannibals, especially in the movies and in the funny papers. White people are the original savages. Look how they enslaved African people and forcefully took this country from the Indians. And all of the Indians they didn't kill were put on reservations. They had the nerve to label the Indians savages and portrayed them in the movies as such."

Paige asserted, "Yes, they do get their kicks with all that comic book jive. The funnies show little half-naked African people with bones in their noses, hovering around a pot of boiling water, cooking some cracker for dinner—as if his funky ass taste good."[5]

Devising a Philosophy

In earlier COBRA meetings, we discussed pertinent and political topics, but a direction that would define us as a collective had not been formulated. In a particular meeting in October 1968, we focused specifically on that subject. Jeff spoke philosophically regarding a direction that we should pursue. "All of us in this studio can make art, but we have to program our minds so that we think revolutionary. What I mean is, we have to purge European concepts and introduce non-Western ideas related to our heritage. We have to make art that will jar the senses of our people."

I asked, "What will we put emphasis on, African American features or color? Are we talking about creating our own stylization of expression that instantly identifies our art?"

Jeff responded without hesitation: "We are talking about exactly that, devising art with new concepts. We are not interested in the least of our art containing the same lame concepts of European artists. If they have any influence on our art, you can bet it will be unimaginative and emasculated—look what they have done to Leontyne Price."

Paige added, "Yeah, look at her now. She's in the big house."

Jeff continued, "You know she is singing at the request of white people to practically a white audience. They get off because in their eyesight, she is nothing more than a big ol' monkey performing for them."

Bob Paige remarked, "Whites in the audience probably think, 'look, they let the maid sing.'"

Jae heatedly responded, "This discussion has completely crossed the line and offers no tangible value to ideas and methods of how to construct a pro-Black revolutionary art movement. We are veering off course. There is no reason for a personal attack to tear down a Black sister. Let's get back to the art."

Gerald's statement put the meeting back on track. "Jarrell spoke about color. That is an important subject that we need to address, because color relates directly to all Black people because collectively we are a colorful people."

"Hey," Paige responded, "the brothers and sisters in the streets are wearing clothes with all those 'hip' bright colors, you know, like in Chicago, New York, and other cities around the country, and they call them Cool Ade colors. They are trying to pull our coats to what's happening."

Gerald asked with concern, "That's not related to the drink Kool-Aid, is it?"

Paige laughed. "Naw baby, it might sound like that name, but these dudes got their own thang going—you dig? These cats ain't concerned about no silly colored-water drink. Their whole thang is about color and style. That would be a 'hip' name for the colors COBRA will use."

Paige's suggestion precipitated laughter. At first it was perceived as a joke because of street vernacular connotations, but it embodied the Chicago grittiness and fittingly coined the name for our colors. Everyone agreed that the name was unique and appropriate for our group, and that it reflected lifestyles of African-descended people around the world. It was immediately co-opted into our philosophy as our first principle, and it became a COBRA brand that we spelled "Cool Ade."

The next principle proposed by Jeff was frontal images. He explained the reason for his suggestion. He said, "African images, such as sculpture, are always made to be front views, never three-quarter or profile. Frontal images represented strength and power." Another principle was added—open color. Positive images became another principle. Barbara introduced written statements. The last principle introduced was arbitrary use of light and line. Each principle was discussed in depth.

Jae explained her use of the final principle and how it benefited her in her work. "The principle arbitrary use of light and line will work very well in everyone's work, and in construction of garments. That idea is important. I use line to define specific areas and overlap light- and dark-colored fabric to create intuitive space."

Jeff was impressed with Jae's statement. "Listen at Mama. She knows how to talk about art."

Jae retorted, "This conversation came up before. I told you that at the Institute, I took all of the core courses—drawing, painting, basic design and art history. I didn't just study fashion design."[6]

This was by far our most productive meeting. The challenge ahead for us was to apply our newly created written and mentally internalized principles to actual visuals by making them function compositionally. Importantly, this challenged each artist to surrender established styles, join a cadre of artists embracing new ideas, and produce art under the umbrella of collective ideology. This was a humbling experience for our egos because previously, we worked as loners by making art set by our own principles.

We took a coffee break and put on records of straight-ahead jazz. After returning from the break, Bob Paige made a suggestion. "We need to cover every facet of art in order to control our destiny. Not only in the fine arts, but have something like the Bauhaus artists had, where crafts are combined with fine arts." He opened his portfolio displaying an advertisement that he had made for Kool cigarettes. "We need to get into the whole package so that we affect everything, including advertising."

We listened to his presentation. At that time, I was working in advertising and had learned that it was void of artistic skills except for a minimum of design and an occasional illustration. Advertising fit the mold of technical regimentation, using T squares, slide rulers, and pasted-up photographs, often by people who never attended art schools.

Jeff was perturbed by Paige's remarks. "I don't think that we should be in the business of advertising cigarettes."

At this period, COBRA was composed of three painters, a printmaker, and a fashion designer. We had hopes of recruiting into the group a sculptor who employed the use of color.

Black Family

During the polemical times of the sixties, several groups contested segregation and overt racism. The groups used different approaches to achieve an end, but all were united against the "laws" and policies designed uniquely for African Americans. The aggregation of people included the Southern Christian Leadership Conference (SCLC), led by Martin Luther King Jr., which fostered a nonviolent philosophy; SNCC (Students Nonviolent Coordinating Committee); Revolutionary Action Movement (RAM); the Black Panther Party; and the National Association for the Advancement of Colored People (NAACP). The most assertive group contesting racism and police brutality was the Black Panther Party for Self-Defense. Their philosophy was congruent with that of Malik El Hajj Shabazz (Malcolm X), who also embraced self-defense.

In the sixties, images of African Americans were rarely seen in white media advertisements of products, although some manufacturers' products were largely consumed by African Americans. The manufacturers and retail companies knew absolutely the value and the impact of image. They were making a statement by unapologetically projecting images of the dominant race. Image is perceived as what defines a person as it pertains to being hired for certain jobs or elected to political offices. The COBRA collective also understood the importance of image—the Black image. So, we suggested a project that would present a strong image of a Black family.

In November 1968, on a Sunday afternoon at the WJ Studios and Gallery, COBRA conducted our weekly meeting. All members were excited about the progress we had made in the previous meeting. Attending were Jeff, Jae, Barbara, Gerald, Phil—who had joined COBRA—and I. Bob Paige had dropped out. In an interview of Paige in 2007 in my New York studio, he explained his reason for leaving COBRA: "I left because philosophically J.D. [Jeff Donaldson] and I were not in agreement on certain issues."[7]

At the meeting, we reviewed the principles that we had set in place and thought that we should add more. The conversation turned to making posters of our work. The idea of making posters was influenced by the number of Black artists who were reproducing prints of their paintings and drawings.

Jeff started the conversation: "We should make posters of our work. We need to refute the idea of an original. This way we will have multiples of the piece."

Barbara agreed. "That's a good idea of making prints of our work, because with words written on the art, we could distribute our messages in Black communities across the country."

"Not just words," Jae added, "but whole statements."

"With written statements," Gerald said, "we will be able to define what our work is about."

"Gerald is right," I interjected. "That will be a visual concept that will control what the viewer sees. That would not allow the art to be interpreted. It would explain itself."

Jeff added, "We'll get places like newsstands to sell the posters. We will number them instead of naming them, so all anyone will have to do is say give me number 7, number 12, number 25, and so on. If we are asked if we are painters, we will say, naw, we just make posters."

Jae set out a new platter of cookies and a pot of coffee. Jeff put some money on the table and said, "Jarrell and Jae have been paying for the refreshments. We all need to put something in the pot. Cookies, coffee, and cheese and crackers cost money."

We added two more principles, visibility and clarity of form, which increased our number to eight. We now had the following:

COOL ADE COLOR

FRONTAL IMAGE

OPEN COLOR

ARBITRARY USE OF LIGHT AND LINE

POSITIVE IMAGES

WRITTEN STATEMENTS

VISIBILITY

CLARITY OF FORM

"Now," Jae stated, "We need to concentrate on making art that includes Black men."

"Excellent idea," Barbara responded. "We need to praise our men. They have been labeled with such a negative image."

I laughed. "Yeah, like lazy and shiftless and don't want to work. That's because as slaves, Black people resented and sometimes refused to work for free in the blazing sun. Whites attached that label to people who were victims of forced labor. Their rationale, of course, was frivolous, by assuming that people in captivity should be happy and spry while being abused and working for nothing."

"Jarrell's right," Jeff said. "We came here with jobs. So it ain't about jobs, because the jobs that Black people get, the pay is less than whites who work alongside them doing the same thing. So, in this revolution we are going to have to take out some of these hunkies."

"You are right there," Jae replied. "We are going to have to take all of them out. There is no peace living among them, not even for trees."

"That's right," Gerald said. "In this revolution we are going to have to kick some ass in order to get respect."

Phil added, "Whitey has ripped us off for everything, including the way we walk and talk."

"It's interesting you would say that," I said, "because the very people that were ripped off are the same people that whites labeled buffoons, apes and jesters."

Jeff laughed. "The perception that Black people went quietly into slavery is the biggest lie ever told. There were uprisings of Black men on ships in shackles that were brought on deck for exercise. In some instances, they pushed a few white overseers overboard or went upside their heads. Some people jumped overboard that rather drown than become slaves. All of that jive about us being docile and willingly accepted slavery and that Black people being loyal to whites is a damn lie." (Historians' accounts of slavery, citing day-to-day resistance of slaves, are parallel with Jeff's argument.)[8]

Jae stated, "Why don't we work collectively on a piece that represents a Black family."

Barbara became excited. "Great idea, great idea! We could all work from that theme by making a work of a Black family."

"That's a hip idea," Jeff agreed. "Black families were split apart by slave owners the minute we arrived in America. That was their way of breaking our spirits and having control over us. We need to turn this mess around by making art that represents a whole family, with a husband, wife, and children."

"I like the idea of a Black family," Gerald agreed. "That sounds real cool."[9]

The Black family was the first step that gave direction to creating our concept of a Black aesthetic, and it gave us the opportunity to emphasize the phrase that extolled African Americans—Black is beautiful. So, all COBRA members executed a work comprising a Black family.

Each member had included the newly created principles in their work. Jae created *Ebony Family* out of collaged and appliqued cotton velvet and velveteen, which she said was influenced by the dashiki, its flat surface and similarity to a canvas. The composition consists of the image of a father holding a baby, with the other hand holding an older child. The mother is also pictured within the family. The figures were constructed of patchwork, with different colors of appliqued ribbon. That procedure defined details of facial features. The father's and mother's hair were constructed of woven black ribbons to indicate texture. The baby's hair is also of ribbon, which is raised to indicate a curly effect. The ribbons bordering the bottom of the garment present irregular shapes to constitute continuation of rhythm. The letters *E* and *F*, which appear on the front and back of the garment, stand for "Ebony Family."

Gerald Williams's Black family, *Say It Loud*, is a portrait of a father, mother, and child. He used vibrant colors and stylized letters and words to depict a compact composition. His use of space conjures what John Coltrane and Albert Ayler did in music by using the complete space, which later became the COBRA principle horror vacui. The words "Say It Loud" appear in

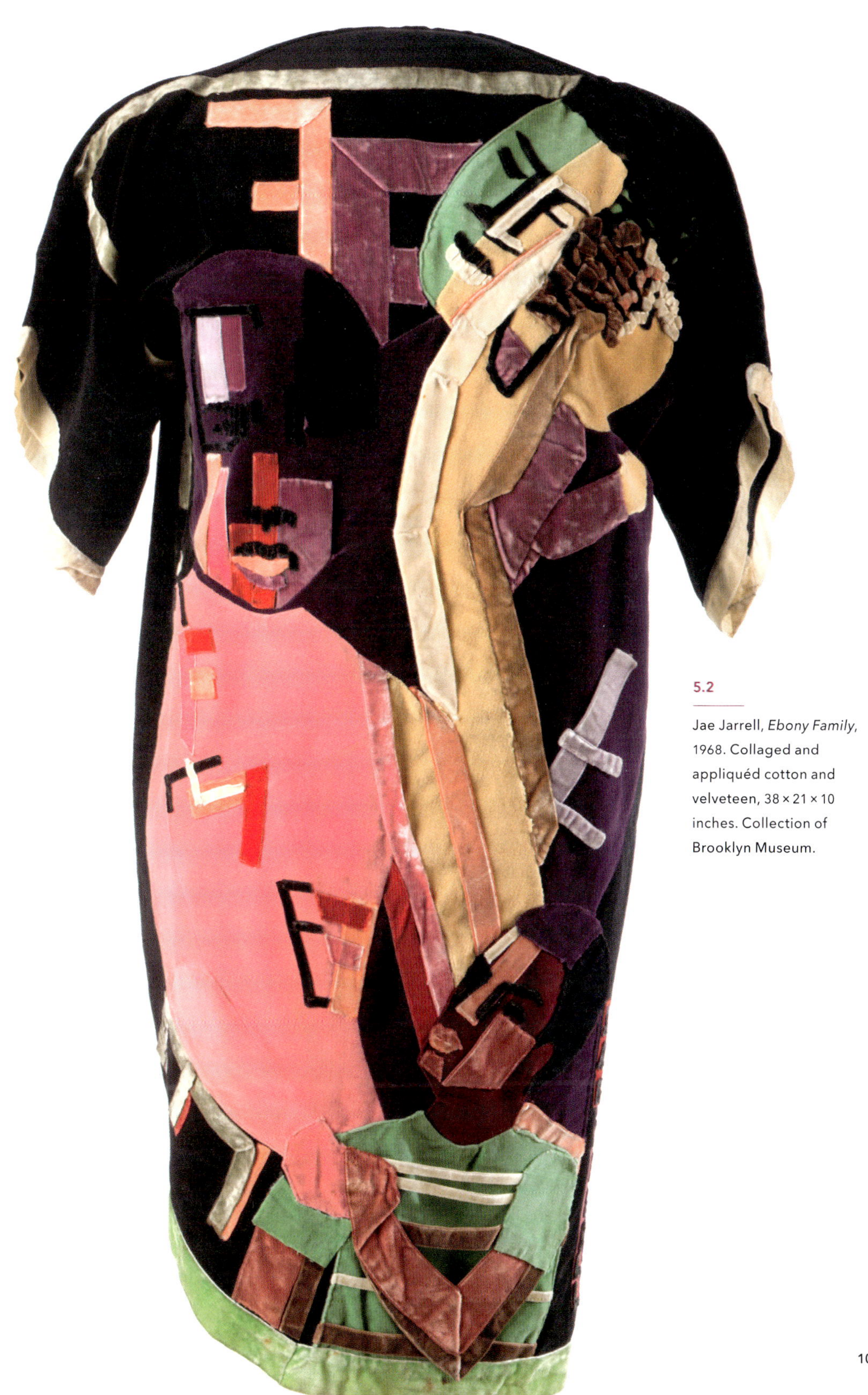

Jae Jarrell, *Ebony Family*, 1968. Collaged and appliquéd cotton and velveteen, 38 × 21 × 10 inches. Collection of Brooklyn Museum.

the composition, referring to the title of James Brown's song "Say It Loud, I'm Black and I'm Proud."

My *Black Family* is executed in acrylic on canvas, with pastel and hot wax. The wax was applied to achieve a degree of texture and translucency. The painting shows a family of four—a father, a mother, and two children. The male child is sitting on his mother's knee, with her arms around him, expressing that he is loved. One arm of the father is cuddling the female child, and the other arm is around his wife. He is making a strong statement that he is the provider and protector of his family. The phrase "Black Prince" appears in the painting, denoting the life of a strong-willed man whose life is lived with profundity. The letter *B* is prevalent in the painting, and it refers to the statement "Black is Beautiful."

Jeff's painting of a Black family is in watercolor. His shows a father, a mother, and a child. The images are skillfully crafted, presenting a happy and strong family. The positive image of a father represents a complete family. Watercolor was Jeff's medium. He had mastered it by including flowing lines that visually constituted musical movement.

Barbara's *Black Family* was executed in silkscreen, with a family of three. With a father, mother, and child, Barbara's print presents a positive statement. Her print joins the rest of the work by addressing the importance of two parents' love and input guiding a meaningful direction for growing children.

COBRA on Television

In the sixties, organizations sponsored films of African American communities, such as interviews of Black artists, social functions, and Black businesses. Television stations supplied sixteen-millimeter cameras for African American photographers to go into Black neighborhoods and film events. One particular example was WGN Television Corporation, which acquired reams of film shot in Black neighborhoods that did not present a cogent story. So, it contacted Jeff Donaldson and asked if he would bring COBRA artists to WGN studios to be part of the presentation, and if he would narrate the film so that it would appear attractive to viewers. It was thought by the television directors that COBRA's presence would add an artistic touch to the program, which they entitled *Black Pride*.

5.3

Gerald Williams, *Say It Loud*, 1968. Acrylic on canvas, 36 × 26 inches. Collection of the Studio Museum in Harlem.

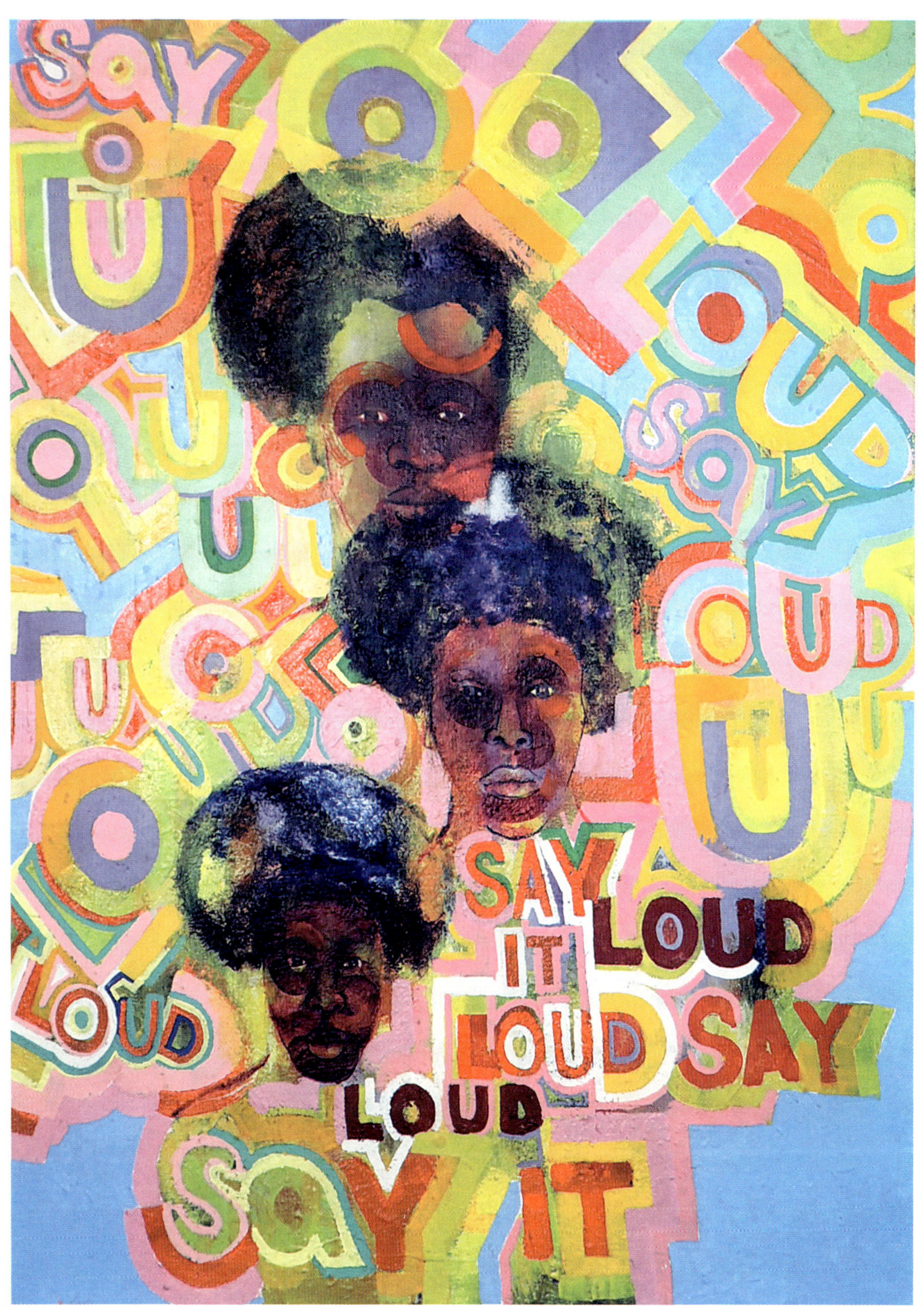

Say
U
LOUD
SAY IT LOUD
IT
LOUD SAY
LOUD
SAY IT

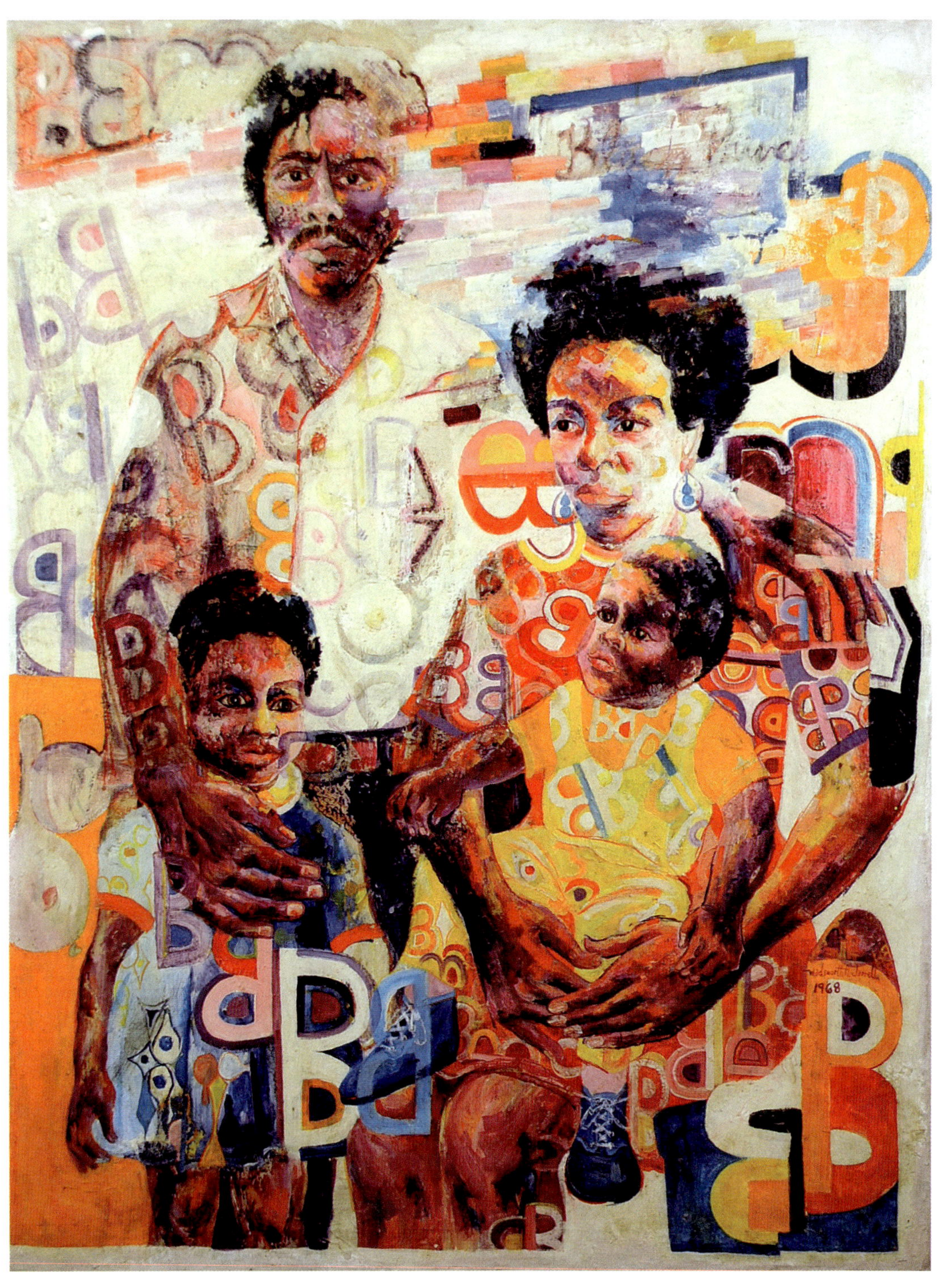

The scenario proposed by the director was for the cameras to zoom in impromptu on COBRA conducting a meeting, while Jeff walked around reciting lines about Black artists and Black businesses and community functions. The COBRA members at that time included Jeff, Jae, Barbara, Gerald, Phil, and me.

Somehow the planed program went awry, as they usually do when a camera or a microphone is placed in front of people unfamiliar with public appearances. Phil and Barbara took the conversation away from the idea of a meeting and proceeded to discuss at length an article in *Rampart* magazine about the Black Panther Huey P. Newton.

Phil said, "We should be into posters. That's what we should be doing." He then asked, "Did y'all see the picture of Huey in that magazine?"

Barbara responded, "You mean the one in *Rampart*?"

"Yeah," Phil replied, "the picture of Huey sitting in the throne-like chair, with a gun in one hand and a spear in the other. You know the white man don't want to see a Black man with a gun."

As a result, although our work was shown in bright Cool Ade colors, a COBRA meeting never materialized during the thirty minutes of filming. In my opinion, I don't think the film served any value to viewers. This was a time when it seemed, or was assumed by whites, that Black people would be happy to see someone on television that looked like them, even in a poorly constructed film.

5.4

Wadsworth Jarrell, *Black Family,* 1968. Acrylic on canvas, with pastel and hot wax, 46 × 36 inches. Collection of the artist.

In September 1968, COBRA was invited to exhibit at the Wadsworth Upper Grade Center, which was an elementary and junior high school in Woodlawn, on the South Side of Chicago. The exhibition was part of a conference whose focus was education, community affairs, and the civil rights struggle. Wadsworth Upper Grade Center and Hyde Park High School were chosen as the model schools that would participate in the Woodlawn Experimental Schools Project (WESP). The experimental schools project focused on progressive learning techniques for Head Start, elementary, junior high, and high school students. The WESP was a community-based organization that partnered with the University of Chicago. COBRA's works were hung in a U shape around the walls of the conference hall, and the panel sat in a semicircle on the stage, comprising notable people from the Chicago area: the principal of Hyde Park High School, Anna Kolheim; the astute educator and director of WESP, Barbara Sizemore; the cofounder of COBRA and PhD candidate at Northwestern University, Jeff Donaldson; the director of Black studies at Cornell University, James Turner; and the director of Operation Breadbasket, Jesse Jackson. Additionally, the panel included teacher and member of the Coordinating Council of Community Organization (CCCO) Al Raby; attorney Duke McNeil; the director of The Woodlawn Organization (TWO), Rev. Arthur Brazier; and the chief of the street gang Black Stone Rangers, Jeff Fort.

The Association for the Advancement of Creative Musicians (AACM), headed by Muhal Richard Abrams, provided the music. Each COBRA member exhibited the first assignment, the Black Family, along with other works. People from the audience said that our art was impressive, and that they were overwhelmed by our presentation, which comprised African American imagery, and our aggressive use of color. Additionally, the audience showed appreciation for the content of the art, which focused on Black political awareness. The room was filled with teachers and workers from the two schools involved in the WESP, a cross-section of people from the city, and those living in the immediate community.

James Turner spoke about the civil rights movement, stating that "Black people are less foolish" than in the past. He was referring to the timbre set by the civil rights movement, which espoused Black assertiveness and awareness as well as Black people controlling their own community. He also asserted, "Black people should be self-reliant and refrain from the idea of being referred to, or viewing themselves as, victims."[1]

Jesse Jackson imparted the functions of Operation Breadbasket, which was the economic arm of SCLC (Southern Christian Leadership Conference). He spoke of using boycotting as a weapon that could force businesses to include products on their shelves manufactured by African Americans. Jackson argued that some of the money earned by white merchants should remain in the community: "Money made by white merchants from Black consumers leave the community on a hundred and eighty degree radius, because their money is only spent in white communities. What they give back to the Black community is nothing."[2]

There were numerous complaints from parents in the Woodlawn community about recruitment of young boys into the Black Stone Rangers' gang. Additionally, businesses in that community complained about the gang's methods of extorting money for protection. The gang offered the merchants security, for a weekly fee, guaranteeing that no display windows would be broken and that their stores would not be robbed or vandalized.

Jeff Fort delivered a speech in defense of the gang. In a moderately low voice, he said, "Everybody saying things about the Black P. Stone Nation, I want to let you know we are here to stay. We are all up in your neighborhood, all up in your homes, and all up in your kitchens."[3]

With their experimental music, the AACM provided the artistic connection with the COBRA artists. Their music was parallel to the COBRA collective in freshness and unconventional methods. COBRA and the AACM's approach displayed a new direction in visual art and in music. The AACM musicians included Muhal Richard Abrams on piano; John Stubblefield on tenor saxophone; Phil Cohran on the frankiphone; the young sensation George Lewis on trombone; Steve McCall on drums; Lester Lashley on acoustic bass; Henry Threadgill, Joseph Jarman, and Roscoe Mitchell on saxophones; and Jose Williams on clarinet. All the AACM musicians were multi-instrumentalists. Williams was not an official member. He said that he wanted to see if he could play the music of the AACM.

Exhibiting our work at the conference was successful in several ways: exposure of COBRA's experimental art to an African American community, and Jae and I being hired by the director of night classes, Allan Collard, to teach in WESP's night program. Jae taught fashion design, and I taught drawing, painting, and photography.

COBRA's Second Exhibition and the Second Group Assignment

Our second exhibition was held at Notre Dame University in South Bend, Indiana. The work was transported there by station wagon and in Barbara's car. The exhibit space was a well-lighted gallery with ample wall space. The audience consisted of faculty and students at Notre Dame. Jeff and Barbara returned a month later and picked up the work.

One week after the Notre Dame exhibition was installed, in November 1968, in a meeting at WJ Studios and Gallery, we discussed our next assignment. We had completed our first group assignment Black Family, and we were excited about our forward progress. It was not imperative to incorporate every principle into a work as long as some of them were applied. The principle of arbitrary use of light and line added great contrast to the art, and it also gave the work an interglow.

We discussed thievery of Black artists' work, namely performing artists, who have been blatantly copied and co-opted, with their white copiers receiving all the accolades. For example, we discussed the talent and inventiveness of tap dancers Bill Robinson and the Nicholas Brothers, who were master dancers extraordinaire. Unfortunately, two white dancers with much less talent, Fred Astaire and Gene Kelly, garnered the attention of the world and were awarded the title greatest tap dancers.

"If it were not for Black people," Jeff mentioned, "I don't know what white people would do. They ripped us off for our creativity and co-opted all their stolen booty into their society and called it theirs."

Gerald laughed. "Well, you know, Benny Goodman is king of swing, and Artie Shaw is king of the clarinet."

I bristled and responded, "Benny Goodman was not a great musician as touted by the white media, and he didn't have a clue about putting together arrangements of music. I read in a report that in 1934, Goodman was unemployed and learned that NBC was planning a new three-hour Saturday night radio program called *Let's Dance*. There were several Black bands, Chick Webb, Fletcher Henderson, or Benny Carter that could have filled the bill, but because of racism, the network studios were closed to them. Goodman attempted to put together a band, but it sounded too much like the Dorsey Brothers and Glen Gray's bands. So, he visited the singer Mildred Bailey, and she said, 'What you need is a Harlem Book.' She urged Goodman to talk with Fletcher Henderson. I read that with Fletcher was having financial problems, and he was forced to break up his band, so he gladly sold Benny Goodman several jazz arrangements. What I am getting at, if it were not for Fletcher, Benny Goodman would not have gotten that job with the network and would not be considered as an important musician."

Jeff said, "You noticed that Goodman formed a combo instead of his original big band and hired three dynamite Black musicians, Teddy Wilson on piano, Lionel Hampton on vibes, and Israel Crosby on bass. He and Gene Krupa were the only white guys in the combo. And you know, Teddy, who was a musical scholar, said that Benny had very little knowledge about music. He said that he played mostly by ear, but his whiteness outweighed his talent."

"What about Elvis Presley?" Jae asked. "He is the king of rock 'n' roll. He became famous with his first hit 'That's All Right, Mama,' when we all heard that tune in the 1940s sung by better musicians like Joe Turner, Louis Jordan, and the man who wrote it, Arthur 'Big Boy' Crudup."

Jeff asked, "Remember one of those senators from Mississippi, I can't remember which one, Eastland, Stennis, or Bilbo, said about Elvis? He said that Elvis is famous because he is the first white man to get up on stage and act like a nigger."

Jae laughed. "We need to make art that will refute those false claims of white people being the kings of music we created."

"What we need to do is make a bold statement that will highlight Black folks' achievements," Barbara stated.

Jeff proposed that we make a work of art that compares a Black person to a white person, with the bold statement written on it, "I Am Better Than Those Motherfuckers and They Know It."

That statement brought laughter. "That is a pretty bold statement," Jae said.

Gerald responded, "That would be difficult for me to write those words on a painting."

Jeff was persistent with getting approval of whatever he proposed and continued arguing his point. "We can't be concerned with what is proper to put on our art. We are not mainstream artists. We are revolutionaries. It's Nation Time. And if we are serious about making a change in art, we will have to be about the business of taking bold steps."

The meeting ended on that note, but the painting with the bold statement remained on our minds. The words in the statement were familiar to everyone, but they were not included in the everyday vocabulary of some members. Therefore, those members, namely Jae and Gerald, thought that it would be out of character for them to write such a statement on their art.

Two weeks later, in the next meeting, three members displayed examples of work in progress. The idea of critiquing work in progress was not easy for professional artists. COBRA was attempting to expand the idea of benefits received from peers' critical analysis by hearing opinions of fellow artists striving for the same goal. The opinions were on how the artist's work could improve technically, positively, and aesthetically. More importantly, we were attempting to mold our collective so that it coalesced around a singular ideology. The process of peer critiquing of art is probably unprecedented in the customarily loner, single-minded field of visual art. Unlike art students, professional artists make their own decisions. COBRA was striving to find the purpose and the significance of making art, and to introduce the idea that artists should have a passionate need to create something unique, powerful, historical, and celestial that could change the accepted norms and the political landscape, as opposed to concerns about monetary values.

Jeff reiterated this concept in the meeting: "We all have jobs. Jarrell and Jae own businesses, so we are not depending on making a living from our art. Our goal should be to make art, not to make money. We should only be concerned with making art that will change the dynamic of what has already been created."

COBRA members knew that successful works of art are not necessarily made only for monetary value, not even portraiture, for example: the Egyptian pyramids at Giza; traditional art such as the wood, terracotta, and bronze heads created in Benin; and the sculpture and masks created in West, Central, and South Africa for ritualistic ceremonies. We knew that the serious artist has to create and realize his or her own vision to make art, rather than just make art for sale. But we also knew that some artists indulged in making art only for sale. Those artists had no vision. COBRA artists understood that to become a serious artist who was dedicated, the profession alone dictates what you are and who you have become.

Barbara, Jeff, and I presented our unfinished work. Barbara's silkscreen print was finished. It depicts a Black woman and a white woman sitting on the beach. The white woman is applying suntan lotion on her body, with her head turned toward the Black woman. The stylized words in Barbara's print are resolved artistically into the composition so that the profound statement is not obvious. Barbara had adhered to the assignment. She chose to compare a permanently tanned person to a person with skin pigmentation that required rays from the sun to tan.

Jae asked, "In what way is this sister better than the white chick?"

Barbara answered, "You might notice that the sister has nice smooth brown skin that is natural for her. But the white girl is sitting in the sun rubbing tracks in her body with suntan lotion in an attempt to achieve the pretty tan. It makes the Black girl better because she is comfortable with herself, and the white girl is not. The white girl is looking at the Black girl, envious of her pretty tan."

"They are all trying to get like us," Jeff interjected. "They lay in the sun and burn blisters in their bodies trying to brown."

We all knew that Jeff had bold ideas and was outspoken. It did not surprise us that his statements were almost always profound. But he was the brainchild of our revolutionary movement. Without his input and leadership, for us, the idea of a Black aesthetic would not have existed.

My painting *Compared to What: I Am Better Than Those Motherfuckers and They Know It* was critiqued. The form consists of graffiti-style words and

Wadsworth Jarrell, *Compared to What: I Am Better Than Those Motherfuckers and They Know It*, 1969. Acrylic on canvas, 34 × 42 inches. Collection of the artist.

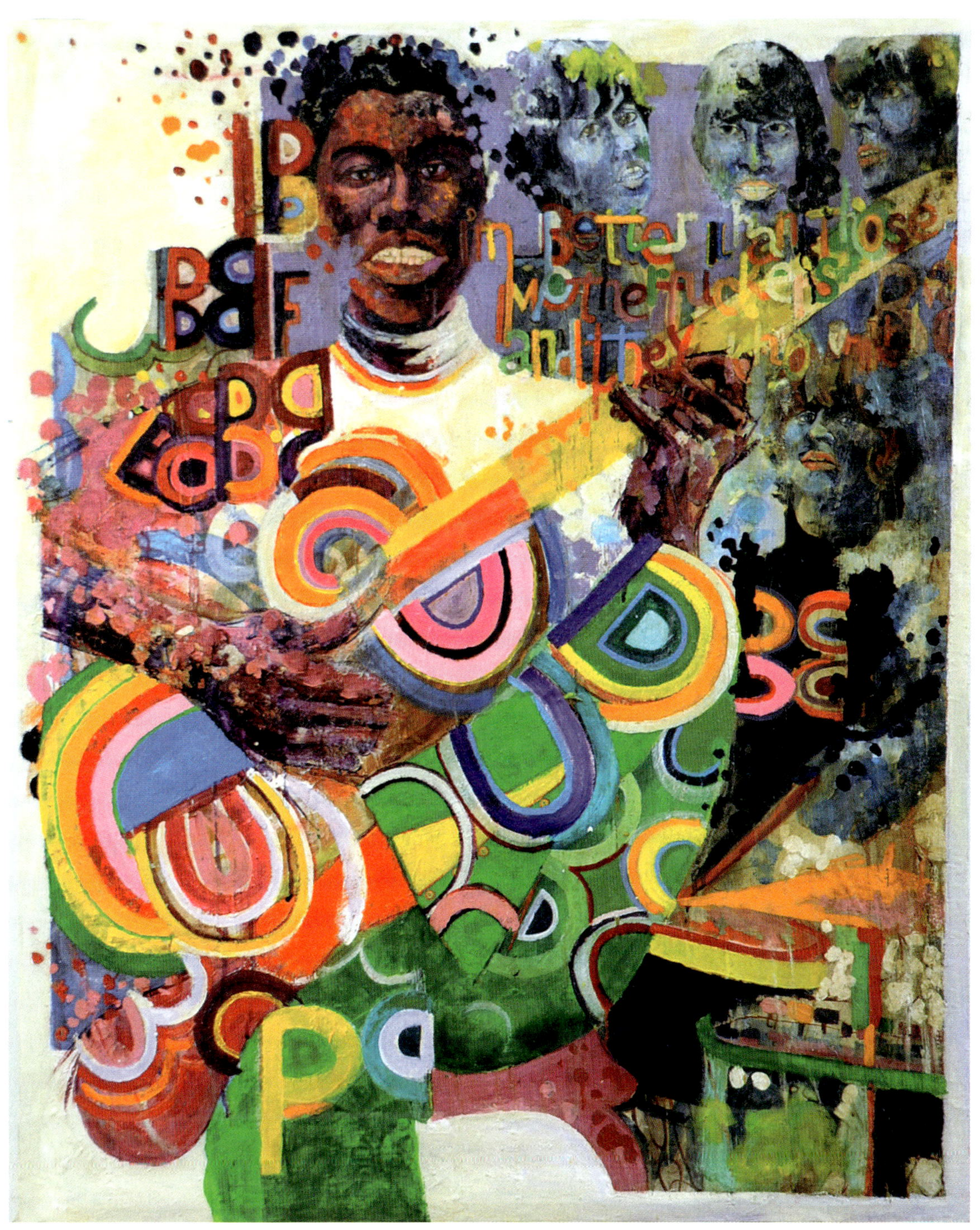
I'm Better than those
Motherfuckers
and they know it

letters, mostly of the letter *B*—for Black is beautiful—and five figures in Cool Ade colors. The dominant figure in the painting is an African American man sitting with his legs crossed, playing a guitar. The four figures in the background represent the European music group the Beatles. The words and letters, especially those near the end of the canvas, explode and fragment into multiple colored shapes. The white borders that rim the painting indicate that it is a poster. The statement "I Am Better Than Those Motherfuckers and They Know It" is difficult to read, because it is an intricate component of the form. Everyone agreed that the idea was well executed, and that it embodied excellent qualities.

Jeff became excited. "Man, that is Wilson Pickett. I hope you don't lose the red and yellowish-brown coloring in the corner of his eyes. You know that plenty of brothers have that coloring in their eyes. Man, you captured that Black thing."

I acknowledged his compliment. "I am comfortable with the statement on my painting. COBRA needs to expose the overwhelming claim of white superiority that is espoused by mouth, by books and the news media, the movies and by the funny papers. My painting is no fantasy—it's the absolute truth. Black folks are superior blues musicians. If not, name one white musician who is equal to, or one who surpasses, Muddy Waters, Buddy Guy, Jimmy Witherspoon, Little Esther Phillips, B. B. King, Ma Rainey, Bobby Bland, Dinah Washington, Howlin' Wolf, Joe Williams, or Jimmy Rushing."

With my comparison between a Black person and a white person, I chose a genre that was created by Black people. I chose a bluesman. More importantly, in my opinion, the blues is something that can only be successfully performed by Black folk. And any attempts thereafter are copycats aping what has already been supremely done.

From 1955 to 1958, I worked after school in a paint factory in Chicago. My position was head paint mixer. The majority of African American employees there hailed from Mississippi—the bedrock of the blues. A fellow employee was from Laurel, Mississippi, which is in the heart of the Delta (an area that lies between the Mississippi and Yazoo Rivers). The Delta starts in Memphis, Tennessee, and stretches into Helena, Arkansas, and Natchez and Vicksburg, Mississippi. The employee at the factory that I am speaking of had worked in Mississippi as a sharecropper and on logging crews for sawmills, and he had worked building levees along the Mississippi River. He said that as a child he had witnessed his dad and uncle play music in their backyard with bluesmen such as Charley Patton, Howlin' Wolf, Skip James, and Bukka White. Those blues musicians defied "proper learned" finger placement on the frets of guitars and challenged the boundaries of chord use. According to my coworker, he watched blues musicians playing twelve-bar blues with their thumbs only. He also said that the blues musicians created the turnaround that sometimes consisted of one or two notes. The former Mississippian expressed his views: "Whatever white people thank they've sangin', I don't know what it is, but I do know dain't no blues. I ain't never heard no white man that could sang the blues."

The factory worker's statement reminded me of a story told to me by the late Nathaniel Beck Sr. of Chicago, the father of my best friend, Nathaniel Beck Jr.:

> In 1919 in Chicago during the race riot, on the South Side a group of black men surrounded a man that they thought was white. They threatened to whip him with steel pipes. The man cried out, "I am a Black man." One of the men in the group said, "If he is a Black man, surely he can sing the blues." The man that appeared white eloquently sung the blues. The men all agreed. "Yeah, he's Black all right."[4]

The African American bluesmen were inventors, archetypes, and trendsetters. They set their own standards, which would be analyzed and copied but never replicated. That is because the blues represents something more than mere music-like chord progressions. Muddy Waters, when he was questioned about Billy Butterfield sitting in on some of his jam sessions and the possibility of him emerging as a bigger star than he, said, "He can play the music because the music is notes, but he can't sang like me."

Jeff presented a collage of nude white women cut out of *Playboy* magazine, the agent benzene used to deface and distort them. The critique of his work was not favorable. One reason was that he was a terrific draftsman but did not apply the skills that he had mastered. Pasted on the collage is the statement "I Am Better Than Those Glitzy Bitches." Jeff's justified his collage: "This collage shows that they love sadomasochism. White people are literally masochists. They love rough sex and love to be tied up and whipped like sex slaves." Our objections were that his entire work was cutouts of scantily clad women that were not compared to anything.

Jae and Gerald opted out of applying the profane statement on their work. Gerald said, "I think that the idea of declaring anyone better than another person is a bit pompous."

"Listen," Jeff retorted. "We are in a hard ball game. That's the game white people play. This is no time to wimp out with some soft-padded jive. Either we are revolutionaries, or we are not. We might as well start a Boy Scout art movement. Maybe we should pitch a few pup tents over there in Jarrell's painting space and practice tying some square knots."

Phil's painting was the last to be critiqued. The subject of his painting consists of a white policemen standing near a Black man with his head tilted downward. The policeman seems to be in the process of arresting the Black man. The painting is representational, and it was executed in brilliant colors. The background is solid green. There are indications of words, but the work was unfinished. Phil was asked to explain the relationship between his painting and the theme that we chose.

He explained, "This is a situation where a brother is about to be arrested by this cop, but the brother has other ideas."

I asked, "What ideas?"

Phil responded, "The brother has the idea of not going to jail."

I asked, "How is the brother going to circumvent that?"

Phil's replied, "The brother has power in both hands, and he is about to flatten this cop."

A week later, in the next meeting, Gerald brought a new painting, *I Am Somebody*. It depicts a large head of a Black man with the statement "I Am Somebody." His painting was a departure from the theme.

Jeff presented a sensitive watercolor painting of a young Black woman from South Africa who was a competent singer and a student at Northwestern University. Written on the painting was a soft version of the proposed statement: "Miotta Famboule Is Better Than All."

Barbara's print and my painting were the only works with the bold statement. We decided that there would be no more assignments. We also decided that our art was about Black people, and in all future works, those were the people we would present.

7

RECRUITMENT

COBRA wanted to expand to include artists working in various mediums. We were already a multifaceted group, with Jae as a fashion designer and Barbara a printmaker, but we were willing to embrace other mediums as well. A total of eight artists were invited to attend a COBRA meeting at different times.

In January 1969, Napoleon Henderson, a weaver, was invited to a COBRA meeting. He came to the meeting with Phil, who had known him when they both were students at the School of the Art Institute. Napoleon presented a tapestry that was woven with intricate shapes in analogous colors. His skills were obvious. We were impressed with his workmanship and ideas, and having him as a member of our collective would complement our desire to become more multifarious. We invited him to become a member of COBRA.

In March 1969, Nelson Stevens, a painter, came to a COBRA meeting. He was invited by Jeff, who had met him at a College Art Association conference. Nelson was an assistant professor at Northern Illinois University in Dekalb. At the conference, Nelson, who had recently received his MFA from Kent State University in Kent, Ohio, had been looking for employment. He said that Jeff had advised him to seek employment close to Chicago, because that was the mecca for Black artistic endeavors.

Nelson presented a painting entitled *The Brother Who Knows*. The image consists of a man who appears to be entangled in a barbed-wire fence. His mouth is open as if screaming in pain. The concept Nelson's painting

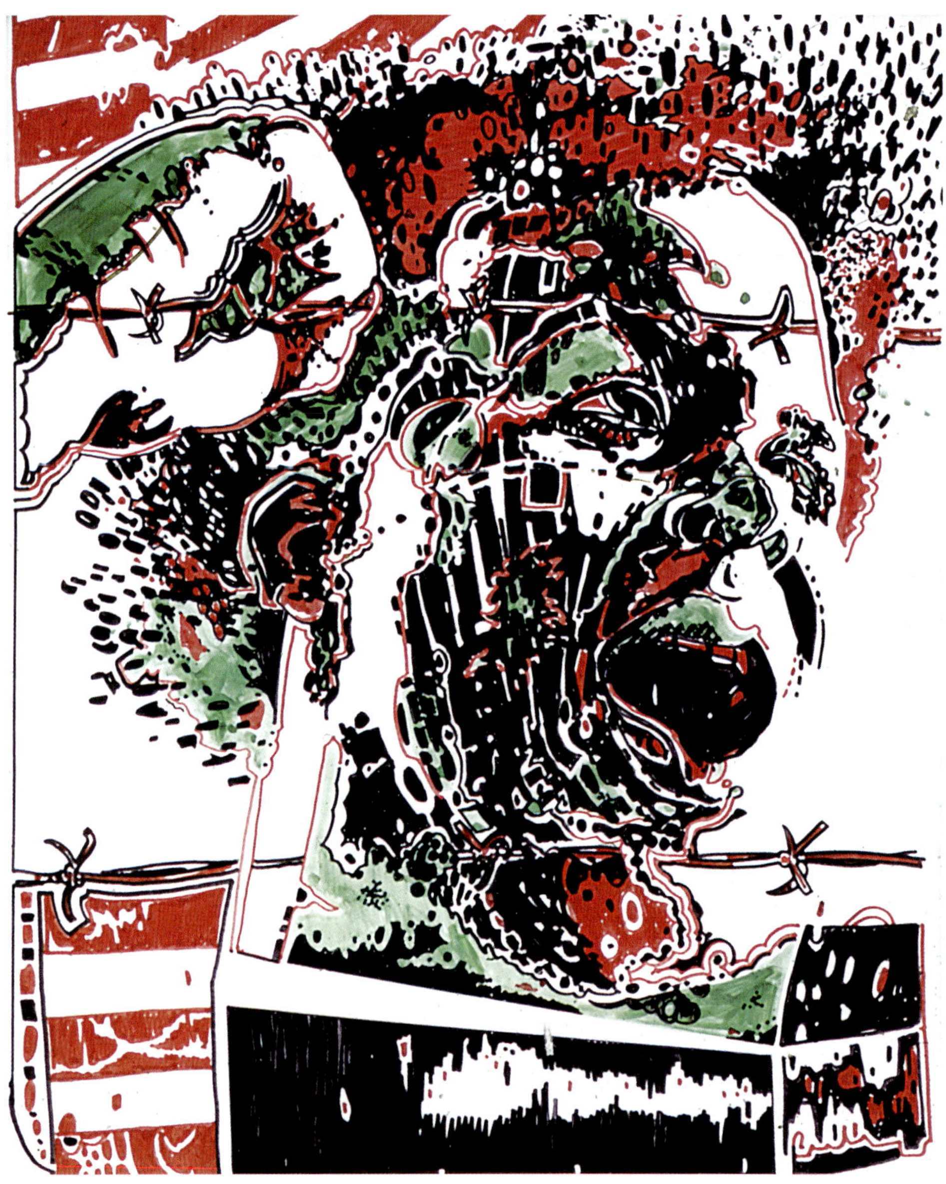

7.1

Nelson Stevens, *The Brother Who Knows*, 1969. Acrylic on canvas, 48 × 48 inches. Collection of Bobby and Carol Braddock.

portrayed did not fit our philosophy of positivism. Jeff asked him, "Is that as negative as you are going to get?" Nelson answered. "Yes, but I have other paintings that's different from this one." Nelson accepted our invitation and became a member.

In June 1969, Carolyn Lawrence, a painter, came to a meeting. Jeff knew her perhaps from the Conference on the Functional Aspects of Black Art (CONFABA), which he created, but most COBRA members knew her from her participation in painting the *Wall of Respect*. She presented an oil painting and asked whether COBRA was similar to the OBAC artists. She was informed that COBRA was a collective with a philosophy whose goal was to create a new language in art. Carolyn became the eighth member of COBRA. In August 1969, COBRA became African Cobra.

In March 1970, Sherman Beck, a painter, came to an African Cobra meeting. The representational oil painting and drawings he presented showed that he was a superb draftsman. Sherman also became an African Cobra member.

In April 1970, three artists were invited to an African Cobra meeting: Elliott Hunter, Keith Morrison, and Bertrand Phillips, all painters. We knew them because they had attended the School of the Art Institute. None of them brought work. They came to observe our work and to learn about the direction of our collective. Jae and I went downstairs to get refreshments, and Elliott followed. He said, "I need something to drink that's stronger than coffee. I am going out to get some cream sherry. I may not be back because the last thing I need is to join a group." Keith and Bertrand did not come to any more African Cobra meetings either.

Other artists attended African Cobra meetings, including a calligrapher and a sculptor, but neither showed interest in joining our collective. (The calligrapher, Bromletter, don't remember his first name, seemed more interested in the art of philosophizing than learning more about African Cobra's tenets.) Scholars like sociologist Abdul Alkalimat and the director of the National Center of Afro-American Artists, Edmund Barry Gaither, came to our meetings. Gaither brought a ceramic sculptor from Sudan, Amir Nour, who was a recent graduate of Yale University. Nour presented some of his work, but I think that he came only as an observer, with no interest in joining a collective. Barry showed great interest in our work and the direction we were going. He was fascinated with the colors on the art and our use of words written directly on the art. He invited us to exhibit at the National Center of Afro-American Artists.

In May 1970, Omar Lama, a draftsman, came to an African Cobra meeting. Jeff invited him mainly because Omar had reproductions of his work, and Jeff wanted to increase our ranks to ten. Omar's medium was pen and ink. He presented a black-and-white print of an exquisite drawing of the dancer Darlene Blackburn. He also showed an illustration for the cover of Haki Madhubuti's book *We Walk the Way of the New World*.

African Cobra's membership was now ten. That was a perfect number because searching for artists interested in creating a new language was difficult. In my opinion, that feat was more attainable with a smaller group of artists.

CONFABA

CONFABA—CONFERENCE ON
THE FUNCTIONAL ASPECTS
OF BLACK ART
Evanston, Illinois, May 1970
by Jeff Donaldson

Jeff explained the purpose of the CONFABA conference in an introductory statement: "As a faculty member at Northwestern University in the spring of 1970, with the invaluable support of students from my African American art history class, I convened the first working conference to 'organize the study of African American Art, and provide a firm foundation whose superstructure, when completed, will properly preserve, protect and project African American visual art history.'"[1]

A diverse group of fifty historians, educators, visual artists, and scholars from other disciplines met at Northwestern University in Evanston, Illinois, from May 7 to May 10, 1970. The conference schedule encompassed objectives and future goals for the advancement of visual art and art history. The function of the conference was to bring together African American art historians, educators, scholars, and students interested in the preservation of Black people's visual art legacy in America. In addition, the goal was to explore the nature and scope of African American art history.

The artists, scholars, and art historians were organized into groups labeled Task Force 1 to 6. The task force groups sought to establish a philosophy of African American art history that defined the field and to respond affirmatively to the quest for self-knowledge and self-esteem throughout African American discourse. The groups also discussed methods of disseminating information about the true history and significance of African American artistic production and its relationship to world art history.

The program containing the schedule was distributed among participants, clarifying the different groups. People asked questions throughout the conference, such as "What makes Black art Black?"

For Task Force 1, the agenda was education: the participants were Theresa Christopher, David Driskell, Eugenia Dunn, Carolyn Lawrence, Malkia Roberts, Frank Smith, Arlene Turner, and Carole Ward.

Task Force 2 was responsible for research: participants included Edmund Barry Gaither, Allan Gordon, Eugene Grigsby, Donald Joyce, Willie Moore, Hughie Lee-Smith, and Shirley Woodson Reid.

Task Force 3 was assigned the agenda resources: it was composed of Chester Bolden, Harold Dorsey, Tritobia Hayes Benjamin, Ademola Olugebefola, and Ann Taylor.

Task Force 4 was assigned the agenda dissemination: the participants were Tom Feelings, Caroll Green Jr., Samella Lewis, E. J. Montgomery, Yvonne Edwards Tucker, Charelene Tull, William Walker, Lawrence Rushing, and Nelson Stevens.

Task Force 5 focused on philosophy: the participants were Aba (Cecille McHardy), Skunder Boghossian, Marie Johnson, Barbara Jones, Paul Keene, Columbus Kepler, Valerie Maynard, Larry Neal, Edsel Reid, Josephus Richards, and Faythe Weaver.

Task Force 6 was assigned the agenda aesthetics: the participants included Sylvia Boone, David Bradford, Dana Chandler, Floyd Coleman, Sylvia Kinney, and Ibn Pori Pitts.

Other guests to the conference invited as observers were a diverse group of scholars, writers, musicians, and artists: musician, composer, and cofounder of AACM Muhal Richard Abrams; poet, music critic, music historian, arts administrator, and author A. B. Spellman; singer, composer, scholar, and social activist Bernice Reagon; photographer Roy Lewis; author, speaker, and scholar of African American politics Ronald Waters; writer, producer, teacher, and activist Barbara Ann Teer; visual artist and musician Jose Williams; sociologist, academic, and psychologist Nathan Hare; scholar, author, sociologist, and activist Abdul Alkalimat; and poet, community activist, musician, and performance artist Ebon Dooley. Here are extracts from conclusions arrived at by all six task forces:

> Black art should be concerned with the African Heritage as much as with our contemporary reality; the heart of the Black artist's ideology is the dedication of his art to the cultural liberation of Black people; when we addressed ourselves to morality and ethics we concluded that Black art seeks also to posit the possibility of a liberated future; the human values with which the Black artists are concerned is his greatest source of spiritual and cultural power—his foundation for a Black Aesthetic.[2]

Cherilyn Wright wrote in "Reflections on CONFABA: 1970": "Myself along with other students that were enrolled in Jeff Donaldson's African American art history class, we mailed out a basic letter to art historians, scholars and artists all across the country. Also, letters were mailed out to Elders of Distinction: Romare Bearden; Elizabeth Catlett; John Howard; Margaret Burroughs; Hale Woodruff; Aaron Douglas; Lois Mailou Jones; John Biggers; Jacob Lawrence; and Hughie Lee-Smith. They all came."[3]

A distinguished invited elder, sculptor Elizabeth Catlett, was unable to physically attend the conference, but her voice and her spirit were there. She was a resident of Mexico, with dual citizenship in Mexico and the United States, and confusion and political issues between the Mexican and the US governments restricted her travel. Nonetheless, Jeff cleverly arranged a conference call that was audible to everyone in the room, making Catlett the keynote speaker for the conference.

In May 1970, Jeff Donaldson sent this notice to all African Cobra members:

SPECIAL CALL MEETING

Reason: There will be a conference of some 60 Black Art historians, distinguished Black artists, and Black Art history students at Northwestern University.

    a. This will be an opportunity for us to meet them.
    b. And an opportunity for them to get to know us, our work, and the Gospel of African Cobra.

In a March 2014 telephone interview, Nelson Stevens said:

In 1969, when I was an assistant professor at Northern [Illinois] University and teaching a course in African American art history, my only reference materials were James A. Porter's book *Modern Negro Art* and Cedric Dover's book *American Negro Art*. People in the history department at Northern approach me and challenged the validity of the history course. Their claim was that the course had no academic standing in the canon of art history. The white professors said that I needed more reference books. Programs in African American history were attacked all across the country. After attending CONFABA, I gathered all of that printed material and dumped it on the professors' desks. After that, no one challenged my history courses.[4]

Around 3:00 P.M. on May 6, approximately seventy-five folding chairs were delivered to WJ Studios and Gallery to accommodate the visitors from the conference. At 6:50 P.M., the visitors arrived on a chartered bus. Several curious people in the neighborhood came out to investigate the reason for the bus on their street. They knew about WJ Studios and Gallery because some of them had visited and had met my family. This event, with all the people visiting WJ Studios and Gallery, reinforced the pride that they felt to have artists and a gallery in their neighborhood.

Five of the guests, Tritobia Benjamin, Lois Mailou Jones-Pierre Noel, David Driskell, Malkia Roberts, and Anna Smith, reunited with us a year later in Washington, DC. Anna Smith was a holdover from James Porter's administration at Howard University, the former chair of the Art Department. She had served as Porter's secretary and had come to the conference to recruit Jeff Donaldson for the open position of chair. She remained at Howard and served as secretary in Jeff's new administration.

In both galleries was an exhibition of African Cobra's work, and each member took turns discussing aspects of his or her art. The dominant audience

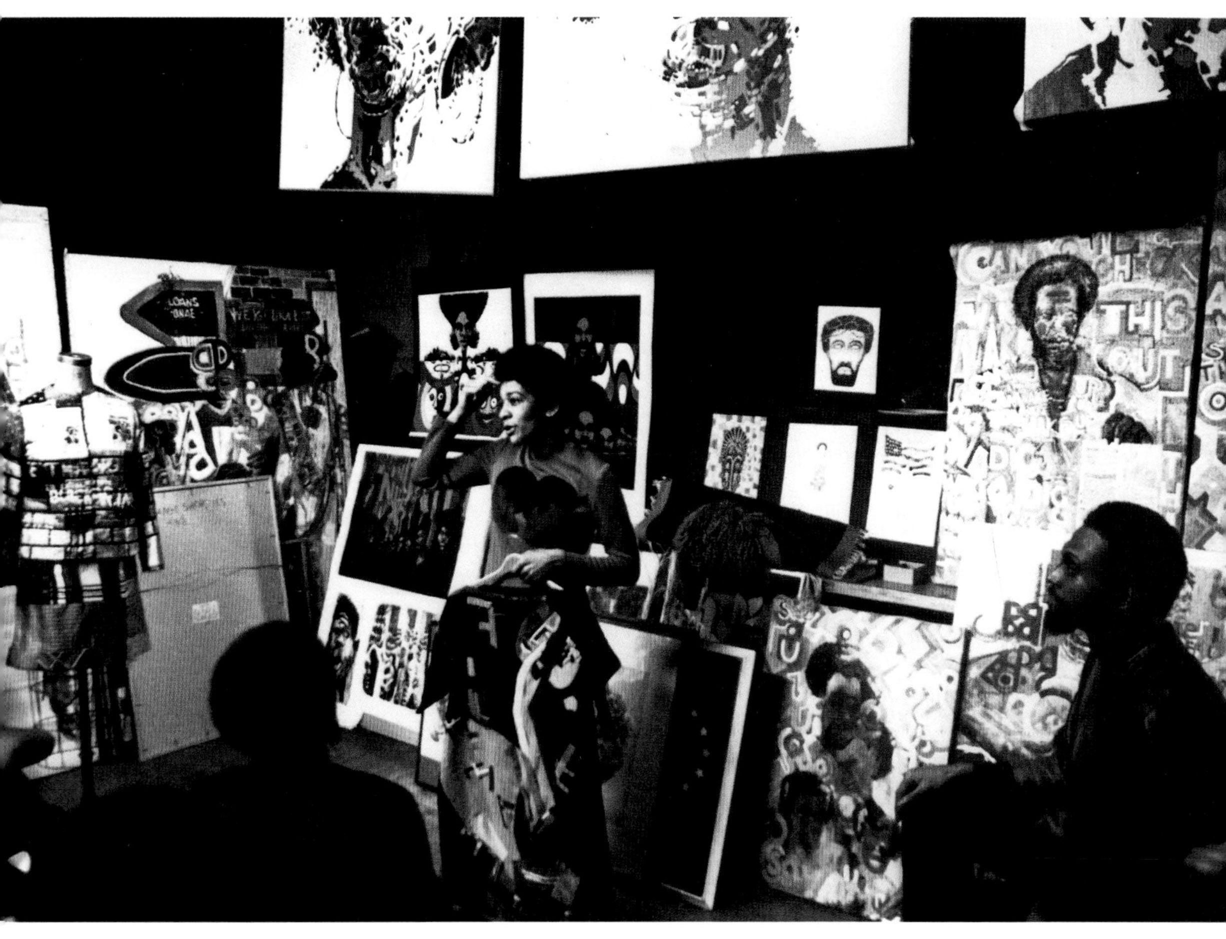

questions were about painting processes, the silkscreen-printing process, and the direction of our collective. Art historian Tritobia Benjamin later wrote: "During an evening tour to the studio of Wadsworth Jarrell, CONFABA participants were introduced to African Cobra and an art form that was direct, authoritative and didactic in its presentation and in its manner of execution. Little did we know that we were bearing witness to a phenomenon destined to impact both stylistically and philosophically the American and the international art scenarios and remain active as an art movement or school of thought to this day."[5]

7.2

Photograph by Roy Lewis. *Jae Jarrell Speaking at CONFABA*, WJ Studios and Gallery, Chicago, 1970. Gelatin silver print.

Made in Chicago

In May 1970, African Cobra became AFRICOBRA (African Commune of Bad Relevant Artists). The new name was only mechanics—the wording change and the abbreviation of African. Additionally, principles in the philosophy were completed in that same month to bring the total to thirteen. Newly added was the following:

FREE SYMMETRY

PROGRAMMATIC

SHINE

EXPRESSIVE AWESOMENESS

MIMESIS AT MIDPOINT

HORROR VACUI

On a Sunday afternoon that month, all ten AFRICOBRA members gathered for a photo shoot at WJ Studios and Gallery. The Studio Museum in Harlem had scheduled an exhibition, AFRICOBRA I, for June 21. The museum was informed that I would make the photographs of artwork and of each member for the official exhibition poster, which would be printed in WJ Studios and Gallery's darkroom facilities. We also agreed to assemble the two-sided poster and to present it camera ready for printing.

The collective assembled at the end of East 61st Street at the concrete wall created by the Illinois Central Railroad for a group photograph. My lab assistant, Ann, was our official photographer, and curious neighborhood children gathered to watch the proceedings. Ann and I took various photographs. We invited a group of neighborhood children to appear in some of them. Later, we moved in front of the WJ Studios and Gallery for another group photograph. Omar asked Ann to use his camera. His idea was to use the photograph as a model for a drawing that he wished to make of the group, but as it turned out, his was the second one unanimously chosen from the selection of photographs for AFRICOBRA use.

In the studio, I proceeded to set up a tripod, background paper, and studio lights to create an atmosphere for portraits. Jeff's large-format Hasselblad camera was used to make individual head shots. My brother Judson, who was a professional portrait photographer, came by and offered pertinent advice. His advice was ignored. The scenario was to have all of the portraits shot with Rembrandt lighting to achieve a dramatic effect. Rembrandt lighting always comes from the left side of the subject, but in my arrangement the main lighting source came from the right side.

Judson advised, "You have the lighting arranged wrong for Rembrandt lighting. It always comes from the left side. What you have now is side lighting."

Being stubborn and a professional photographer myself, I regrettably rejected his advice. "It doesn't matter. Rembrandt, side, what's the difference?"

After development of the film, each negative was transferred to high-contrast film to accommodate the line-printing process for the poster. After viewing the group pictures, we discovered that a photograph of choice for the poster was the one that did not include me holding my son. That was because I shot the photograph of choice. I suggested that the group picture that included me holding my son, shot by my assistant, Ann, could be grafted onto the photograph of our choice. The image of me holding my son was stripped from one negative and added to the group negative that everyone had agreed on. Some expert retouching was required on the negative and on the paper print.

Jeff brought a Gelede mask from his African art collection to the photo shoot. Omar noticed it hanging on the wall and put a pair of sunglasses on it. The mask assumed another appearance, like a baptism in African American urban hipness. We immediately co-opted the Gelede mask with sunglasses as an AFRICOBRA brand and included it on our poster.

The finished artwork for the poster was in black and white, and I suggested that it should remain that way. I said that black and white would make a stronger impact. Most members disagreed and suggested that the poster be printed on colored paper, and I went along with the majority. After we received final printed copies from the Studio Museum, Jeff admitted, "Jarrell was right. This would have been much stronger in black and white. Next time we are going to listen to him."

8

AFRICOBRA I

In April 1970, Edward Spriggs, director of the Studio Museum in Harlem, curated the exhibition AFRICOBRA I: *Ten in Search of a Nation*, scheduled for June 21 through August 30. AFRICOBRA exhibited fifty-two works: paintings, drawings, serigraphs, fashion designs, and weavings. After two years of intense meetings devising a philosophy, and after presenting two local exhibitions in and around Chicago, this was our first major event.

The exhibition drew the attention of the media, including *New York Magazine*, *Amsterdam* newspaper, *Black World* and *Jet* magazines, and a French publication whose name I can't remember. AFRICOBRA works that included bandoliers on the art appeared in an article written by the staff of *Jet* magazine, "Black Revolt Sparks White Fashion Craze." That publicity helped catapult the collective to the attention of national and international audiences. The AFRICOBRA I exhibition was the genesis for showcasing a fresh new direction, introducing viewers to an uplifting experience and awareness of contemporaneous social, cultural, and political concepts. In an essay, Edward Spriggs wrote, "When we first encountered AFRICOBRA in Chicago, they had a name and a philosophy that was infinitely much slicker than anything we had in the shadows of Madison Avenue. Harlem had to have some of what they were offering."[1] Spriggs's essay chronicled components of AFRICOBRA's philosophy, such as words used to construct images and our unconventional applications of color. He described the components that identified the essential form of the collective's art: "AFRICOBRA had harnessed the energy of the

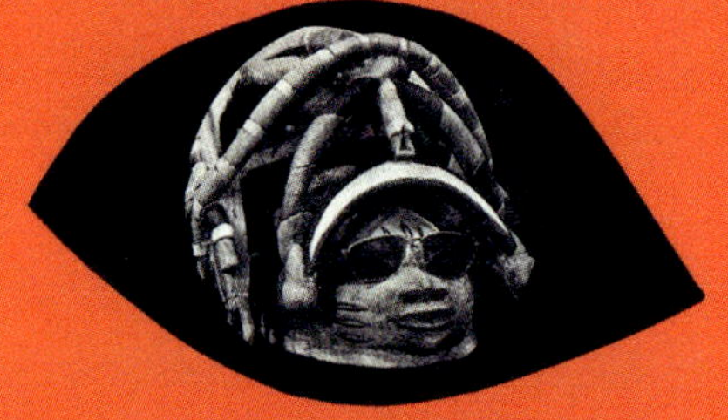

8.1

Brochure for *AFRI-
COBRA I* exhibition
at Studio Museum in
Harlem, 1970.

socio-political ferment of the urban experience during the 1960s and was directing it back to the community. Their creations were rapping visually. Their use of color and words on the canvas was fascinating. With colored words, they articulated visually an aesthetic that is uniquely theirs. They borrowed from nobody's tradition with this use of words and letters in paintings, textile, and graphic compositions."[2]

AFRICOBRA had an understanding of color rooted in our newly devised principle Cool Ade color. In addition to bright colors, some members' palettes contained earth colors, silver and gold, and black for strength and stabilization. White was applied as a color and as a component for mixing colors, but not to the extent of graying so that the colors lose identity. Everyone in the collective agreed to the process of intensifying colors for warmth, including colors in the cool spectrum. That brought luster into the art, as later stated in an essay by Cherilyn Wright for the *AFRICOBRA II* catalog: "with bright/survive/stay alive colors that come poppin' out at you like a galaxy in the night sky."[3] Part of our philosophical constructs were interpreting and knowing color functions, like color complements and secondary colors, and anticipating how adjacent colors react when another color is placed in close proximity or is surrounded by that color. The Cool Ade colors were why the exhibition was labeled "A Dazzling Show of Negro Art" by the art critic for the *Amsterdam* newspaper, Harry Long: "AFRICOBRA created images that

Photographs and graphic design by Wadsworth Jarrell. Poster for *AFRICOBRA I* exhibition at Studio Museum in Harlem, 1970.

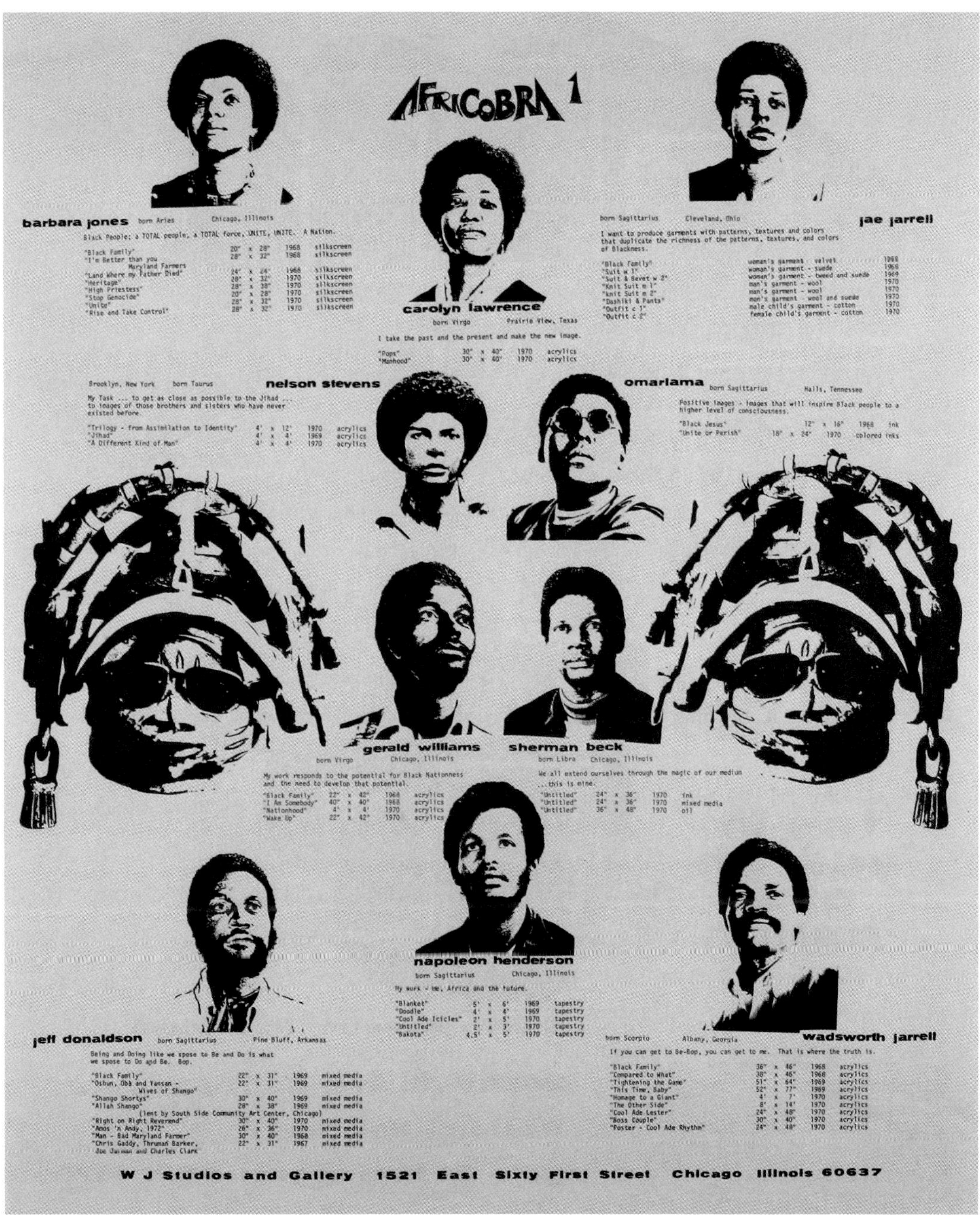

are pertinent to urban black people, their art is designed to be useful and appealing to them, regardless of any formal training or prior experience with art. . . . Perhaps the most important component of their art is color. . . . The collective searched for colors that shine, dazzling brilliant colors, and colors that defines and identify."[4]

In "The Big Bad Relevance," John Gruen, art critic for *New York Magazine*, described the show:

> The work in the exhibition is far from being ethnically inspired derivatives. The four principles of AFRICOBRA, Cool Aid Colors, Shine, Free Symmetry, and Living Form, all of the works easily fall within one or another of these principles. Clearly the stars of the group are Nelson Stevens, Napoleon Henderson and Jae Jarrell. *Stevens's Trilogy: From Assimilation to Identity,* is a vibrant triptych of dazzling color, in which a series of black faces emerges as potent-visual explosions.
>
> The tapestries by Napoleon Henderson—lively abstractions of vivid and bold design—accurately conform to the group' s law of Free Symmetry. Particularly arresting in the series [are] garments designed by Jae Jarrell, a young Ohio-born fashion designer, who says, "I want to produce garments with patterns, textures and colors that duplicate the richness of the patterns, textures and colors of Blackness." Miss Jarrell uses cloth surfaces as picture planes. She paints or appliques images relevant to today's black urban America. One quite elegant dress features a suddenly shocking bullet-belt across the chest. The bullets are actually many-colored pellets that shine ominously against the somber brown-gray of the fabric.[5]

AFRICOBRA I: *Ten in Search of a Nation* was not only a manifestation of dazzle and shine as described by Long, but it also embodied aesthetic imperatives and assertive statements addressing the dire condition of African Americans. The work also offered solutions to that condition. The art was profound. In 1980 in an essay entitled "AFRICOBRA/Farafindugu," written for the AFRICOBRA/*Farafindugu* exhibition held at the Neighborhood Art Center in Atlanta, Georgia, Larry Neal wrote, "This artistic ideology springs from the ethos of African American and Pan-African spiritual and political culture."[6] AFRICOBRA's focus was for our art to advocate and strongly suggest ideally what should be. Those suggestions called for self-love and a proud

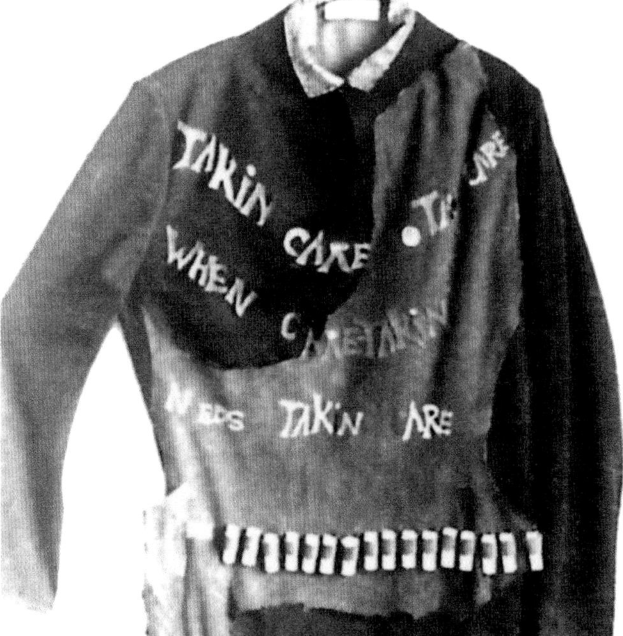

8.3

Jae Jarrell, *Takin' Care
to Take Care When
Takin' Care Needs
Takin' Care*, 1970.
Hand-painted cotton
and leather bandolier
with faux bullets.
Collection of the
artist. Photograph by
Wadsworth Jarrell.

cohesive nation of Black people who would stubbornly resist unfounded rac-ist laws, traditions, and customs. AFRICOBRA believed that to create a new language—a Black aesthetic—African heritage was required to transcend protest art and European aesthetics. As Larry Neal proclaimed in the same 1980 essay, "The aesthetic ground for this approach to making art seems to be rooted in the rhythmic values of African aesthetics, what Leopole Senghor called the 'vibratory shock.'"[7]

AFRICOBRA's approach to making art and labeling it Black art was different from that of other Black artists in the sixties, seventies, and eighties. Most of those artists' work was rooted in European aesthetics. AFRICOBRA's art was grounded in the philosophy of creating a brand new language. Significantly, our art proposed a diversion from the moribund protest art produced in the sixties (the avalanche of weepy, lamenting, negative, woe-is-me, and look-what-they-did-to-us art), grounded in European procedures. This negativity refers to the Middle Passage as well, art depicting captured Africans bound and constrained in neck bracelets and leg irons, tightly huddled together in the bellies of ships, and sailing unwillingly to America to be sold in the market as commodities, as chattel.

The AFRICOBRA collective viewed that genre of art as extremely negative, characterized by images perpetuating self-deprecation, domesticity, docility, surrender, self-hatred, and violence: portrayal of the Ku Klux Klan; of the use of power water hoses, police dogs, and billy clubs on civil rights marchers; and of Black men and women with syringes embedded in their arms. Additionally, our art was definitely different from that which identifies with the Black experience by glorifying "Black memorabilia." Art fitting this description only brings attention to the violent acts themselves and identifies existing infelicities in African American communities. Those works of art provide only framed memory of those injustices, bolstering the gloating wishes of the oppressor, who is better served by these images.

The art in AFRICOBRA I lived up to the principle shine, introduced by Nelson Stevens. In an AFRICOBRA meeting in September 1969, Nelson said, "One thing is for sure, in order for Black people to fully embrace and sanction our efforts, the work has to shine."[8] Nelson's idea of shine, I thought, represented exemplary achievements of the highest order in a profession, a beacon that shines to lead the way. When Nelson introduced shine as a principle, apparently Jeff took it literally. He championed it and wrote about it by interpreting it to have other meanings. As a result, in my opinion, the meaning was reduced figuratively to signify the luster apparent in African American lifestyles, like gold teeth, silver and gold threads in clothing, hair pomades, plastic covering on upholstered furniture, shiny cars, spit-shined shoes, and so forth. My opinion of the meaning of shine versus Jeff's interpretation, unfortunately, was minimized by my silence and the silence of other members when the principle was introduced. Consequently, Jeff's interpretation has overwhelmingly played out in the media and in books and essays by scholars who accepted his as the true meaning.

My understanding of shine emanates from an expression I heard my father, Solomon, say when I was a young boy. He would often say, "I have to shine today." Another expression he frequently used was "I have to turn around today." My father's use of those terms suggested accomplishing an important feat and moving rapidly to accomplish that feat. In 1950s Chicago, my sister Alesie was a door-to-door salesperson for Fuller Products. She said that in their morning pep rallies, before each salesperson departed for their itineraries, the rallying cry was, "We gonna sell, we gonna shine—we gonna shine!" In Black communities, the expression has taken on another sense: "I [or we] have to throw down."

In June 1970, in the last AFRICOBRA meeting in Chicago, while planning for the forthcoming exhibition in New York City, we discussed staging a barn-fire book-burning event on 125th Street and Lenox Avenue in Harlem. We labeled it "The Great Book Burning" (the GBB). We thought that this demonstration would be timed perfectly to coincide with the AFRICOBRA I exhibition, purging from our psyche European literature that we had learned in schools. We proposed burning books by the following authors: Dostoyevsky, Kierkegaard, Sartre, Camus, Nietzsche, and Descartes. Additional books that were destined for the furnace were by authors Aldous Huxley, Plato, and Aristotle. The much-anticipated event did not occur because to stage events of that magnitude, an advance permit from the city is required, which we never pursued.

When AFRICOBRA artists arrived at the Studio Museum in Harlem two days before the opening of the exhibition, we discovered that our request had not been honored. Our policy required the walls of galleries and museums to be painted in our traditional Cool Ade colors. To fulfill that requested policy, AFRICOBRA artists along with museum staff—including Valerie Maynard, who was artist-in-residence at the museum—joined in to help paint the walls. Jeff, Jae, and I had unfinished work, and our time was used to complete it. My unfinished painting *The Other Side*—a diptych, measuring eight feet by eight feet—was literally finished there. Edward Spriggs did not approve of artists completing works at the museum. He seemed a bit perturbed but was also pleasantly satisfied to have all the work completed for the exhibition.

Droves of visitors dropped by the museum impromptu, and finishing work allowed me very little time for socializing. Two people from my school days at the School of the Art Institute of Chicago came by: LeRoy Neiman, my former instructor, and Benny Andrews, a former classmate. Other visitors of note were the photographer Roy DeCarava and the painters Frank Smith, James Phillips, and Ademola Olugebefola.

On Sunday June 21, 1970, the Black Repertory Theater opened the exhibition in a celebration of grandeur, with a spirited call-and-response performance. The first sound heard was the word "Black" voiced in baritone and built to a crescendo of contralto, tenor, alto, and soprano—"Black! Black! Black! Black! Black!" The actors recited assertive lines expressing Black awareness reflecting the times. The performance lasted approximately five minutes, and the theater group invigorated the audience with the spiritual intensity of Baptist ministers' sermons on Sunday mornings. The celebration was in concord with the art of AFRICOBRA appearing in a blaze of brilliant Cool Ade colors, positive black images, expressive awesomeness, free symmetry, and syncopated rhythm.

With the lights on, the art took center stage, and overwhelming excitement and awe were visible on faces in the audience. The AFRICOBRA artists realized that this event was special. This was perceived undoubtedly as a milestone in art. The exhibition communicated boldness and originality in concept, profound elegance in presentation, and proficiency in execution. This was AFRICOBRA's first attempt to present work related to what avant-garde musicians embodied in their music—an egalitarian concept.

The collective was asked to participate in a film made by an independent film crew, and photographers from around the world assembled, waiting anxiously for permission to shoot a group photograph. The moment permission was given, the room exploded with floodlights and flash bulbs. One photographer representing a French magazine literally jumped in front of the crowded field and fired away at rapid-fire speed.

The five founding members exhibited the first theme assignment, Black Family. Barbara Jones and I also exhibited the controversial second theme assignment, I Am Better Than Those Motherfuckers and They Know It. In addition, Barbara exhibited *Unite, Heritage, Land Where My Father Died, High Priestess, Stop Genocide,* and *Rise and Take Control.* Her signature piece was *Unite,* with colors of red, black, green, and gold, depicting rows of African American men and women with raised clenched fists.

Jae Jarrell's work consisted of a total of eight garments, including three outstanding works: *Revolutionary Suit (Bullet Belt Suit), Urban Wall Suit,* and *Brothers Surrounding Sis.* Her signature piece, which garnered national and international attention, was *Revolutionary Suit,* a woman's garment elegantly designed in gray tweed, with a yellow leather bandolier of colorful faux bullets.

Nelson Stevens's paintings were *Trilogy: From Assimilation to Identity, Jihad,* and *A Different Kind of Man.* His signature piece was *Trilogy: From Assimilation to Identity*—a quadrisect. It consists of three panels of larger-than-life heads of African American women and a half-circle altar piece atop the middle panel.

Jeff Donaldson's watercolors manifest his knowledge of Yoruba aesthetics: *Allah Shango, Oshun, Oba, Yansan,* and *Wives of Shango.* Other works were *Black Family, Shango Shorties, Man,* and *Amos 'n Andy.* His signature piece, capturing an enormous amount of attention, was *Wives of Shango.* The painting is composed of three stalwart African American women, armed, with bandoliers of painted bullets—worn crisscrossing the middle of one woman's chest and slung low, like gunfighters, around the waists of the other two women. Jeff's painting presents quite a departure from the collection of Aunt Jemima paintings by other African American artists attempting to portray a defiant Black woman.

Carolyn Lawrence explained that she takes the past and the present to make new images. She exhibited two paintings: *Pops* (a painting of an old man representing the past), and *Uphold Your Men.* Her signature work was *Uphold Your Men,* portraying a strong Black woman with arms folded, defiantly asserting, "Uphold Your Men, Unify Your Families."

I presented eight paintings, including five that stood out: *Black Family, Compared to What, Homage to a Giant, Cool Ade Lester,* and *Boss Couple* (a portrait of my son, Wadsworth Jr., and I). My signature piece was *Homage to a Giant,* which includes four images of Malik El Hajj Shabazz (Malcolm X), and one each of Kwame Ture (Stokely Carmichael), Jesse Jackson, and Huey P. Newton—who is shown wearing a bandolier across his shoulders.

Gerald Williams's vibrant paintings displayed his interest and knowledge of graffiti: *Say it Loud, I Am Somebody, Nationhood,* and *Wake Up.* His signature painting in the exhibition was *Wake Up.* The painting is of an African American man who seems to be peeking from behind or through an intricate network of highly stylized letters, with some letters forming words.

Napoleon Henderson presented tapestries that functioned as wall hangings. Titles of his works were *Blanket, Doodle, Cool Ade Icicles,* and *Bakota.* The tapestry *Bakota* was influenced by aesthetics of the Bakota in Lobaye, Central African Republic. His signature work was *Cool Ade Icicles,* a tapestry of strips of colored cloth, encased with aluminum foil in one area.

Sherman Beck's artist statement for AFRICOBRA I catalog was "We all extend ourselves through the magic of our medium, and this is my medium." All three of his works were untitled. One painting was in oil, and the others were gouache, pen and ink, and color markers. The painting rendered with color markers shows the face of a man emerging from a background of

Barbara Jones-Hogu, *Unite*, n.d. Silkscreen on wove paper, 22 × 30 inches. Collection of Brooklyn Museum.

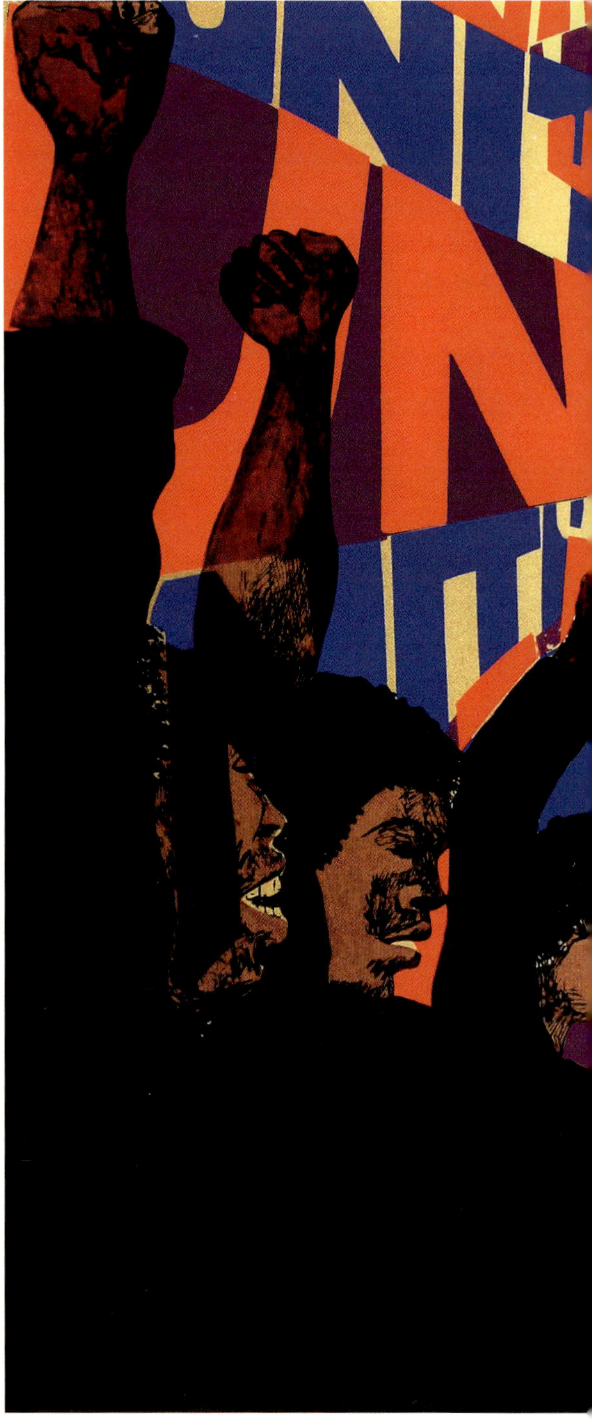

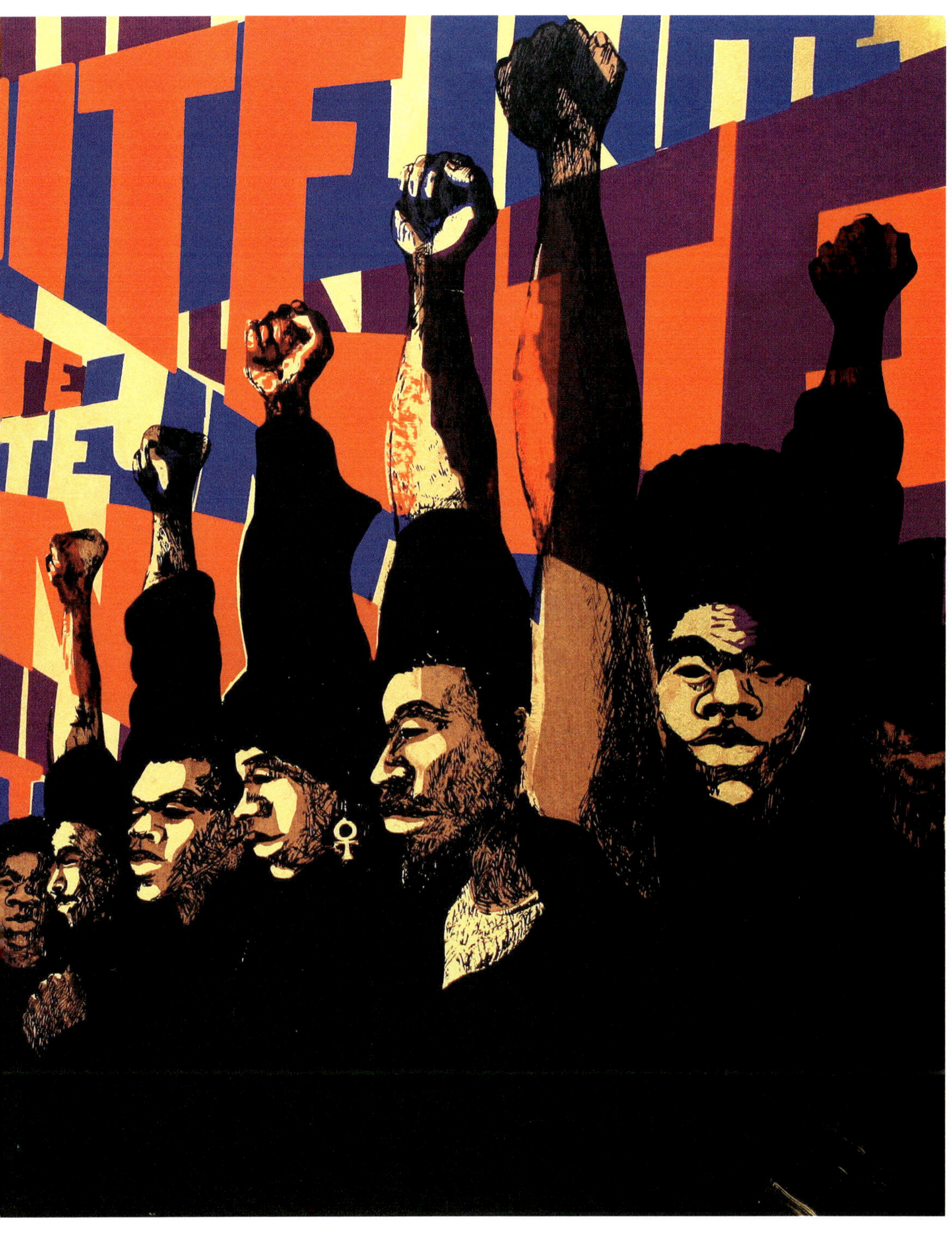

8.6
—————
Barbara Jones-Hogu,
High Priestess, 1970.
Silkscreen on paper,
22 × 30 inches. Collection
of Jae and Wadsworth
Jarrell.

8.5
—————
Barbara Jones-Hogu,
Rise and Take Control,
1970. Silkscreen on
paper, 22 × 38 inches.
Collection of David
Lusenhop.

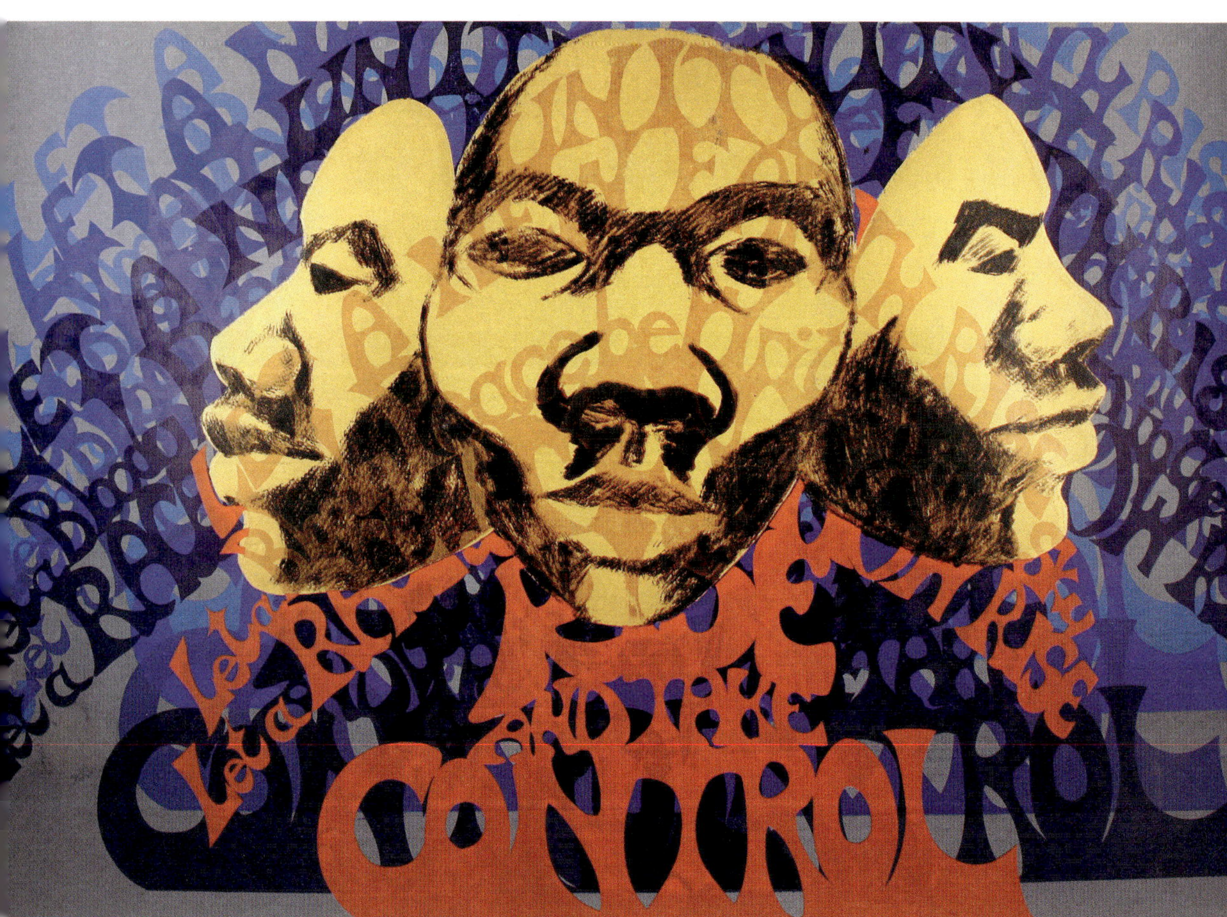

RISE AND TAKE CONTROL

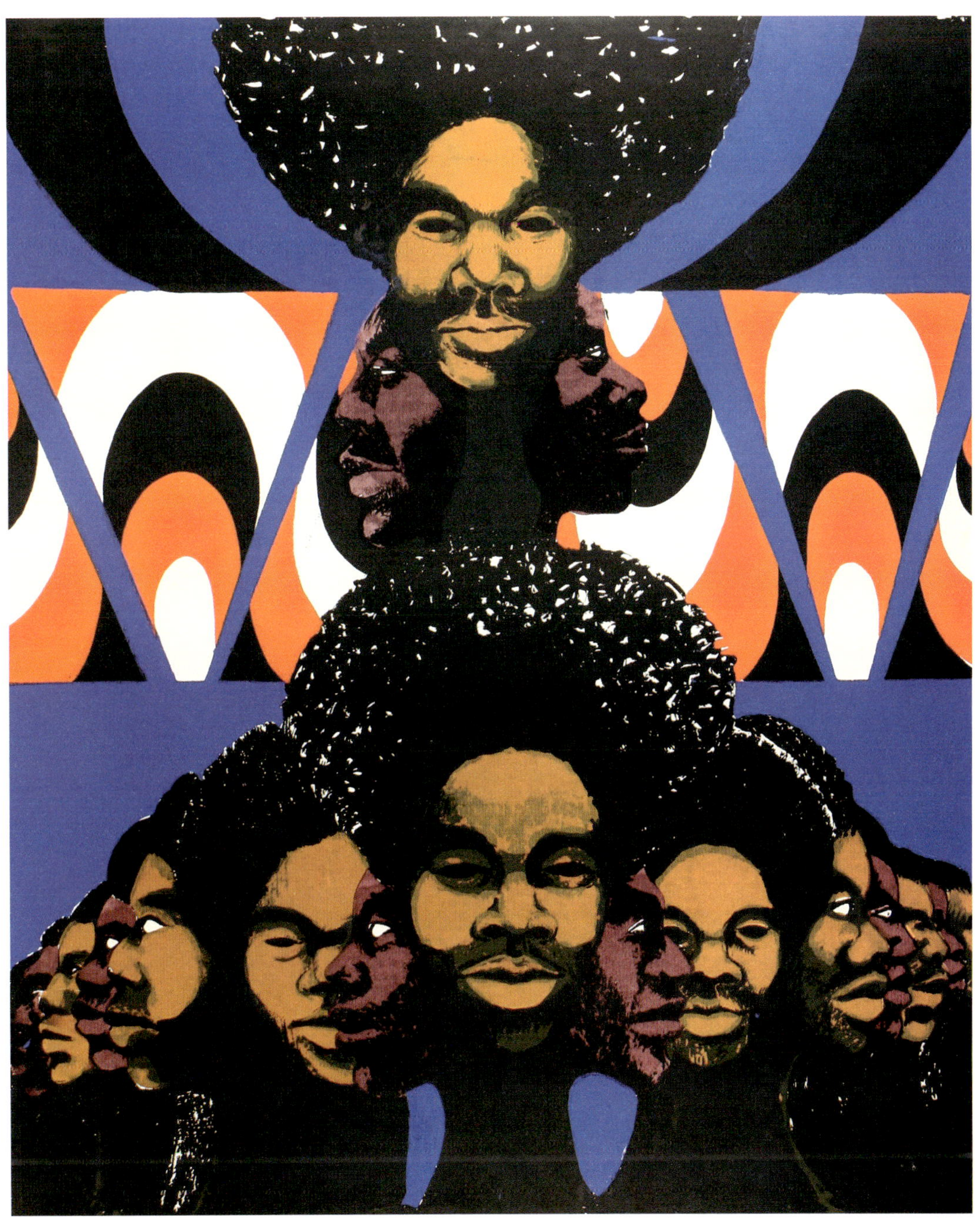

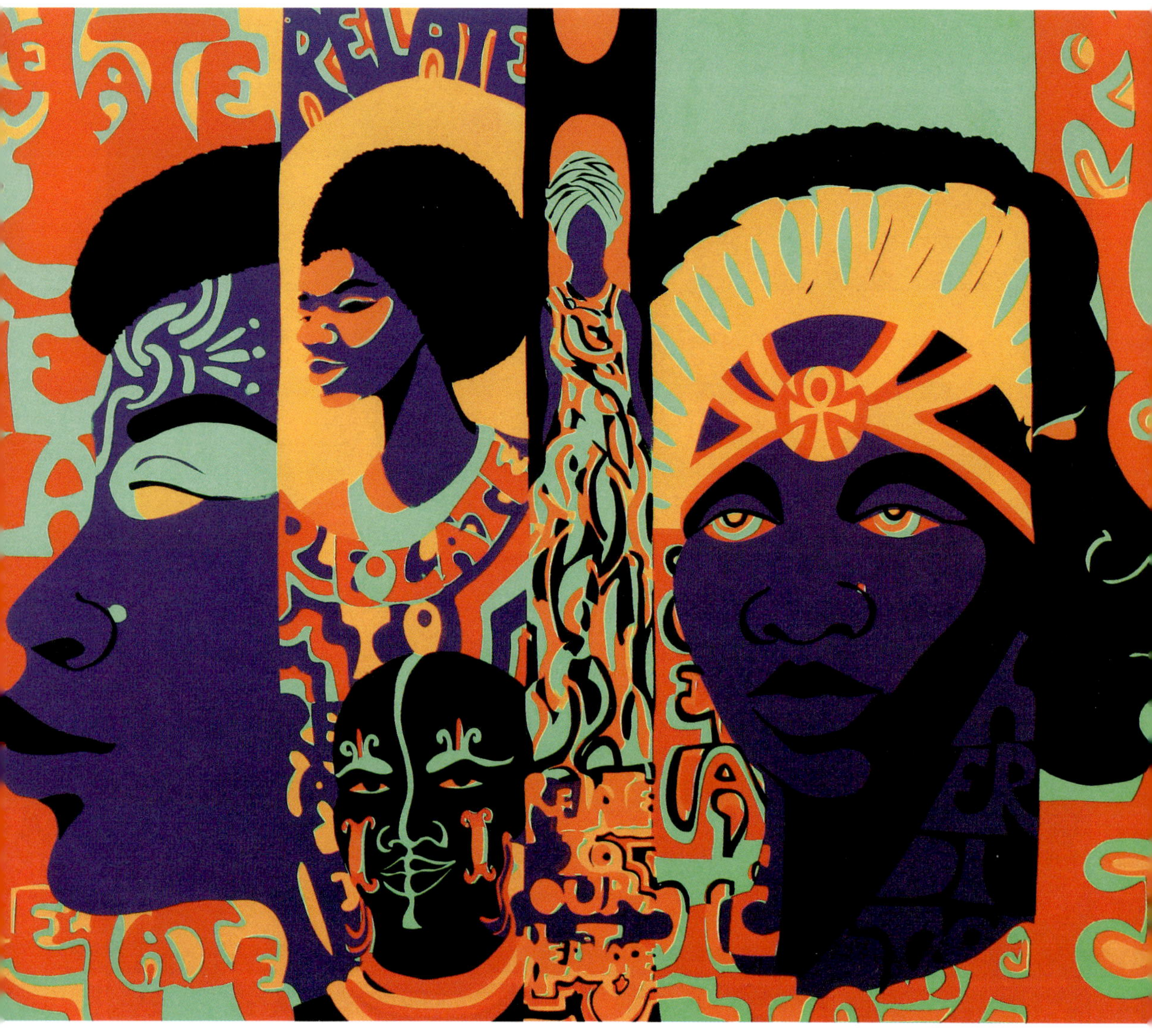

8.7

Barbara Jones-Hogu, *Heritage*, 1970. Silkscreen on wove paper, 28 × 38 inches. Collection of David Lusenhop.

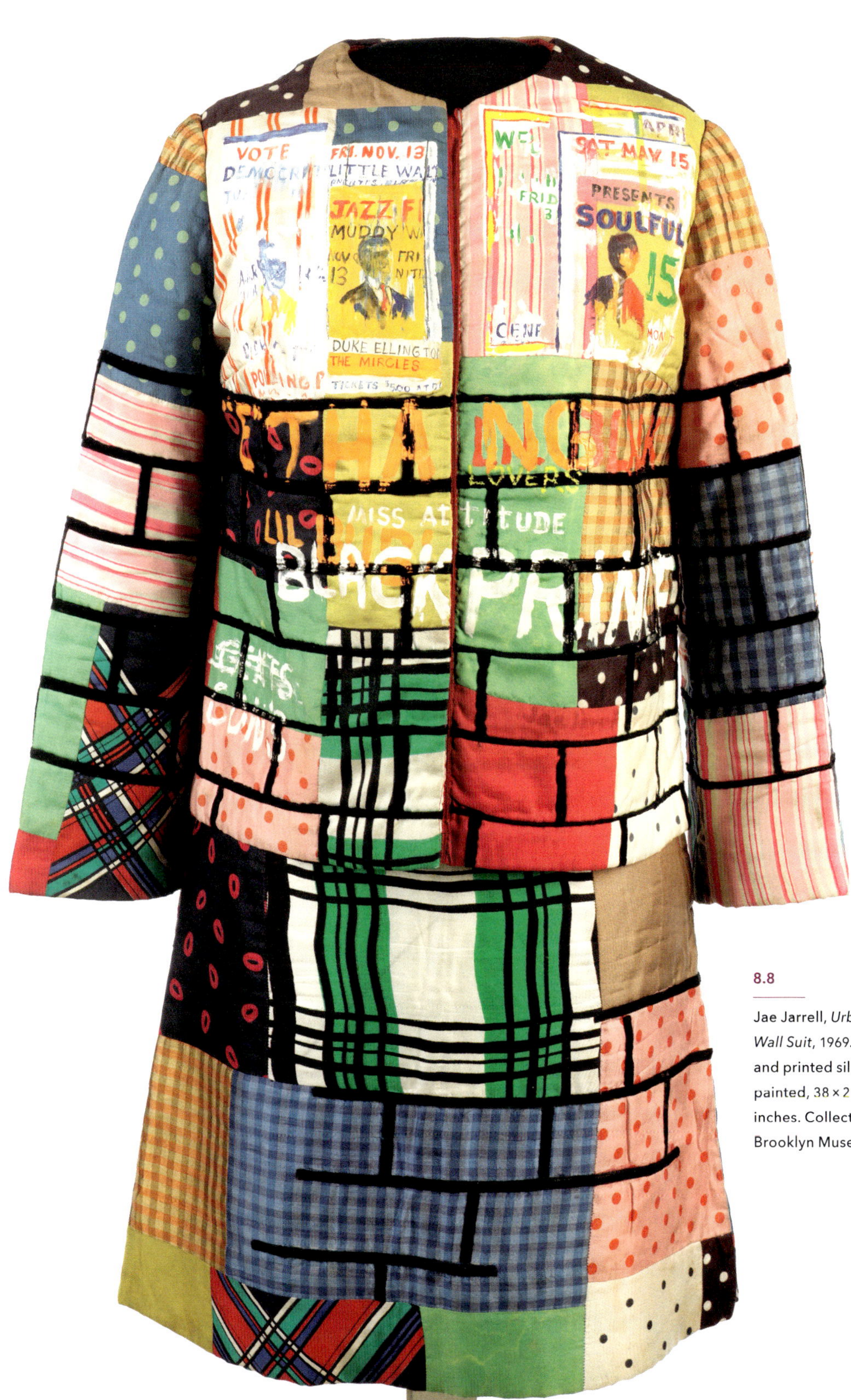

8.8

Jae Jarrell, *Urban Wall Suit*, 1969. Dyed and printed silk, hand painted, 38 × 21 × 10 inches. Collection of Brooklyn Museum.

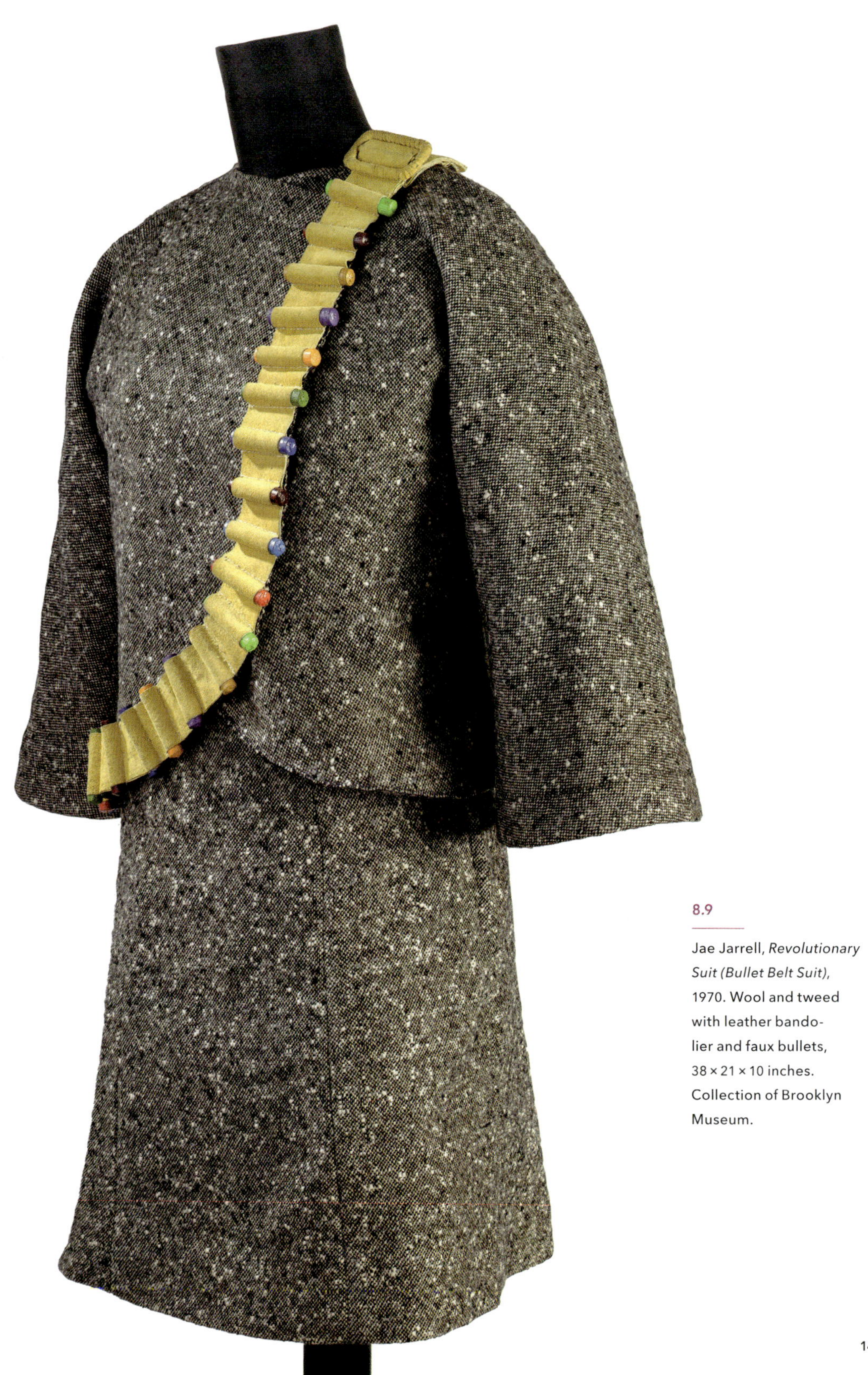

Jae Jarrell, *Revolutionary Suit (Bullet Belt Suit)*, 1970. Wool and tweed with leather bandolier and faux bullets, 38 × 21 × 10 inches. Collection of Brooklyn Museum.

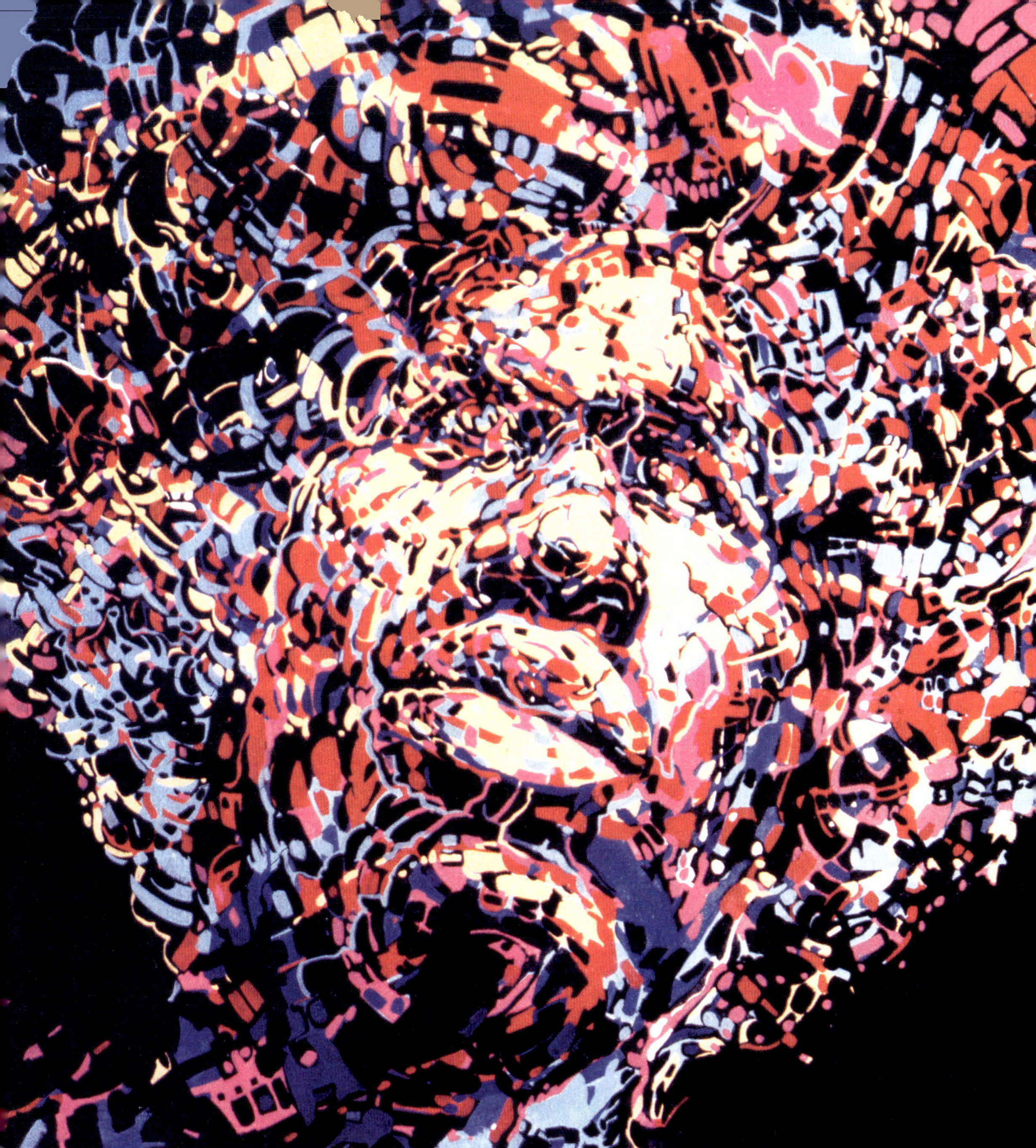

8.10

Nelson Stevens, *A Different Kind of Man*, 1970. Acrylic on canvas, 48 × 48 inches. Collection of the artist.

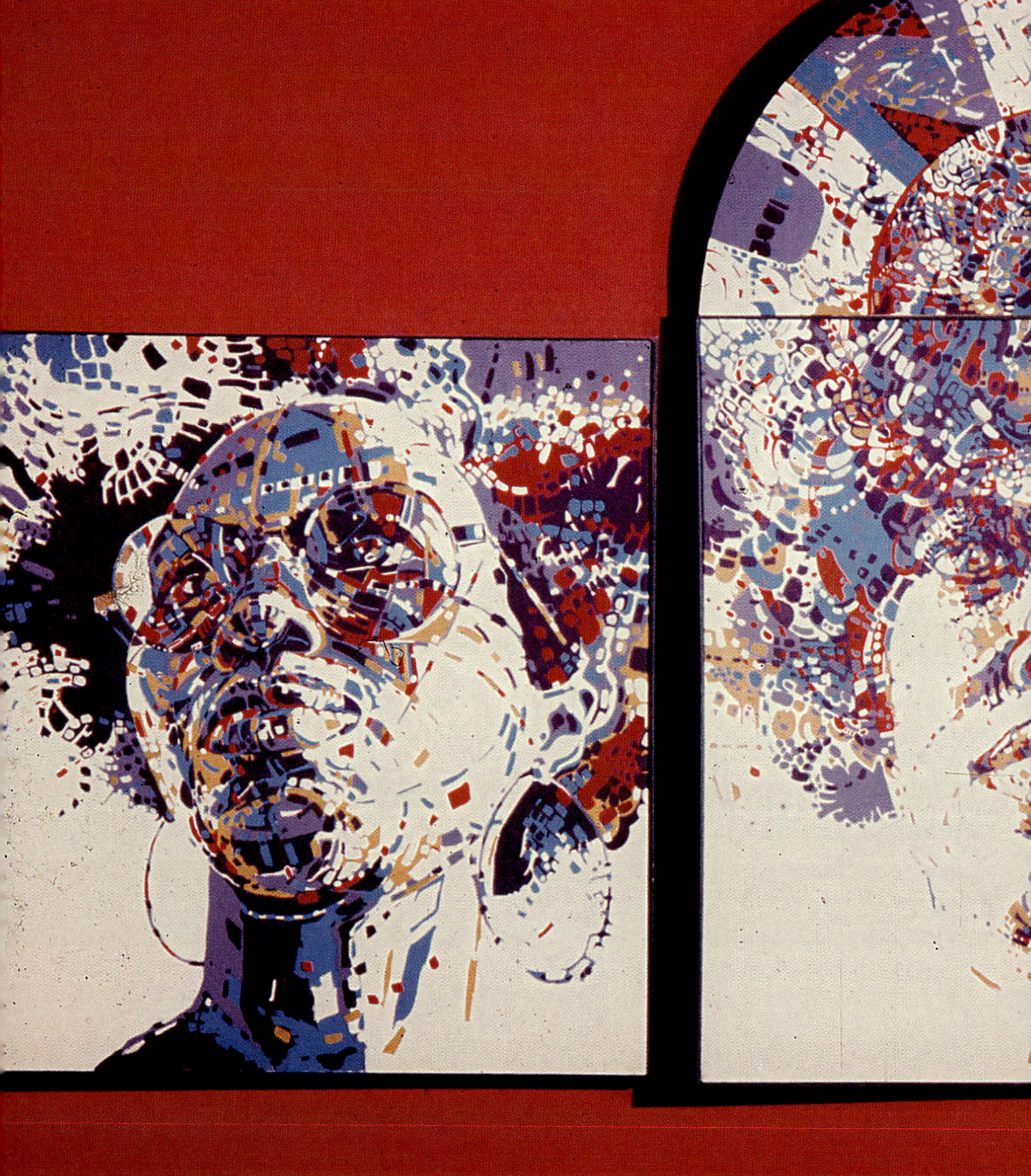

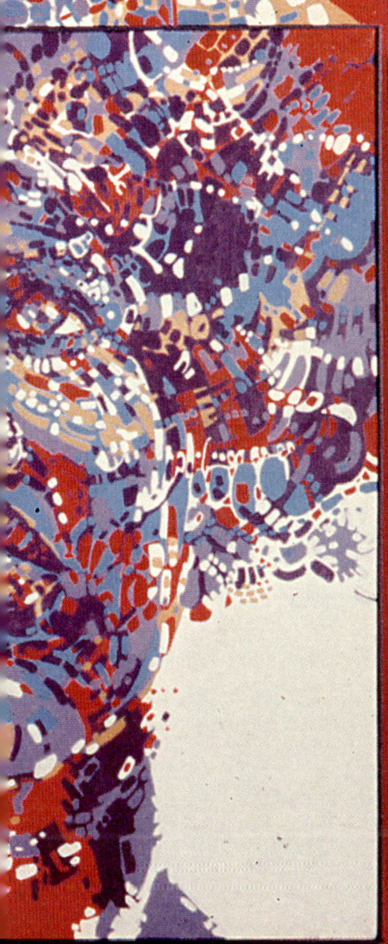

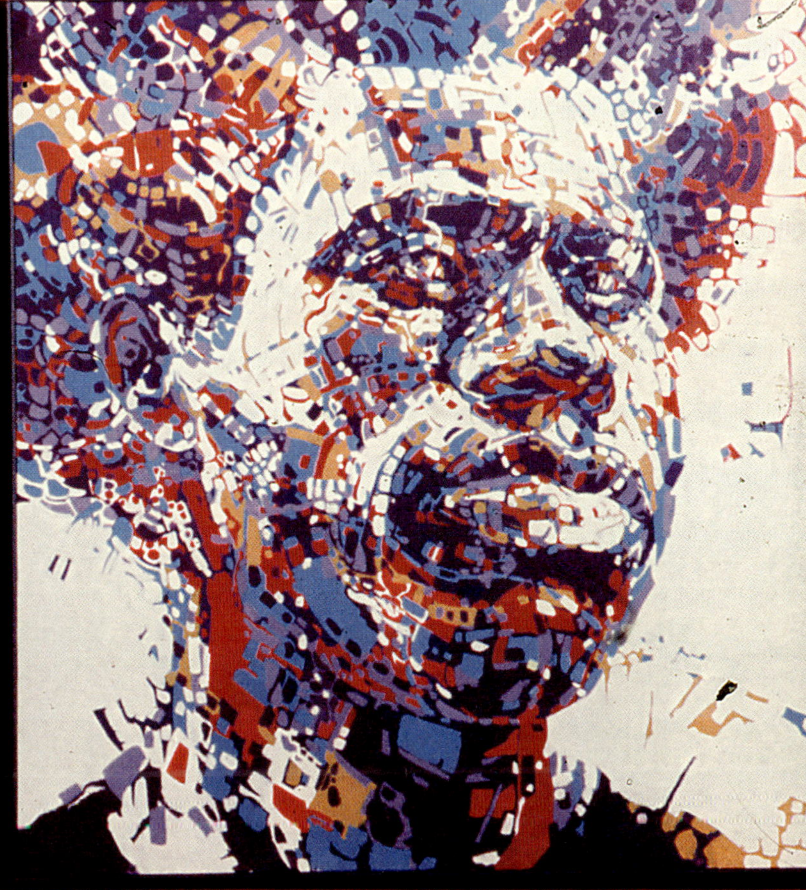

Nelson Stevens, *Trilogy: From Assimilation to Identity*, 1970. Acrylic on canvas, 48 × 144 inches. Split collection of the triptych, National Museum, Washington, DC, and The Art Institute of Chicago.

8.12
—

Carolyn Lawrence, *Pops*,
1970. Acrylic on canvas,
30 × 40 inches. Collection
of the artist.

8.13
—

Carolyn Lawrence,
Uphold Your Men, n.d.
Acrylic on canvas, 30 × 40
inches. Collection of the
artist.

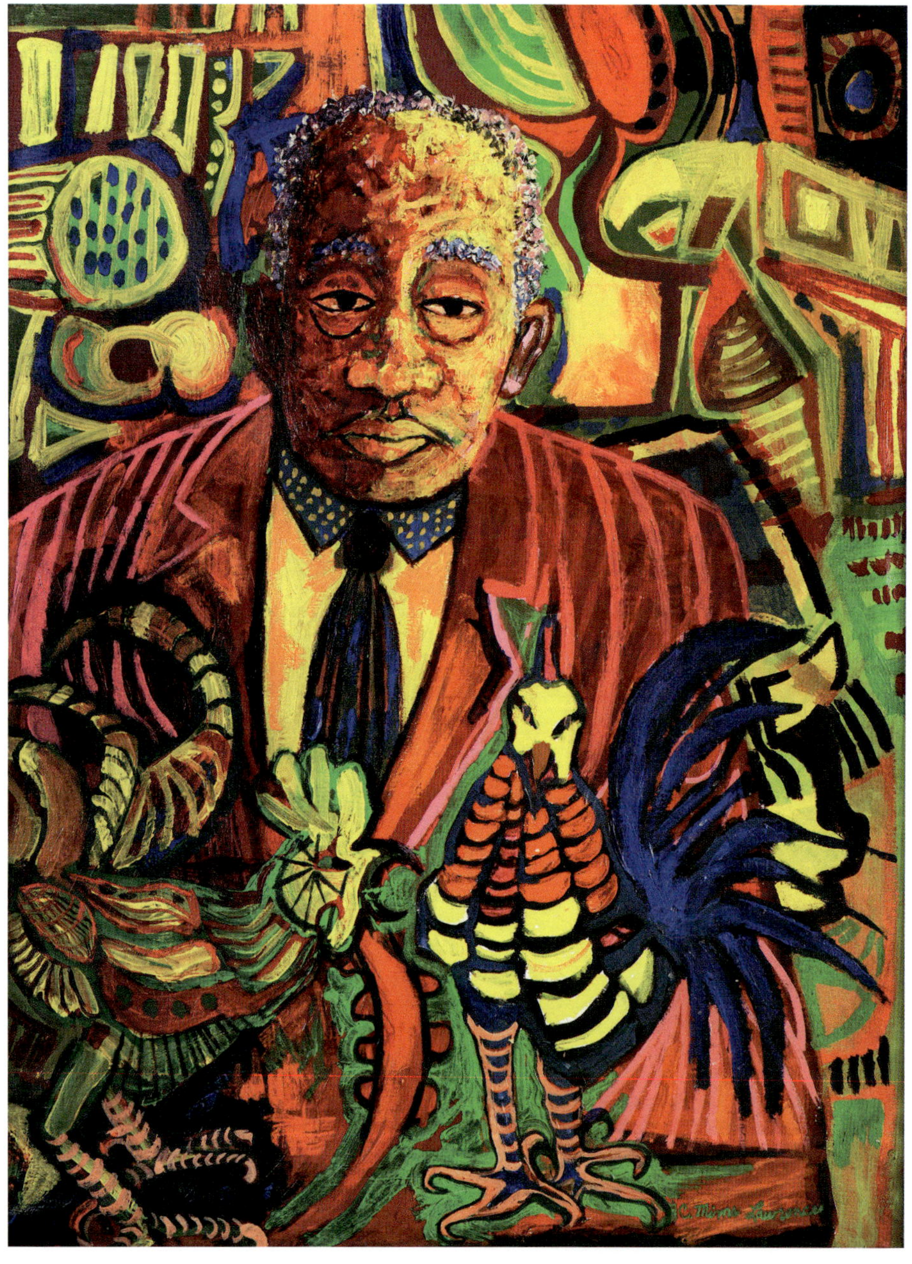

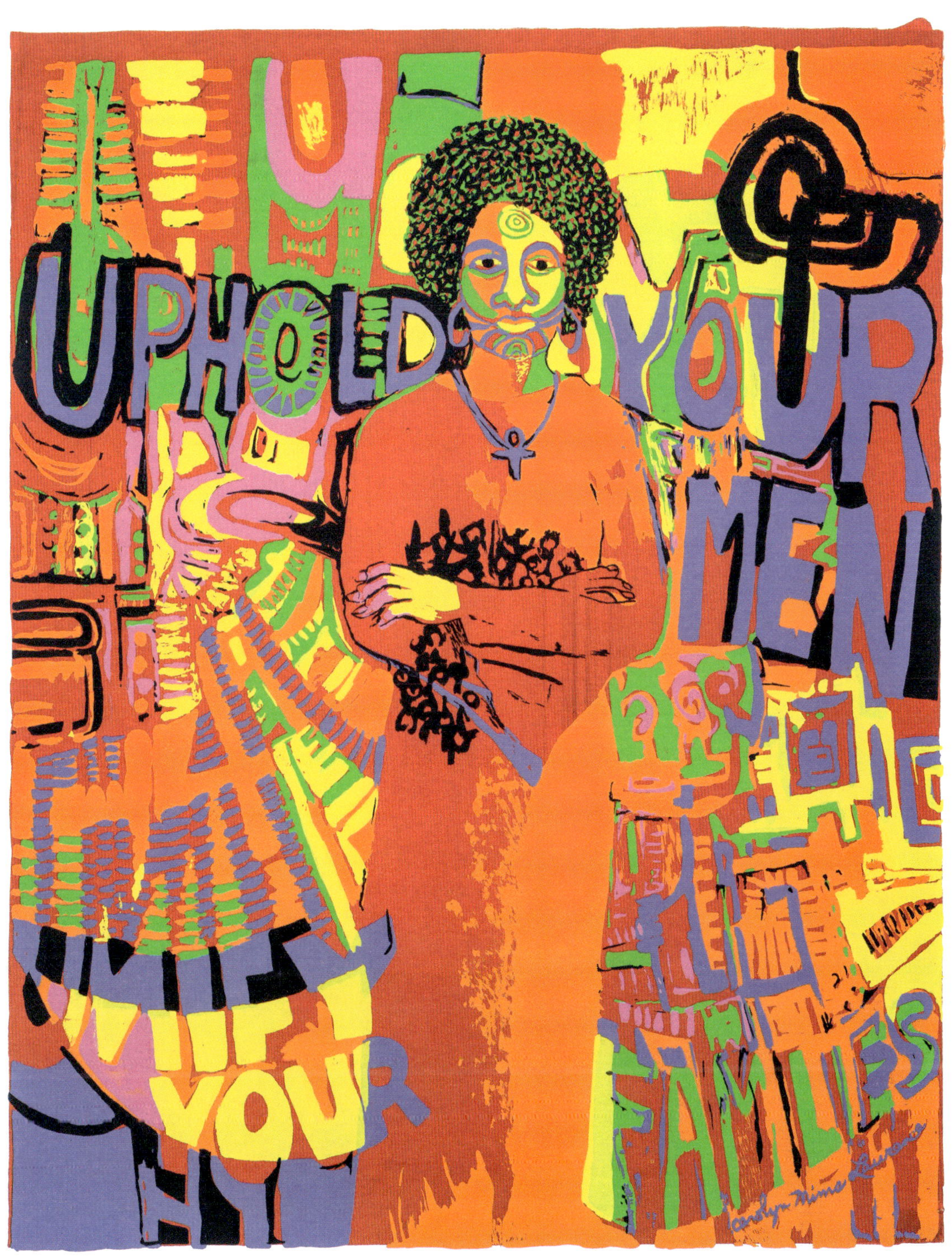

UPHOLD YOUR MEN
UNIFY YOUR FAMILIES
Carolyn Mims Lawrence

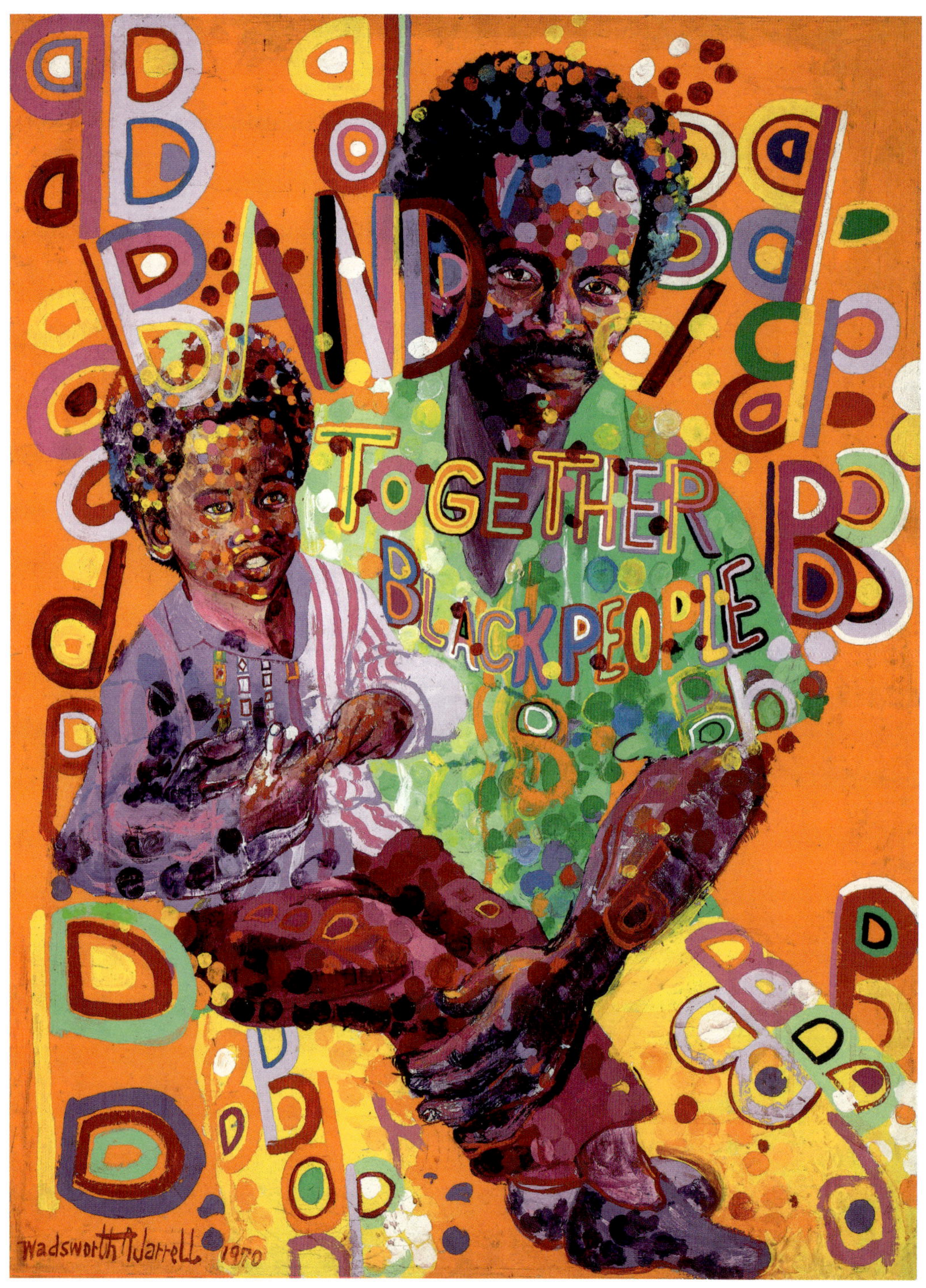

BAND
TOGETHER
BLACK PEOPLE
Wadsworth Jarrell 1970

8.14

Wadsworth Jarrell, *Boss
Couple*, 1970. Acrylic on
canvas, 30 × 40 inches.
Collection of the artist.

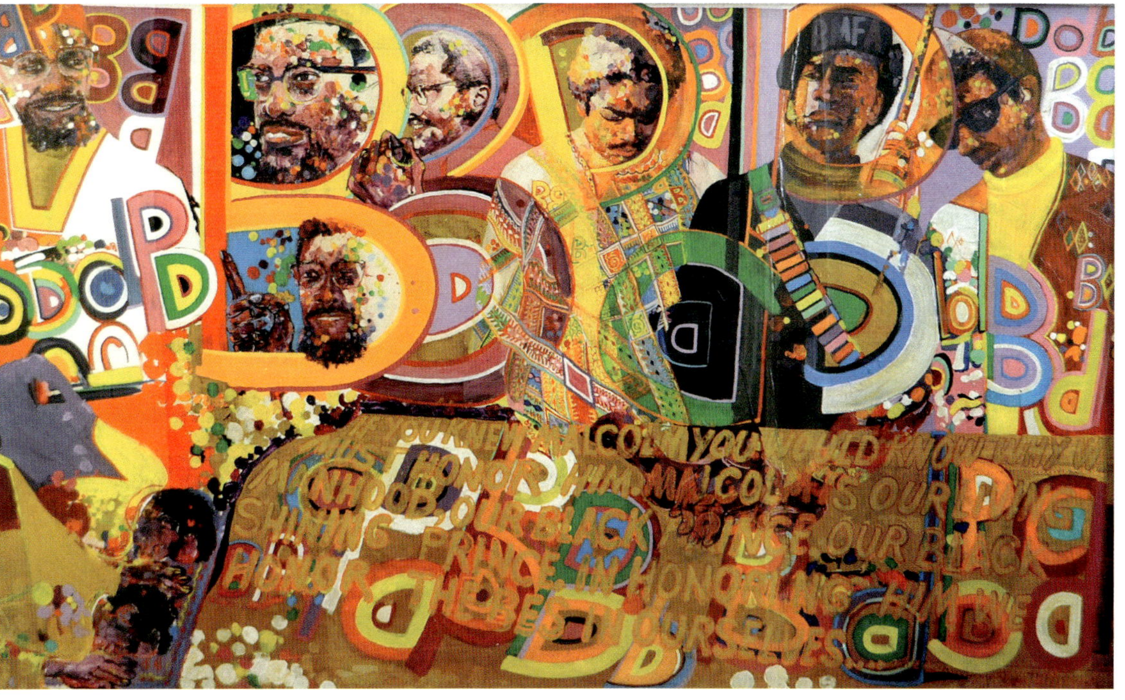

8.15

Wadsworth Jarrell,
Homage to a Giant,
1970. Acrylic on board,
48 × 90 inches. Collection
of the artist.

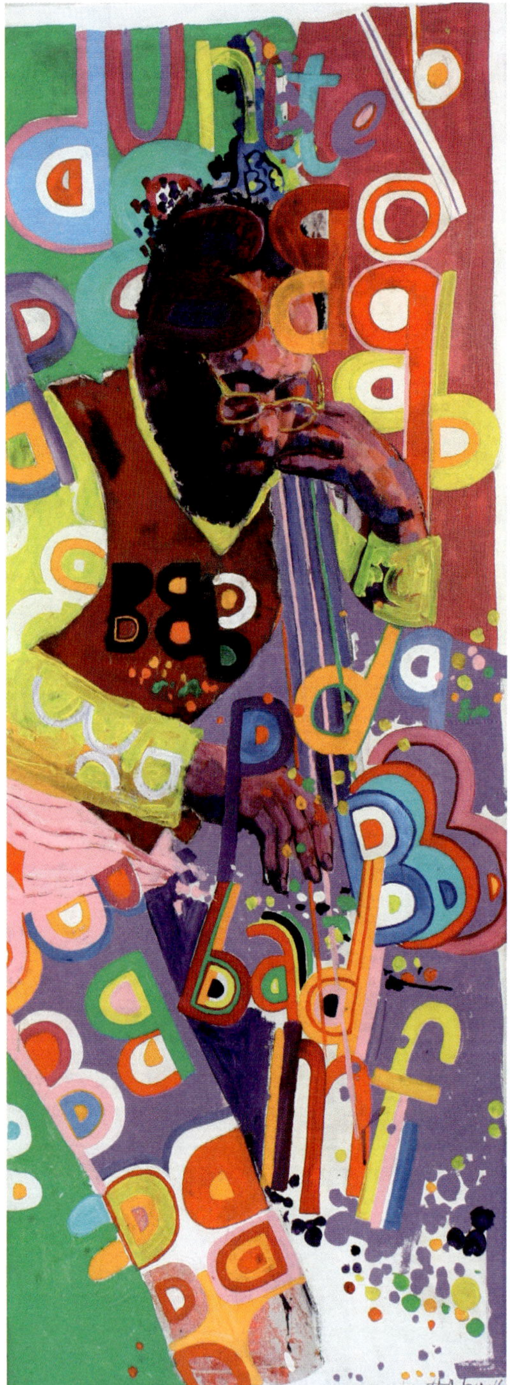

8.16

Wadsworth Jarrell, *Cool Ade Lester*, 1970. Acrylic on canvas, 50 × 24 inches. Collection of Mr. and Mrs. Michael and Christa Brinson.

spiraling bright colors. Beck's signature painting was the one in oil, displaying a man with a bald eagle atop his head, near an expired parking meter with a sign that reads, "No Parking Anytime."

Omar Lama's artist statement was "Positive images—images that will inspire Black people to a higher level of consciousness." He entered two pieces: *Unite or Perish*, rendered in color inks, and a black-and-white ink drawing of a resolute figure entitled *Black Jesus*. His drawing of Jesus has historical implications as well as possible truth, because the part of the world where Jesus is said to have been born is the area now known as Israel. Inhabitants who occupied that region were also Palestinian, so the place was basically filled with dark people. Omar's signature work was *Unite or Perish*. It illustrated two figures as Siamese Twins joined at the head, with the words "Unite or Perish" scrolled on each side of the figures.

After the opening celebration of the exhibition, we attended a buffet-style dinner of vegetarian cuisine at a restaurant owned by Kimarko Baraka, sister of Amiri Baraka. In addition, we were invited to visit the workshop and gallery of the Weusi Nyumba Ya Sanaa Collective (*weusi* in Swahili means "house of art"). The Weusi Collective was found in 1965, and their works were filled with symbols, patterns, and images of African sculpture. Much of their art was in black and white, reproduced into prints that could be readily distributed in shops, in galleries, and on street corners. The artists who formed Weusi were former members of the disbanded group the Twentieth Century Creators. Weusi Artists Collective was later renamed Weusi Nyumba Ya Sanaa. Founding members as well as artists who joined the group later were Ademola Olugebefola, Abdullah Aziz, Bill Howell, Taiwo DuVall, Otto Neals, Gaylord Hassan, Okoe Pyatt, Abdul Rahman, James Phillips, Kay Brown, Falcon Beazer, Rudy Irwin, Milton Martin, James Sepyo, and Emmett Wigglesworth. The Weusi artists were committed to exposing ordinary Black folk to art through sidewalk exhibitions in Harlem.

AFRICOBRA I: *Ten in Search of a Nation* was scheduled next for September through October at the National Center of Afro-American Artists in Boston, Massachusetts, and in November at Black Expo in the Amphitheater in Chicago. Jeff returned November 1970 from Washington, DC, to Chicago to participate in an AFRICOBRA meeting held at WJ Studios and Gallery. The agenda for the meeting was dispersing information concerning the upcoming Black Expo exhibition and critiquing current work. Jeff brought a new painting

Gerald Williams, *Malcolm*,
1970. Acrylic on canvas,
45 × 27 inches. Collection
of Kyoko Pamura.

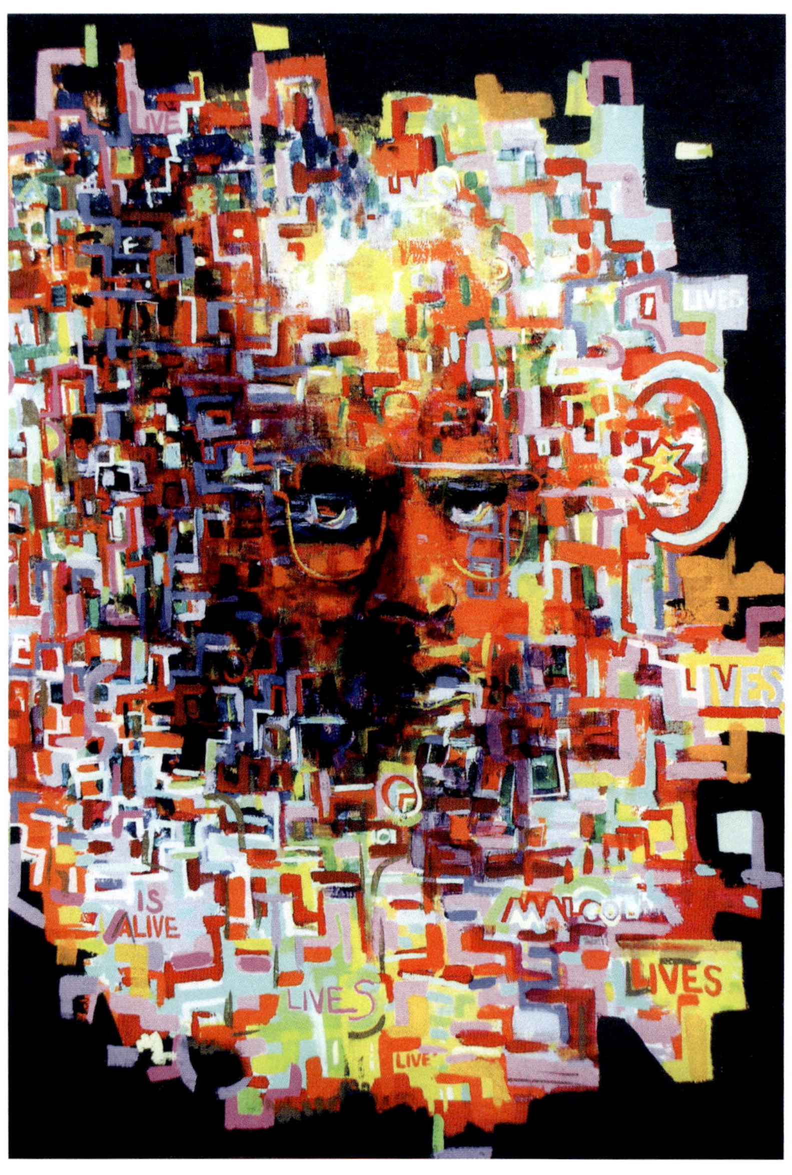

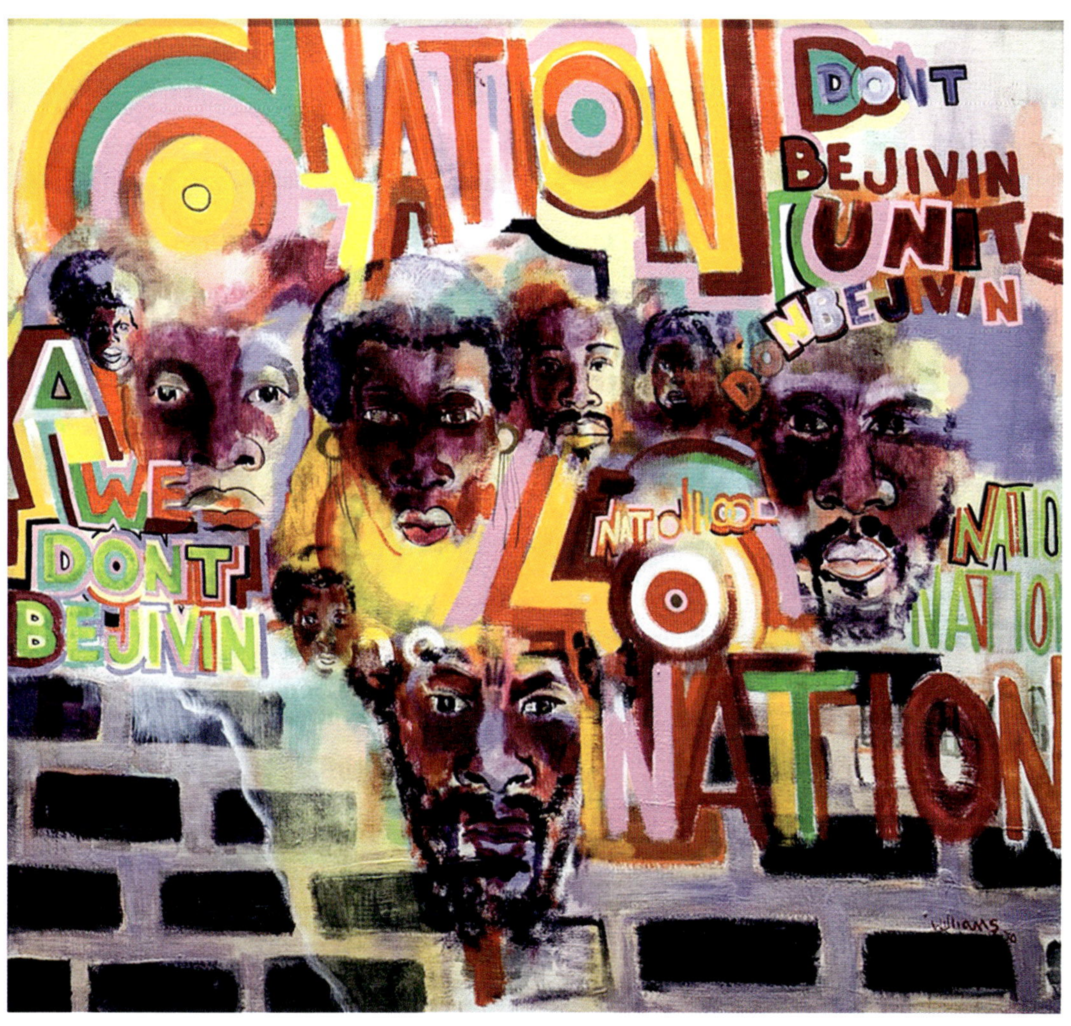

8.18

Gerald Williams,
Nationtime, 1969. Acrylic
on canvas, 48 × 48 inches.
Collection of John and
Susan Horseman.

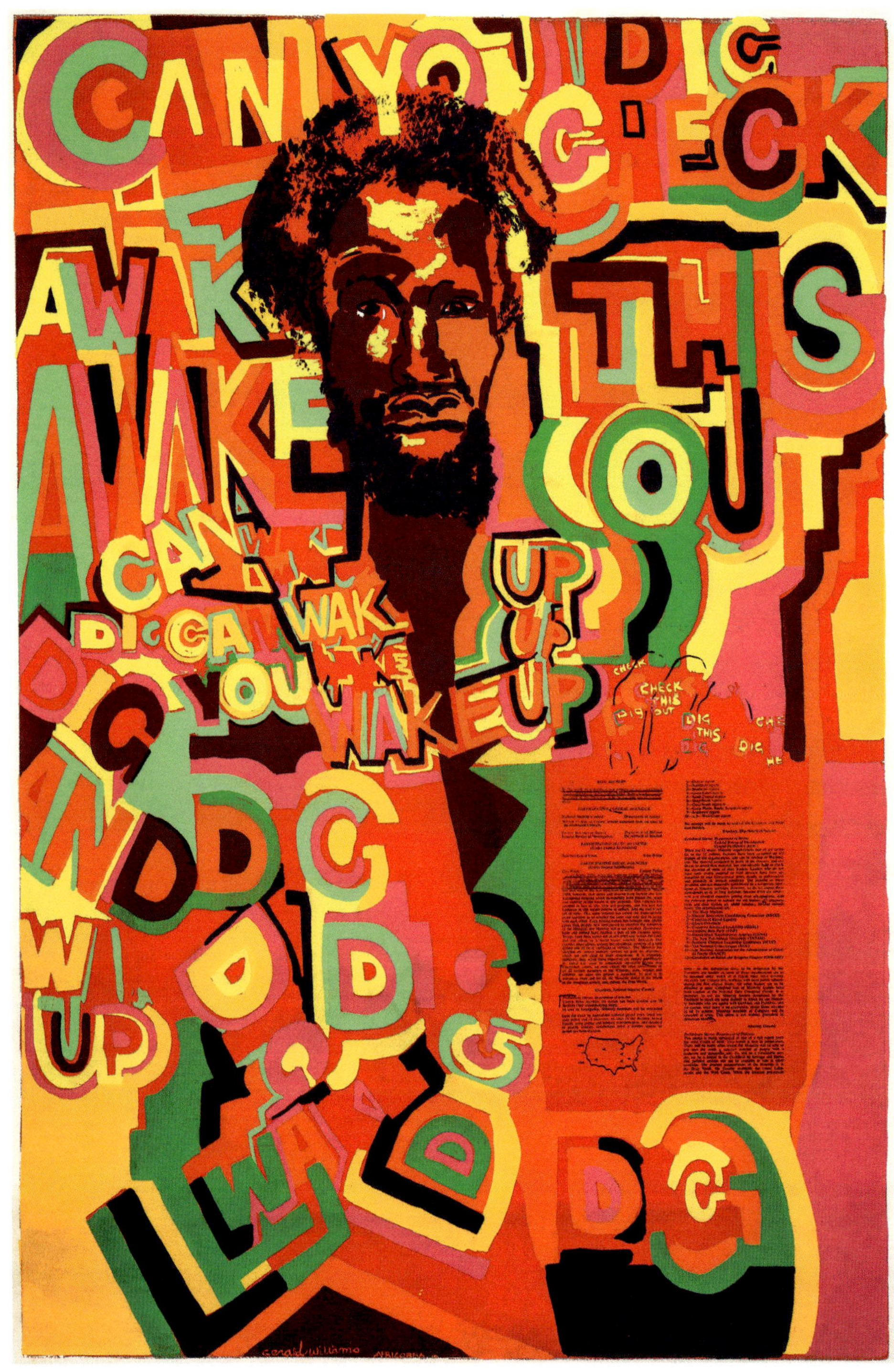

CAN YOU DIG
CHECK
AWAKE
THIS
AWAKE
OUT
AWAKE
A
CAN
DIG CAN WAK
WAKE UP
DIG YOU
WAKE UP
AND
UP
UP
CHECK
CHECK
THIS
DIG OUT
DIG THIS
AND D D C
DIG DIC
W UP D D
AND UP
W A D D C

that he had recently finished: *Here Comes the Judge* interprets a scene from the tragic incident on August 7, 1970, when Jonathan Jackson attempted to negotiate the freedom of the Soledad Brothers, which included Jonathan's older brother, George.

The plan was to kidnap superior court judge Harold Haley and use him as a bargaining chip to free the prisoners. The judge was taken from the Marin County Civic Center in San Rafael, California, where a shootout ensued that left four men dead, including both Jonathan Jackson and Judge Haley. This violent incident precipitated the incarceration and eventually the criminal trial and acquittal of Angela Davis. She was accused of owning the guns used in the attempted breakout.

Jeff's painting shows an image of the judge with a Black man holding a handgun to his head. The judge's face is rendered as a skeleton, implying that he was a dead man walking. The painting is rendered mostly in black and white and is void of Cool Ade colors, one of our important principles. His painting contains large areas of white, alluding to illustrations seen in magazines. I spoke to that effect: "Where is the color? The negative spaces of white along with the painting being basically in black and white gives the appearance of a magazine illustration."

It became obvious that my choice of words infuriated Jeff. My critique was merely an inquiry about an AFRICOBRA principle regarding color. Instantly, we learned that Jeff did not accept criticism well, because he became animated and went into a rage.

"What do you mean it looks like a magazine illustration? As far as I'm concerned this painting is finished. My painting has as much quality and AFRICOBRA essentials as any other works in this room. What do you think we should do, put *B*s on our paintings like you do?"

His remarks startled me. "No, I am not saying your painting as well as anybody else's work should contain *B*s. I am speaking of the negative spaces in white, and your decision to paint it void of color. Color is what we are about."

"Look at BJ's [Barbara Jones's] work," Jeff retorted. "It isn't exactly saturated with color and doesn't necessarily offer any new ideas. Look at her work: raised fists appear regularly in a lot of her work—that's not inventive. That is a common gesture appearing in several black artists' work today. She was making prints like this before we started AFRICOBRA. Maybe we should

Gerald Williams, *Wake Up*, 1969. Acrylic/collage on canvas, 30 × 44 inches. Collection of the Smart Museum, Chicago.

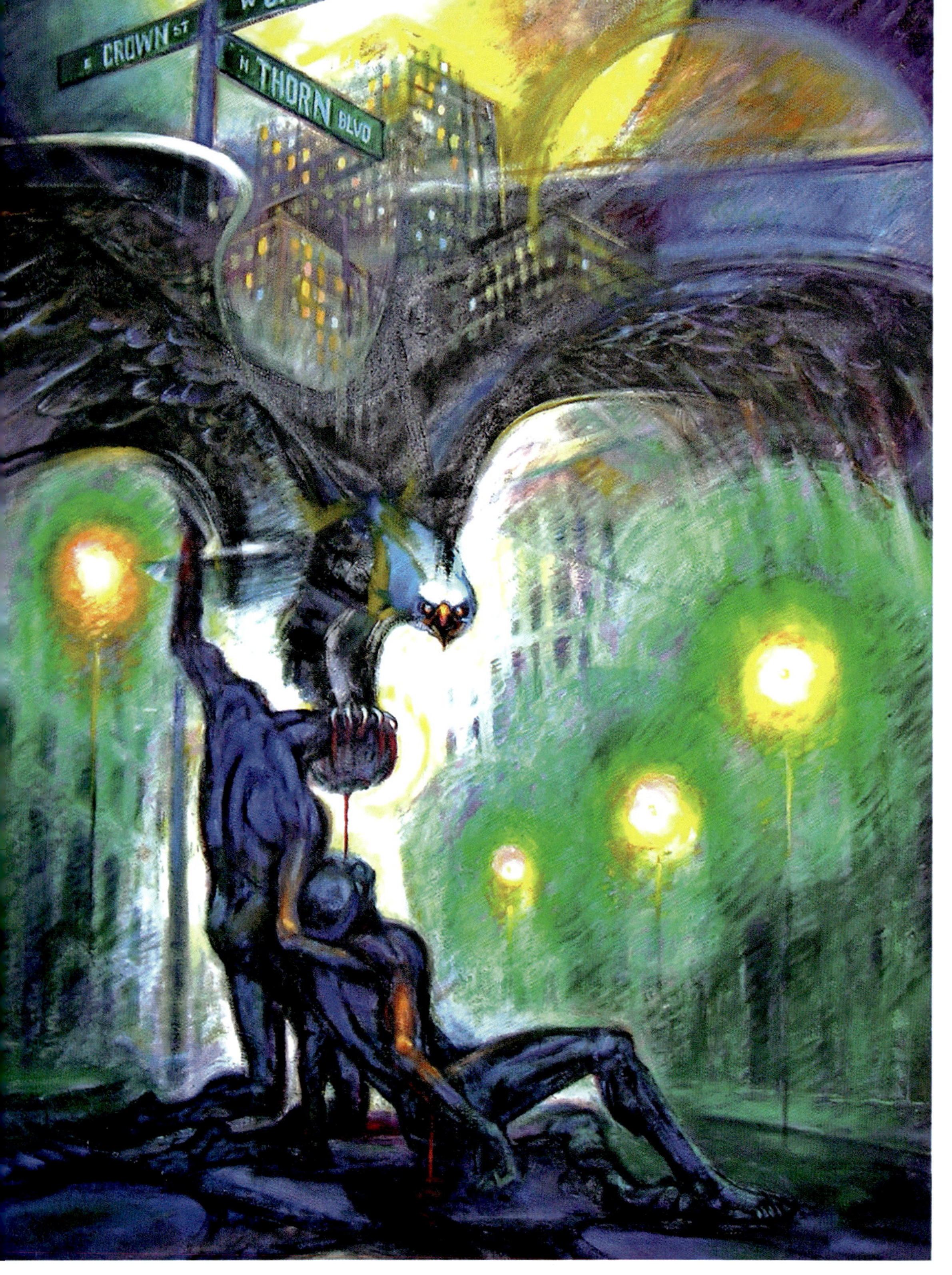
E CROWN ST
N THORN BLVD
W CRO...

be about much more than making art. Perhaps we should be about real revolution, like learning how to break down and reassemble some MI rifles. We
should use Baraka's group in Newark as an example."[9]

Jeff's remarks were perceived as bombastic and vengeful. AFRICOBRA's interest was in making art—creating a Black aesthetic—and not about physical
warfare. AFRICOBRA was a collective of revolutionary artists striving to make
a change in art. It was alarming to hear Jeff's vicious critique of Barbara's
work. In the past he had been so complimentary of everything she produced.
No one mentioned Jeff's painting again for the remainder of the meeting.
We knew that in the future it would be important to offer criticism along
with praise. After the meeting, Jeff left his painting to be entered into the
exhibition at Black Expo and departed for Washington, DC.

A week later AFRICOBRA artists gathered at WJ Studios and Gallery and
waited for several hours for the arrival of our art by transport truck from our
last exhibition at the National Center of Afro-American Artists in Boston. Jae
was on the telephone during a portion of the time, directing the transport
driver to the studio. Around 9 o'clock at night, the work arrived and was
immediately loaded into a station wagon and Barbara's car and driven to the
Amphitheater on Halsted Street. Instead of being painted with Cool Ade
colors, the false walls at the Amphitheater were covered with colored display
paper. The installation of the work consumed the remainder of the night.

The exhibition opened the next day, with all AFRICOBRA artists present
and standing near their work. The duration of Black Expo was ten days. Our
collective was warmly welcomed to Chicago, as it was the first time the Chicago community had the opportunity to view the AFRICOBRA I exhibition.
Designated members represented the exhibition while others took time off.
Nelson Stevens along with his students from Northern Illinois University
sold a reproduction of one of his works for a fundraiser designated for student scholarships. The group labeled their organization the Color Wrappers.

Jae and I were the representatives for the exhibition when Harold Haydon,
art critic for the *Chicago Sun-Times*, stopped by for an interview. He knew us
from his visits to the WJ Studios and Gallery. He asked why we called ourselves Bad Relevant Artists. He found humor in the name. We explained that
"Bad" implied imperative meanings like bold, certainty, and integrity. Haydon
responded with a question: "You mean, bad is good, huh?" The next day, his
article appeared in the *Chicago Sun-Times* entitled "Right On, Art Lovers."

Sherman Beck, *Crown of Thorns*, 1970. Oil on canvas, 36 × 48 inches. Collection of the artist.

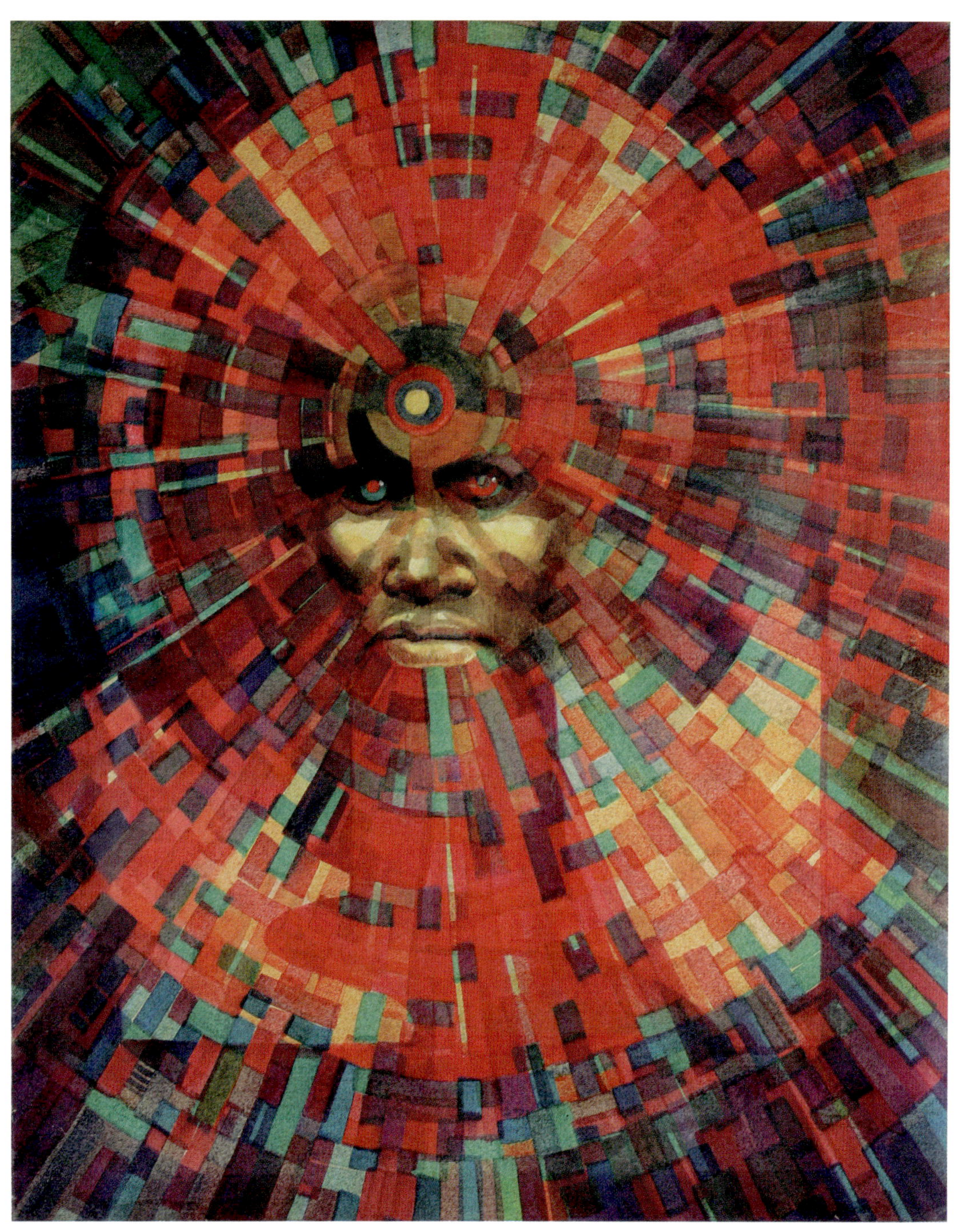

8.21

Sherman Beck, *Untitled*,
1970. Color markers on
paper, 24 × 36 inches.
Collection of the artist.

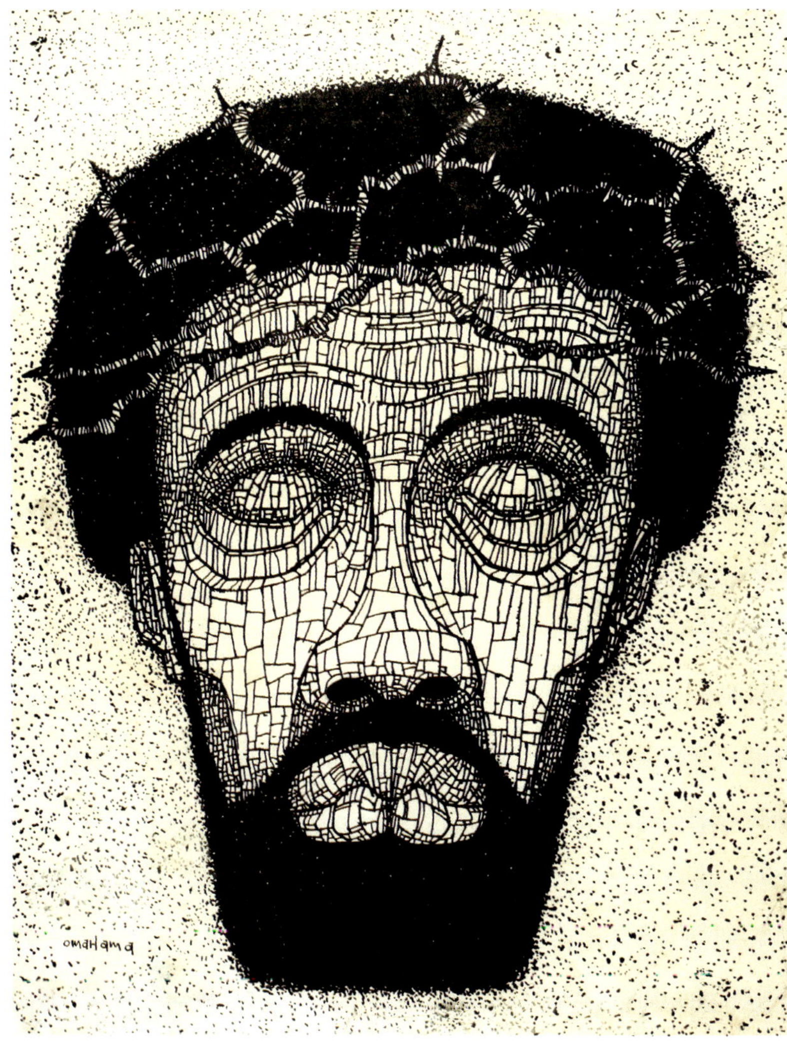

8.22

Omar Lama, *Black
Jesus*, 1968. Ink on
paper, 12 × 16 inches.
Collection of the artist.

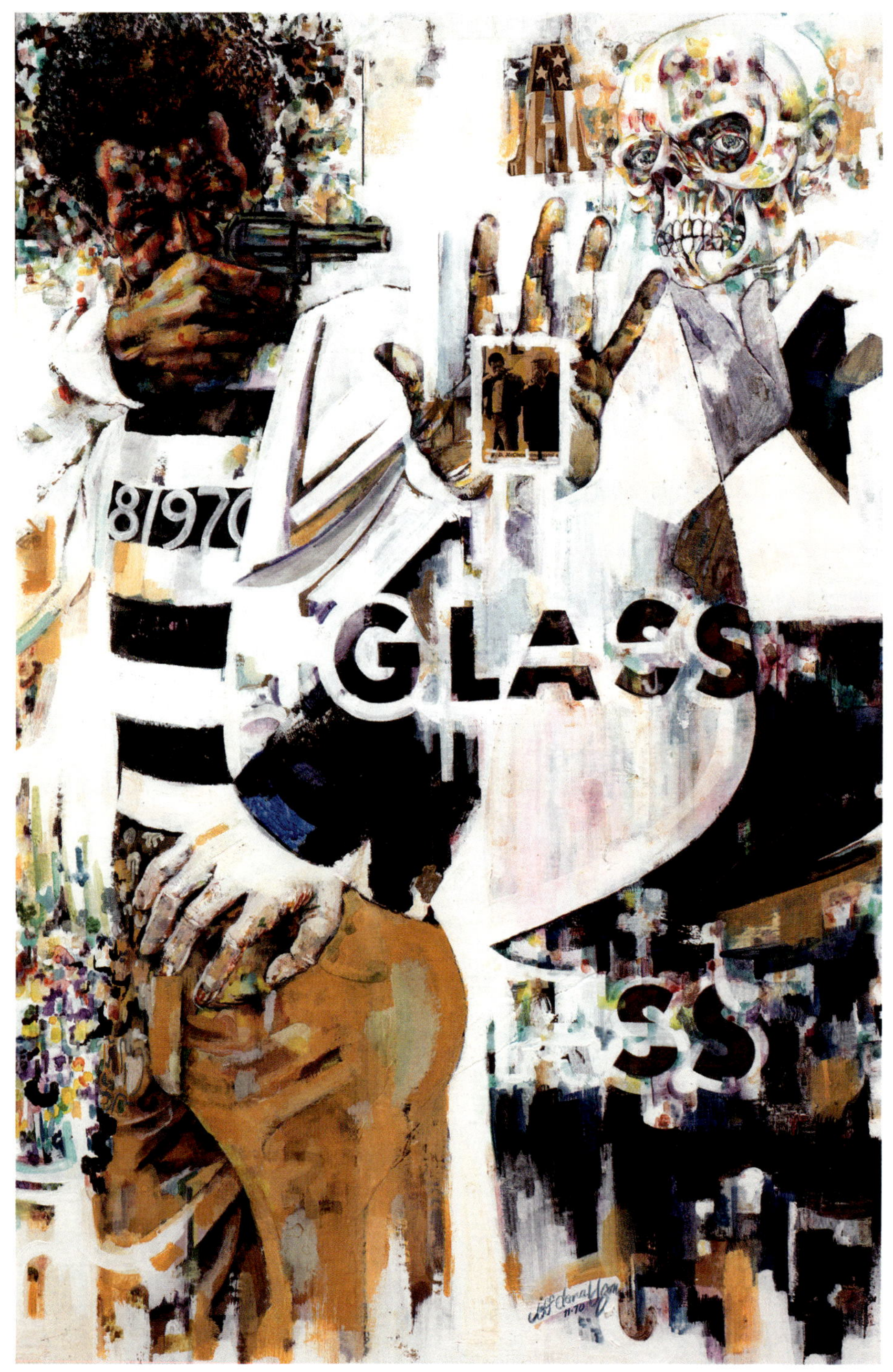
81970
GLASS
ASS

He wrote, "The work is brilliant in color, and filled with messages. The AFRI-COBRA images are making a positive and hopeful approach to the young hip black generation, and it is people's art with a real punch in its message."[10]

The Black Expo in Chicago was the last stop on the itinerary. We then directed our energies toward making new art and inducting a new member. The ceramist Howard Mallory Jr. joined the AFRICOBRA collective in 1971. His membership increased our ranks back to nine. Sherman Beck and Omar Lama had left in 1970 after the *AFRICOBRA I: Ten in Search of a Nation* exhibition. Mallory's beliefs were related to family and Black unity, and his political and cultural ideology was parallel to AFRICOBRA's. His acceptance was significant because it added a ceramic sculptor.

Ripped Off: Co-opted

In *Jet* magazine in early 1971, AFRICOBRA works, including bandoliers on the art, appeared in an article written by the staff of *Jet* magazine: "Black Revolt Sparks White Fashion Craze." The article stated:

It had to happen. White fashion designers have finally gotten hip. For years white Americans of all sorts have been plagiarizing Black art, music and dance, and laughing all the way to the bank. And now the fashion world, long a haven for creative larceny, is getting into the act. It is "borrowing" from the Black Revolution. The bandolier is the latest fashion accessory to sweep the country, and two white women along the Atlantic seaboard are raking in the cash hand over fist, trying to capitalize on their "discovery" three months after the style was featured in a leading Black monthly publication. The bandolier, a cartridge belt with mock 30 caliber bullets, is selling for $25 to $50 at top fashion boutiques across the country.

The October (1970) issue of *Black World* exposed the style to the public through a painting by Jeff Donaldson that he said he created in 1969. The same issue included a picture of a "revolutionary suit," designed by Black couturiere Jae Jarrell, with the bandolier sewn across the shoulders.[11]

AFRICOBRA I: Ten in Search of a Nation displayed bandoliers on *Wives of Shango,* by Jeff Donaldson; *Revolutionary Suit* and *Takin' Care to Take Care*

When Takin' Care Needs Takin' Care, by Jae Jarrell; and my *Homage to a Giant*. This AFRICOBRA tour de force was announcing that the real America is a violent place, and when African people engage in protecting themselves against the oppressor, they need something more potent than a song, a prayer, and the Bible.

The two white women claimed to have spotted the cartridge belt in a shop in London and then persuaded their businessmen husbands to manufacture and carry them in their stores. The article continued:

> By pricing the belts so high, the fashion houses have virtually assured themselves that Black masses will never possess the creation. But not if designer Mrs. Jarrell has her way. "The driving force behind the AFRICOBRA philosophy," she says, "is isolating strong Black images that relate to the times, then making the resulting creations available at prices the masses can afford."
>
> Mrs. Jarrell says, the strong, relevant Black images in her designs have been compromised by white commercialism. "We were saying something when we used the belts," she says. "We're involved in a real revolution."[12]

In March 1971, AFRICOBRA embarked on the commitment to produce quality hand-pulled silkscreen prints from our work. The prints would be sold at reasonable cost to encourage purchases from African Americans. Barbara, Gerald, Carolyn, Mallory, and I gathered at Napoleon's studio for a print workshop. Being a printmaker, Barbara had expertise in the silkscreen process. The serigraphy process was new to the remainder of the members but not a new process per se. History testifies that it existed for centuries, dating back to the Song Dynasty in China (AD 960–1279). In 1971, J. I. Biegeleisen wrote in *Screen Printing*: "Not many years ago, pictorial compositions that were evolved by means of screen stencils were ineligible for submission to major print shows. The primary reason that they weren't acknowledged as authentic prints was that they weren't produced with traditional printing plates."[13]

Scholars and informed, serious print collectors rigidly adhere to the codified canon of fine print making and consider intaglio to be the finest among prints, followed by lithographs and silkscreen prints. Included in their evaluation are total numbers in an edition: limited editions are finely crafted original hand-pulled prints on quality paper, and the edition does not exceed

8.24

Photograph by Wadsworth Jarrell. *AFRICOBRA Print Workshop*, Chicago, 1971. Napoleon Henderson (*left*) and Howard Mallory.

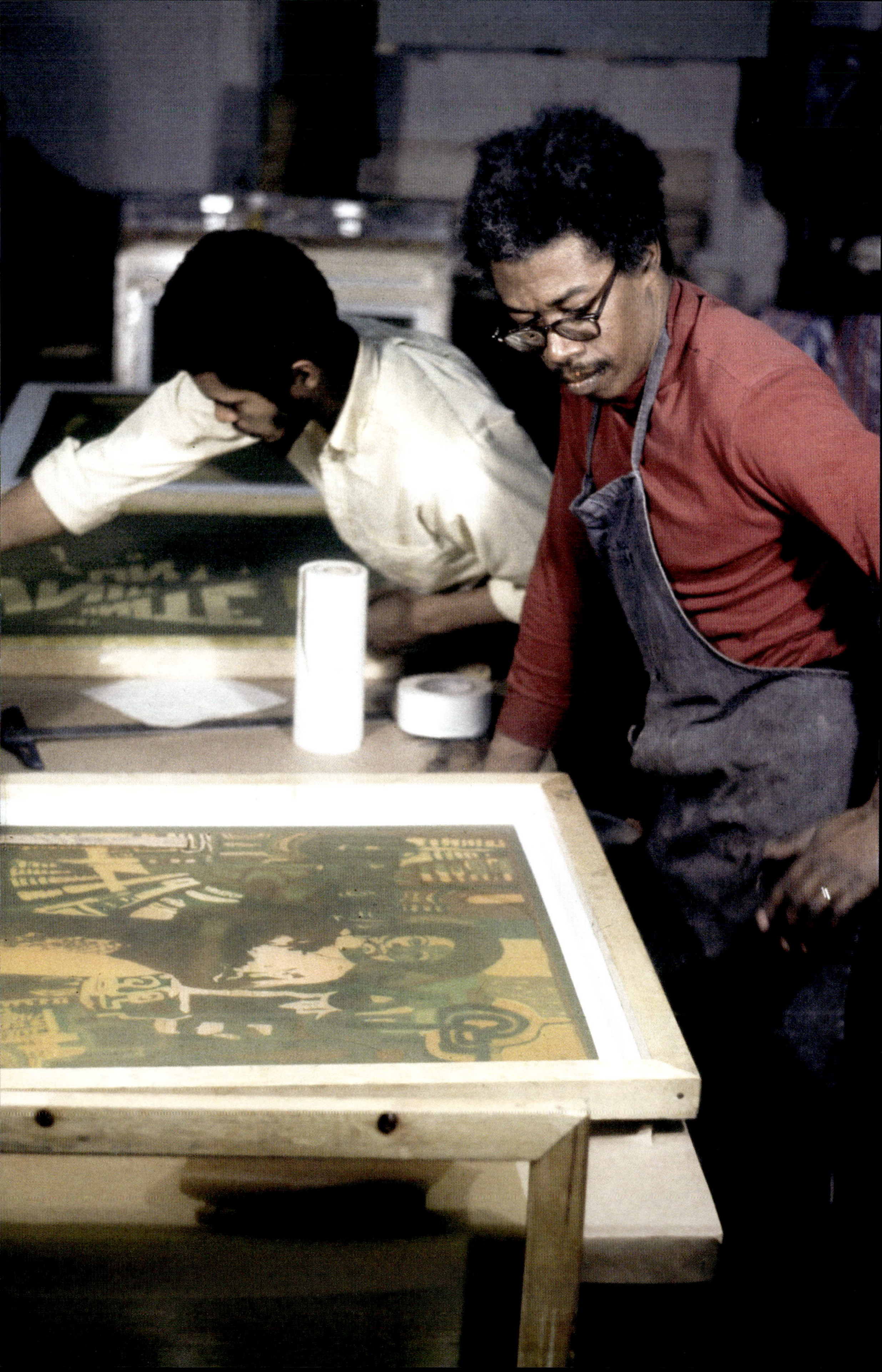

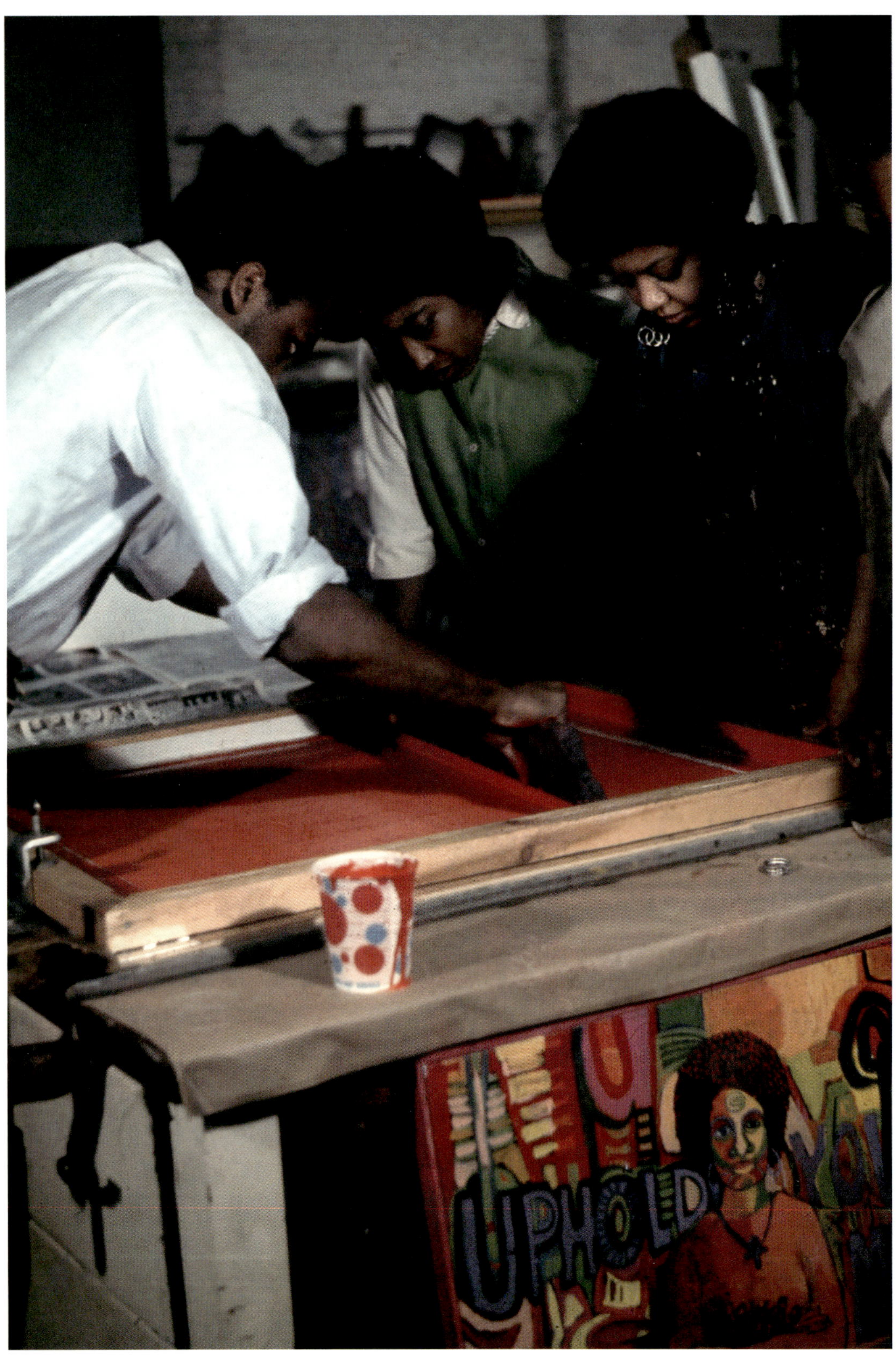

Photograph by Wadsworth Jarrell. *AFRICOBRA Print Workshop*, Chicago, 1971. Gerald Williams (*left*), Carolyn Lawrence, and Napoleon Henderson (*right*). Ektachrome transparency.

Photograph by Gerald Williams. *Wadsworth Jarrell, AFRICOBRA Print Workshop*, Chicago, 1971. Ektachrome transparency.

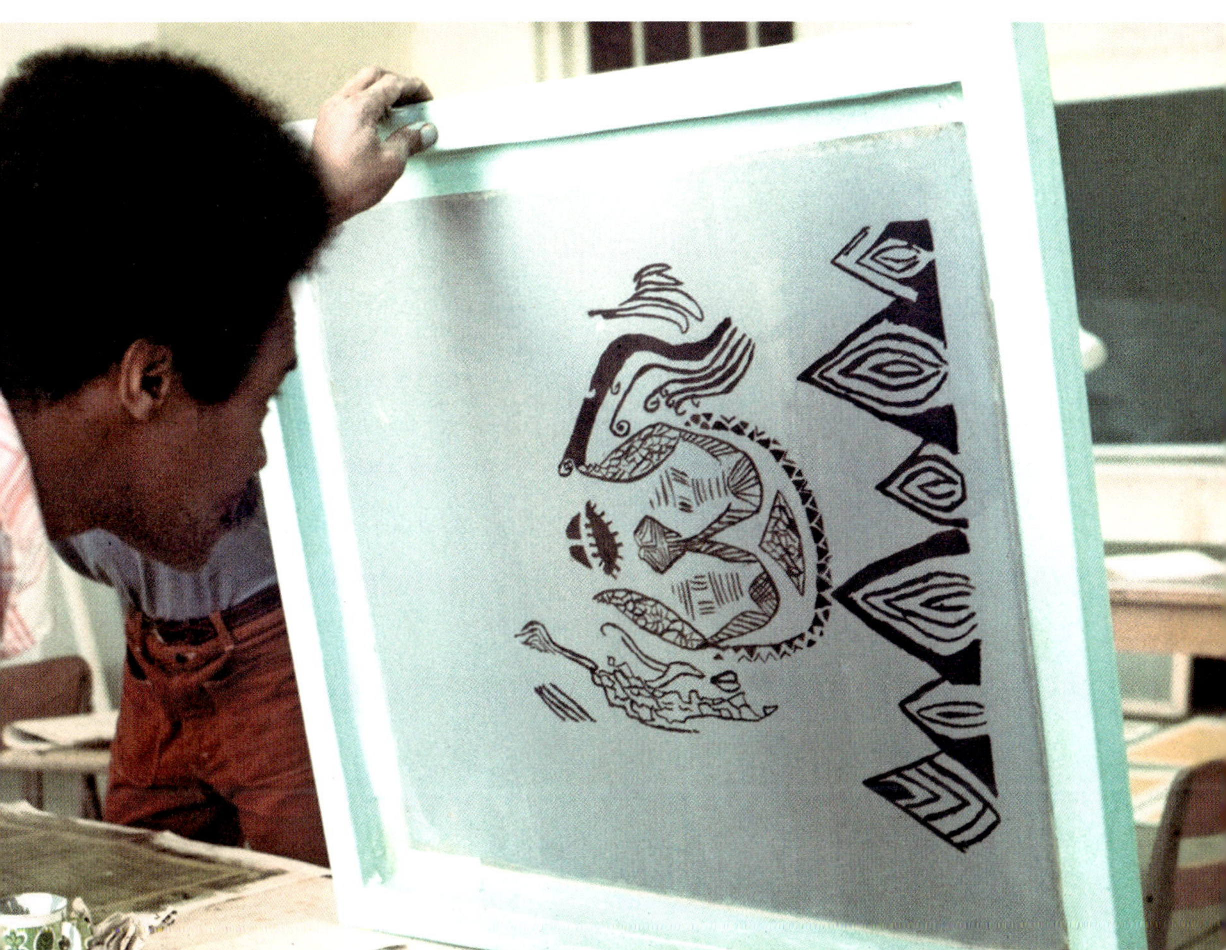

one hundred. AFRICOBRA questioned the rules because we produced prints for mass distribution without labeling them limited editions.

Carolyn Lawrence's painting *Uphold Your Men*, containing seven colors, was chosen to be the first print produced. Barbara's print *Unite* concluded the printing session. Both prints were stamped with the AFRICOBRA logo (the Gelede mask), and all six members signed them.

Shortly after the print workshop took place, Jae and I decided to move from Chicago. The safety of our son, Wadsworth Jr., who was three, and our daughter Jennifer Carol, three months old, was important given the amount of gang violence. We wanted to live in an area near New York that provided a substantive art and fashion environment, but in April 1971, we briefly lived in Waterbury and New Haven, Connecticut, and then Boston, Massachusetts, before finally settling in Washington, DC, where I accepted a teaching position at Howard University.

We arrived in New Haven at the peak of the widely publicized trial of two Black Panther members: Bobby Seale, cofounder and chairman, and Ericka Huggins, the New Haven field marshal. They were charged with the murder of suspected FBI informant Alex Rackley. Both were acquitted some time in May. With us living in Chicago at the time, Jae and I were familiar with Huey P. Newton's trial in California in 1968, and the 1969 shootouts between the Black Panthers and policemen on the South Side of Chicago. We also knew of the killing of Fred Hampton and Mark Clark by law officers on the West Side. In Boston, I purchased books that provided a pertinent history of the Black Panthers: *The Black Panthers*, by Gene Marine; *Free Huey!*, by Edward M. Keating; and *The Vanguard*, a photographic essay by Ruth-Marion Baruch and Pirkle Jones.

The books inspired Jae and me to respond artistically to situations we considered unjust. From study of the books, I made drawings that resulted in a painting entitled *Liberation Soldiers*. The trial in New Haven of the Black Panthers and information from the books motivated Jae also to make drawings, which served as models for her design *Free Black Political Prisoners*.

Jae and I were pleased to leave Boston for Washington, DC, because we found the city of Boston unattractive—a cultural shock, where African Americans, at least the ones we met, did not proclaim any allegiance to Black consciousness or the Black power movement. They did not have a revolutionary bone in their bodies. In 1971 while Jae and I were living there, we

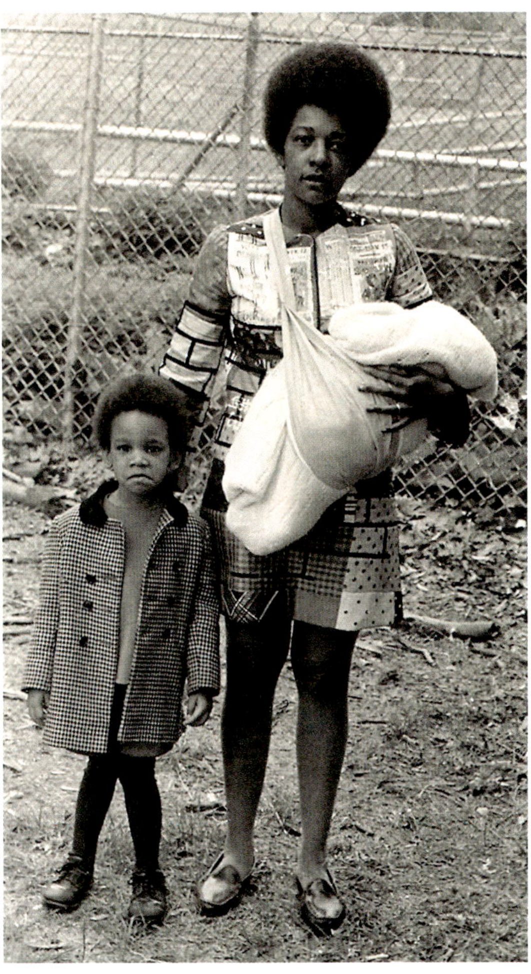

8.27

Photograph by
Wadsworth Jarrell. *Jae
Jarrell, Wadsworth Jr.,
and Jennifer*, Boston,
1971. Gelatin silver print.

had a telephone conversation with Howard Mallory in Chicago, and he asked, "How are the people in Boston? I am talking about Black people, because I know how the white people are."

I answered, "Coming to Boston straight from Chicago was a huge cultural shock for me and Jae. Boston is dirty, the sidewalks in our neighborhood are covered with dog feces, potholes are in the streets, and the Black people that we have met since we moved here seem not to be interested in Black consciousness in any way. They act as if they can blend in with whites and not be noticed, you know, not stand out in a sea of white people."

Washington proved to be an asset to Jae's and my artistic development because moving there helped influence the direction of our art.

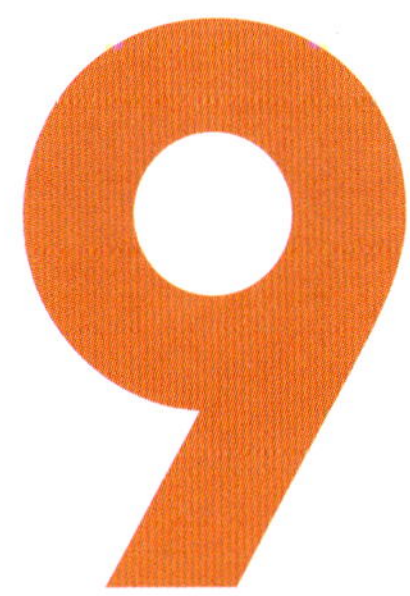

AFRICOBRA II

AFRICOBRA was extremely significant during the era of the 60s and 70s because artists were working collectively in a group to solve some of the problems of the previous generation, namely, how to make art more accessible to more people, and secondly, to precisely formulate systems of a Black Aesthetic. —Rosalind Jeffries

In 1971, Edward Spriggs scheduled a second AFRICOBRA exhibition, *AFRICOBRA II*, at the Studio Museum in Harlem, from November 19, 1971, to January 21, 1972. In an essay titled "AFRICOBRA: An Intermediarily Pro/position," he wrote for the exhibition catalog:

> It was by no accident that AFRICOBRA was presented for two consecutive years during my tenure as director of the Studio Museum in Harlem. They are here for the second time because we believe that they present one of the most dynamic combinations of thought, talent and commitment that we know of in the visual arts during this era of the "Black Aesthetic" in America. By 1970, we had become aware of AFRICOBRA as a new phenomenon, and were struck by the potential of their credo, as well as the evolving stylistic manifestation of the then Chicago-based collective.[1]

Photographs I had taken of two young ladies in Cambridge, Massachusetts, along with a photograph of a young lady in Chicago, were made into a painting entitled *Three Queens*. Preparing two paintings for the upcoming exhibition AFRICOBRA II took so much time that I finished them virtually at the deadline for the exhibition. Jae was pregnant with our third child, Roslyn Angela, but diligently continued producing her designs for the coming exhibition. Jae; Frank Smith, who was a professor in the Art Department at Howard; Jeff's wife, Arnicia; and I rode in a station wagon from Washington, DC, to New York for the exhibition. Frank was not yet a member of AFRICOBRA.

Minutes taken by Carolyn Lawrence, secretary, November 29, 1971, stated that "the entire AFRICOBRA collective attended a special meeting held at the Harlem, New York, apartment of poet Larry Neal and his wife, Evelyn. Members from Chicago included Barbara Jones, Napoleon Henderson, Nelson Stevens, Carolyn Lawrence, Gerald Williams, and Howard Mallory." The meeting opened with Carolyn giving a report of the minutes, which included the state of silkscreen prints, venues that carried them, and the amount of sales. (Two venues were Zeno Gallery in Chicago and Rainbow Sign Gallery in California.) She stated that a large number of prints had been sold at WJ Studios and Gallery, where Barbara had set up a printing workshop. (Barbara had moved there after Jae and I left for Washington, DC.) Carolyn also mentioned a new location on East 71st Street, which AFRICOBRA rented and where we had moved the print workshop.

AFRICOBRA attempted to adhere to the agreement that we had made ("We want everybody to have some") by pricing all prints at ten dollars each. That price was to encourage purchases from an African American audience. All print sales and fees charged for each exhibition, four hundred to five hundred dollars per exhibition, were deposited into a bank account. Each member owned a share. This was by no means a business to acquire a financial advantage for members; it was absolutely a labor of love for the people. AFRICOBRA members were satisfied to redeem funds that had been invested in materials and felt fortunate to be in a position to offer inexpensive fine art to African Americans.

Jeff brought a supply of his new print *Victory in the Valley of Eshu*, printed by the Washington-based master printer Lou Stovall. Jeff's print was at the center of an intense argument lasting practically the duration of the meeting. He withstood an avalanche of criticism, with accusations of deception

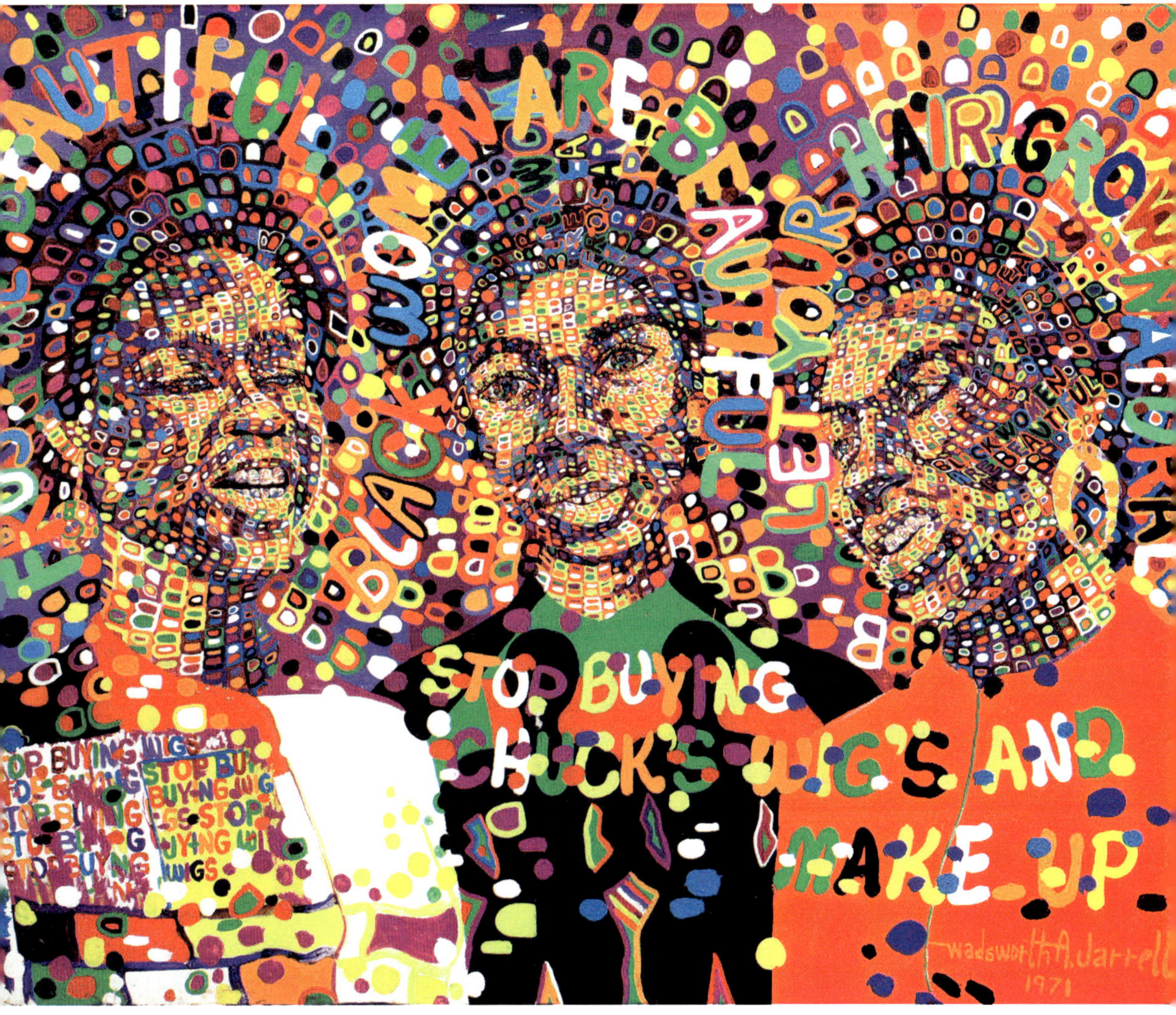

9.1

Wadsworth Jarrell, *Three Queens*, 1971. Acrylic on canvas, 30 × 38 inches. Collection of Detroit Institute of Art.

and selfishness. Jeff was accused of not adhering to rules of the collective by independently financing his own print edition and controlling the price, which was not in accord with other AFRICOBRA prints. Jeff priced his prints at $15.25 each. He was not one to accept ridicule, and his rebuttal was cogent and fiercely stated: "My print can not be marketed at that price. The materials—ink, paper, brushes, and so forth—cost seven hundred dollars, and the printing cost four hundred dollars. The original run was 300, and only 280 good prints were salvaged. In order to remain in the black, it sells for that price, and the $.25 is the cost of the plastic sleeve that housed the print. At $10.00 a print, I would suffer a loss."

Nelson was visibly perturbed. He confronted Jeff regarding a previous conversation between them. "I asked you was your print going to be an AFRICOBRA print? And your answer was, yes. You said, Yeah man, you know it's going to be an AFRICOBRA print."

Jeff retorted, "Man, I thought you meant was it going to be in the spirit of AFRICOBRA. It most certainly is an AFRICOBRA print. Your entire argument is based on the cost of the print, and me not turning over the edition to the group to be sold for the same price as the other prints. I will tell you, I invested an enormous amount of time and money into this edition of prints, and to think that I will allow them to be marketed at a loss is absolutely absurd."

Jae spoke in defense of Jeff. "I agree that he should have ownership of his entire edition of prints because he personally financed all costs of printing and materials. And don't mention the task of labor of doing all the color separations of nineteen colors."

Nelson, Barbara, Mallory, Napoleon, and Carolyn adamantly expressed their views of disapproval. Carolyn addressed what she saw as deceitfulness in Jeff's decision to independently produce a print. She said, "There is always a rotten apple in the barrel."

Jeff perceived Carolyn's remark as utmost effrontery. "Why do I have to be the rotten apple? I am the one who had the vision to start and name AFRICOBRA in the first place, and I am the one who brought you into the group." Jeff threw his glasses from his face to the floor to add emphasis. "I can cut the head off of AFRICOBRA anytime I choose. It was conceived by me, and it would wither on the vine if I don't keep promoting it."

The conversation then focused on the prints and the printing process, as well as the wear and tear on individuals. It was concluded that:

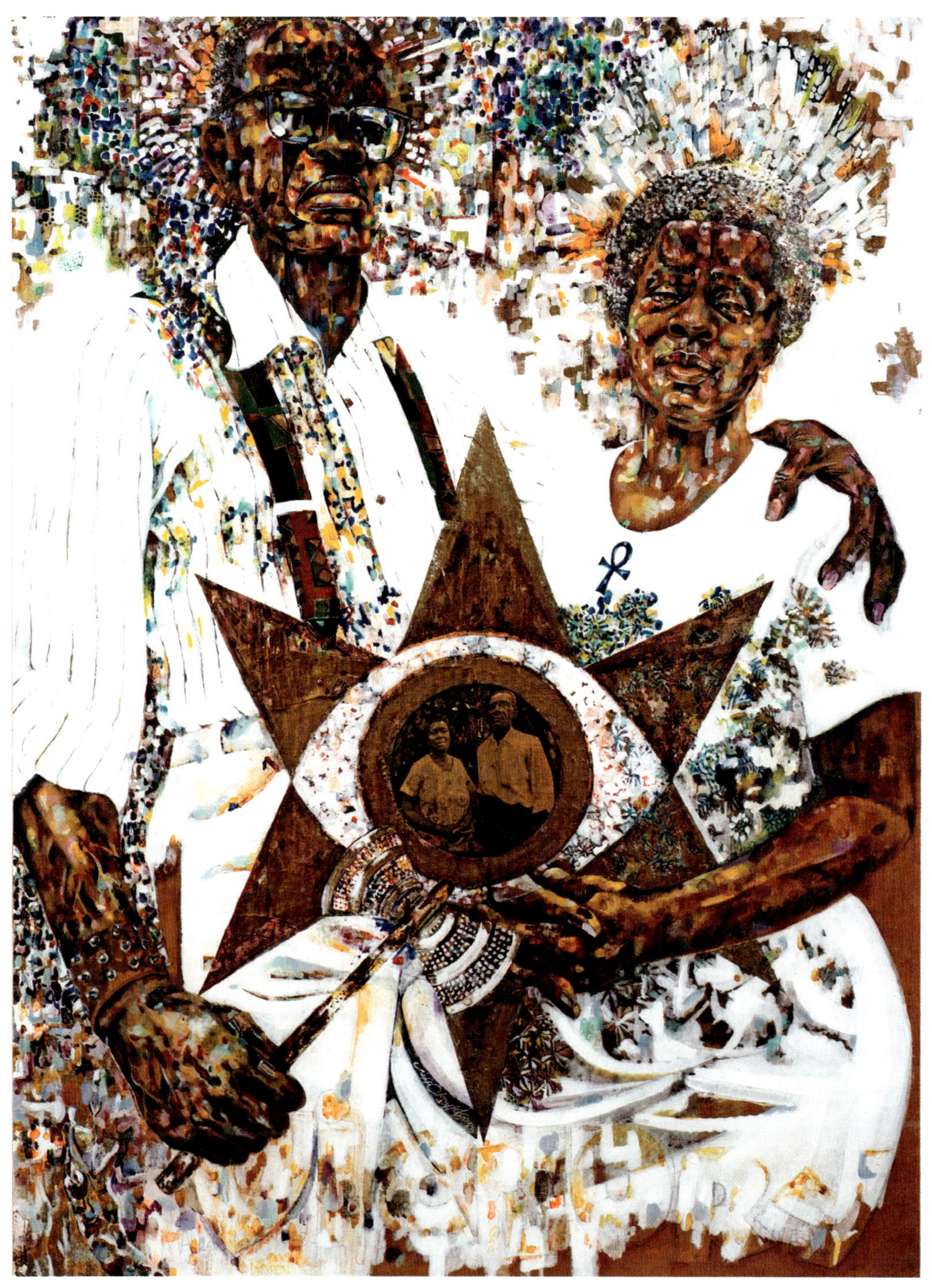

1   Things to be printed should be approved by the group.

2   Production of the prints would be farmed out.

Jeff gave us a breakdown on what he had spent for his prints to give us a guideline for the cost of farming out work to a business. He said that the size of the paper was thirty by forty inches and cost three hundred dollars, at one dollar a sheet. It was proposed that the individual artist put up two-thirds of the cost of printing. The profit would be divided up annually:

1   50 percent to the indiviual member whose print is being produced

2   40 percent to AFRICOBRA

3   10 percent to some outside struggle or to an organization contributing to the building of a nation (That organization would later be identified.)

As money came into the treasury, it would be earmarked to be put into separate funds.[2]

The meeting was concluded on that note, except for a later agreement by the collective to purchase prints from Jeff and resell them. His print created a perplexing situation because of the disparity in price between his and the other artists' prints. In the final analysis, the print situation was resolved, and the results of that meeting were sent in a memo to all AFRICOBRA members:

Jeff sent a special delivery letter to members in Chicago, and it was decided that the members of AFRICOBRA in Chicago should offer the following alternative solution for Jeff to consider. In a memo dated December 5, 1971, Carolyn and other Chicago AFRICOBRA members wrote, "In the spirit of harmony, we AFRICOBRA, agree to pay $3.25 for the sale of each of Jeff's prints. This is the figure originally requested by mail for *Victory in the Valley of Eshu*. Money for the sale of posters sold in New York should be forwarded to the treasurer of AFRICOBRA, Gerald. Jeff will receive $3.25 for each one of the posters sold, and Jeff's print will remain with AFRICOBRA II exhibition until it closes, and all future prints will be sent to Gerald, the AFRICOBRA treasurer."

Members present:

Barbara

Gerald—Treasurer

Nap

Mallory

Nelson

Carolyn—Secretary.

Shortly after the contentious AFRICOBRA meeting, we entered the Studio
Museum and found that this time the walls had been painted in Cool Ade
colors. All the art had been delivered to the museum except three of my
paintings, which were in storage: *Revolutionary*, *Black Prince*, and *The King*.
Frank and I drove down to Waterbury, Connecticut, on Saturday afternoon
to retrieve the paintings. The frame molding had been removed in Chicago
from the selected paintings because I had been deciding which of the three
would be color separated to produce a print. When I saw the unframed paintings, I immediately thought about the letter Spriggs had written to all AFRI-
COBRA members:

August 11, 1971.

Dear Members of AFRICOBRA:

For the exhibition, *AFRICOBRA II*, please bring all work to the museum
finished and ready to hang, unless it is a performance work that's part of
the exhibition.

Thank you,
Edward Spriggs, Director of the Studio Museum in Harlem

Frank and I arrived back in New York in a torrential rainstorm and proceeded to hang my work with raw edges. Spriggs came over to view the space
where my work would hang. He asked, "How are you going to circumvent the
raw edges? Are you going to put striping around them?"

My reply was vague. "Perhaps I can put some black tape around the ones
with raw edges."

Outside, there still was a downpour past six o'clock in the evening, and
businesses such as lumberyards were closed. As a result, the work was hung
without black tape covering raw edges and without further concern. Spriggs
donned his hat and raincoat and announced: "I'm taking my lady to a play. I
don't have time to watch AFRICOBRA hang artwork all night."

He was referring to the length of time it had taken to get the work ready to
hang in AFRICOBRA I. My family (Jae, me, Wadsworth Jr., and our new addition,

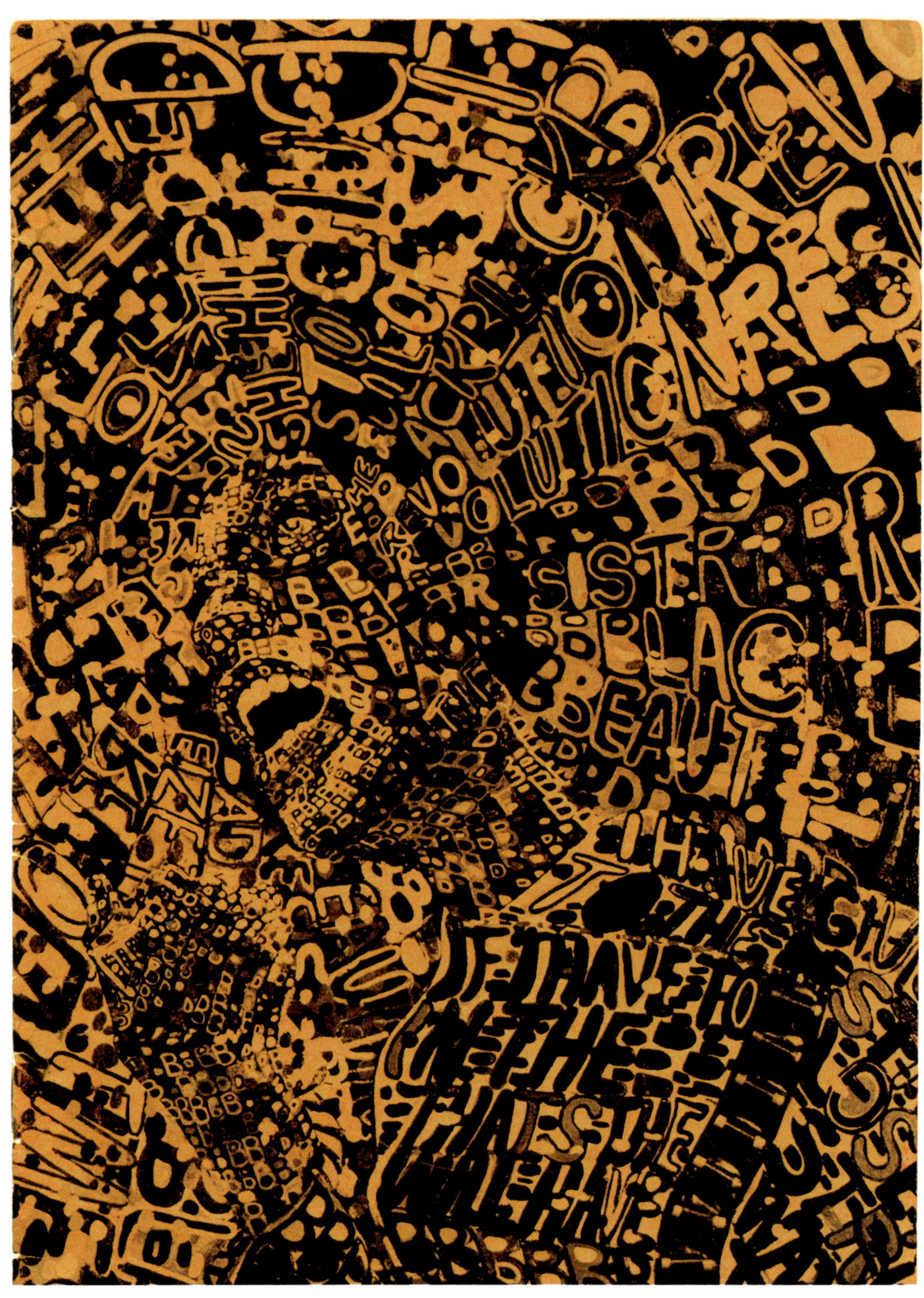

Jennifer Carol) were invited to lodge at Spriggs's apartment on Morningside Avenue a second time.

The next day, on Sunday, the exhibition opened with protracted pomp and splendor in comparison to our first exhibition. The New York audience was receptive and welcomed us back for a second appearance. The body of sociopolitical work presented created a harmonious synthesis and identified the collective as more unified toward a new language. The new work revealed the development of personal stylistic approaches, as well as cerebral and emotional essentials, like improvement in defining subject matter, form, and color combinations, as well as a direction of expression. In the AFRICOBRA II exhibition, viewers witnessed an artist consortium imbued with contextualized precepts and creative resolve, spiritually and vocally in concordance with the Black power movement. Also revealed in the exhibition: AFRICOBRA artists alone set their own standards of procedure. In my opinion, AFRICOBRA dictating our art and aesthetic ideas was the factor that drew a parallel between avant-garde music and visual art, because both are fresh, inventive, and experimental. Encompassing such fundamentals as use of color, letters and words creating the form, and the implementation of our created principles moved the art and the music beyond categorization, with both subscribing to unconventional constructs. Even though the musicians and the AFRICOBRA artists were skilled in standard precepts of both crafts, to create and expand, those rules had to be broken. When experimental art and music are stripped bare of intellectual supportive text (opinions of art historians and critics), what is then left naked for the viewers and listeners are the art and the music themselves. Both remain constant, and both individually can speak volumes.

AFRICOBRA artists' work was designed with the unlearned spectator in mind—to see the work and respond accordingly. Viewers were invited to internalize our clear messages in the art. Consequently, art critics were circumvented because they were not needed for analysis or input that might influence the opinions of viewers. Jeff Donaldson wrote: "We strive for images inspired by African people/experience and images that African people can relate to directly without formal training and/or experience. Art for people and not for critics whose peopleness is questionable. We try to create images that appeal to the senses—not to the intellect."[3]

The *AFRICOBRA II* exhibition brought to New York—the art mecca—a degree of verve and gritty hardcore Chicago confidence. Some permanent residents of New York did not hesitate to remind AFRICOBRA members, "The Big Apple is a big bite!" They assumed our collective from Chicago was naïve and defined us as minnows, with New York critics as sharks. In September 1971 in Washington, DC, the late Murry N. DePillars, scholar, educator, artist, and AFRICOBRA member, said to me in my studio, in a causal conversation about Chicago being called the second city in comparison to New York, "Statements such as those about New York make my Chicago come down on me."

When I was a resident of Chicago, it was common to hear Chicagoans say, "If it ain't happening in Chicago, it ain't happening; said in Chicago and heard in New York." In the sixties, when Jae and I had mailorder businesses, she said, "Made in Chicago and marketed in New York." Contrary to expectations, AFRICOBRA took a respectable bite out of the Big Apple.

My painting *Revolutionary* appeared on the cover of the catalog for the exhibition, and Jeff's painting *Victory in the Valley of Eshu* was on the back cover. Inside, the catalog included images of *Nation Time*, by Barbara Jones; *Don't Forget the Struggle*, by Gerald Williams; *Spirit Sister*, by Nelson Stevens; *Unite Wholy People*, by Napoleon Henderson; *From These Roots*, by Howard Mallory; and *Be Worthy of Your Brother's Trust*, by Carolyn Lawrence. In addition, the catalog contained essays: "AFRICOBRA: An Intermediarily Pro/position," by Edward Spriggs; "AFRICOBRA I: Ten in Search of a Nation," by Jeff Donaldson; and "Ten in Search of a Nation," by Cherilyn Wright. Jeff's statement about membership in the AFRICOBRA collective also appeared in the catalog:

> *at first we were five. Jeff Donaldson, Jae Jarrell, Wadsworth Jarrell, Barbara J. Jones and Gerald Williams. 1968. ***Then we were seven. Napoleon Henderson came in Fall of 1969, and Nelson Stevens brought us shine during that period. ***Then we were ten. . . . ***Now we are nine. Sherman Beck and Omar Lama left in 1970 and we added Howard Mallory Jr. in 1971.[4]

Jae Jarrell exhibited designs produced in improbable fabrics seldom used by fashion designers, namely, felt and burlap. The fabrics are not particularly revolutionary, but with her sewing equipment unavailable, she artfully fringed edges of burlap to weave garments together. On the ensemble *Sisters*

Adorn to Reflect, she hand painted Black women with their hair in braids, wearing clothing of non-Western influence. Here, she speaks to African American women about the importance of adornment that reflects pride in one's heritage. Jae was also defining revolutionary fashion. On a felt design, Jae painted images in bold colors of Black brothers and sisters addressing the disproportionate preponderance of Black people unjustly incarcerated in American jails. Words on her design demanded their release, thus inspiring the title *Free Black Political Prisoners*. The messages are distinct and run along the edge of the design, cut to give a lacy effect.

Gerald Williams displayed paintings entitled *Black Day Is Coming* and *Don't Forget the Struggle*. *Black Day Is Coming* is an acrylic on paper showing the face of a Black man in front of a red, black, and green flag. The painting contains amorphous shapes and is outlined in white against a solid chromium-oxide green background. Brilliant colors dominate a portion of the face of the man. The words "Black Day Is Coming" and "Uhuru" are written within the biomorphic white shape in the picture. *Don't Forget the Struggle* is a painting of the head of a man in orange and red, surrounded with small circular and semicircular shapes in varied colors. The words "Unite" and "Cooperation" are skillfully meshed into the composition.

I presented four paintings: *Revolutionary, Black Prince, The King*, and *Three Queens*. *Revolutionary* is a large portrait of Angela Davis wearing a replica of Jae Jarrell's *Revolutionary Suit*. (The *Revolutionary Suit* was Jae's vision.) I was merely paying tribute to a creative AFRICOBRA member, who was way out front of fashion designers.

Davis's face and hands are constructed of *only* the letter *B*—for Black is Beautiful—and words, namely, "Revolution," "Black Is Beautiful," "Resist," "Seize the Time," "Bad," and "She Hipped Us to Chuck . . . He Full of It." Words and letters compose her endless afro hairstyle, which explodes into fragmentations of the letter *B* (which gives the illusion of also being other letters). The letters, words, and shapes are layered over an orange and yellow background. Written on the garment she is wearing are remnants of a speech she delivered in 1970 in California: "I have given my life to the struggle. . . . If I have to lose my life in the struggle, that's the way it will have to be." Also attached to her suit is a red leather bandolier of colorful faux bullets. Size and scale in the painting are emphasized in an attempt to capture the aura of her power and strength as an activist, educator, scholar, politician, revolutionary,

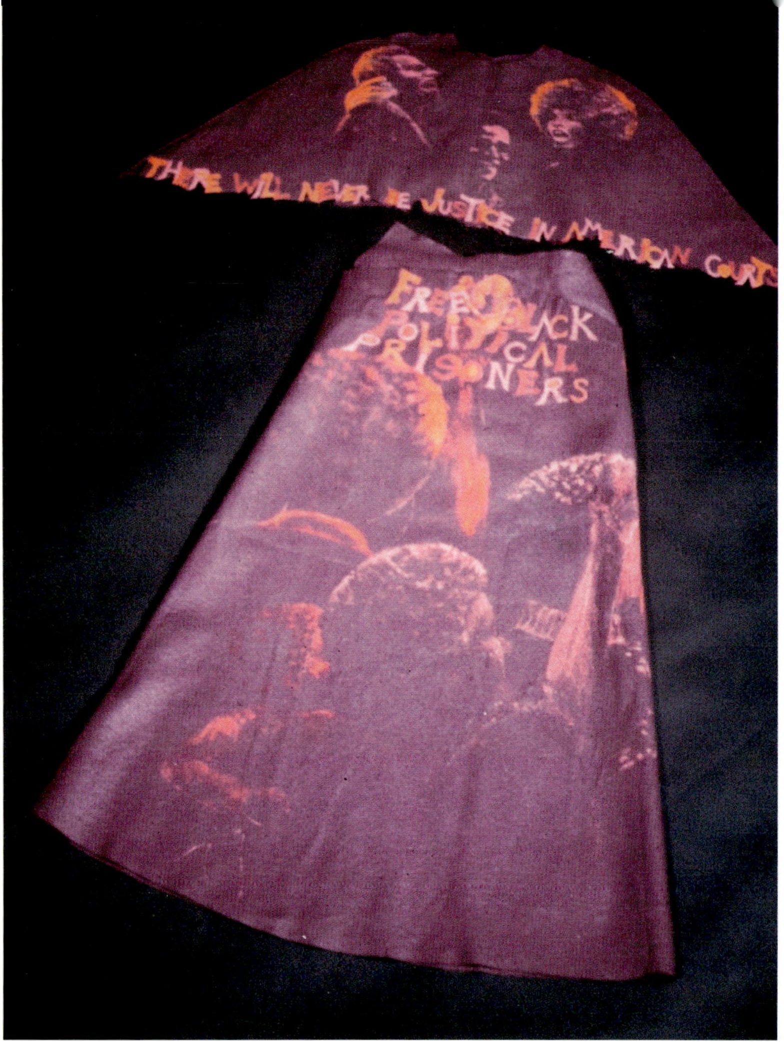

9.4

Jae Jarrell, *Free Black
Political Prisoners*, n.d.
Hand-painted felt.
Collection of the artist.

9.5

Gerald Williams, *Don't
Forget the Struggle,*
1971. Acrylic on canvas,
48 × 48 inches. Collection
of the artist.

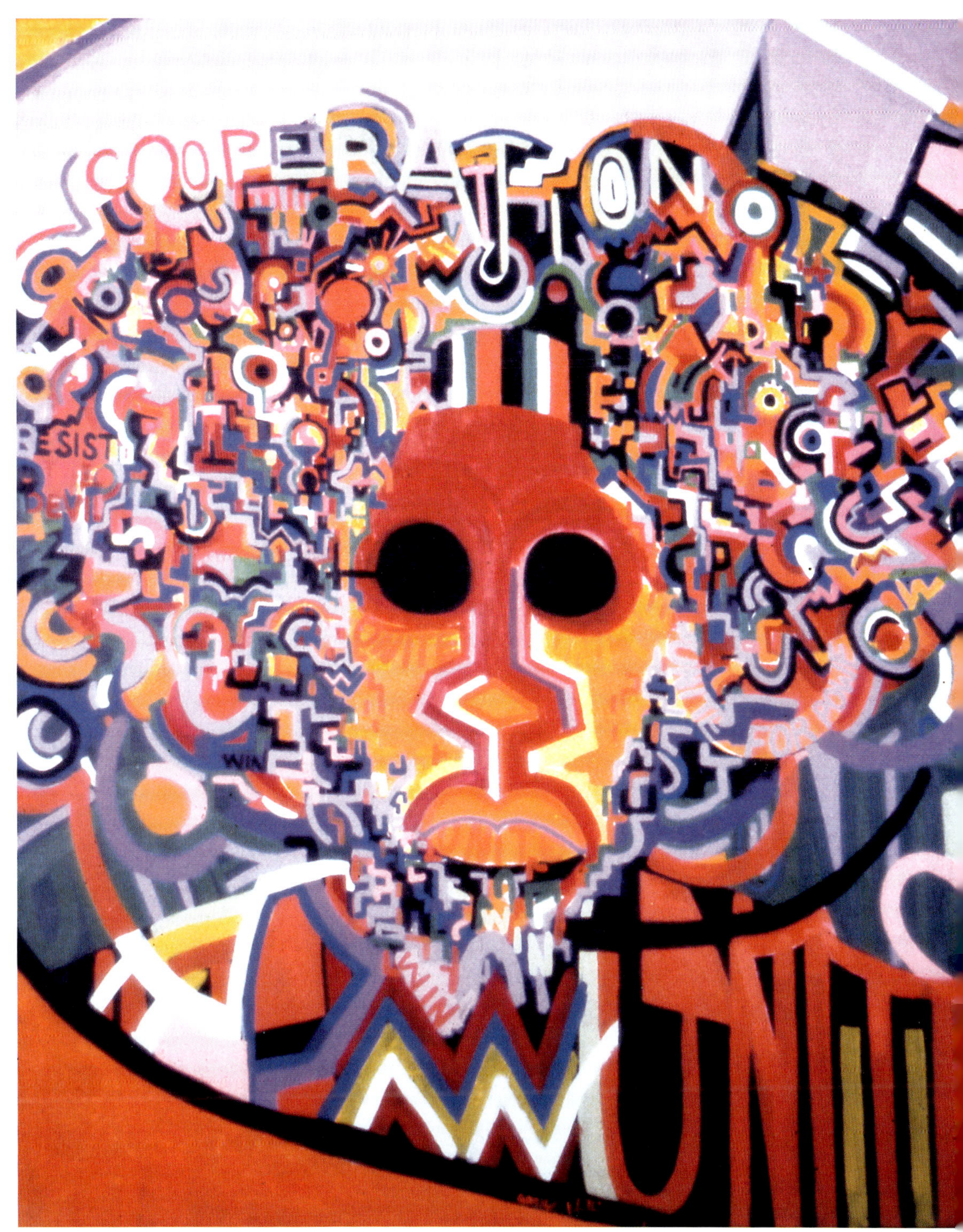

COOPERATION
RESIST
DEVIL
WIN
WIN
WIN
UNITY

9.6

Wadsworth Jarrell, *Black Prince*, 1971. Acrylic on canvas, 64 × 44 inches. Collection of Mr. and Mrs. Munson and Christina Steed.

9.7

Wadsworth Jarrell, *Revolutionary*, 1971. Acrylic and collage on canvas, 63.5 × 50.5 inches. Collection of Brooklyn Museum.

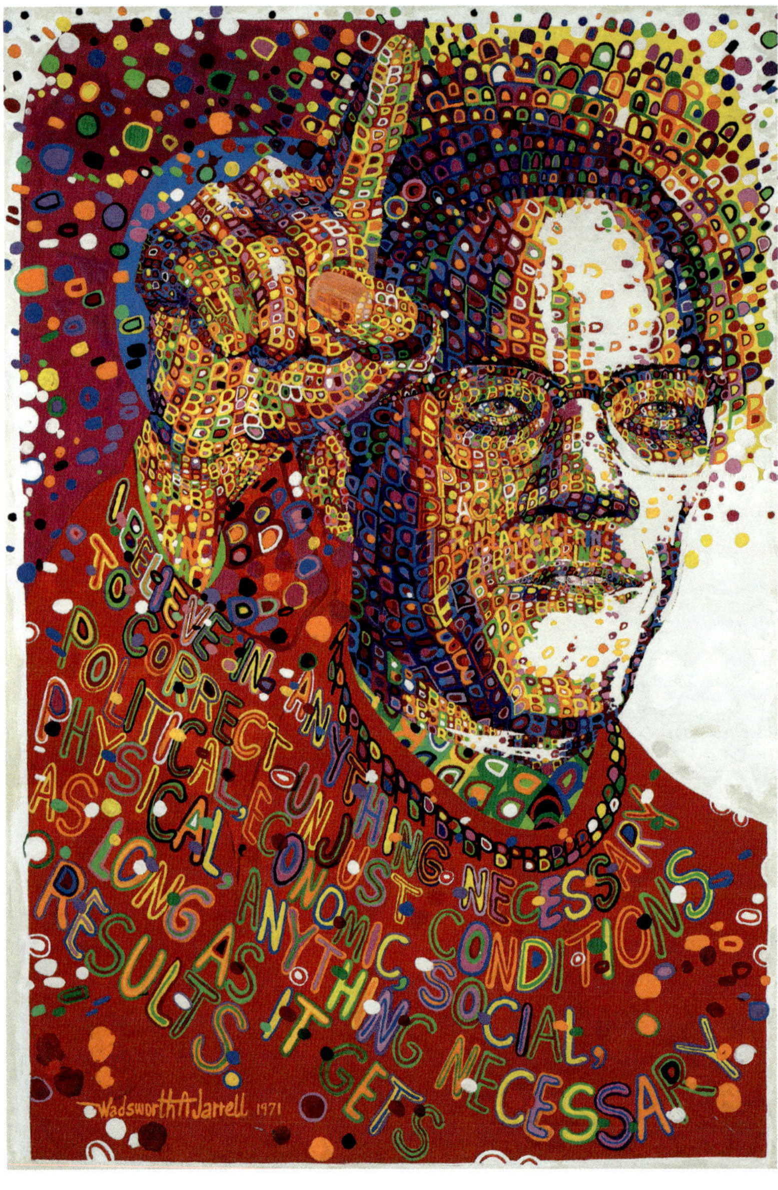

I BELIEVE IN ANYTHING
TO CORRECT UNJUST
POLITICAL, ECONOMIC CONDITIONS
PHYSICAL, ECONOMIC
AS LONG AS ANYTHING SOCIAL,
RESULTS IT GETS NECESSARY
Wadsworth A Jarrell 1971

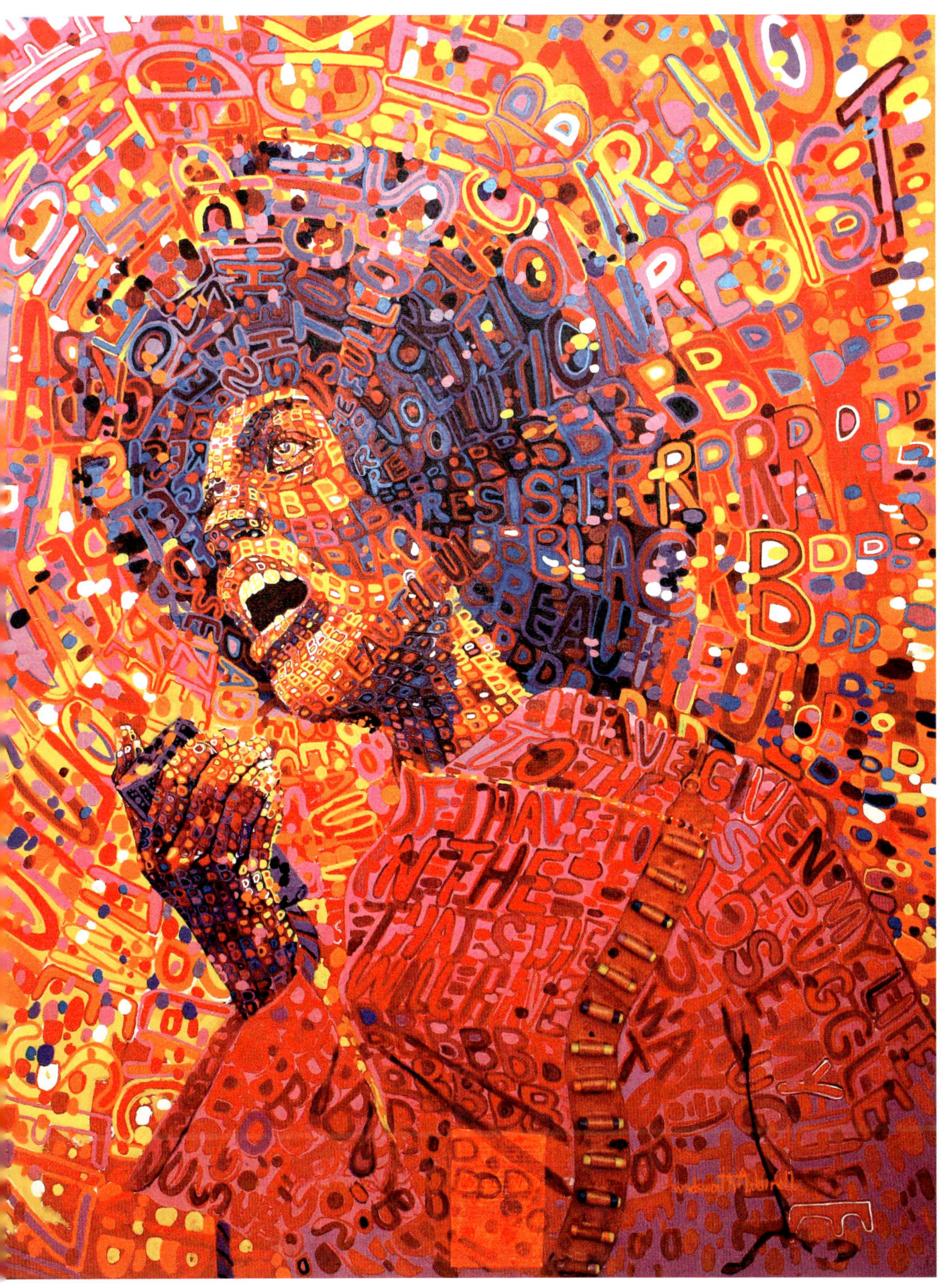

member of the Communist and the Black Panther Parties, with her own agenda encapsulating radical change.

Black Prince is a portrait of Malik El Hajj Shabazz (Malcolm X) constructed of words and letters that partially turn the form against a stark flat background. The words "Black Prince" are visible on his face and raised hand. Malcolm is wearing a red robe and a red, black, and green tie, unlike the traditional blue suit and solid red tie he wore when making important speeches. In the introduction to the book *Malcolm X: The End of White World Supremacy*, Benjamin Goodman described giving an opening speech in December 1962 at Mosque Number 7, where Malcolm was the main speaker: "I also noted as I talked that day he was wearing his blue suit and red tie. This was his 'burning suit,' which he wore when he was fully prepared and intended to give a very deep lecture."[5] Written on Malcolm's red robe in *Black Prince* is a paraphrased version of one of his speeches: "I believe in anything necessary, political, economic, social, as long as it gets results." On one side, the white background breaks into the form, signifying that it addresses the AFRICOBRA principle open color. The edge of the painting is rendered in broad white lines, indicating that it is poster art. The name *Black Prince* derived from the statement in Ossie Davis's eulogy of Malcolm. With the juxtaposition of bright Cool Ade colors, colored letters with an outline and an inline, and the deliberate scale of the painting, I aspired to capture the charismatic persona of this bright Black prince.

The King is a portrait of Martin Luther King Jr. delivering a fiery speech. It captures him adorning ecclesiastic regalia, hands extended, with one holding a book entitled *Mahatma Gandhi*, and the other with fingers spread in a rigid pose. The painting, like other paintings in this grouping, consists of words and the letter *B*. Large versions of the letter *B* are across the top of the painting, extending behind his head, creating overlaps. Written on one sleeve and across the breadth of his robe are portions of a profound statement that was part of a speech: "I may get crucified. I may even die, but I want it said, that he died to make men free." In this painting, color and scale are important in an attempt to capture the majestic charm, seriousness, and leadership of an astute drum major for freedom.

Three Queens shows large portraits of three young women flaunting their natural hair, indicating pride and confidence in their Blackness. Written in a circular arch around the heads of the figures are the phrases "Black Women

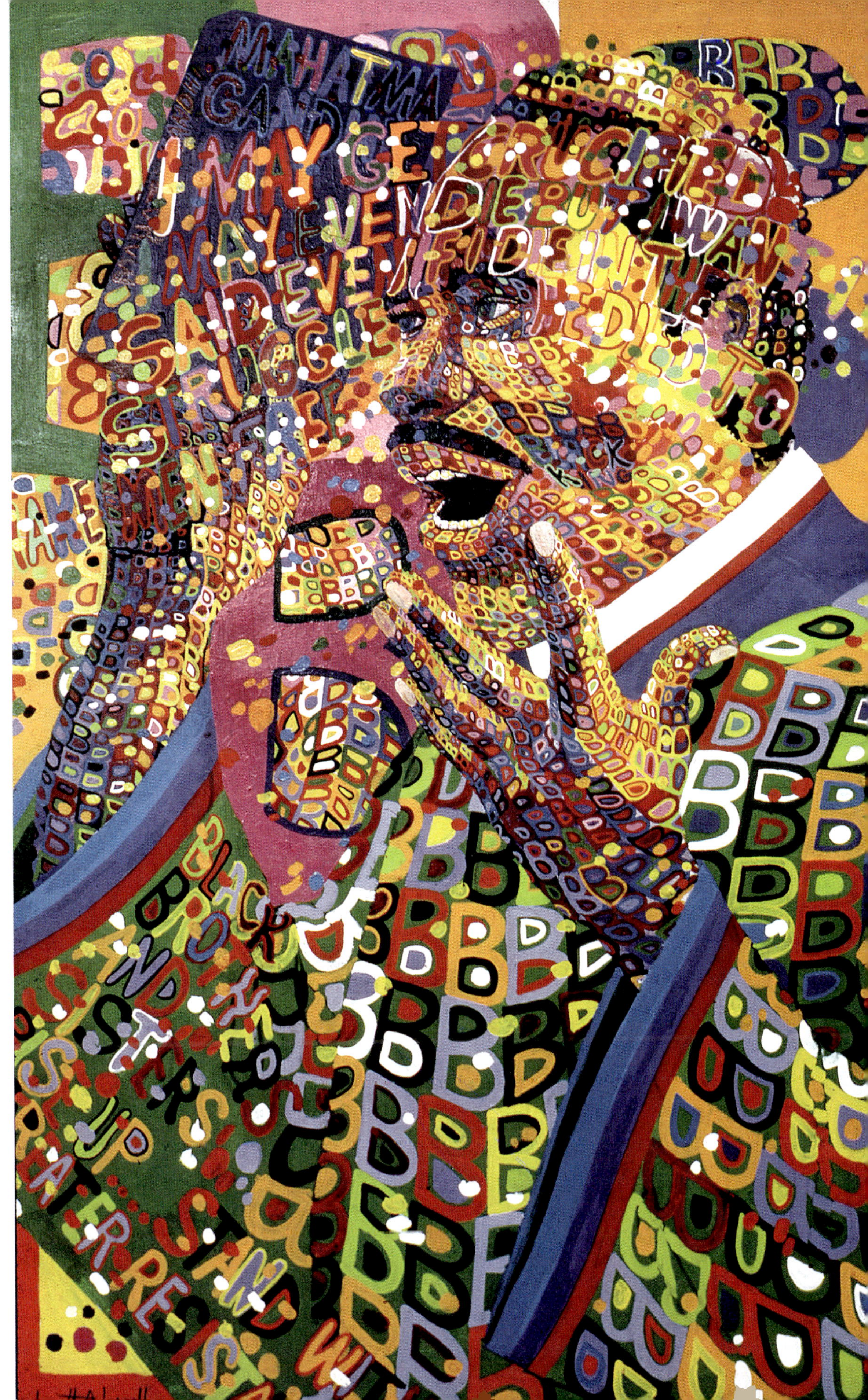

MAHATMA GANDHI
I MAY GET CRUCIFIED
I MAY EVEN DIE BUT I WANT
IF I DIE IN THE STRUGGLE
BLACK
BLACK AND
STIR UP
GREATER RESISTANCE WI

Are Beautiful. Let Your Hair Grow Natural. Stop Buying Chuck's Wigs and Make-Up." These statements are concurrent with heart-felt jargon of the civil rights and Black power movements, suggesting that Black women do not need artificial Euro-American influences because they are endowed with natural beauty.

Barbara Jones's silkscreen prints included *Nation Time* and *To Be Free*. In *Nation Time*, the picture is imperiously composed of the head of an African American, implicit with thick lips and flat nose, reddish-orange coloring representing the pupils of the eyes, also indicative of Africans and African Americans. Barbara uses her inventive multiple cartoon-graffiti-style lettering to characterize the theme *Nation Time*. The combination of powerful image and designed words explicitly presents poignantly a work of high quality, inventiveness, and high visibility.

To Be Free (which was covered later in a tapestry by weaver Napoleon Henderson) displays a head and shoulder view of an African American with a large afro constructed of words and stylized letters. In a circle in the forehead of the image are inscribed the words "To Be Free." Once again, Barbara had mastered her own style, using a font for the lettering that displayed artistic imperatives itself. Her art always encompassed themes of Black consciousness.

Nelson Stevens presented images that were saturated with more color than his previous works. His increase in color demanded a much larger presence for his highly developed style of art. Paintings he exhibited were entitled *Spirit Sister, Unite,* and *Wholy. Spirit Sister* reveals only a head and neck view of a figure dominating the picture plane. The head is cropped at the top of the painting to enforce power and visibility. It was executed deliberately with the appearance of a low angle, with the subject's head tilted as if looking up.

Another painting by Nelson is a portrait of Nina Simone entitled *Nina*, which is also cropped across the top. An intense application of bright colors constructed of elusive and amorphous shapes make up the form. The word "Nina" is written in stylized letters along the side of Nina's face.

Nelson's painting *Wholy* is a large-scale portrait of a woman's head. The image is larger than the frame it is housed in, and it seeks to break out. He presented this painting in a spectacular arrangement of colored squares, lines, rectangles, and organic shapes. The shapes are actively assimilating movement, juxtaposed side by side as well as overlapping. A silver-rimmed circle with a red line surrounds the woman's head.

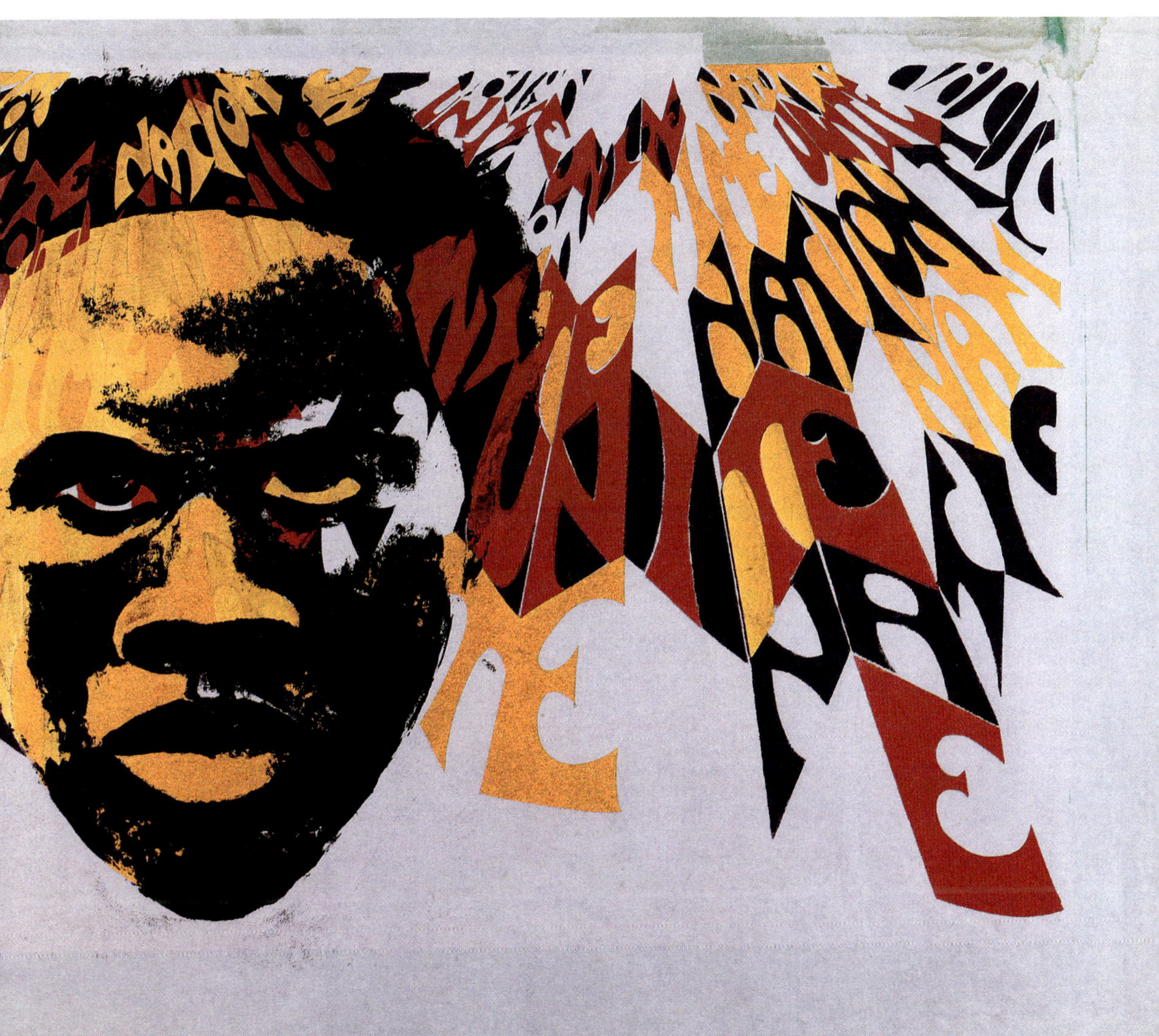

9.9
Barbara Jones-Hogu,
Nation Time, 1970.
Silkscreen on paper.
Collection of Brooklyn
Museum.

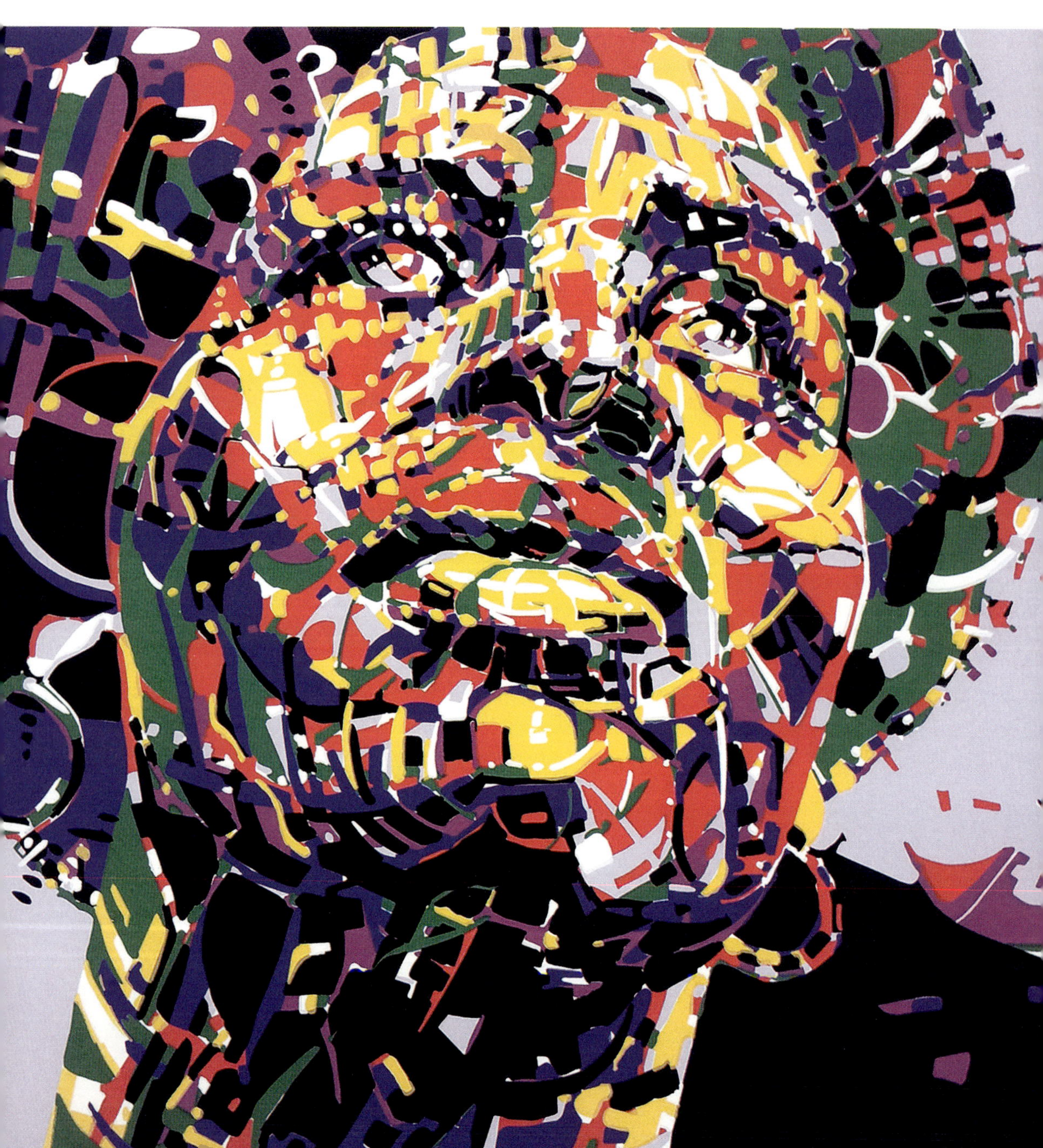

9.10

Nelson Stevens, *Spirit Sister*, 1971. Acrylic on canvas, 48 × 48 inches. Collection of Mr. and Mrs. Michael and Christa Brinson.

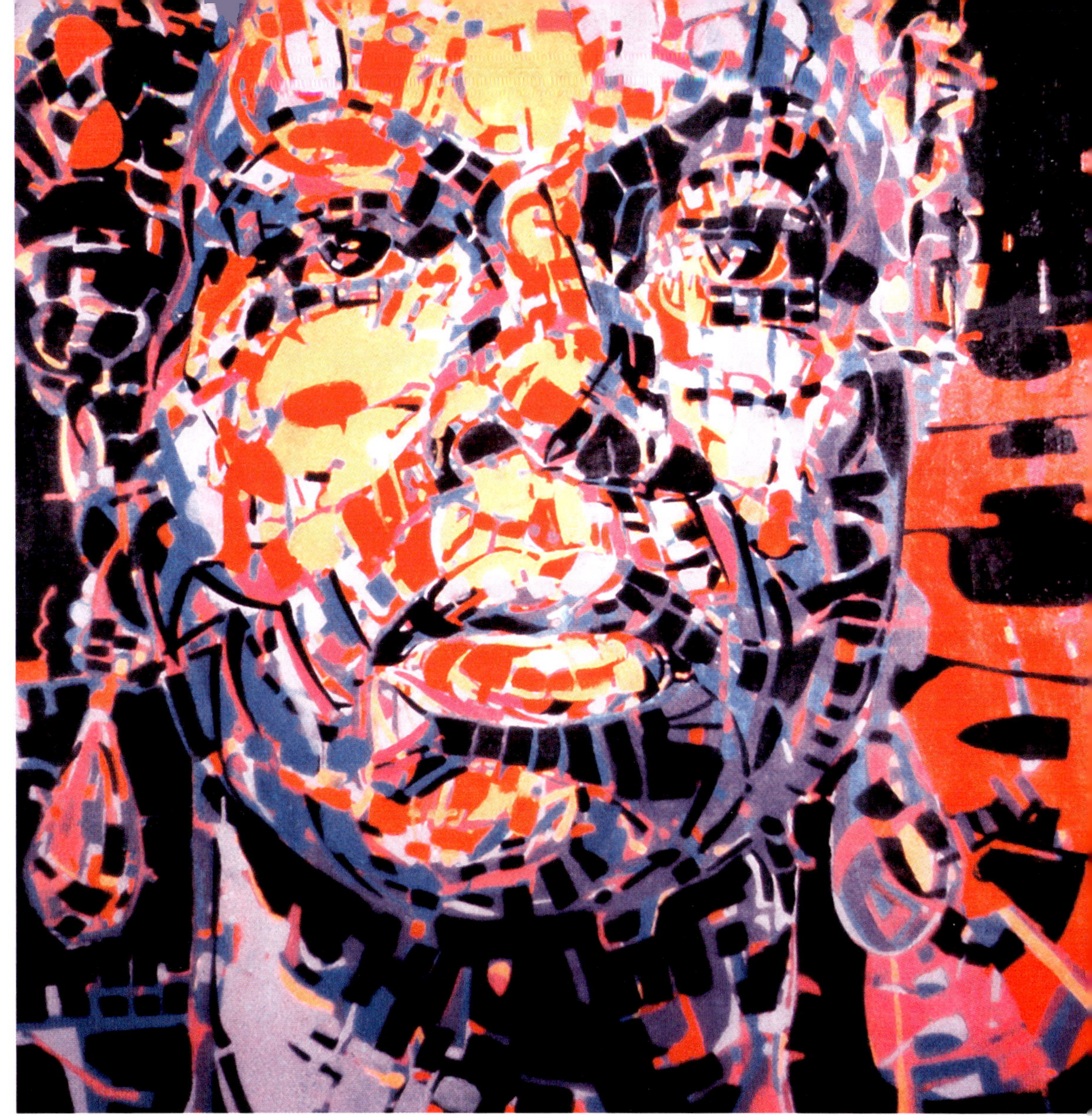

9.11

Nelson Stevens, *Nina*,
1972. Acrylic on canvas,
48 × 48 inches. Collection
of Henry Dawson.

Carolyn Lawrence exhibited two paintings, *Be Worthy of Your Brother's Trust* and *Get Some Land, Black People*. Her painting *Be Worthy of Your Brother's Trust* shows a grouping of young people standing together socializing. Behind the images is a broken circular shape that creates radial balance, with lines spiraling out from the center. She inscribes the statement at the top of the painting: "Be worthy of your brother's trust, your young are watching you."

Carolyn's work exhibited great internalization of AFRICOBRA's philosophy and revealed her extraordinary skills as an inventive artist. In *Get Some Land, Black People*, Carolyn decries the lack of ownership of land by African Americans. She not only advises in print, "Get Some Land, Black People," she also writes, "Keep Your Land, Black People." And as a final important suggestion, she writes: "Our Survival Is Dependent Upon Land." Carolyn is cognizant of the importance of land ownership, and the degree of freedom and power it embodies.

Napoleon Henderson showed two weavings, *Unite Wholy People* and *Egyptian Solar*. His tapestry *Unite Wholy People* is in large format, consisting of strips of material and colors that expand the length of the work. At the bottom of the tapestry is a pyramid shape containing faces, which is another departure from nonobjective works exhibited in AFRICOBRA I. Napoleon used his weaving surfaces as canvases, where he created intricate and skillfully rendered images and complementary abstract shapes. Napoleon owned the medium of weaving as if he had invented it. *Egyptian II* is a woven tapestry with aluminum foil, consisting of linear horizontal and vertical shapes, a primordial animal, and an ankh. Both works by Napoleon are remarkable achievements.

Jeff Donaldson abandoned the watercolor medium that he had made his own and presented new works in acrylics. This change displayed his versatility. He exhibited four paintings: *Victory in the Valley of Eshu*, *Wedding Unit Portrait*, another version of *Wives of Shango* in acrylics, and *Here Comes the Judge*. (Note: *Allah Shango* and *Shango Shorties* had been exhibited in AFRICOBRA I in 1970).

The painting *Victory in the Valley of Eshu*, which was reproduced into a silkscreen print, depicted a middle-aged couple in a warm embrace. They are painted mostly in earth colors, with inflections of bright colors surrounding them. Spraying out from the heads in a radial format are patterns of color resembling crowns of royalty. The man is wearing suspenders and in one hand holding a Shango ax (representing the God of Thunder). In the center of the painting is a large star painted gold. Affixed inside the star are images of the couple from a newspaper clipping that was his inspiration. The painting portrays the story of a Washington, DC, couple who was victorious in a land dispute regarding encroachment by the city. Here, Jeff captures the joy and celebratory atmosphere of the regal couple basking in triumph. At the bottom of the painting, meshed into the composition in block letters, is the single word "Victory."

The painting *Nation Unit—Wedding Portrait* is of him and his wife, Arnicia. She is seated cross-legged in a thronelike chair, with Jeff standing behind her holding a shotgun. Their eyes seem to be fixed in solidarity on someone or on an object beyond the picture plane. A halo of colors jets out from around the heads of the figures, indicating divinity. Written on the barrel of the gun is the statement "Control, Land, Mines, Goods, and Nation." The gun is symbolic for Black revolution, informing America of the truth behind Frantz Fanon's statement: "Decolonization is always a violent event."[6]

Howard Mallory presented a brilliantly executed ceramic relief work, *We Must Go Home with Something*. Its depiction of five figures includes a large one that is only a head and four smaller figures with head and shoulders, juxtaposed and overlapping one another—all seem to be set in the composition separately.

That procedure makes the picture plane multidimensional, and each image appears outlined. The color glazes consist of blue, green, yellow, brown, and black. Written in bold letters on the left side of the relief, from top to bottom, "WE MUST GO HOME WITH SOMETHING TO BUILD A NATION." On one figure is a partial map of Africa with the word "Home" written on it, and on another is the symbol of life, an ankh. Howard's explanation for the title is clearly explained with inscriptions on the figures. On the larger figure is written "Engineer," and separately on three of the smaller figures, "Scientist," "Educators," and "Technicians." Here, Howard is implying that if African Americans intend to compete for a piece, or the whole pie, preparation is imperative. This work is in clay, the medium Howard has mastered. The work exhibits brilliance of concept and mastery of the artist's calling—mystic man of fire.

9.13

Napoleon Jones-
Henderson, *Egyptian
Solar*, 1969. Tapestry,
60 × 72 inches. Collection
of the artist.

9.12

Carolyn Lawrence, *Be
Worthy of Your Brother's
Trust*, 1971. Acrylic on
canvas, 36 × 44 inches.
Collection of the artist.

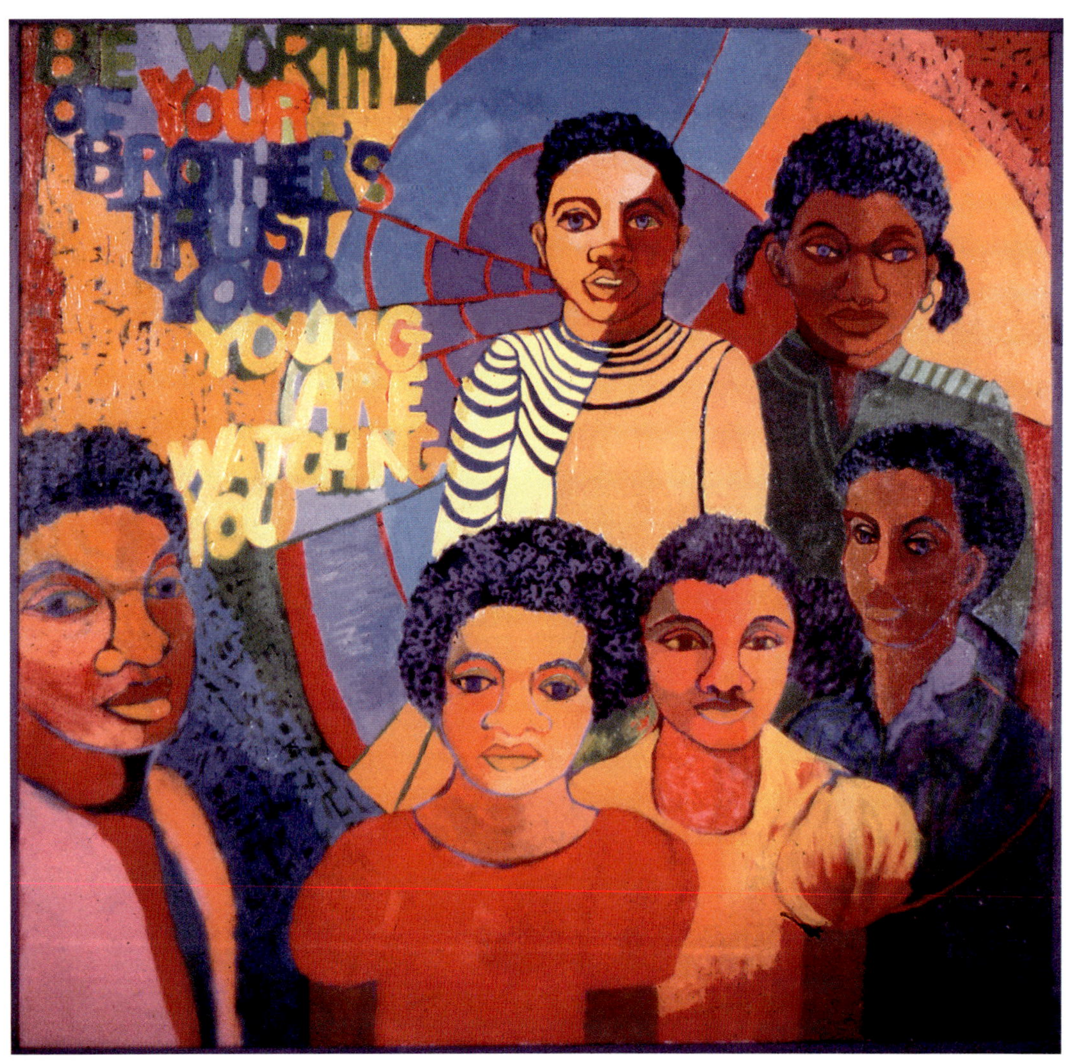
BE WORTHY
OF YOUR
BROTHER'S
TRUST YOUR
YOUNG ARE
WATCHING
YOU

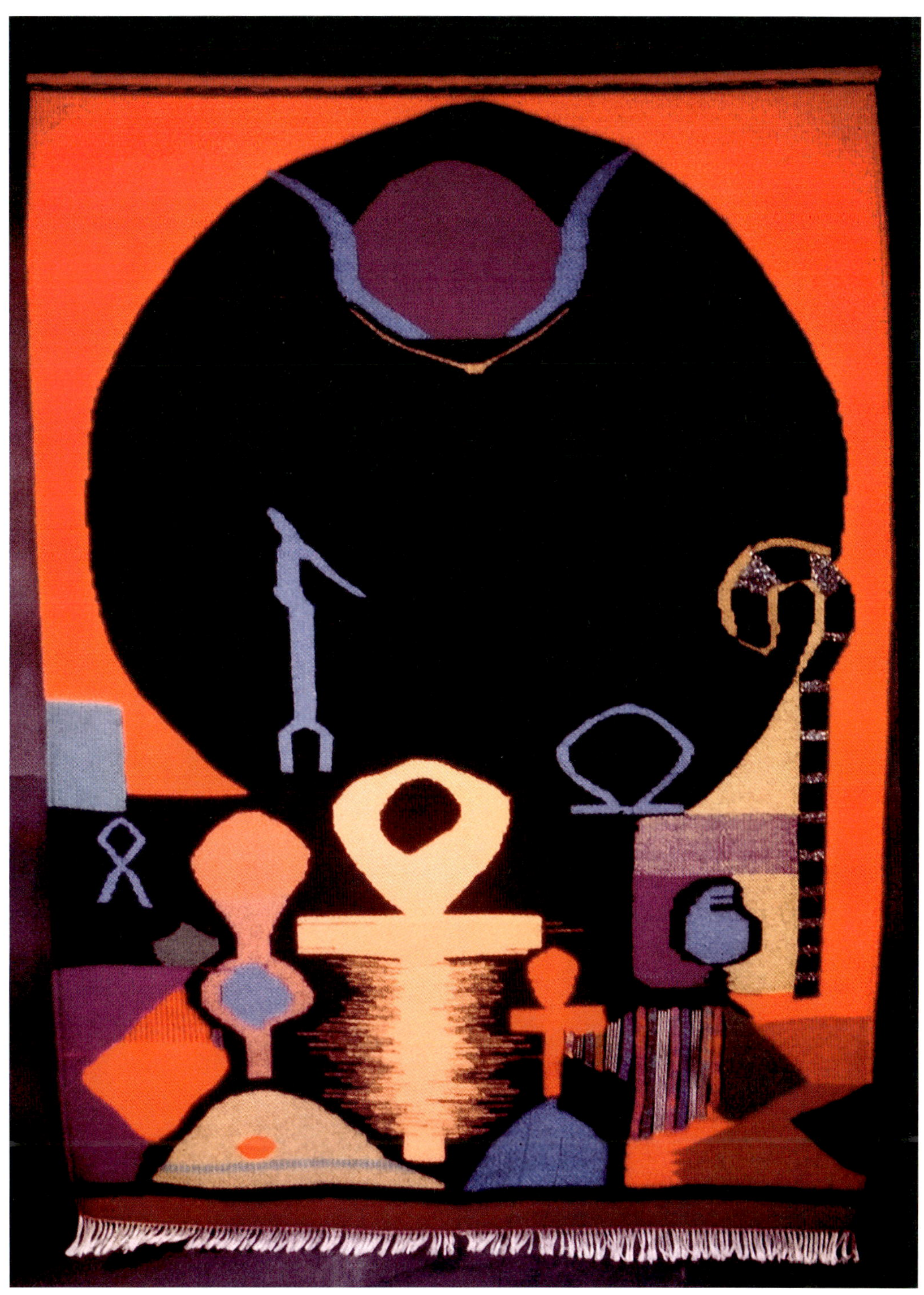

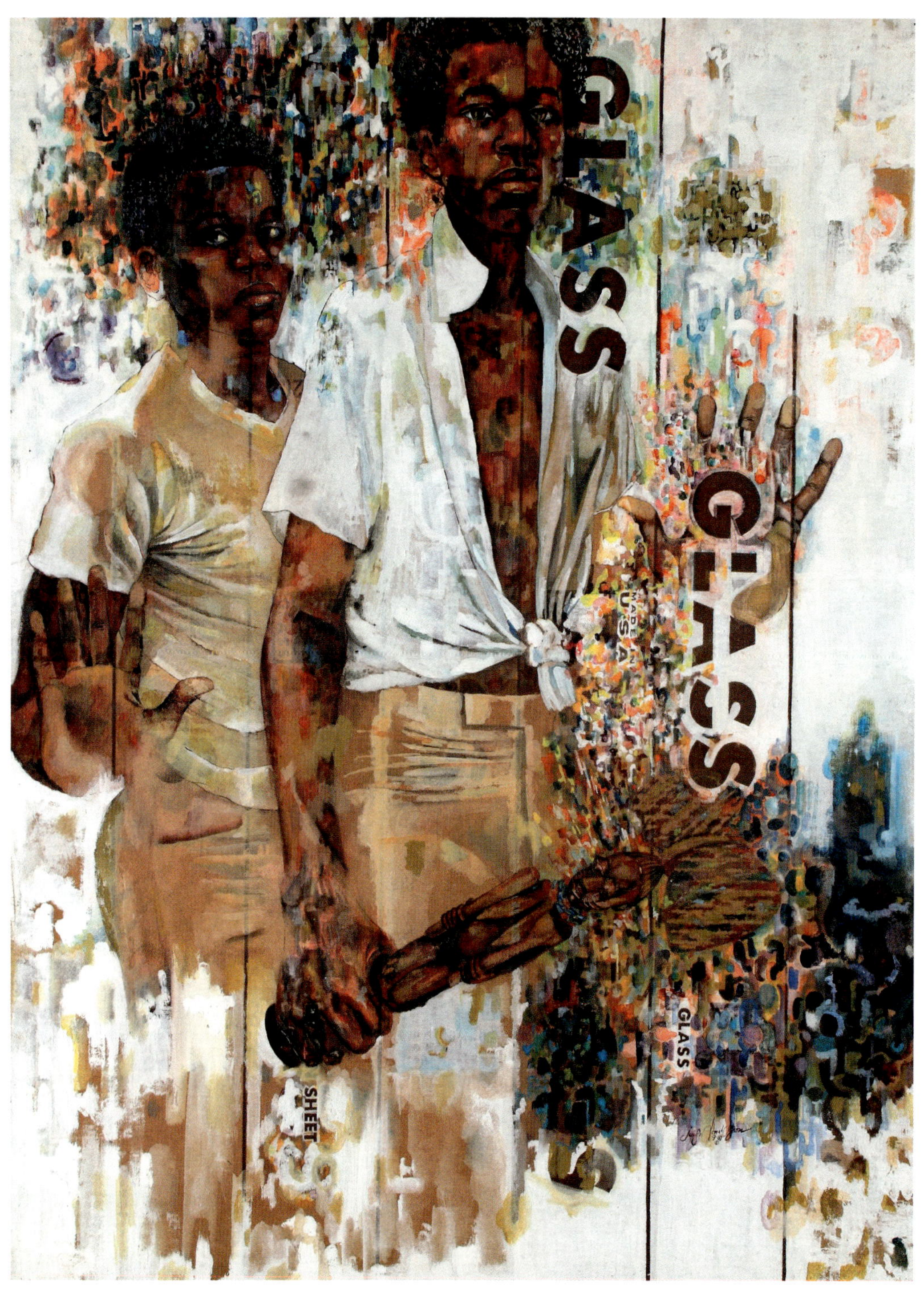

GLASS
GLASS
MADE IN U.S.A.
GLASS
SHEET

AFRICOBRA in Boston

The Museum of the National Center of Afro-American Artists in Boston was next on the AFRICOBRA itinerary. The director, Edmund Barry Gaither, invited AFRICOBRA a second time and gave the Boston audience a view of our more mature work. The museum walls were painted in our traditional Cool Ade colors, and according to Gaither, the exhibition was well attended and successful.

In September 1972, Gaither wrote in "Nationhood," "AFRICOBRA is an authentic artistic movement presenting the opportunity for renewed purposefulness within the Afrocentric world, which is the proper domain for an African people. It was in support of this understanding of AFRICOBRA as both an authentic art historical movement and a prime element of a larger growth of black people toward nationhood, that the Museum of the National Center of Afro-American Artists has valued the work and place of AFRICOBRA artists."[7]

AFRICOBRA in Washington, DC

The Howard University Gallery of Art in Washington, DC, was the third stop for *AFRICOBRA II*, on February 25, 1972. The walls of the gallery were painted in Cool Ade colors. The exhibition provoked a measure of excitement along with skepticism. Both doubt and curiosity occurred because of prepublicity that filtered out of New York City about our exhibition there in 1970. The uniqueness of a multifarious artists' collective and the accompanying printed literature declaring AFRICOBRA the paradigm for Black art, or the Black aesthetic, as described in essays by Spriggs and Gaither, caused great expectations and concern for the Washington audience.

AFRICOBRA II was our first exhibition in Washington, DC, at Howard University—the exemplary institution among Black colleges, which housed the exhibition gallery within the College of Fine Arts. Included in the college was the School of Music, staffed with accomplished musicians, and at that time, Donald Byrd was chair of Jazz studies. There was a proficient Drama Department, where once the charismatic Howard Dobson, poet and playwright, chaired the department. Other significant professors who once taught in the Drama Department were the important playwright Paul Carter Harrison and playwright Joe Walker, who won a Tony award for his off-Broadway/Broadway play *River Niger*. The Department of Communications had its own radio station, WHUR, and the department was chaired by the

Jeff Donaldson, *Allah Shango*, 1969. Mixed media, 28 × 38 inches. Collection of Johnson Publishing Co.

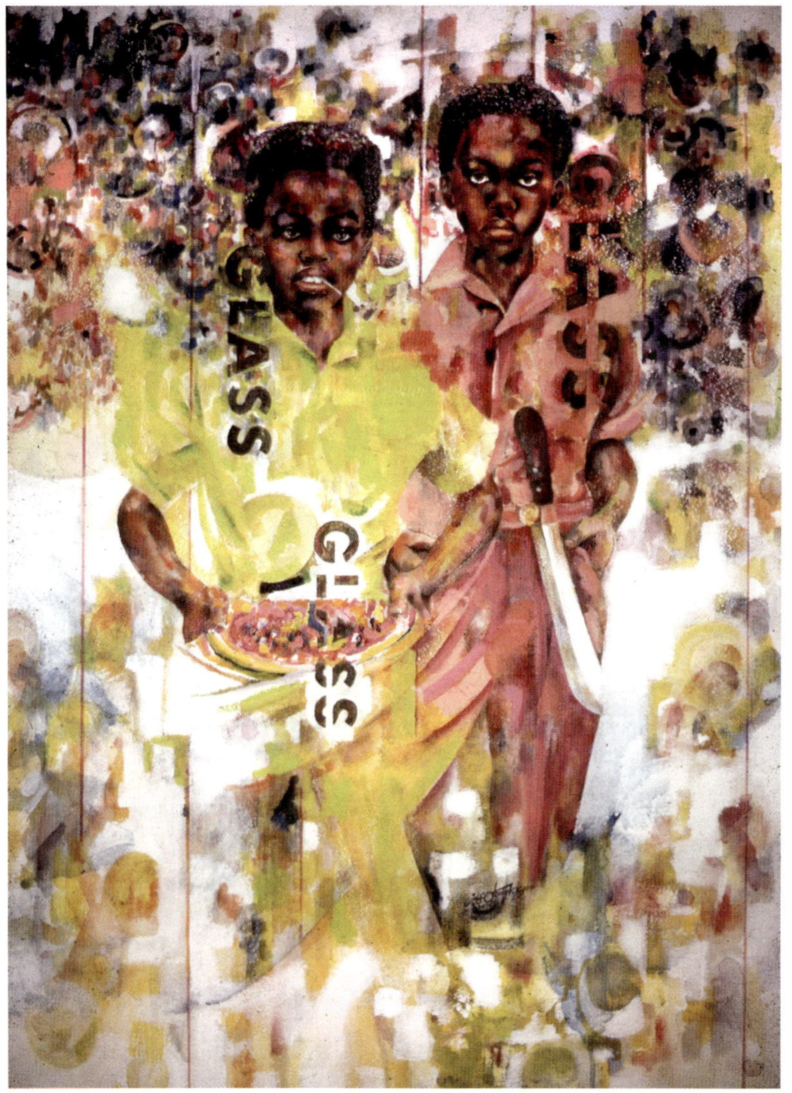

9.15

Jeff Donaldson,
Shango Shorties, 1969.
Watercolor on paper,
30 × 40 inches. Collection
of the artist.

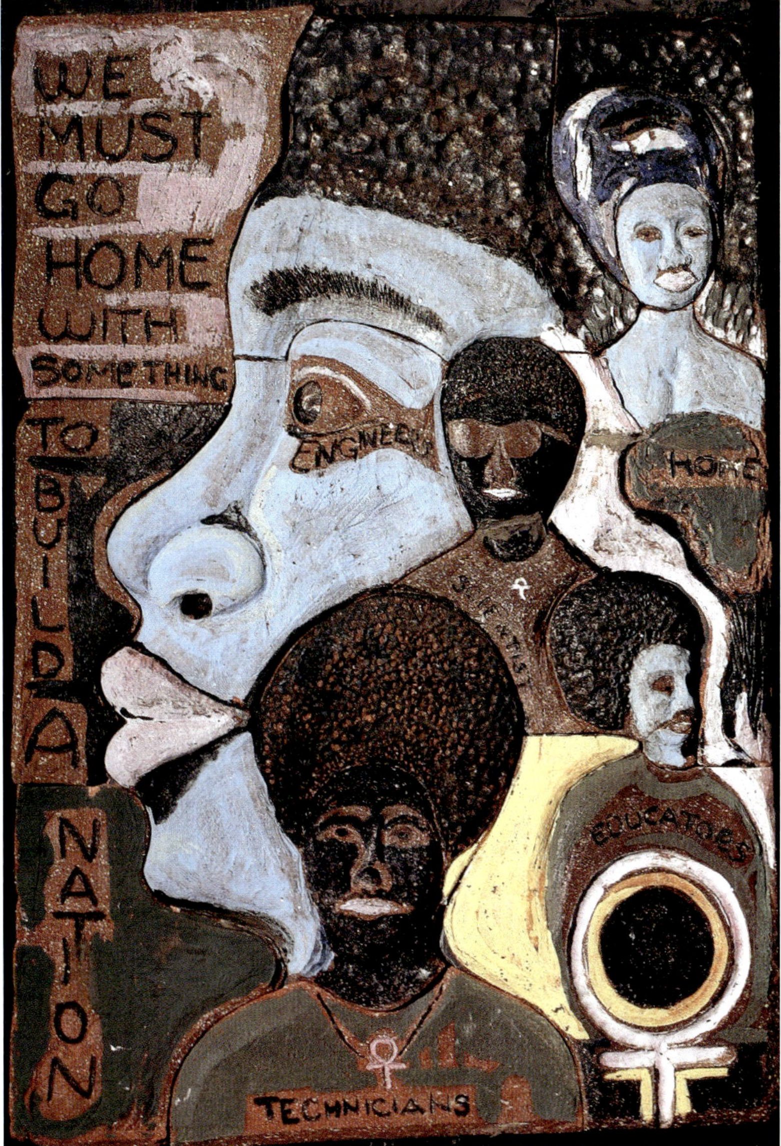

Howard Mallory, *We Must Go Home with Something*, 1971. Ceramic relief, 30 × 40 inches. Collection of Brooklyn Museum.

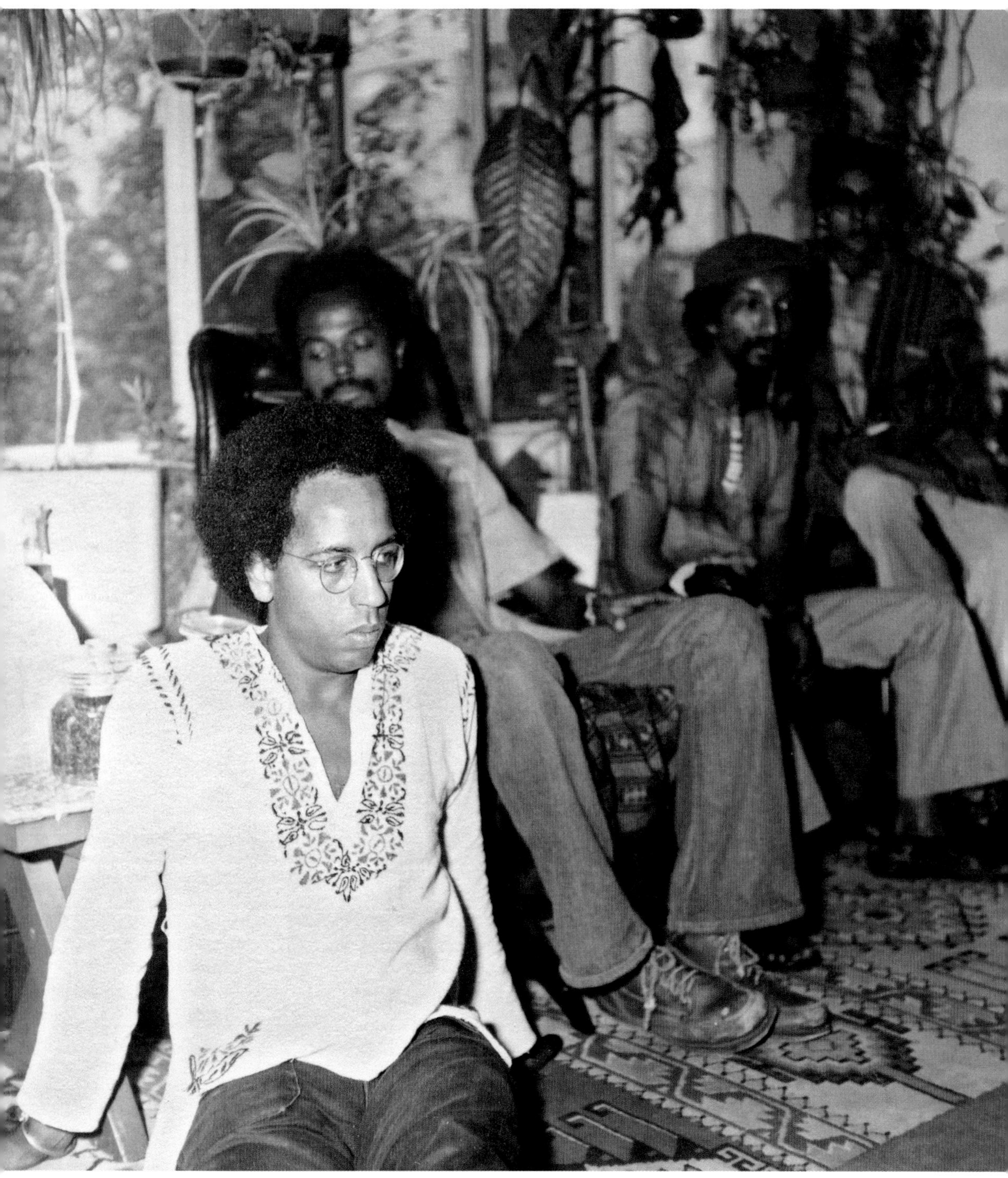

activist and colorful television personality Tony Brown. Rounding out the college complex was the Visual Art Department, chaired by Jeff Donaldson and staffed with nationally and internationally acclaimed artists.

Presenting an exhibition at a Black historical institution such as Howard, which had an association with known scholars, was a thought-provoking undertaking. Among scholars associated with Howard, to cite a few, are Amiri Baraka, Toni Morrison, Thurgood Marshall, Sterling Brown, Zora Neale Hurston, Alain Locke, Ossie Davis, John O. Killens, Stephen Henderson, E. Franklin Frazier, and Haki Madhubuti.

AFRICOBRA II met the challenge. Explicitly revealed was that AFRICOBRA was an efficiently constructed, authentic artistic movement. AFRICOBRA philosophically represents the only US-based movement since the Harlem Renaissance that responds to the collective needs of African American artists who are motivated by their African heritage.[8] Most importantly, the work was proficiently executed and steeped in brilliant colors, which manifested visibility and mimesis at midpoint, and disclosed a new inventive approach that bent the standard canon of art. Some of our most suspicious critics from the Howard faculty were convinced that our collective was important mainly because of publicity we had received. Two colleagues of mine approached me with praise of my work. One stated, "I see you made the [*Washington*] *Post*. You have to be pretty good to make the *Post*." The other faculty member expressed great admiration for my painting *Revolutionary*. "I like your painting of Angela. That is a great work." Thurlow Evans Tibbs Jr., then director of the Evans-Tibbs Collection in Washington, DC, went as far as to say in an essay: "AFRICOBRA is an important and original art movement in the Black and in the American community."[9]

The catalyst that was largely responsible for all the praise and ovations was the comprehensive review written by Paul Richard, art critic for the *Washington Post*. Jae was in charge of publicity and graciously extended an invitation to Richard to visit Howard and review the exhibition. In kind, he professed gratitude for the invitation and mentioned that it was his first visit to Howard University Gallery of Art. He came and interviewed Jeff and me before the opening of the show. Richard admitted that he was awestruck by the beauty of the art.

Jeff gestured toward a wall containing AFRICOBRA's art and said to Richard, "You're not seeing them. All you see is pictures on the wall. Everything is together, religion, tradition, dancing and song. James Brown doesn't just stand there and sing. You can't see AFRICOBRA unless you're in the struggle, unless you hear the music. But if you hear the music, at least if you are white, you hear Ray Charles sing the Beatles and Otis Redding sing the Stones and not just vice versa."[10]

Richard retorted, "I see these works because they resemble European things."

Jeff asked, "What is European about them?"

"They are categorized as easel art on flat surface canvases that is displayed on gallery walls."

"How do you know that Africans did not make paintings on flat surfaces? You only know what has been recorded by white historians because Europeans plundered everything that wasn't nailed down, and paintings in caves they couldn't handily steal."

"I am familiar with fine carvings of African art, and I do see some of the things mentioned in your manifesto, like Free Symmetry and Shine that perhaps relates to those carvings. But manifestos are European things."

Jeff was perturbed. He disliked anyone categorizing anything that he wrote, said, or painted, and worse, by a white art critic. "What do you mean, manifesto? I never said that I wrote a manifesto. You said that."

"AFRICOBRA's art was designed with disregard for mainstream art principles," I interjected. "Our art and our guidelines address Black people everywhere."

"I can clearly see that," Richard responded, "because of that note you attached to your painting *Revolutionary*. That makes it explicitly clear, that AFRICOBRA art is not for Chuck—for hunkies, as you call them."

The following Sunday, February 27, 1972, Richard's article appeared in the Entertainment and Style section of the *Post*. Included were two five-by-seven-inch full-color images on the front page of the section: *Revolutionary* and *Black Prince*. Inside the paper, the article continued and included one five-by-seven-inch full-color image: *Nation Unit—Wedding Portrait*. The exhibition was labeled "AFRICOBRA: African Art for Africans Only." Richard wrote: "The show is called AFRICOBRA: there is blackness in that word, coiled menace. This is a show for us, it seems to warn. If you are white, or worst, a white critic, this is not a show for you. The show's a knockout, but if you're white you cannot righteously review it, not because its blackness makes you tiptoe, not because you're tempted to compromise or condescend, but the paintings bar you everywhere."[11]

I would argue that, as a white art critic for an acclaimed nationwide news-paper situated in Washington, DC, which contains all-white neighborhoods, like Georgetown, and many important art museums and galleries mainly exhibiting white artists, this was the first art exhibition containing unapologetic themes of Blackness that he'd had the opportunity to write about. Possibly, it was the first exhibit of in-depth and concentrated positive Black art, excellently executed and presented, that he had ever seen. The art, with inscriptions on it calling for revolution and stating that it was created with only Black people in mind, he could very well surmise as a white person that the art barred him everywhere. But bear in mind that AFRICOBRA artists were creating art for and about Black people.

Richard continued:

Wadsworth Jarrell's fiery portrait of Angela Davis is the first one that you see. She's a mosaic made of colored letters, mostly of the letter B, for Bad, for Black, for Beautiful, and her Afro is an endless halo and she wears a belt of 3-D cartridges and a raspberry and orange suit. You study it awhile, admiring its passion, its power, its inventiveness, but then you lean a little closer and it warns you: keep away. A piece of paper with a typed notation is fastened to the canvas against the suit she wears. This is what it says: "This is a replica of a revolutionary suit designed by Jae Jarrell. . . . When chuck jump on and bastardize it as he does everything else we do, I want you to know he stole it from black giants (AFRICOBRA).

This suit is not for hunkies, strictly for Black people in the present revolution." If you read that and you're black, you might say, yeah, right on.

If you're Chuck, if you're a hunkie, you may recoil at those words. And you're supposed to. Throughout this show you sense a bounce, a confidence, a brightness and a joy, but it is theirs, not yours.[12]

Richard's description of the exhibition held some truths, but parts of his article expressed the opinionated views of an art critic. But with the interview of Jeff and me and his viewing the show, his article was on point and had a good amount of credibility. But as an art critic, he took liberties describing and literally giving his version of the meaning of words on the painting. His version did not represent the true meaning of letters and words on the painting *Revolutionary*, for instance: B for Black, for Bad, and for Beautiful. Although those words were on the painting, I constructed the painting of the letter *B* to represent *only* the profound statement of praise extolling our people at that time—"Black is Beautiful."

Richard continued: "How do you make art for blacks that blacks can only understand? Wadsworth Jarrell, Jeff Donaldson, Nelson Stevens and the other AFRICOBRA artists have settled on a set of qualities, a style that is shared. Donaldson describes the qualities that it includes: The expressive awesomeness that one experiences in African art . . . the Holiness Church . . . the demon that is the blues, Jabbar's dunk and Sayer's cut, the Hip walk and the together talk."[13]

Jeff is a dramatic composer of words and myths—that's one of his strengths. He also embellishes. Once he gets rolling, it's literally impossible to stop him. But, as one of the founders of such a dynamic pro-Black collective as AFRICOBRA, creating myths—Black myths, emphasizing unequivocal aesthetic principles, with an attitude embodying opinionated thoughts—are germane to being a creator and a member in the era of the Black aesthetic. As the saying goes in Black communities, "You gotta have 'tude." The following statement describing shine could be considered overreaching in the context of the meaning of the word:

> Symmetry that is free, based on African music and African movement . . . the rhythm rhythm rhythm. This is the big one. . . . Shine. . . . We want the things to shine, to have the rich luster of a just-washed-'fro, or spit-shined shoes . . . the Shine who escaped the Titanic, the 'lil light of mine,' patent leather, Dixie Peach, cars, shineum. Color color color. . . . Superreal color for Superreal image Coolade colors for Coolade images for Superreal people.[14]

On February 28, 1972, approximately a week after the opening of *AFRI-COBRA II*, Larry Brown, from a television station in Washington, came to the exhibition to interview Jeff and me. His interview was aired on a local television station at 10:00 P.M., when Brown presented *Black News*. One incident that stands out vividly in my mind is that of a cameraman from the television station taking a meter reading of the work, whether it was reflected or incident light. He was shocked that the meter reading was constant for all the work.

The cameraman asked, "Why is that?"

I explained to him, "That is because we subscribe to a common philosophy. It doesn't make a difference whether the dominant colors are dark or light. We use Cool Ade color, which is mixed with the purpose in mind of intensifying cooler colors to bring the intensity up to match the warmer colors."

While the exhibition was still in their art gallery, the student body of Howard University invited Paul Richard there for a discussion. The entire Art Department—students, faculty, and the curator of Howard's art collection—attended. Richard was invisible in this part of town, only known through his articles about art, which did not include Howard University Gallery of Art. The exhibition was discussed, including the mediums on display—paintings, prints, fashion design, and weaving. A student from the audience asked Richard, "What do you think of the exhibition?" Richard responded, "The AFRICOBRA artists' work is executed with such decisive skill and perception that it is not deadlocked in what is known as protest art. Theirs falls under the category of fine art."

AFRICOBRA II continued its itinerary to Northern Illinois University, in Dekalb, where Nelson Stevens was a professor in the Art Department. According to him, students and faculty were deeply impressed, and some students were influenced by the art. The final stop on the midwestern itinerary was Black Expo in Chicago. This was our second time to visit there. Two AFRICOBRA members, Napoleon and Gerald, informed me that the exhibition created as much, or more, excitement among the Chicago audience as had AFRICOBRA I. Silkscreen printing was executed on the spot as a workshop demonstration for educational purposes and to enhance sales of prints.

AFRICOBRA Traveling Exhibitions

After the Chicago Expo exhibition, Edward Spriggs requested selected works from each AFRICOBRA member for a traveling exhibition. The itinerary was for the duration of one year. It was presented at the State Museum of New York, Albany; the Haiti Gallery, Rochester, New York; Everson Museum of Art, Syracuse, New York; and Langston Hughes Center for Visual and Performing Arts, in Buffalo, New York. In Buffalo on October 8, 1972, the exhibition provoked comments from art critic Nancy Tobin Willig of the *Buffalo Courier Express*. She wrote:

> An exhibition at the Langston Hughes Center for the Visual and Performing Arts presents the 10 members of AFRICOBRA II, in media which range from woven hangings, to clothing design, to paintings. It is an Angry Exhibit—a bit too Angry. Artwork scream out their messages: Unite! Freedom! Revolution, "Resist," Control of Our Land is the Key to political Power. They were not content to paint subjects only—to let the artwork carry the statements—each artist has added his own personal form of calligraphy, letting the angry words become a part of the painting or silk screen, or tapestry like a poster.[15]

To understand the aesthetic principles of AFRICOBRA, letters and words were important components of our philosophical constructs, and we labeled the art poster art. In addition, to understand the era of the Black revolution and the Black aesthetic, words and statements in AFRICOBRA's works were an implicitly germane conduit for disseminating our messages to African people. Those words and statements on our art were as important and served the same purpose as the drum—to deliver the word, secrets, to Africans, and later to African slaves in America.

Willig continued:

> What is beautiful about the exhibit is a sense of people, beautiful people, full of life and vigor. But it is not praise to humanity[,] it is a pageant to black humanity only. If these paintings are meant to turn blacks on, they are equally intended to turn whites off. "Revolutionary" (Angela) by Wadsworth Jarrell is a portrait of a young black woman screaming slogans—with a bandolier with real bullets slung over her shoulder. Jarrell's painting is an over-statement. It is not art as the weapon. It is the weapon as art.[16]

Willig also addressed beauty that she saw in the work: "If the viewer could remove himself from the barrage of slogans in the paintings, some beautiful things are happening. For example, Barbara Jones's silkscreen prints maximized the Egyptian–African curves and mystery of a black woman's face. It is a beguiling and sensuous beauty, too long ignored."[17]

The critic's comments about the beauty of Black women are interesting on analysis. Dark women worldwide—in Africa, the Americas, including the

United States—are the embodiment of standard beauty: shapely hips and beautiful skin with full mouth. But by European standards, dark women's beauty is categorized as exotic, and only women with fair skin are the standard for their concept of beauty.

Willig's review critiqued works of individual artists: "Nelson Stevens' paintings resemble stained glass and he achieved a unique sensitivity for portraits so large. Jeff Donaldson is the talented one in the collective[;] his paintings could be considered illustrations. [In] his painting *Victory in the Valley of Eshu*, the background mysteriously works to create what might be halos around the heads of the dignified, unified elderly couple that are most certainly not figments of the artist's imagination."[18]

Willig described the exhibition as an "attempt at the creation of an artistic black identity," and she said that it is the genesis of a separatist movement for "Black Aesthetics" to be enjoyed by blacks only. In addition, she said that AFRICOBRA's pursuit of creating a Black aesthetic was a result of being rejected by white artistic establishments, namely, museums and galleries.

On the contrary, in 1972, AFRICOBRA had refused invitations to exhibit in mainstream museums, including the request from curator Brownstone to exhibit at the Musee d'Art Moderne de la Ville de Paris, and one at a museum in Germany. Edward Spriggs had traveled to Europe with a congregation of museum directors from the United States, and he took with him examples of works of African American artists. According to Spriggs, when he showed examples of AFRICOBRA's work, that motivated Brownstone and a curator of a museum in Germany to extend invitations to exhibit our collective.

Additionally, years before the inception of AFRICOBRA, in Chicago and surrounding areas, some members of AFRICOBRA, Barbara, Jeff, Jae, and I, individually achieved recognition in mainstream galleries and museums, to cite a few: Main Street Gallery, the School of the Art Institute's Biennial Watercolor and Print Show, Allan Fumpkins Gallery, the Chicago Show, the Union League Show, the Chicago Fine Art Gallery, and Lakeside Gallery. Our work was also the subject of critical analysis from local newspapers and magazines. Jae's designs were featured in her debut show, *Fashion Safari*, in 1963; in several seasonal shows at Jae of Hyde Park; in numerous newspaper and major magazine articles; and in a commission by Sunbeam Corporation to design a garment representative of Lady Sunbeam hair dryer. That garment was exhibited in the 1963 National Ebony Fashion Fair.

10

AFRICOBRA III

Bright color is an enduring element found in all forms of African art dating back to the ancient Egyptian murals that after thousands of years of interment still incredibly retain their brightness. Whether or not AFRICOBRA's colors will last that long is a question for the future. What is certain now is with their construction of an Afrocentric aesthetic AFRICOBRA has built a school of art no less significant and instructive than the temples of Egypt. —Nubia Kai, *AFRICOBRA: The First Twenty Years*

In May 1972, AFRICOBRA called a meeting in Washington, DC, to induct a new member, Frank Smith, into the collective. The meeting held at Howard University consisted of AFRICOBRA members residing in Washington: Jeff, Jae, and me. Our work was displayed on walls of the meeting room to point out specifics that would help Frank understand our philosophy. Chicago is Frank's hometown, where he was born into an artistic family of music and visual art. Chicago was always known for its intensely organized hard-nosed politics, and he lived there active as an artist at the dawn of the sixties. Margaret Burroughs's political stance and involvement had been instrumental in helping establish the South Side Community Art Center in the thirties. Frank said that in the forties, as a child, he regularly visited the South Side Community Art Center, where his parents were involved, and he remained actively involved there as an adult artist. Immersing himself in Chicago's artistic community and witnessing the civil rights struggle there enabled Frank's seamless transition into a collective of artists whose base was originally Chicago, and whose agenda was political.

Works were randomly chosen for discussion. One of Frank's paintings was collaged with aluminum foil, which caused another discussion about methods. We were fascinated with what he said: "I used foil as a color and as a source of bringing light into my painting." His application of foil was immediately co-opted into our philosophy, complementing the AFRICOBRA principle shine.

Jeff chose my painting in progress *Liberation Soldiers* for critique, and pointed out methods of approach. "For an example, check out Jarrell's painting. It starts a distance before he reaches the canvas, and when he hits it, the colors and words explode upon the canvas."

Frank waved his hand toward the painting. "It looks like he took a single color and extended it all the way across the canvas."

Jeff laughed. "Yeah, it looks that way, but he didn't do that because that is impossible to do without knowing how other added colors will react."

"Jeff's right," I responded. "That would be complicated to take a color and run it from end to end on a painting. As a matter of fact, all of my paintings start out as a layout indicating shapes and colors. Some colors I go back into the painting to intensify, and some shapes may change, but the foundational blueprint is there from the beginning."

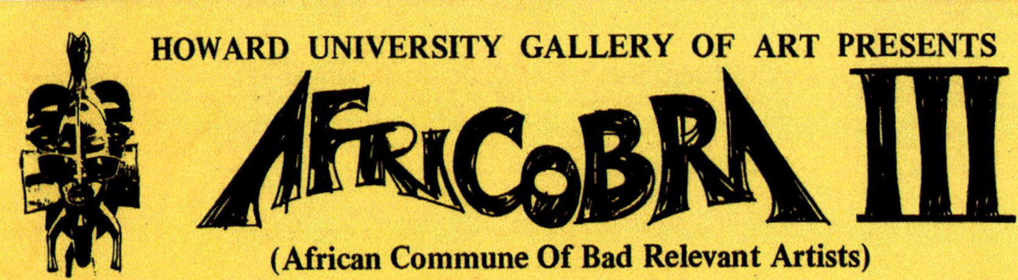

Jae presented two garments in progress, *Gent's Great Coat* and *Dahomey Spirit Ensemble*. She explained how she began a work. "I start a garment the same way as Jarrell does a painting, by laying out the entire garment. In that way I know where every appliqué, image, gusset, and seam goes."

Jeff's painting in progress *God Bless the Child That's Got His Own* was discussed. He pointed to the bandoliers on the two images. "AFRICOBRA is about revolutionary art and not about presenting statements that's passive, revengeful, or about wait until next time. We are about this time in this revolution. The philosophy is basically set because we are not planning to add any more principles right now. We will work with what we already have in place."[1]

The conversation returned to the aluminum foil collaged on Frank's painting. Frank advised what adhesive was appropriate to keep it permanently in place. He told us that it would have to be an adhesive other than acrylic medium gel or varnish, because a water-based medium was not sufficient to hold it in place. Although in 1970, Napoleon was first to use aluminum foil on his tapestry *Cool Ade Icicles*, Frank's painting put the use of the foil in perspective for painters.

In April 1973, Jeff scheduled the AFRICOBRA III exhibition to open at Howard University Gallery of Art so that it would coincide with the National Conference of Artists (NCA), who had chosen Washington, DC, for the site of their annual meeting. Howard University was the central meeting place for the NCA's lectures and art workshops. It was a perfect situation for the exhibition, because in the conference attendees we had an audience of artists and historians from across the country.

On April 4, 1973, a day before the exhibition opened, AFRICOBRA conducted a meeting. We sat on benches in front of the College of Fine Arts. Those AFRICOBRA members present were Jeff, Barbara Jones (now Jones-Hogu), Napoleon Henderson (now Napoleon Jones-Henderson), Jae Jarrell, Carolyn Lawrence, Howard Mallory, Frank Smith, Nelson Stevens, Gerald Williams, and me.

The meeting opened with a discussion of the current exhibition and its itinerary. Nelson was concerned about our new member, Frank Smith. He said, "I don't have any objections of this brother being a member of AFRICOBRA, but it is the first time I heard anything about Frank Smith being a member. I think that at least I or we should have been consulted."

"You are right," Jeff replied. "It's my fault. I should have informed everybody. Frank's a good artist and a good brother. When you get to know him, I'm certain you will agree. I'm sure he will work out fine."

The art critic Paul Richard from the *Washington Post* accepted Jae's invitation to review the AFRICOBRA exhibition for the second time. The heading of his article read, "Black Art, Politics, Messages." In his review, Richard wrote: "Art, art history, art gallery, critic and collector—the words themselves imply a kind of segregation. Art it sometimes seems is manufactured for the few, for the sophisticates, for the connoisseurs, for those with leisure, cash and education. If you're poor and black forget it. Art is not for everyone; art's for the elite. The artists of AFRICOBRA are not willing to accept that. They are aiming at an art that is accessible to everyone, particularly blacks."[2]

Richard had read Jeff's essay in *Black World* magazine, in which he had declared, "AFRICOBRA is creating images that relate to Black People and one that they can relate to. Color color color that shines, color that is free of rules and regulations—color that is expressively awesome. Color that defines, identifies, and directs."[3] Richard's article continued:

> Their shared ideology is everywhere apparent. Their art is filled with messages, with raised-fist rhetoric and slogans. In almost every work they celebrate with pride and ardor the beauty they see in blackness. It is not their imagery that moves me, perhaps because I'm white. I receive their messages at something of a distance, but one need not be black to see the beauty of these pictures. That beauty is uncanny.
>
> Three AFRICOBRA artists—Jeff Donaldson, who heads Howard's art department, Wadsworth Jarrell, who teaches there, and Nelson Stevens, who lives in Massachusetts—together contradict something I have long believed: that art that is so blatantly political is not art at all. Donaldson's pictures, and others in this show, despite the half-familiar black pride images they offer, are painted with such conviction, such pleasure and such skill that they manage to escape the deadly look of propaganda.[4]

AFRICOBRA never used the word "propaganda" to describe our purpose, but we did use the power of images and words to help disseminate our philosophy of art for the people—which included, basically, Black communities—and the idea of creating a new visual language. Our goal was for the art of AFRICOBRA to encompass an aesthetic that was not rooted in a dishonest political structure but that overwhelmingly affected the lives of all Black people. Richard did not say that our art was propaganda art; he said that ours managed to escape it, with images "painted with such conviction, such pleasure and such skill," but reading between the lines, and by his description of the art with raised fists and rhetorical slogans, I would argue that there are implications. By his praise, Richard was clearly impressed with the art. His article continued:

> Look, for instance, at *"Oneness"* by Nelson Stevens. It is not that noble couple that gives this work its power. What is remarkable about this picture is the way it is drawn. Stevens has given us not just an inspirational image, but a colored penciled surface on which the eye can graze for hours.
>
> Donaldson's African freedom fighter merges with the black map of Africa that he carries as a shield. It is not the message of the picture, but at least for me, the way it has been painted, the use of broken color and of gleaming gold, that makes that warrior seem so god-like.
>
> Wadsworth Jarrell's "Together We Will Win" shows us not just black warriors and black workers and black mothers and black children, but a picture that simultaneously brings to mind Western portraiture, African carvings and the shimmering mosaics of religious art. His images are built of countless Bs—for Black, for Bad, for Beautiful. His figures are hewn from color as a carving is hewn from wood. These Bs are facets and they organize themselves to form not just the heroes he portrays but the glowing auras that surround them. His painting is at once solid and ethereal. It is beautiful as well.[5]

In his description of the painting *Together We Will Win*, the art critic returned to his former description of the painting *Revolutionary* in assuming the meaning of the *Bs* that the form is constructed of. This was an art critic's concept, not mine.

The exhibition opened on a Friday at 7 P.M. On view were AFRICOBRA works replete with experimental materials and procedures, including the newly adopted method of using aluminum and gold foil. For some AFRICOBRA members, especially those living in Washington, DC, the AFRICOBRA philosophy had expanded to embrace aesthetics and influences of the South Pacific and several African countries. In 1993, artist, educator, and scholar

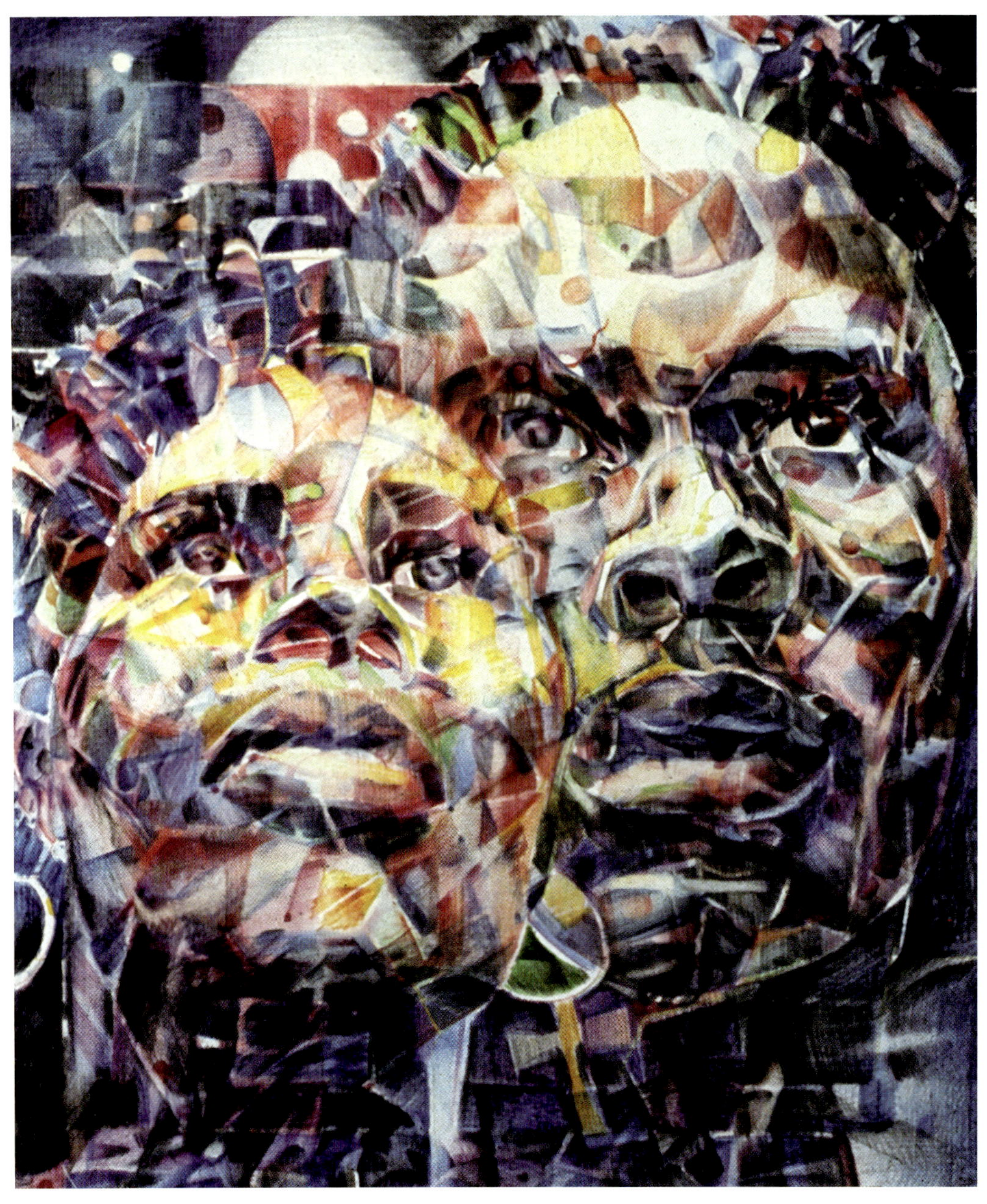

Nelson Stevens, *Oneness*, 1972. Color pencil on paper, 48 × 48 inches. Collection of Ed Mazer.

Robert L. Douglas curated and wrote an essay for my solo exhibit *Edge Cutters*, in which he coined the term "multidominant cultural theory": "AFRICOBRA's pioneering experiments with an African based visual aesthetic have aided AFRICOBRA members in creating a *Multidominant Cultural Theory* born of an African aesthetic. Africa's significant expressive cultural forms are composed of multi-dominant elements. The multi-rhythmic music, the multi-movements of its dance, the multiple use of colors and/or patterns of its fabrics, as well as the colorful mixed media presentation of the intricately ornamented surface of African masks and sculpture, exhibit the African aesthetic of multidominant cultural elements."[6]

Works in the *AFRICOBRA III* exhibition were among the first for the artists to incorporate those influences from West, North, South, and East Africa and New Guinea. The African and Oceanic influences originated from in-depth cultural studies of African countries, the association with African cultural communities in Washington, DC, and some AFRICOBRA members' travel to African countries. Important also was study of aesthetics and woodcarvings made by people living in New Guinea along the banks of the Sepik River. History has attested that the people who inhabited that area were African descendants, namely Australian Aboriginal people, who came to New Guinea around 1500 BCE. The progenitor clearly reveals that Aboriginal art embodies African characteristics even though altered to incorporate their own culture. Compositionally and spiritually, AFRICOBRA's art has influential ideas inspired by African and New Guinea culture. Therefore, I would ague that AFRICOBRA could be looked at as a kind of a bridge between African, South Pacific, and Western culture. But our exploration into African culture did not rest with, and never intended to be mimicry of, African art. Our vision extended beyond their physical art to capture what Leopold Sedar Senghor described:

> Art itself is taken to be perishable, to be made again each time it disappears or it is destroyed. What is clung to is the spirit which makes art possible, and the African idea of this spirit is very different from the European idea. European art attempts to imitate nature, African art is concerned with reaching beyond and beneath nature, and itself become a part of *la force Vitale*. The artistic image is not intended to represent the thing itself, but, rather, the reality of the force the thing contains.[7]

That is precisely what the AFRICOBRA artists sought. Our interest and focus were on capturing the power and spirit, and grasping the precepts and attitudinal characteristics that so abundantly permeate African art. We concentrated on making those intangibles an AFRICOBRA brand by successfully incorporating them into our art. Achieving those slippery qualities requires keen intellect and extraordinary skills. Metaphorically, those intangibles were as elusive as dust or electronic waves in the air, and as difficult as catching lightning in a bottle. In viewing the work of AFRICOBRA artists, I would argue that this feat was accomplished and was a large part of the success in establishing an African American aesthetic.

Barbara Jones-Hogu exhibited three serigraphs: *Black Men We Need You, Rise and Take Control*, and *When Styling*. The print *Black Men We Need You* depicts a Black man holding a baby in his arms, with an older child standing nearby. Written on the print is the statement, "Black Men Preserve Our Race, Leave White Bitches Alone." The color white was applied only as specificity, to emphasize and identify the antagonist that she describes as "white bitches."

Her print *When Styling* shows a couple dancing. The male dancer is wearing bellbottom trousers and platform shoes, denoting the style at that time. Circling the couple are irregular shapes and words: "When Styling, Think of Self-Determination—Liberation." Once again, Barbara's concern is about purity of race. She states it boldly and unapologetically. With this print, she appropriated her creative vision, which transcended race, by producing a master work of art—a calque of the German word Meisterstück.

Nelson Stevens's statement in the catalog for AFRICOBRA III read:

As a Black image maker, it seems to me that my work cannot be about the sterility of the red, white and blue life-style but rather about exploring alternatives. I am dealing with the cool and casual rhythms in us. Like the rhythms we walk when we believe the ground we walk on belongs to us . . . and cool like the posture we strike when we are letting a sister know our point of view on a matter of primary importance. Sometimes I deal with the hot screams of the sweet thunder and the fire sirens, which cause us to explode . . . but always with rhythm. Like we be doin'.[8]

Nelson displayed four paintings: *Together, Uhuru, Oneness*, and *After She Removed Her Street Disguise*. His painting *Together* is an extraordinary work of art by a remarkable artist that not only presaged a new direction in art, but embodied visionary constructs of conceptualization. The painting is composed of a large male head Nelson said is looking east, conjoined in unison with an equally adept rendition of a female head that he said is looking west. This painting conforms to the AFRICOBRA principle mimesis at midpoint.

In the painting *After She Removed Her Street Disguise*, Nelson abandoned his signature large head portrait format for an elegant full figurative portrayal of a nude woman. The painting is rendered in pastel and color pencils, displayed in sweeping delicate lines and planes. Nelson evocatively captures an intimate moment of an African American woman seen in her beautiful Black nudeness.

In Gerald Williams's artist's statement, he said: "Before becoming a part of AFRICOBRA, I was interested in creating landscapes, still lifes, and abstractions. But in light of growth in our people's position in the world, and challenges that we were involved in, doing landscapes and abstractions seemed too ridiculous. Painting became a meaningless activity."[9]

Gerald displayed two paintings, entitled *Live for the Life* and *Angela*. *Live for the Life* is a larger-than-life portrait of an African American man with a wide nose, full mouth, and expressive eyes. The image is juxtaposed over a dark orange background, and at the bottom is written "Live." On the head of the man is a circular shape resembling a crown, composed of colored squares, rectangles, lines, and black oval shapes, rimmed in the colors yellow and blue. The shapes are reminiscence of a Batcham mask of Cameroon.

The painting *Angela* is a large-scale painting of Angela Davis, captured in the moment of one of her fiery speeches. The painting includes only her head rendered in basically one flat color and cropped at the top. Her afro-styled hair is structured with vibrant Cool Ade color circles, semicircles, crescent lines, letters, ankhs, and programmed shapes resembling skeleton keys. Extending from her 'fro and beyond are the words "Unite," repeated twice, and "Don't Be Jiving." This painting is remarkable and dramatically, skillfully composed. It reveals the artist's vision and sense of seizing the time.

Jae Jarrell said that she came from a bloodline of tailors, and her inspiration and influences were her grandfather Robert S. Koiner; her mother, Adleyn Koiner Johnson; her aunt Alice Koiner Wilson; and her sister Carol Johnson King. They all were highly competent in clothing construction and creative fashion design. Jae wrote in her artist's statement: "Preservation of

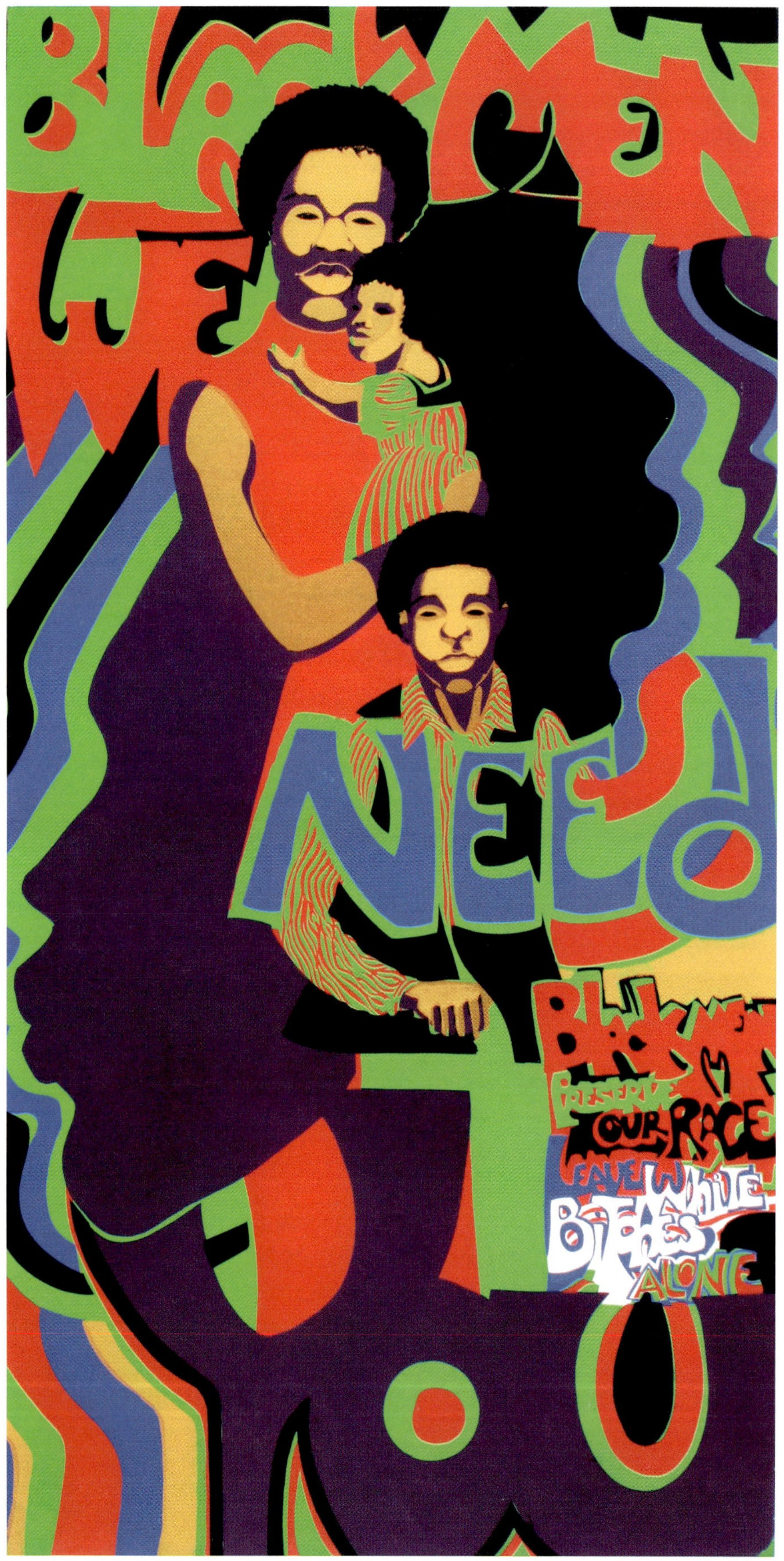

10.3

Barbara Jones-Hogu, *Black Men We Need You*, 1971. Silkscreen on paper, 28 × 38 inches. Collection of Jae and Wadsworth Jarrell.

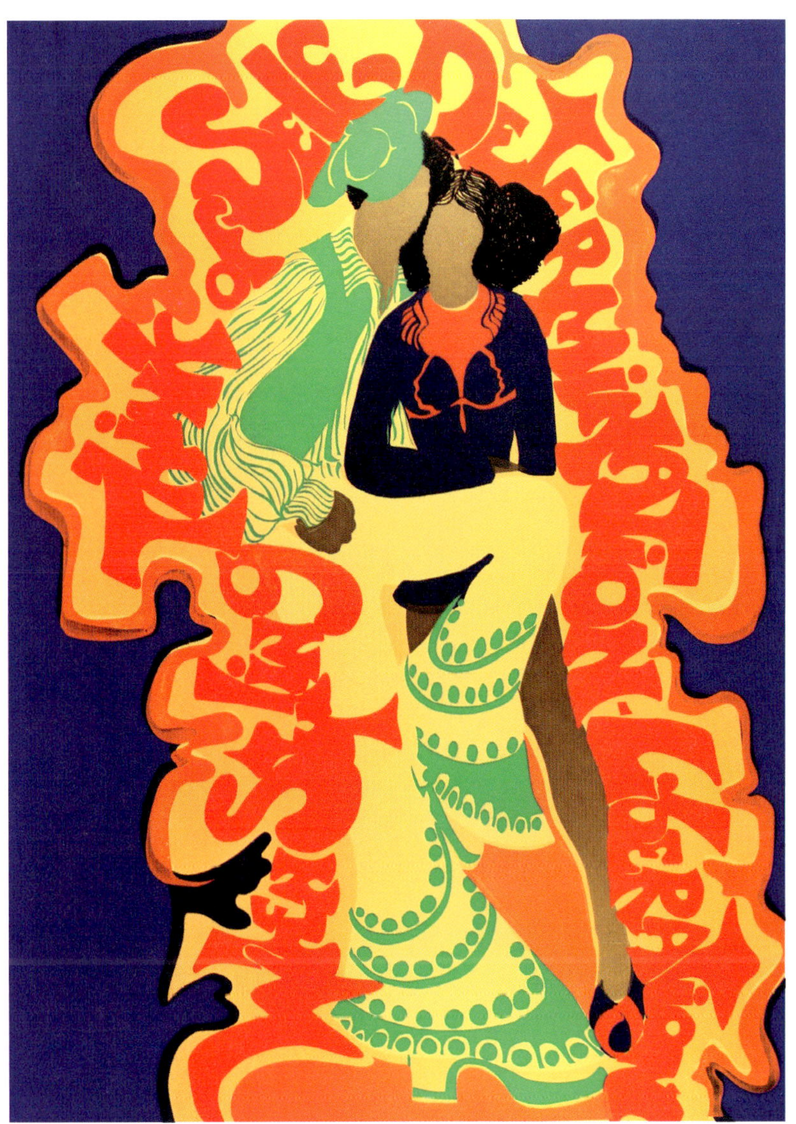

Barbara Jones-Hogu, *When Styling*, 1971. Silkscreen on paper, 22 × 30 inches. Collection of David Lusenhop.

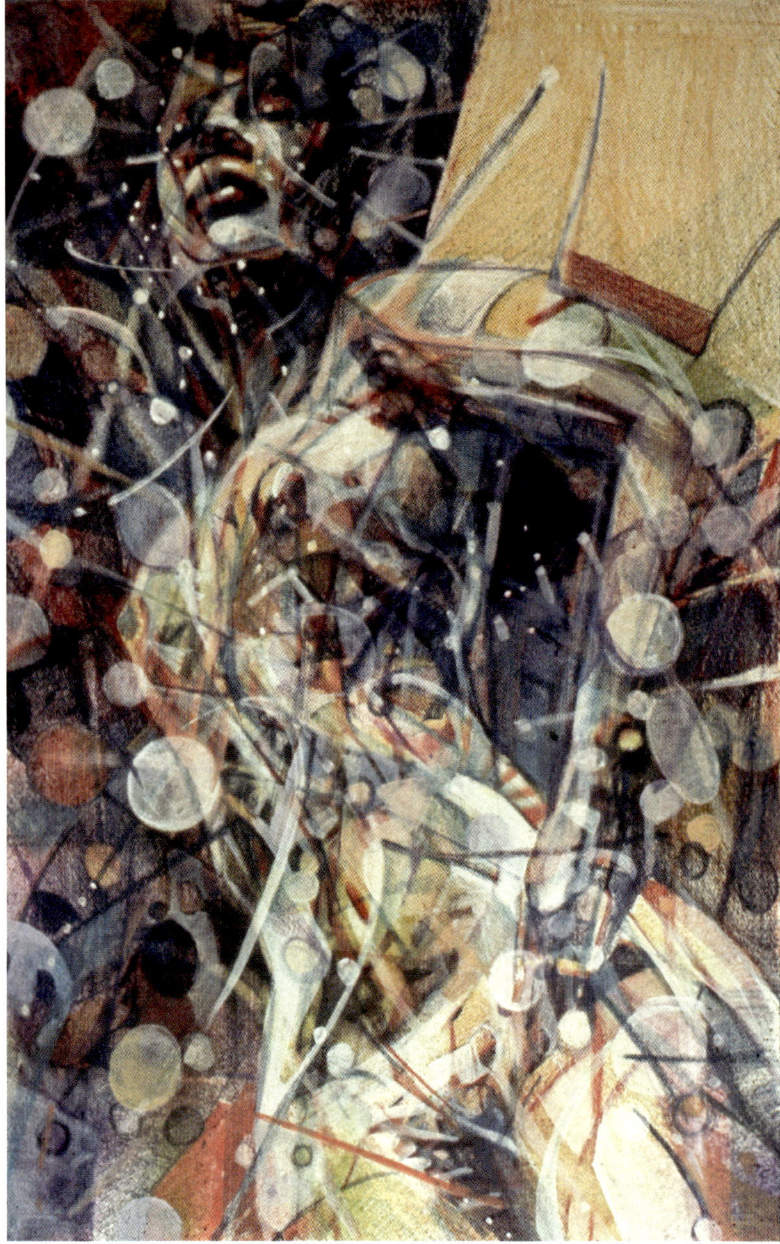

Nelson Stevens, *After She Removed Her Street Disguise*, 1973. Color pencil on paper, 24 × 36 inches. Collection of Betty Webb.

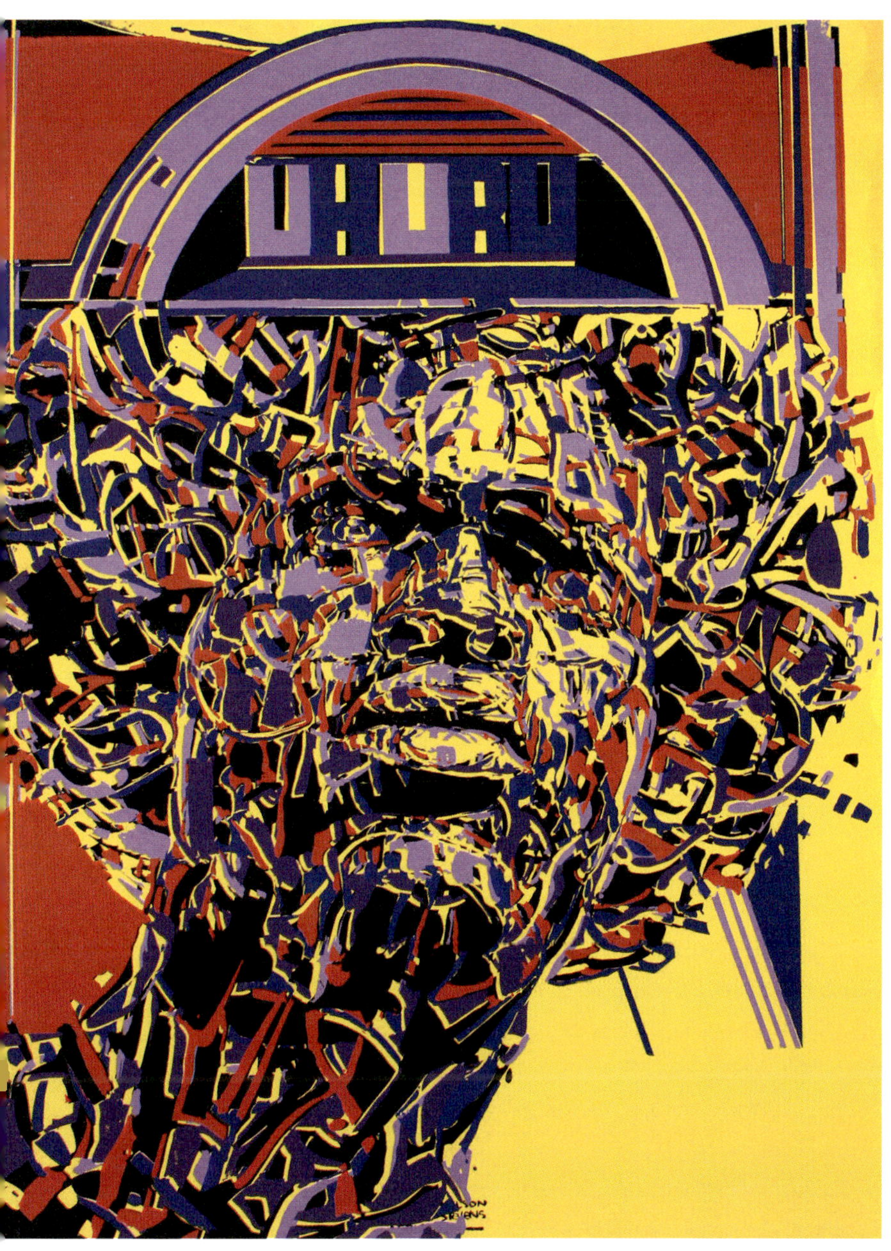

10.6

Nelson Stevens, *Uhuru*, 1971. Acrylic on canvas, 48 × 48 inches. Collection of Max Roach.

our heritage motivates me to design for my sisters and brothers' adornment that reflects out beautiful culture."[10]

She displayed four designs, *Gent's Great Coat*, *Dahomey Spirit Ensemble*, *Woman's Great Coat*, and *Coat for Little Fella*. The design *Gent's Great Coat* made a bright, bold statement in fashion design. The coat was constructed of outside seams, bell sleeves, and ribbons of colored leather that she cut into zigzag strips and woven into the collarless coat. Jae's designs are inspired by African fashions with elaborate embroidery and other intricate emblazonry on collarless V-neck garments. The coat has large patch pockets and a zip-up front, with a shockingly colored patterned lining that serves as a foil against the stark black suede coat.

Jae said that her *Dahomey Spirit Ensemble* was influenced by Dahomey mudcloth prints. The green suede jacket is appliquéd in leather geometric shapes, which repeat in the full-length skirt. Here, she unfurls her harbinger abstract vocabulary in fashion design, with repeated designs, completing a beautiful and creative composition that is revolutionary in concept—*novus extraordinarius*.

Jeff Donaldson's statement for the AFRICOBRA III catalog was his essay written in 1970 for *Black World* magazine. It read in part:

> We are a family—COBRA, the Coalition of Black Revolutionary Artists, is now AFRICOBRA—African Commune of Bad Relevant Artists. It's NATION TIME and we are searching.
>
> Our guidelines are our people—the whole family of African People, the African family tree. And in this spirit of familyhood, we have carefully examined our roots and searched our branches for those visual qualities that are most expressive of our people/art. Our people are our standard for excellence.[11]

Jeff contributed three paintings to AFRICOBRA III: *African Liberation Day*, *In The Blooming Time*, and *God Bless the Child That's Got His Own*. *African Liberation Day* shows a warrior wearing sunglasses and gripping an automatic weapon. The lower part of the warrior's face is hidden by a map of Africa, rimmed in gold. Written in circular shapes around the warrior's head are names of African liberation leaders: Cabral, Mondlane, Nkrumah, and Lumumba. Also written on the painting is "African Liberation Day," connoting the first Pan-African conference held in 1958 on African soil, in the city of

Accra, Ghana. But more specifically, it addresses the mass demonstration held in Washington, DC, on September 19, 1981, with 260,000 people in attendance, in solidarity with the African revolution.

Jeff's painting *God Bless the Child That's Got His Own* is an art clinic in draftsmanship. It shows two well-developed muscular African American males face to face, arms folded, with bandoliers of realistically rendered bullets slung over the shoulders of each warrior. One of the men is a corporal in the US military, and the other male is dressed in street wear, representing the people's warrior. The phrase "God Bless the Child That's Got His Own" was taken from a Billie Holiday refrain, but in this case, the men possess necessary ammunition and weaponry for self-defense and conquest.

Napoleon wrote an artist statement for the AFRICOBRA III catalog that read in part: "We must be about the business of expressing what is 'Beautiful,' ourselves. I am not the 'CREATOR,' but the instrument, endowed with his knowledge of harmonious interlocking."[12] He exhibited two tapestries, *To Be Free* and *A Word from the Prophet Stevie*. Both works are exceptional—each a *magnum opus*. His tapestry *To Be Free* is composed of words circling an image of the head of an African American. Written across the top are the letters TCB (taking care of business), and written in the forehead are the words "To be free." Napoleon's weaving is a tribute to Barbara Jones-Hogu's serigraph *To Be Free*. As a replica of an original idea, the work loses some inventiveness. The weaving also includes Barbara's signature cartoon-font-style lettering and her colors.

The tapestry *A Word from the Prophet Stevie* is an intricate design of words and images. The picture plane is broken up with an amalgam of shapes, colors, stripes, and rows of linked images, seemingly representing stars and stripes in a flag. On one side is a stylized image symbolizing the magnificent mask *Sacrosanct Kingdom of Benin* from the sixteenth century. Across the top of the tapestry is written "In God We Trust? All Men Are Equal." Included is a line from a Stevie Wonder song, "If you want to hear our view, you ain't done nothing."

In Carolyn Lawrence's statement for the AFRICOBRA III catalog, she said:

Presently I am interested in the relationship of our Black children to the Movement as they participate in it. I feel it is very important that children be allowed to develop as children, but that Black youngsters

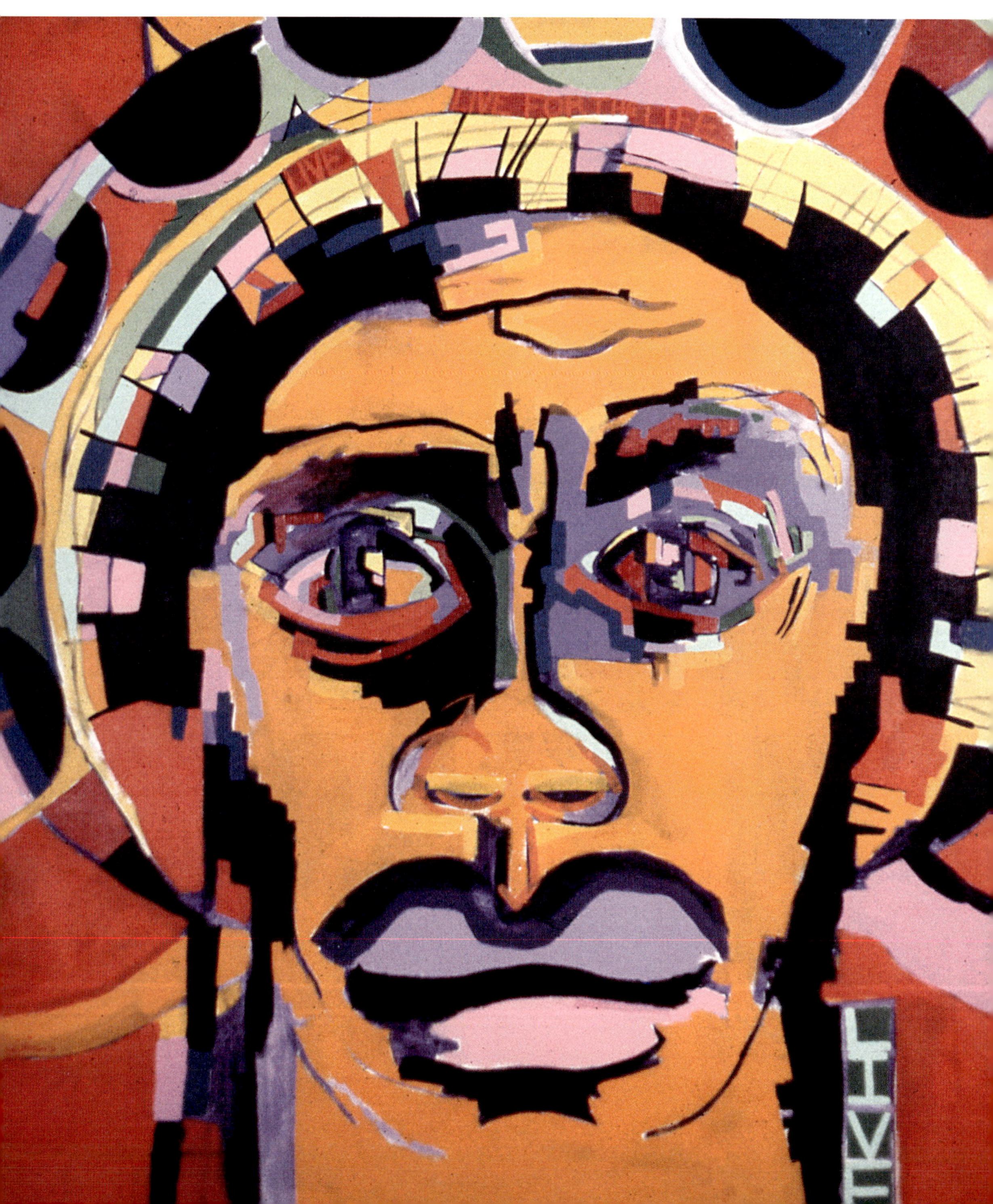

10.7

Gerald Williams, *Live for the Life*, n.d. Acrylic on canvas, 48 × 48 inches. Collection of the artist.

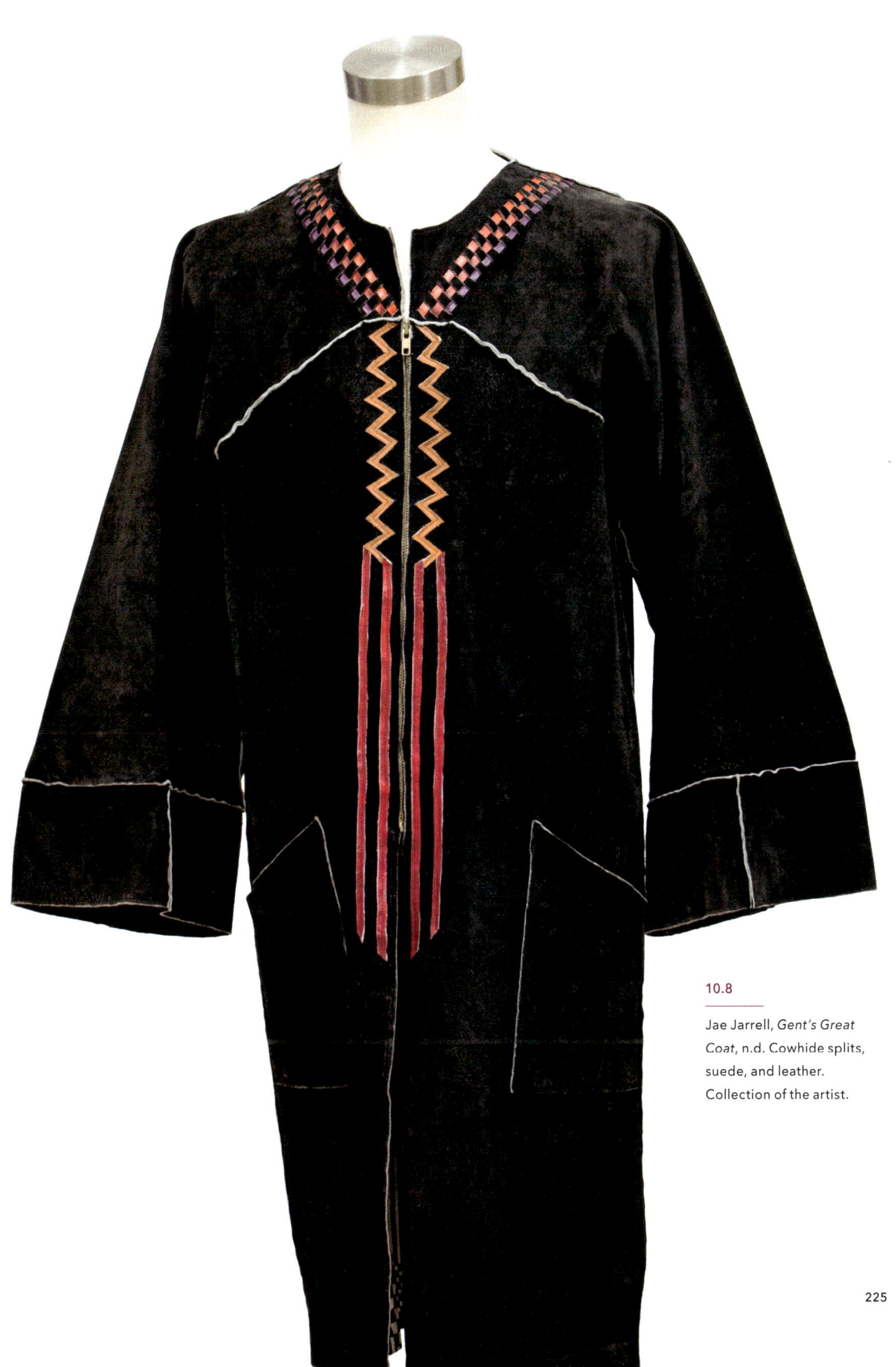

10.8

Jae Jarrell, *Gent's Great Coat*, n.d. Cowhide splits, suede, and leather. Collection of the artist.

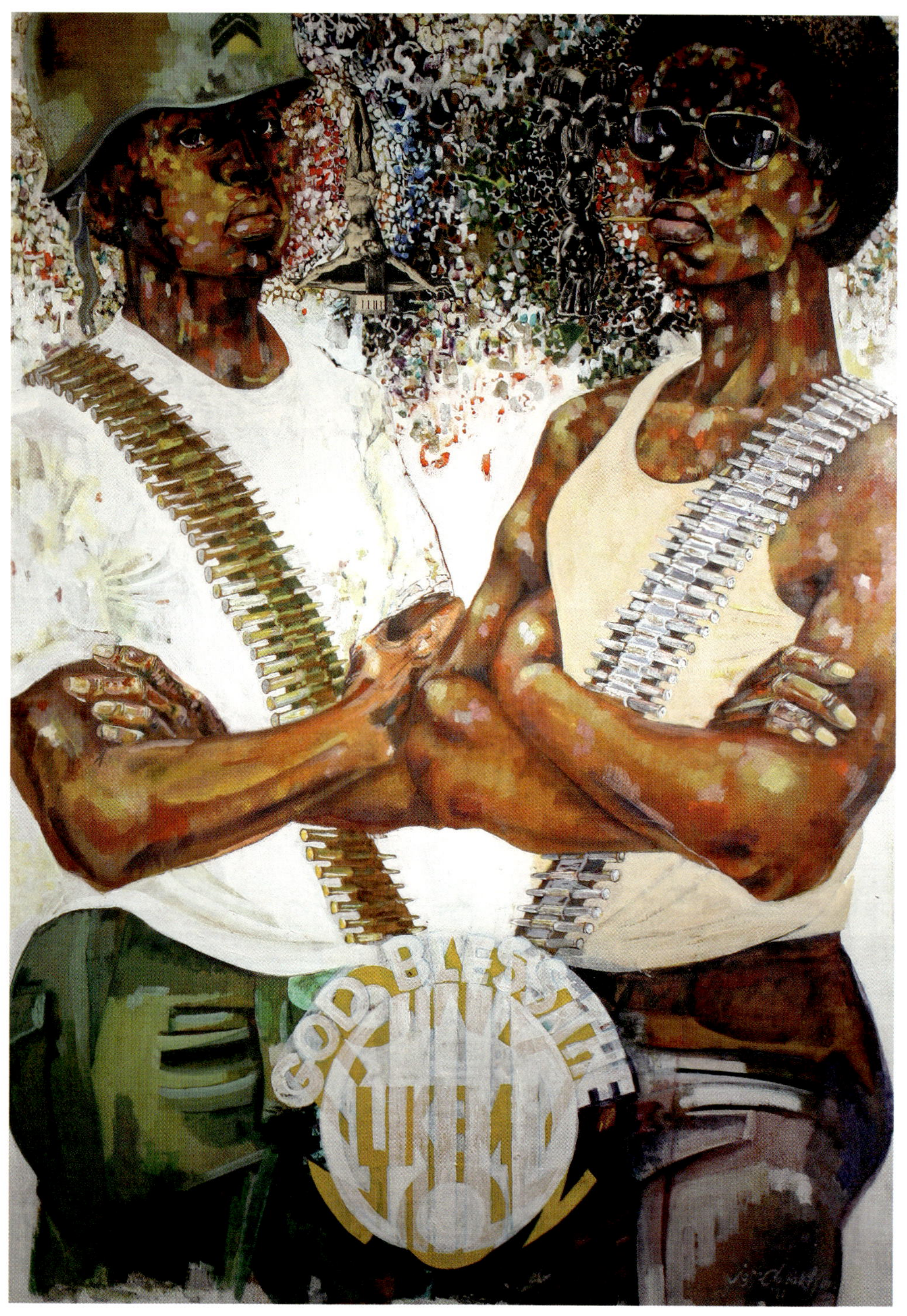
GOD BLESS

Jeff Donaldson, *God Bless the Child That's Got His Own*, 1971. Gouache and acrylic on board, 36 × 25 inches. Collection of Mr. and Mrs. Michael and Christa Brinson.

10.10

Napoleon Jones-Henderson, *To Be Free*, 1970. Tapestry, 72 × 54 inches. Collection of the artist.

in particular must be made aware of their responsibility to retain their ethnic identity as well as their personhood as they strive for excellence in every way. It is our responsibility as adults to be sure that our young are not consumed in the struggle but that they are made stronger because they understand how they must function in a racist society.[13]

Carolyn exhibited two paintings, *Black Children Let Your Spirits Be Free* and *Legacy*. Her painting *Black Children Keep Your Spirits Free* is an excellent study in communal socialism. She includes the allegory of a ram's head atop the body of a man playing an accordion. Scattered in the background are gregarious children dancing. In addition, words are combined to emphasize the statement: "Keep Your Spirits Free."

Legacy is a portrait of a male child sitting affectionately on his mother's lap, against a background of bright linear colors containing a density approximating a rainforest. Here, Carolyn made use of AFRICOBRA's declaration of family unity and procedural principles in unique and inventive ways. This work is powerful, and it is making a powerful statement in an attempt to engage the African American community.

In my artist's statement for the AFRICOBRA III catalog, I wrote:

Through my years of experience and observation of people, I have found that African people are the forerunners, innovators, creators and the hip. African people are my motivation. So, in my art, I must reflect the attitude of my people—the colors, the style, the hip and the rhythm. My role is to make social imagery that intrudes upon the thoughts, and jar the senses of African people. My attempt is to produce Art that is as warm and awesome as the songs and prayers of Sunday Morning Baptist meetings . . . and Art that's getting into the color and sound of those prayers and songs.[14]

My two paintings were titled *Together We Will Win* and *Liberation Soldiers*. *Together We Will Win* is a quadriptych (a four-part painting) that is a tribute of solidarity to South Africans living in apartheid. On one panel are children representing future warriors-liberators. On two other panels are men armed with automatic weapons and architects and engineers viewing plans designated for future progress. The half-circle top panel shows a rooster crowing in front of a setting sun, representing the symbol on the flag of the political party UNITA (Uniao Nacional Para a Independencia Total de Angola, or National Union of the Total Independence of Angola). Written in Portuguese are three words: Patria (meaning homeland, or fatherland), Unidada (unity), and Liberdada, (freedom, or liberty). Although, the message in the painting is advocating freedom for the people of Angola, the painting itself and the methods and structure are still saturated with the AFRICOBRA principle relating to African American urban street wear—Cool Ade colors—together with aluminum and gold foil representing the principle shine.

Liberation Soldiers is imbued with African and Oceanic influences. It is a painting of the Black Panthers, depicting Huey P. Newton, Bobby Seale, and other Panther members in the background. They are dressed uniformly in blue turtleneck sweaters, berets, and black leather jackets. Newton is armed with a shotgun and a bandolier over his shoulder, and Seale is equipped with a sidearm holstered in a bullet belt. One side of the jackets worn by Newton and Seale are built up of impastos of paint and collaged on aluminum foil, with circles and scrolls of color reminiscent of art and culture in Papua, New Guinea. The Panthers bore arms in defiance of law enforcement, interrupting a city council meeting while bearing arms in protest of a proposed gun control law.

In Howard Mallory's statement for the catalog, he wrote: "I seek to do the best with my ability. I seek to be a positive force with Black people. I'm a spoke in the wheel, which grinds away at the oppressive forces that are against Black people. We are tied to each other and will be responsible for the suffering. Our responsibility is in giving personal direction toward total liberation. Malcolm said, 'By Any Means Necessary.' To me, this means—art, pen, gun, or labor of any kind."[15] Howard's two works in the exhibition were *Liberation (or Liberation Door)* and *From These Roots. Liberation* is a remarkable work constructed of clay in relief and mounted on a wood panel and a wood frame. The form of the work is in the shape of a key pointing in the direction of a lock. Howard wrote at the top of the construction "Liberation." On the art itself, he wrote, "Quit Shaking Your Fist. Quit Rapping. Do Something Now!" His statements refer to Black street poets and other pontificators speaking from podiums to a captive audience, saying that only rhetorical words be used as weapons of change.

Howard's *From These Roots* represents a change in medium. Instead of clay he chose cloth. He stitched together a figure in various colors, mostly red,

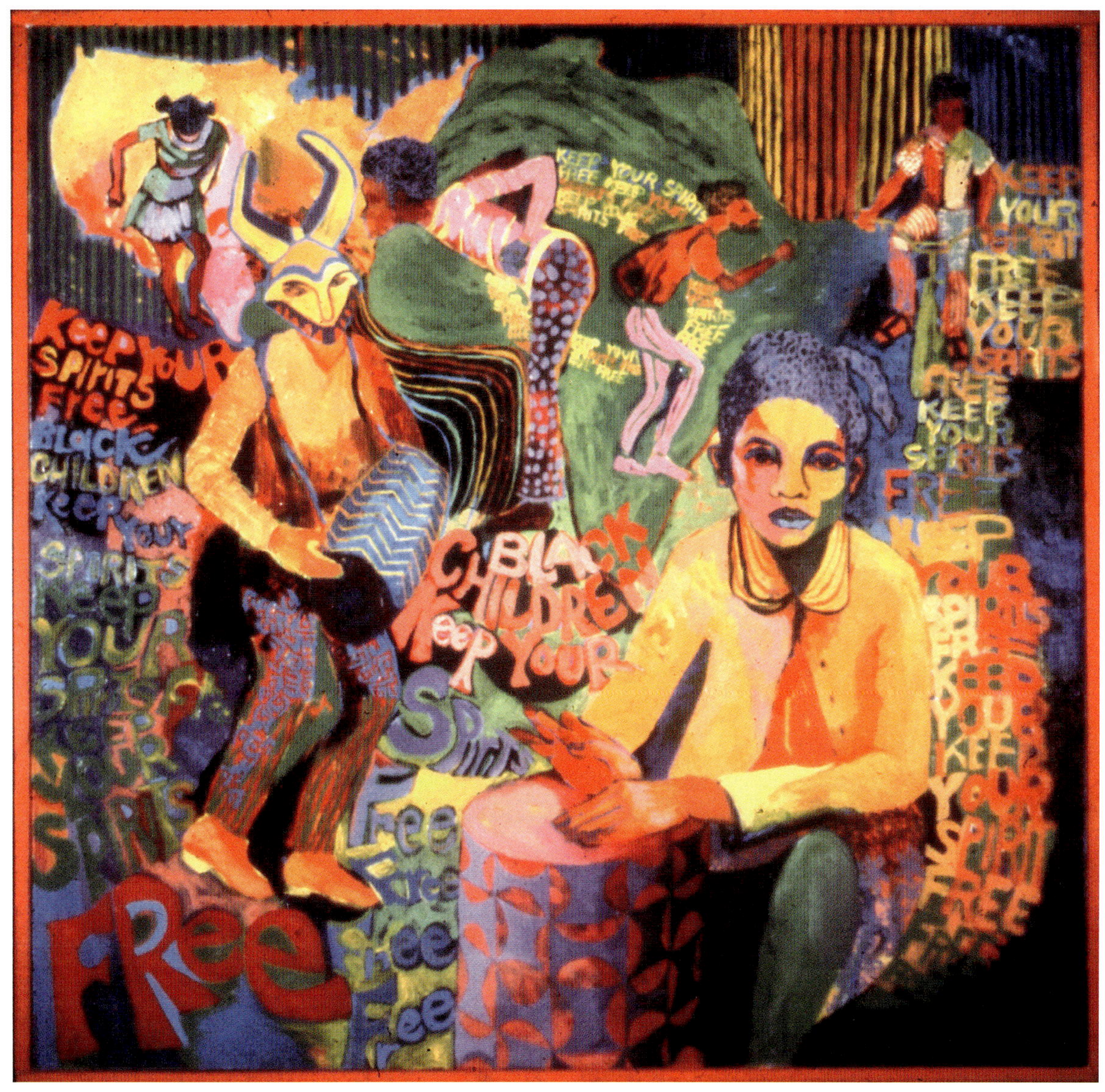

10.11

Carolyn Lawrence, *Black Children Keep Your Spirits Free*, 1972. Acrylic on canvas, 30 × 40 inches. Collection of the artist.

230

10.12

Carolyn Lawrence,
Legacy, 1973[?]. Acrylic
on canvas, 30 × 40 inches.
Collection of the artist.

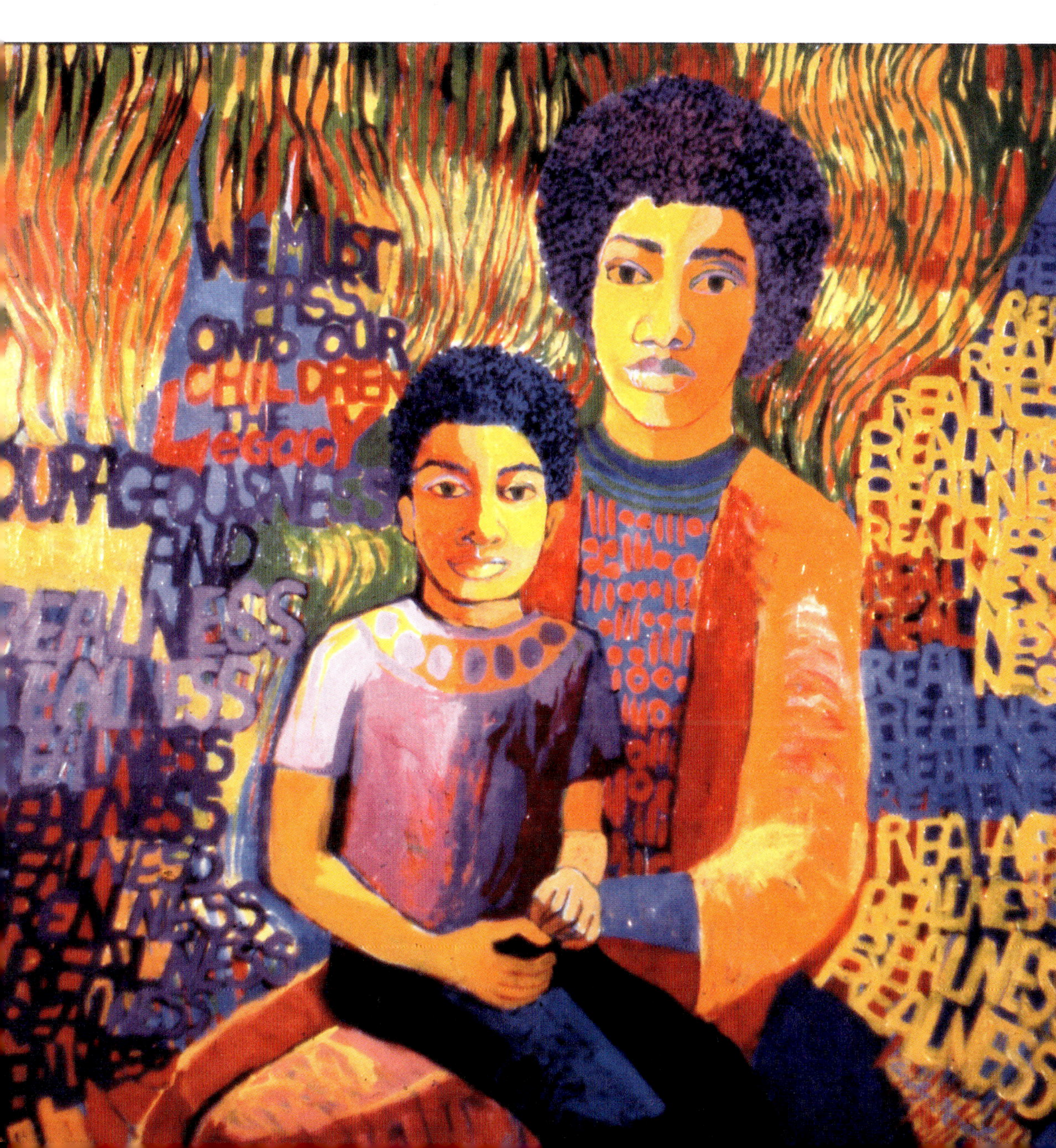
WE MUST
PASS
ONTO OUR
CHILDREN
THE
Legacy
OF
OURAGEOUSNESS
AND
REALNESS
REALNESS
REALNESS
REALNESS
REALNESS
REALNESS
REALNESS
REALNESS
REALNESS
REALNESS
REALNESS
REALNESS
REALNESS
REALNESS
REALNESS
REALNESS
REALNESS
REALNESS
REALNESS
REALNESS

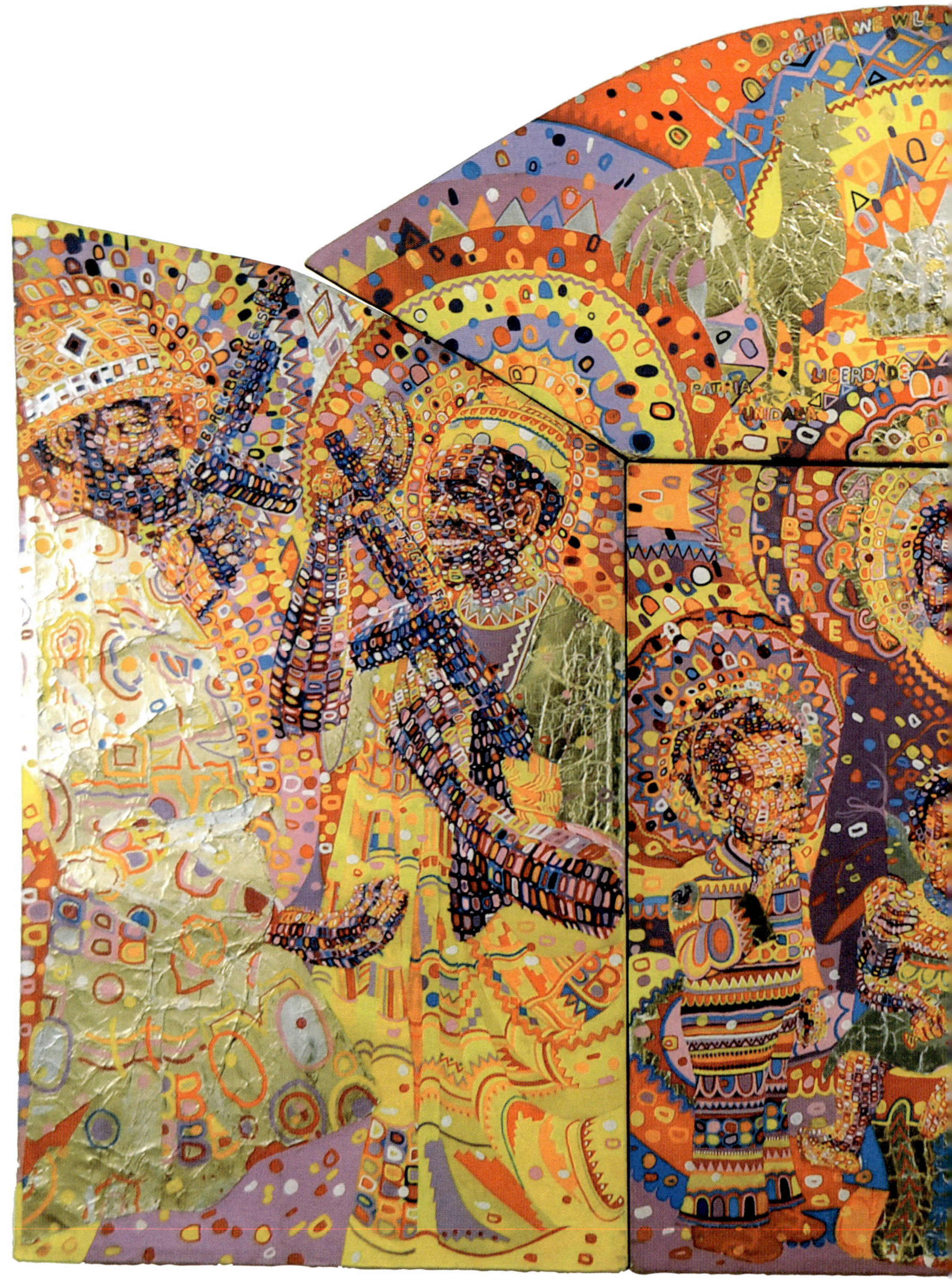
TOGETHER WE WILL
BLACK BROTHERS
PATRIA
UNIDAD
LIBERDADS
SOLIDERATE

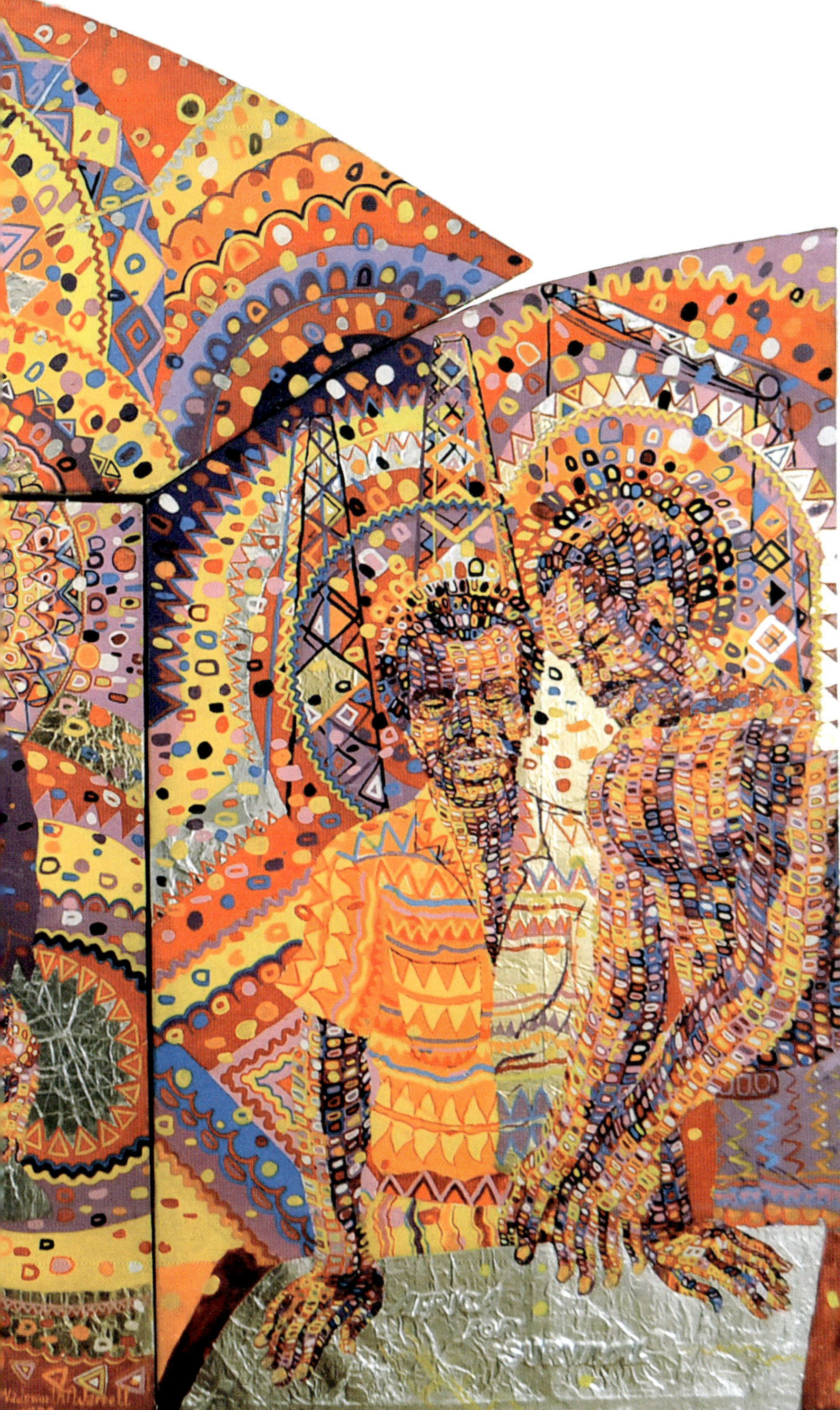

10.13

Wadsworth Jarrell, *Together We Will Win*, 1973. Acrylic and foil on canvas, 60 × 70 inches. Collection of the artist.

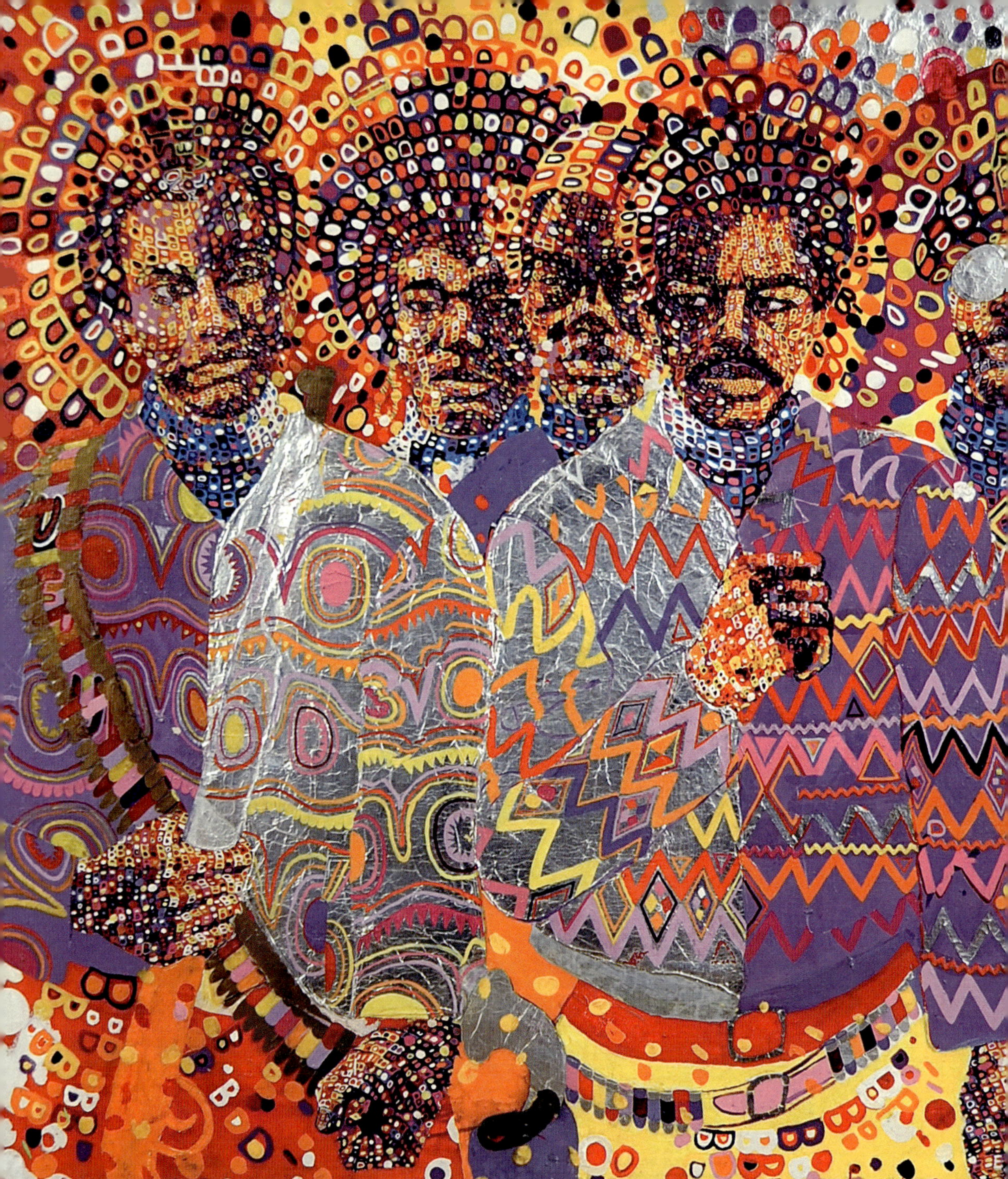

black, and green. In addition, it contains words and two symbols, an ankh and th Islamic symbol of a quarter moon and a star.

AFRICOBRA III was the first time Frank Smith exhibited with the collective. His work evolved toward understanding AFRICOBRA's philosophy. In his artist's statement for the catalog, he wrote:

> I think of my work the same as my teaching. Believing that image/ culture/education are functional instruments for reinforcing the values of the society that produces them and believing further that Africans in the diaspora should retain their social and cultural identity to Africa. I look home to Africa for sources of my work. The traditional symbols of African societies and the symbolic use of color are fundamental to each piece. In that sense, works are masculine or feminine, instructional or hymns of praise to those who have dedicated their lives to the cause of Pan-Africanism.[16]

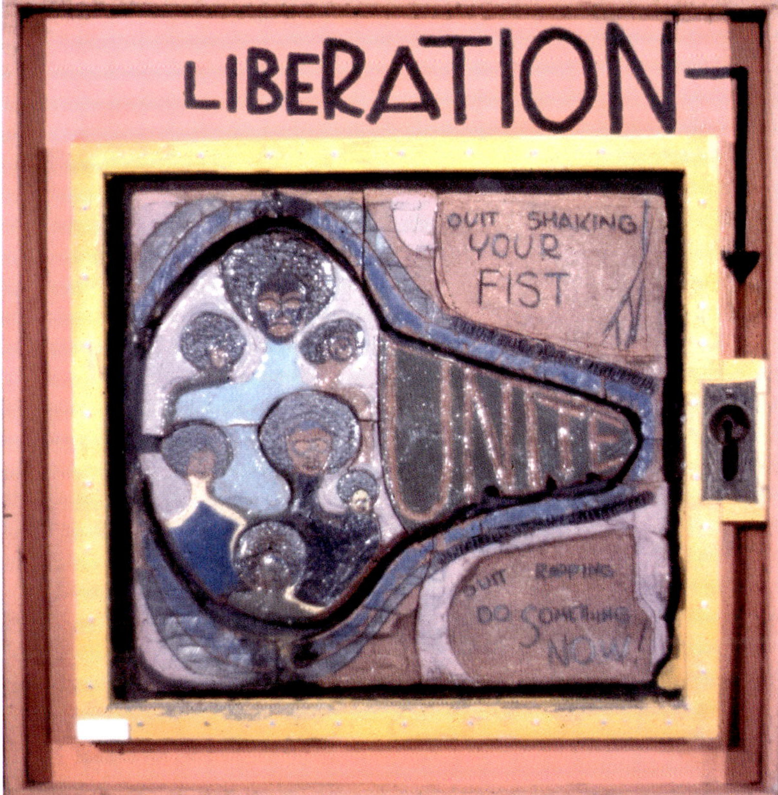

10.14

Wadsworth Jarrell,
Liberation Soldiers,
1973. Acrylic and foil on
canvas, 50 × 48 inches.
Collection of Mr. and
Mrs. John and Susan
Horseman.

10.15

Howard Mallory,
Liberation, 1971[?].
Ceramic on wood,
pictures and bro-
chures, 48 × 48 inches.
Collection of the artist.

He contributed three paintings, entitled *A Revolution Starts with One Black Family*, *The Profit*, and *Vanguard*. His painting *A Revolution Starts with One Black Family* shows a family of four: father, mother, and two children. The father and mother are seated, and the children (two boys) are standing. The painting is saturated with brilliant colors and restless brush strokes. Frank's painting is a straight line drawn between art and music, and it embraces the statement by Larry Neal: "AFRICOBRA present to us an iconography bestowed on them by the pressing and always exciting culture of the African American community."[17]

On September 7, 1973, *AFRICOBRA III* opened at the University Art Gallery at the University of Massachusetts at Amherst, and continued to September 30. Edward Spriggs wrote an essay for the catalog that was later published in the 1973 *Compton Yearbook*. Spriggs wrote:

> With AFRICOBRA we are witnessing a group of artists, in this era of "the Black Aesthetic," who from their perspective as Afro-Americans are attempting to identify style and rhythm qualities that are expressive of black people everywhere. Theirs is a Pan-African perspective. AFRICOBRA should be looked at more closely as an indication of the direction of black artists in the 1970s. The black artist of the '70s will move beyond the protest art of the '60s and renew the celebration and pageantry of our collective ethos. He will no longer need to avenge personal and collective suffering through art but will direct his energies to articulating the needs, spirituality, direction, and values that will liberate or reorient his own and the colonial mind. This is indeed a new epoch for black Americans.
>
> For many black artists it signals a time for reviving those "ancestral gifts" and "ancient skills" that Alain Locke referred to more than three decades ago. It is an age for moving beyond mere rage—it's Nation Time and black artists are searching. Black artists are immigrating into self, family, and nationhood—and celebrating the process.[18]

Barbara Jones-Hogu wrote an essay for the *AFRICOBRA III* catalog entitled "The History, Philosophy and Aesthetics of AFRICOBRA." She wrote:

> When we [AFRICOBRA] had found our common denominator[,] our next step was to ponder whether a group of Black artists could transcend

the "I" or "me" for the "us" and "we" in order to create a basic philosophy which would be the foundation of a visual Black Art Movement. We wanted to create a greater role as Black Artists who were not for self but for our kind. Could we sacrifice the wants for self and ego in order to create the visual needs of our kind? Yes, we can! In fact, AFRICOBRA can move toward stating and restating repeatedly the needs for organization, purpose, and goals of our people for a stronger cohesive body and the need for racial nationalism. AFRICOBRA will not only state our problems and solutions but also state our emotions, our joys, our love, our attitude, our character, our total emotional and intellectual responses and feelings. Art can be a liberating force—a positive approach concerning the plight and the direction of our people. Visual imagery should bring us together and uplift us as a people into a common—common unit, moving toward a common destination and a common destiny. We in AFRICOBRA shall help bring this about.[19]

This concludes the first five years, 1968 to 1973, of AFRICOBRA. Those were the formative years and the most significant ones, because in that period, the philosophy was constructed, during the pinnacle of the civil rights struggle and the Black power movement, when we created some of our most poignant art. That era of unrest influenced the timbre of events occurring in America, racially, politically, and economically. That era also precipitated the formation of African American artistic groups. This book essentially reports a portion of my experience as a founder of the African Commune of Bad Relevant Artists, affording opportunities for other members and art history scholars to write additional perspectives.

There are many years of exciting activities to write about, such as new members, meetings, national and international exhibitions, stylistic changes, and literally becoming an all-male collective after the resignations of all female members: Barbara and Carolyn left in 1975, and Jae in 1976.

AFRICOBRA extended beyond five years because I was a member for thirty years, from 1968 to 1998. Since then, I have moved on with my art, instituting other ideas and aesthetic stylistic changes that I consider important to my growth. The AFRICOBRA collective—a variety of mostly painters who subscribe to the standard Robert's Rules theory of voting—still exists at this writing, calling themselves AFRICOBRA Now. But they have moved away

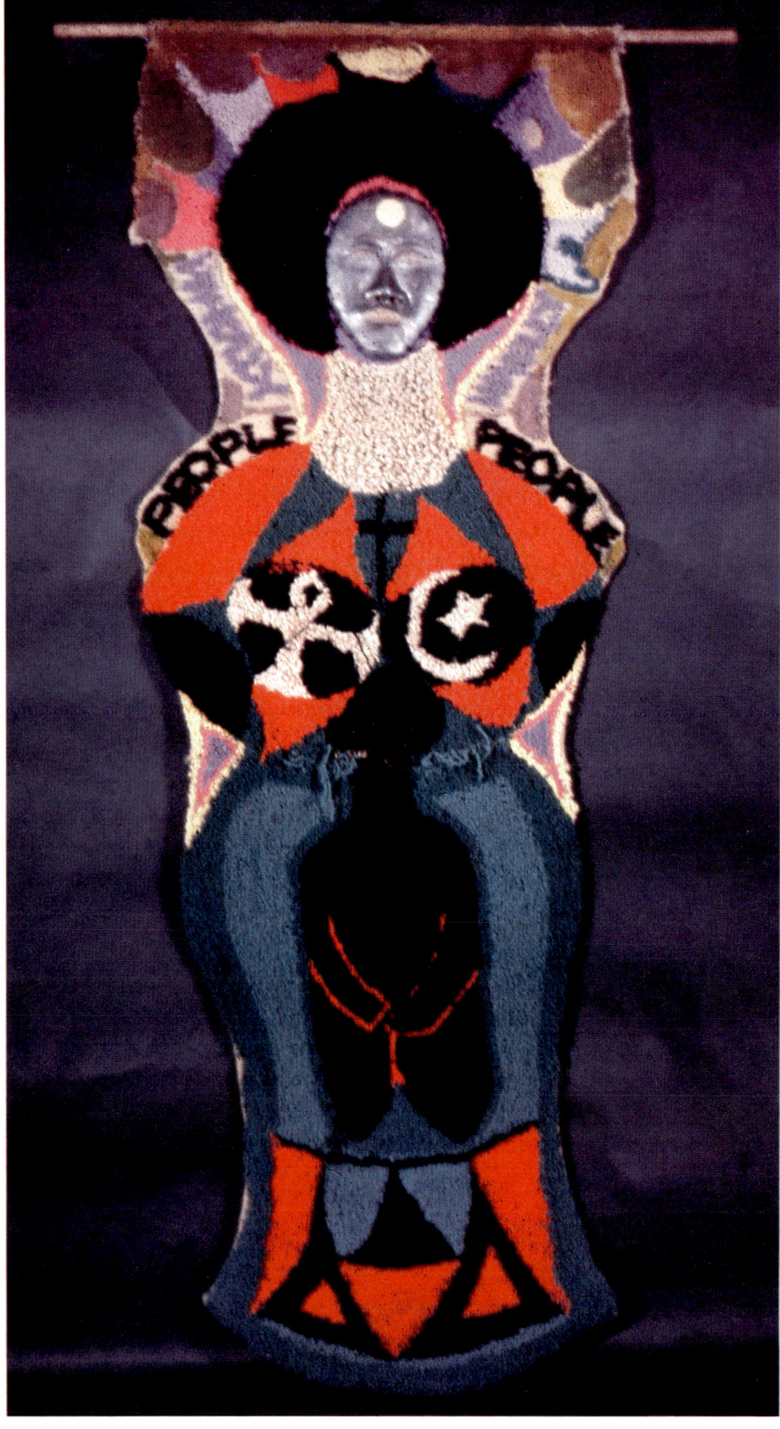

10.16

Howard Mallory, *From These Roots*, 1972. Applique on fabric. Collection of the artist.

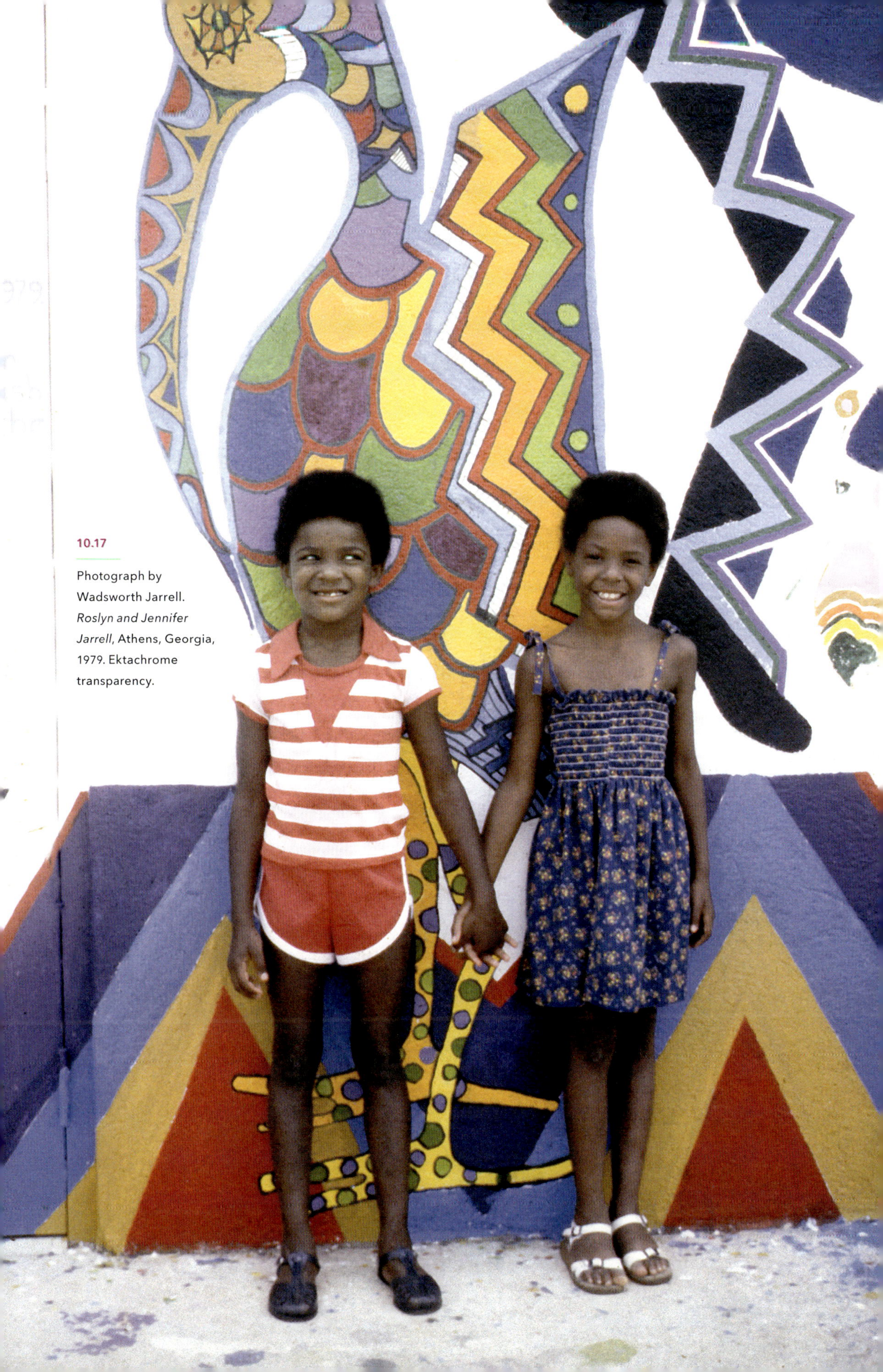

Photograph by Wadsworth Jarrell. *Roslyn and Jennifer Jarrell*, Athens, Georgia, 1979. Ektachrome transparency.

from the original AFRICOBRA tenets and philosophy formed by the founding members in 1968, becoming more of a loosely formed group of individual, independent-thinking artists, who exhibit as AFRICOBRA, with two members who joined in 1969, Napoleon and Nelson. Starting in 1975 into the 1980s, the AFRICOBRA membership expanded to include painter and educator James Phillips; scholar, painter, and art historian Michael Harris; painter, scholar, and educator Murry DePillars (now deceased); painter and educator Akili Ron Anderson; and painter and photographer Adger Cowans. Members added in the first decade of this century include painter and educator Kevin Cole; artist, art historian, and curator Moyo Okediji; and sculptor and painter Renee Stout.

Fifty-two years after the inception of AFRICOBRA, presented here, to the best of my recollection and research (interviews of members and museum directors), is an accurate report. I am humbled and honored to have the privilege to present this collective of talented revolutionary artists, who created a philosophy that we believe was foundational to an African American aesthetic, and who created a body of work that is now a school of thought—which is AFRICOBRA's contribution to world art. I am also grateful to author a book representing a group of revolutionaries who chose such an auspicious name as African Commune of Bad Relevant Artists.

Over the course of the 1960s, Black consciousness moved from an appeal for justice, requesting recognition, raising moral contradictions, and pressing for fair enforcement of the law—or, put differently, asking permission to join and share in the national bounty that Black sweat had disproportionally produced—to an attitude of practical petitions to enjoy enfranchisement, get jobs, and live decently, to, by later years of the decade, an attitude of aggressive self-declaration that screamed, "I am here in all my corporality, creativity, genius, and color. Now you deal with me!"

This shift was from an appeal to a proclamation to undeniable assertion. It charted the change from "Negro" to "Black" to "We are an African people." The spirit of change was inseparable from the collapse of colonialism globally and the rise of a powerful transnational Black consciousness, which was equal parts political and cultural. Just as "Black is beautiful" was impossible without the transformed self-visualization that swept over rural and urban Black communities, as their televisions showed almost daily elegantly outfitted African delegations arriving at the United Nations in New York, Black young people were embracing and transforming their own expression in music, dance, and fashion, and simultaneously creating new palettes and motifs for visual artists.

The use of African patterns, Cool Ade colors, omnipresent values of improvisation and rhythmic complexity had vanquished the staid respectability of middle-class aspirations that threatened to subdue and whiten Black popular expression. Inner city spaces were in turbulent transition, and actions with a spine were required. Riots across the country had given impetus to a new Black subjectivity that would assert itself or crash the temple. The turmoil forced civic, social, and political powers to reckon with it. From the troubled national landscape sprouted Black power, Black shows, and endless Black studies intended to forestall rapid change. AFRICOBRA arose from this transformative energy, harnessing its particular essence in the visual arts, and shaping the visual vocabulary of all that follows it. A manifesto movement of deliberate intentions, AFRICOBRA would change visual art in America, and indeed across the Americas, as well as help build a new bridge to Africa. The outsized impact of this small community of artists arose from its daring to become itself, without apology, and without kowtowing to the prevailing art establishment.

Though not without parallels, such as the Weusi Collective in New York, the emergence of COBRA/AFRICOBRA was significant on several counts and positioned Chicago powerfully in the discussion of African American visual arts. Of particular consequence were influences on (1) art criticism, (2) institutions beyond Chicago, and (3) Black museums. Each of these merits brief discussion. Regarding critical discourse, COBRA and later AFRICOBRA artists were very engaged with African American scholars of art history and art criticism. With the coming of the late sixties and early seventies, the number of academically trained Black art historians was growing. Even among the traditionally important ranks of artists/historians, the shift was strongly toward figures for which art history and criticism were primary. Scholars such as professors Floyd Coleman, Allan Gordon, and many others—I among them—were engaged in trying to name and define what constituted Black art and Black aesthetics. Regular conferences addressing Black cultural issues, such meetings of the National Conference of Artists, were scenes of heated discussion of competing interpretations of Black visual art. AFRICOBRA, because it had substantially codified a position on Black aesthetics, was a central catalyst for such dialogue. Jeff Donaldson, regarded as the chief theorist for AFRICOBRA, provoked fiery discourse within and beyond Black art criticism and history because he so forcefully challenged prevailing assumptions. This was especially true as he became head of art at Howard University, where he directly controlled teaching content.

AFRICOBRA, more than any other movement of the era, reframed the relationship between African—historical and contemporary—art and the art of Black Americans. It moved African influences beyond quotation and appropriating to an imaging color, pattern, and rhythm, as emotive elements reworked to express African American temperament. This is the central idea behind the AFRICOBRA assertion that they wished to make art with all the power of soul music. Additionally, AFRICOBRA sought to marry abstraction, as exhibited through patterns and motifs, with specific narrative messages, expressed through the use of either actual words or images of known significant Black historical and journalistic figures. Here, too, the AFRICOBRA positions forced art historians and critics to reassess how this movement related to other, less probing self-declared Black art forms as well as to American movements such as pop art and hard edge painting.

The COBRA/AFRICOBRA artists and their actions sparked two major impacts. COBRA's disruption of Columbia College's Arts and the Inner City Conference led directly to the founding of the National Center of Afro-American Artists in Boston in 1968, billed as a conference of Black creative intellectuals. Elma Lewis attended from Boston. She joined John O. Killens, Charles White, and many other Black notables who lamented the absence of a place "to be somebody." The conference was upended when COBRA artists led by Jeff Donaldson essentially took control of it and rewrote its agenda. Elma Lewis allied with the insurgents and found common cause with their objections and objectives, but most of all, she responded to their desire to have their own space, control their fates, and define their own critical and creative directions. She left wanting to address those needs, and soon finding herself with expansive properties, she created the National Center of Afro-American Artists as a Black professional entity that would parallel the Elma Lewis School of Fine Arts, which she had founded and operated since 1950. As evidence of the impact of the Chicago conference, the original board of directors of the National Center of Afro-American Artists included Jeff Donaldson, Charles White, and John O. Killens. Donaldson, who deeply impressed her with his pro-Black perspective and assertiveness, she had first met only months before. I joined her center the following year.

A second impact of AFRICOBRA was the disbursal of artists associated with the movement beyond Chicago, especially to Boston and Washington, DC. By the midseventies, Boston's very active Black art scene enjoyed the contributions of Napoleon Jones-Henderson and Nelson Stevens, working within the AFRICOBRA aesthetic. Already profoundly influenced by the *Wall of Respect*, Boston's street mural movement counted, along with the work of Dana Chandler and Gary Rickson, notable contributions from Stevens. Through their teaching locally and regionally, as well as through exhibitions, Jones-Henderson and Stevens established awareness of AFRICOBRA as important elements of Black art in New England. Farther south, Jeff Donaldson's relocation to Washington, DC, where he chaired the Department of Art at Howard University, produced major tremors in art teaching at historically Black colleges and universities. Upsetting the more conservative canons that had prevailed since the long era of James A. Porter, Donaldson aggressively pushed instruction toward a reassessment of what thrusts teaching and critical studies should take in such institutions. In time, he realigned the thinking and practice of a generation of students, bringing many of them into harmony with the aesthetic vision of AFRICOBRA.

At the turn of the seventies, independent Black museums were few. And more generally, most independent Black museums were history driven in their missions. Outside historically Black colleges and universities such as Hampton, Fisk, Howard, Atlanta University, and so forth, there were no Black art museums in major urban centers, with the exception of the newly formed Studio Museum in Harlem, New York, and the Museum of the National Center of Afro-American Artists in Boston, Massachusetts. At the time, Ed Spriggs directed the former, and I headed the latter. Both Spriggs and I were deeply committed to making our institutions places that put Black communities and Black artists in dialogue. We did not want to be simply white museums in "black face"; instead, we wanted to sponsor genuine reciprocal encounters between creative people and publics across the full spectrum of our neighborhoods and communities. I had met Donaldson and attended CONFABA in Chicago, and Spriggs and I spoke occasionally, as we were in the same business.

When the Studio Museum in Harlem committed to presenting an AFRICOBRA exhibition, we quickly followed. In fall 1970, we showed *AFRICOBRA: Ten in Search of a Nation* at the Museum of the National Center of Afro-American Artists, where it was well received and locally reviewed. The exhibition and the young museum were philosophically aligned, as confirmed by a short passage from a press release: "Our guidelines are our people—the whole family of African People, the African family tree. And in this spirit of familyhood, we have carefully examined our roots and searched our branches for those visual qualities that are most expressive of our people/art. Our people are our standard of excellence."[1]

It was this process of growth, self-direction, and responsiveness to an internally recognized cultural imperative that our museum had been founded to foster.

I think *Ten in Search of a Nation* was the first AFRICOBRA show beyond the Midwest. It and subsequent shows would spread the ideas and ideals of the AFRICOBRA group widely, laying the basis for wide influence on the art of Black artists throughout the United States, the Caribbean, and Africa.

Langston Hughes urged Black Americans to tell their own story. Wadsworth Jarrell has undertaken that task with this insightful firsthand account of a truly important visual arts movement of the last half-century. I commend his excellent work, and I am a witness to the veracity of his report and analysis.

Edmund Barry Gaither
Director and Curator, Museum of the National Center
of Afro-American Artists, Boston

1968

Wadsworth Upper Grade Center, Chicago, Illinois

Notre Dame University, South Bend, Indiana

1970

AFRICOBRA I, Studio Museum in Harlem, New York

AFRICOBRA I, National Center for Afro-American Artists, Boston, Massachusetts

AFRICOBRA I, Black Expo, Chicago, Illinois

1971–1972

AFRICOBRA II, Studio Museum in Harlem, New York

1972

AFRICOBRA II, National Center for Afro-American Artists, Boston, Massachusetts

AFRICOBRA II, Howard University Gallery of Art, Washington, DC

AFRICOBRA II, Northern Illinois University Art Gallery, DeKalb, Illinois

AFRICOBRA II, Black Expo, Chicago, Illinois

AFRICOBRA II, Langston Hughes Center for the Visual and Performing Arts, Buffalo, New York

AFRICOBRA II, New York State Museum, Albany, New York

AFRICOBRA II, Haiti Gallery, Rochester, New York

AFRICOBRA II, Everson Museum of Art, Syracuse, New York

1973

AFRICOBRA III, Howard University Gallery of Art, Washington, DC

AFRICOBRA III, University Art Gallery, University of Massachusetts at Amherst, Amherst, Massachusetts

COBRA on WGN Television in *Black Pride*, Chicago, Illinois, November 1968.

Harry Long, "A Dazzling Show of Negro Art," *Amsterdam*, June 1970. Review of AFRICOBRA I at the Studio Museum in Harlem, New York.

John Gruen, "Big Bad Relevance," *New York Magazine*, July 13, 1970. Review of AFRICOBRA I at the Studio Museum in Harlem, New York.

Jeff Donaldson, "Ten in Search of a Nation," *Black World*, October 1970, including images of art from the exhibition. Review of AFRICOBRA I at the Studio Museum in Harlem, New York.

Harold Haydon, "Right On, Art Lovers," *Chicago Sun-Times*, September 1970. Review of AFRICOBRA I at the Black Expo in Chicago, Illinois.

Jet staff, "Black Revolt Sparks White Fashion Craze," *Jet*, January 28, 1971. A review of bandoliers on art, mentioning Jeff Donaldson and Jae Jarrell's art, with a picture of Jae's *Revolutionary Suit*, modeled by AFRICOBRA member Barbara Jones, at WJ Studios and Gallery, Chicago, Illinois.

Paul Richard, "AFRICOBRA: African Art for Africans Only," *Washington Post*, February 27, 1972. Review of AFRICOBRA II exhibition at Howard University Gallery of Art, Washington, DC.

Larry Brown, interviews with Jeff Donaldson and Wadsworth Jarrell on *Black News*, February 1972. Review of AFRICOBRA II exhibition, with images of art, Washington, DC.

Nancy Tobin Willig, "Black Group's Exhibit Is Seen as a Political Weapon," *Buffalo Courier Express*, October 8, 1972. Review of AFRICOBRA II exhibition at the Langston Hughes Center for Visual and Performing Arts, Buffalo, New York.

Paul Richard, "Black Art, Politics, Messages," *Washington Post*, April 1973. Review of AFRICOBRA III exhibition at Howard University Gallery of Art, Washington, DC.

Barbara Jones-Hogu, "The History, Philosophy and Aesthetics of AFRICOBRA," in the exhibition catalog for AFRICOBRA III at the University of Massachusetts at Amherst, Amherst, Massachusetts, September 30, 1973.

Samella Lewis, untitled review, *Black Art* 2, no. 2 (1978). Review of designer Jae Jarrell's work.

Museums

Brooklyn Museum of Art, Brooklyn, New York

Philadelphia Museum of Art, Philadelphia, Pennsylvania

Detroit Institute of Art, Detroit, Michigan

Tate Modern Museum, London, UK

Cleveland Museum of Art, Cleveland, Ohio

Kansas African American Museum, Wichita, Kansas

Minneapolis Institute of Art, Minneapolis, Minnesota

Nelson-Atkins Museum of Art, Kansas City, Missouri

Rennie Museum, Toronto, Canada

High Museum of Art, Atlanta, Georgia

Delaware Museum of Art, Wilmington, Delaware

African American Museum, Smithsonian Institution, Washington, DC

Birmingham Museum of Art, Birmingham, Alabama

Museum of Contemporary Art, Atlanta, Georgia

Kentucky Derby Museum, Louisville, Kentucky

DuSable Museum of African American History, Chicago, Illinois

Georgia Museum of Art, Athens, Georgia

Harriet Tubman Museum, Macon, Georgia

National Civil Rights Museum, Memphis, Tennessee

Hammond House Museum, Atlanta, Georgia

Institutions

School of the Art Institute of Chicago, Chicago, Illinois

Institute of American Indian Art, Albuquerque, New Mexico

Howard University Collection, Washington, DC

Shomberg Center Collection, New York, New York

Rhode Island School of Design, Providence, Rhode Island

Hampton University Collection, Hampton, Virginia

Bureau of Cultural Affairs, Atlanta, Georgia

Atlanta Public Library, Atlanta, Georgia

Burney-Harris Middle School, Athens, Georgia

Coca Cola USA, Atlanta, Georgia

Wieland Homes Collection, Atlanta, Georgia

Harambee House Hotel, Washington, DC

Atlanta Life Insurance Company Collection, Atlanta, Georgia

Johnson Publication Company Collection, Chicago, Illinois

King and Spalding Collection, Atlanta, Georgia

Washington Post, Washington, DC

Kaiser Permanente, Atlanta, Georgia

Metropolitan Atlanta Cardiology Consultants, Atlanta, Georgia

OK Café, Atlanta, Georgia

Many private collections

Adul Alkalimat, Romi Crofard, and Rebecca Zorach, *The Wall of Respect*, Northwestern University Press

H. H. Arnason and Peter Kalb, *History of Modern Art*, 5th edition, Prentice Hall

Gershun Avilez, *Radical Aesthetics and Modern Black Nationalism*, University of Illinois Press

Naomi Beckwith and Dieter Roelstraete, *Freedom Principles: Experiments in Art and Music, 1965 to Now*, University of Chicago Press

David Bindman and Henry Louis Gates Jr., *The Image of the Black in Western Art*, Harvard University Press

Rose Bouthiller, Megan Lykins Reich, and Elena Harvey Collins, *How to Remain Human*, Museum of Contemporary Art, Cleveland

Terasa A. Corbone, Kellie Jones, Connie H. Choi, Dalia Scruggs, and Cynthia A. Young, *Witness*, Brooklyn Museum and Monacelli Press

Robert L. Douglas, *Wadsworth Jarrell: Artist as Revolutionary*, Pomegranate Publishers

Gwendolyn DuBois Shaw and Richard Powell, *Representing: 200 Years of African American Art in the Philadelphia Museum of Art*, Philadelphia Museum of Art

Lisa Farrington, *African American Art: A Visual and Cultural History*, Oxford University Press

Elsa Honig Fine, *The Afro-American Artist*, Holt, Rinehart and Wilson

Michael D. Harris, *Colored Pictures*, University of North Carolina Press

Graham Lock and David Murray, *The Hearing Eye: Jazz and Blues Influences*, Oxford University Press

Valerie J. Mercer and Salvador Salort-Pons, *Art of Rebellion: Black Art of the Civil Rights Movement*, Detroit Institute of Arts

Catherine Morris and Rujeko Hockley, eds., *We Wanted a Revolution: Black Radical Women, 1965–85*, Brooklyn Museum

Rebecca Zorach and Marissa Baker, eds., *The Time Is Now! Art Worlds of Chicago's South Side, 1960–1980*, Smart Museum of Art and the University of Chicago Press

Introduction

Epigraphs: Larry Neal, "AFRICOBRA/Farafindugu," written for the exhibition catalog for *AFRICOBRA/Farafindugu*, held at the Atlanta Neighborhood Art Center, Atlanta, Georgia, March 7 to March 28, 1981. Eddie Granderson, "A Shared Ideology," in *Wadsworth Jarrell: A Shared Ideology* (Atlanta, GA: Bureau of Cultural Affairs, City Gallery East, 1996), 7.

1   Booker T. Washington, Atlanta Compromise Speech, Cotton States and International Exposition, Atlanta, Georgia, September 18, 1895.

2   William Gay, personal conversation with the author at WJ Studios and Gallery, Chicago, Illinois, May 1970.

3   Vincent Smith, speaking at artist Jacob Lawrence's memorial, September 28, 2001, Riverside Church, New York City.

4   Aime Cesaire, opening speech, "The Relationship between Colonization and Culture," at the Conference of Negro–African Writers and Artists, the Sorbonne Amphitheatre Descartes, Paris, 1956. Cited in James Baldwin, *Nobody Knows My Name* (New York: Dell, 1961), 32.

5   Nubia Kai, "AFRICOBRA Universal Aesthetics," *AFRICOBRA: The First Twenty Years*, exhibition catalog (Atlanta, GA: Nexus Press, 1990), 6–7.

6   Barbara Jones-Hogu and Napoleon Jones-Henderson, video interview, for the film *AFRICOBRA: Art for the People*, produced by TV Land and NOLA Film Production, Chicago, Illinois, January 2010.

7   Jae Jarrell, taped interview with the author, New York, April 2007.

8   Molefi Kete Asante, *Afrocentricity* (Trenton, NJ: Africa World Press, 1988), 39.

9   James Baldwin, *Nobody Knows My Name* (New York: Vintage International, 1993), 20.

10 Edmund Burke Feldman, in discussion of a student's doctoral dissertation presentation on mural painting, University of Georgia, Athens, spring 1980.

11 Mural painting dissertation discussion, spring 1980.

12 Professor William Cowans, color class, School of the Art Institute of Chicago, fall quarter, 1956.

13 Lisa Farrington, *African-American Art: A Visual and Cultural History* (New York: Oxford University Press, 2016), 3.

14 Murry N. DePillars, foreword to *Wadsworth Jarrell: The Artist as Revolutionary*,
by Robert L. Douglas (San Francisco: Pomegranate, 1996), v.

15 Michael D. Harris is citing Elizabeth Alexander's collection of essays *The Black
Interior* (Minneapolis, MN: Greywolf Press, 2004), in AFRICOBRA *Now: An Aesthetic
Reflection*, the online catalog for AFRICOBRA *Philosophy*, an exhibition held at the
Logan Center, Chicago, Illinois, June 28–September 22, 2013. Harris's essay was
contracted by Rebecca Zorach, who curated the exhibition and was then an art
history professor at the University of Chicago.

16 Willie Mabon, "I Don't Know" (Chicago: Parrot Records, Blues Label, 1952).

17 Muddy Waters, "Hoochie Coochie Man," written by Willie Dixon (Chicago:
Chess Records, 1948).

18 David Brizan, "Douens," in *Douens*, by Le Roy Clarke, exhibition catalog,
(Washington, DC: Howard University Gallery of Art, 1976).

19 Muddy Waters, in *American Masters*, directed by Robert Gordon and Morgan Neville
(New York: PBS, 2003).

20 Janice Mathews, conversation with the author, in Athens, Georgia, May 1982.

21 Kenneth Rodgers, "The Africobra Collective," in AFRICOBRA/*Fromaje*, exhibition
catalog (Washington, DC: Howard University Gallery of Art, 1989), 17.

22 Thurlow Evans Tibbs Jr., "A National Treasure," in AFRICOBRA/*Fromaje*, 17–18.

23 Edward Spriggs, "AFRICOBRA: Intermediarily," in AFRICOBRA *II*, exhibition catalog
(Harlem, NY: Studio Museum, 1971), 1.

1. Black in Chicago

1 Leonard F. Johnson, personal conversation with the author in his Washington, DC,
studio, April 12, 1976.

2 Quoted in Mike Royko, *The Boss* (New York: Signet Classics, 1971), 134.

3 Jennifer and Roslyn Jarrell, personal conversation with the author, Chicago,
November 23, 1992.

4 Molefi Kete Asante, *Afrocentricity* (Trenton, NJ: Africa World Press, 1988), 12.

5 Carl Sandburg, *Chicago Poems* (New York: Henry Holt, 1916), 3.

6 Amiri Baraka, *Blues People* (New York: Morrow Quill, 1963), 96.

7 Gerald Williams, personal conversation with the author in New York studio,
May 2005.

8 These are Ossie Davis's words but not in the same sequence. Ossie Davis eulogy for
Malcolm X, Faith Temple Church of God, New York, February 27, 1965.

9 Royko, *The Boss*, 144.

10 Haki Madhubuti, *Black Men: Obsolete, Single, Dangerous?* (Chicago: Third World
Press, 1991), 128–29.

11 Bill Borin, conversation with the author at WJ Studios and Gallery, Chicago,
July 1967.

12 Martin Goldsholl, personal conversation with the author at wj Studios and Gallery, Chicago, July 30, 1967.

13 Useni Eugene Perkins, *West Wall* (Chicago: Independent Black Press, 1968), n.p.

14 William McBride, speech at McBride's Gallery, Chicago, July 1967.

15 GerShun Avilez, *Radical Aesthetics and Modern Black Nationalism* (Urbana: University of Illinois Press, 2016), 3.

16 Henry Louis Gates Jr., "Black Creativity on the Cutting Edge," *Time*, October 10, 1994, 74–75.

17 Lerone Bennett Jr., introduction to *Tradition and Conflict: Images Of A Turbulent Decade, 1963–1973*, edited by Mary Schmidt Campbell, exhibition catalog (New York: Studio Museum, 1985), 10.

18 Floyd Coleman, lecture on African American Art at the 9th Annual James A. Porter Colloquium, Howard University, Washington, DC, 1998.

2. Genesis

1   Jeff Donaldson, speaking at an art fair in Hyde Park, Chicago, August 1963.

2   Frantz Fanon, *The Wretched of the Earth* (New York: Grove Press, 1961).

3   Gerald Williams, written statement for AFRICOBRA: *Experimental Art toward a School of Thought,* June 2007.

4   Jeff Donaldson, conversation with the author, art fair in Hyde Park, Chicago, August 1963.

5   Norman Parish, telephone conversation with the author, August 2004.

6   Nelson Stevens, taped interview with the author, Baltimore, Maryland, March 2007.

7   Frank Smith, taped interview with the author, Baltimore, Maryland, March 2007.

8   Fred Jones, conversation with the author at an art fair in Hyde Park, Chicago, August 1963.

9   Murry N. DePillars, foreword to *Wadsworth Jarrell: Artist as Revolutionary*, by Robert L. Douglas (San Francisco: Pomegranate, 1996), v.

10 Jeff Donaldson, conversation with the author and Norman Parish, art fair in Winnetka, Illinois, July 1964.

11 Norman Parish and author conversation, art fair in Winnetka, Illinois, July 1964.

12 Anonymous woman, conversation with the author, art fair in Winnetka, Illinois, July 1964.

13 Donaldson conversation, July 1964.

3. Organization of Black American Culture

Epigraph: Lerone Bennett Jr., introduction to *Tradition and Conflict: Images of a Turbulent Decade, 1963–1973*, edited by Mary Schmidt Campbell, exhibition catalog (New York: Studio Museum in Harlem, 1985), 9.

1 Michael D. Harris, "Urban Totems: The Communal Spirit of Black Murals," in
   Walls of Heritage/Walls of Pride, edited by James Prigoff and Robin J. Dunitz (San
   Francisco: Pomegranate, 2000), 25.

2 Editors of *Ebony*, *Civil Rights Movement to Black Revolution*, vol. 3 of *Ebony Pictorial
   History of Black America* (Chicago: Johnson Publishing, 1971).

3 Bennett, introduction, 9.

4 Norman Parish, written statement on the *Wall of Respect* sent to the author,
   November 2008, 64–65.

5 Gregory Foster-Rice, "The Artistic Evolution of the *Wall of Respect*," *Wall of Respect*,
   Block Museum, operational 1997 to 2017, https://www.blockmuseum.northwestern
   .edu/wallofrespect/, currently archived at https://issuu.com/blockmuseumofart/docs
   /wall_of_respect_website.

6 Jeff Donaldson, "The Rise and Fall and Legacy of the *Wall of Respect* Movement,"
   International Review of African American Art 15, no. 1 (1998): 22–26.

7 Darthard Perry, interview by Gil Noble, *Like It Is*, originally aired November 2, 1980
   (New York: WABC-TV).

8 Carolyn Lawrence, videotaped interview, January 2011, in Chicago for the
   documentary AFRICOBRA: *Art for the People* (New York: TV Land and NOLA Film
   Productions, 2011).

9 Barbara Jones-Hogu, letter to the author about the *Wall of Respect*, November 2008.

10 Norman Parish, letter to the author about the *Wall of Respect*, December 2008.

11 William Walker, letter to the author about the *Wall of Respect*, December 2008.

12 Burleigh Hines, "Mural in the Ghetto," *Chicago Daily News*, August 24, 1967.

13 Donaldson, "Rise and Fall and Legacy," 23.

14 Bennett, introduction, 9.

15 Gwendolyn Brooks, "The Wall," composed specifically for the *Wall of Respect*
   dedication on August 27, 1967. Reprinted by consent of Brooks Permissions.

16 Haki Madhubuti, "The Wall," composed specifically for the *Wall of Respect* dedication
   on August 27, 1967.

4. The Inception

1 Memo to Ray E Brown, folder 13, box 1, the Lorado Taff-Midway Studio's Papers,
   the University of Chicago Library, from research sent to me by Rebecca Zorach,
   December 15, 2015.

2 Jeff Donaldson, discussion in COBRA's first meeting regarding the *Arts and the Inner
   City*, held at Columbia College, Chicago, 1968.

3 Nubia Kai, AFRICOBRA: *The First Twenty Years*, exhibition catalog (Atlanta: Nexus
   Press, 1990), 8.

5. A Visual Art Proposal

1   Jeff Donaldson, "Exploring a Black Aesthetic—A Visual Art proposal," 1968. A copy of an unpublished three-page letter that Jeff had typed was given to each AFRICOBRA member.

2   Donaldson, "Exploring a Black Aesthetic."

3   Conversation at a COBRA meeting, September 1968.

4   Catherine Fox, review of *20 Artists 20 Years*, *Atlanta Journal/Atlanta Constitution*, September 15, 1993.

5   COBRA conversation, September 1968.

6   Conversation at a COBRA meeting, October 1968.

7   Bob Paige, interview by the author in his New York studio, October 2007.

8   See, for example, John Hope Franklin and Loren Schweninger, *Runaway Slaves: Rebels on the Plantation* (New York: Oxford University Press, 1999), 2–3. Franklin and Schweninger wrote about day-to-day Resistance: "Most of what historian have termed 'day-to-day resistance' involved crimes against property. Slaves pulled down fences, sabotaged farm equipment, broke implements, damaged boats, vandalized wagons, ruined clothing, and committed various other destructive acts. They set fires to outbuildings, barns, and stables; mistreated horses, mules, cattle, and other livestock. They stole with impunity: sheep, hogs, cattle, poultry, money, watches, produce, liquor, tobacco, flour, cotton, indigo, corn, nearly anything that was not under lock and key—and they occasionally found the key. . . . Some blacks worked slowly, or indifferently, took unscheduled respites, performed careless or sloppy labor when planting, hoeing, and harvesting crops. Some chopped cotton so nonchalantly that they cut the young plants nearly into fodder, while others harvested rice or sugar with such indifference that they damaged the crops. Slaves feigned illness, hid in out buildings, did not complete their assigned tasks, and balked at performing dangerous work."

9   Conversation at a COBRA meeting, November 1968.

6. First COBRA Exhibition

1   James Turner, speaking on a panel at the one-day Conference on Progressive Education and Civil Rights, Wadsworth Upper Grade Center, Chicago, September 1968.

2   Jesse Jackson, speaking on a panel at the Conference on Progressive Education and Civil Rights.

3   Jeff Fort, speaking on a panel at the Conference on Progressive Education and Civil Rights.

4   Nathaniel Beck Sr., personal conversation with the author, Chicago, April 1962.

7. Recruitment

1 Jeff Donaldson, prospectus for CONFABA, held at Northwestern University in Evanston, Illinois, May 7–10, 1970.

2 Extracts from conclusions reached by all six task force participants at CONFABA.

3 Cherilyn Wright, "Reflections on CONFABA: 1970," *International Review of African American Art* 15, no. 1 (1998): 36–44.

4 Nelson Stevens, telephone interview by author, March 14, 2014.

5 Tritobia Benjamin, introductions and acknowledgments to the exhibition catalog for *AFRICOBRA/Groupe Fromaje: Esthétique Universelle/Universal Aesthetics*, held at Howard University Gallery of Art, Washington, DC, November 6–December 17, 1989.

8. *AFRICOBRA I*

1 In 1989 Edward Spriggs, wrote an essay titled "AFRICOBRA Aesthetics" for the exhibition catalog for *AFRICOBRA/Fromaje*, held at Howard University Gallery of Art, Washington, DC, November 6–December 17, 1989.

2 Spriggs, "AFRICOBRA Aesthetics."

3 Cherilyn Wright, "Ten in Search of a Nation," review for the exhibition catalog for *AFRICOBRA II: Ten in Search of a Nation*, held at the Studio Museum in Harlem, New York, 1971, 6.

4 Harry Long, "A Dazzling Show of Negro Art," *Amsterdam*, June 1970.

5 John Gruen, "The Big Bad Relevance," *New York Magazine*, July 13, 1970.

6 Larry Neal, "AFRICOBRA/Farafindugu," in the exhibition catalog for *AFRICOBRA/Farafindugu*, held at the Atlanta Neighborhood Center in Atlanta, Georgia, 1980.

7 Neal, "AFRICOBRA/Farafindugu."

8 Nelson Stevens, AFRICOBRA meeting, WJ Studios and Gallery, Chicago, September 1969.

9 Conversation at AFRICOBRA meeting, WJ Studios and Gallery, Chicago, November 1970.

10 Harold Haydon, "Right On, Art Lovers," *Chicago Sun-Times*, September 1970.

11 *Jet* staff, "Black Revolt Sparks White Fashion Craze," *Jet*, January 28, 1971.

12 *Jet* staff, "Black Revolt."

13 J. I. Biegeleisen, *Screen Printing* (New York: Watson-Guptill, 1971), 9.

9. *AFRICOBRA II*

Epigraph: Rosalind Jeffries, "Defining a Black Aesthetic," in the exhibition catalog for *AFRICOBRA/Fromaje*, held at Howard University Gallery of Art, Washington, DC, November 6–December 17, 1989.

1 Edward Spriggs, "AFRICOBRA: An Intermediarily Pro/position," written for the

exhibition catalog for AFRICOBRA II, held at the Studio Museum in Harlem, November 19, 1971–January 21, 1972.

2 Carolyn Lawrence's AFRICOBRA minutes, November 29, 1971, New York City.

3 Jeff Donaldson, "Ten in Search of a Nation," *Black World*, October, 1970, 80–89.

4 Jeff Donaldson, statement on AFRICOBRA members, AFRICOBRA II exhibition catalog, 1971.

5 Benjamin Goodman, *Malcolm X: The End of White World Supremacy* (New York: Merlin House, 1971), 13–14.

6 Franz Fanon, *Wretched of the Earth* (Paris: Dammes de la terre, 1961), 1.

7 Edmund Barry Gaither, "Nationhood," in the exhibition catalog for AFRICOBRA/ *Fromaje: Esthétique Universelle/Universal Aesthetics*, held at Howard University Gallery of Art, Washington, DC, November 6–December 17, 1989.

8 Samella Lewis, "A True Movement," in the exhibition catalog for AFRICOBRA/ *Fromaje*.

9 Thurlow Evans Tibbs Jr., "A National Treasure," in the exhibition catalog for AFRICOBRA/*Fromaje*.

10 Jeff Donaldson, interview regarding the AFRICOBRA II exhibition by *Washington Post* art critic Paul Richard, at Howard University, Washington, D.C., February 1972.

11 Paul Richard, "AFRICOBRA: African Art for Africans Only," *Washington Post*, February 27, 1972.

12 Richard, "AFRICOBRA: African Art for Africans Only."

13 Richard, "AFRICOBRA: African Art for Africans Only."

14 Richard, "AFRICOBRA: African Art for Africans Only."

15 Nancy Tobin Willig, "Black Group's Exhibit Is Seen as a Political Weapon," *Buffalo Courier Express*, October 8, 1972.

16 Willig, "Black Group's Exhibit."

17 Willig, "Black Group's Exhibit."

18 Willig, "Black Group's Exhibit."

10. *AFRICOBRA III*

Epigraph: Nubia Kai, "AFRICOBRA Universal Aesthetics," in AFRICOBRA: *The First Twenty Years*, exhibition catalog (Atlanta: Nexus Press, 1990), 8.

1 Conversation at AFRICOBRA meeting, Washington, DC, May 1972.

2 Paul Richard, "Black Art, Politics, Messages," *Washington Post*, April 1973.

3 Jeff Donaldson, "Ten in Search of a Nation," *Black World*, October 1970, 83.

4 Richard, "Black Art, Politics, Messages."

5 Richard, "Black Art, Politics, Messages."

6 Robert L. Douglas, "On the Cutting Edge of History and an Aesthetic," in the exhibition catalog for *Edge Cutters*, held at the Kentucky Derby Museum, Louisville, Kentucky, February 6–March 20, 1993.

7   Leopold Senghor, lecture at the Conference of Negro-African Writers and Artists, Sorbonne Amphitheatre Descartes, Paris, September 19–22, 1956.

8   Nelson Stevens, "Artist's Statement," in the exhibition catalog for AFRICOBRA III, held at Howard University, Washington, DC, and the University of Massachusetts at Amherst, 1973.

9   Gerald Williams, "Artist's Statement," in the exhibition catalog for AFRICOBRA III.

10   Jae Jarrell, "Artist's Statement," in the exhibition catalog for AFRICOBRA III.

11   Jeff Donaldson, "Artist's Statement," in the exhibition catalog for AFRICOBRA III.

12   Napoleon Jones-Henderson, "Artist's Statement," in the exhibition catalog for AFRICOBRA III.

13   Carolyn Lawrence, "Artist's Statement," in the exhibition catalog for AFRICOBRA III.

14   Wadsworth Jarrell, "Artist's Statement," in the exhibition catalog for AFRICOBRA III.

15   Howard Mallory, "Artist's Statement," in the exhibition catalog for AFRICOBRA III.

16   Frank Smith, "Artist's Statement," in the exhibition catalog for AFRICOBRA III.

17   Larry Neal, "AFRICOBRA/*Farafindugu*," in the exhibition catalog for AFRICOBRA/*Fromaje*, held at Howard University Gallery of Art, Washington, DC, November 6–December 17, 1989.

18   Edward Spriggs, "Towards a True Black Aesthetic," in *Compton Yearbook* (Chicago: F. E. Compton, 1973).

19   Barbara Jones-Hogu, "The History, Philosophy and Aesthetics of AFRICOBRA," in the exhibition catalog for AFRICOBRA III.

Postscript

1   The entire press release reads: "We are a family—COBRA, the Coalition of Black Revolutionary Artists, is now AFRICOBRA, African Commune of Bad Relevant Artists. It's NATION TIME, and we are searching. Our guidelines are our people—the whole family of African people, the African family tree. And in the spirit of familyhood, we have carefully examined our roots and searched our branches for those visual qualities that are most expressive of our people/art. Our people are our standard of excellence. We strive for images inspired by African people/experience and images that African people can relate to directly without formal art training and/or experience. Art for people and not for critics, whose peopleness is questionable. We try to create images that appeal to the senses—not the intellect. It is our hope that intelligent definition of the past and perceptive identification of the present will project nationful direction in the future—look for us there, because that's where we're at. We hope you can dig it—its about you, and as Marvin Gaye says, 'You're what's happening in the world today, baby.'" Jeff Donaldson, "Ten in Search of a Nation," written for the exhibition AFRICOBRA I: *Ten in Search of a Nation*, held at the Studio Museum in Harlem, June 21–August 30, 1970.

Jeff Richardson Donaldson. Education: Northwestern University, Evanston, Illinois, PhD; Illinois Institute of Design and Technology, Chicago, MS; University of Arkansas, Pine Bluff, BA.

Jeff Donaldson was born in 1932 in Pine Bluff, Arkansas, to Frank and Clementine Richardson Donaldson. His father worked for the Union Pacific Railroad, and his mother was a high school principal. He was youngest in a family of three, two boys and one girl. Donaldson was a painter, an art historian, a scholar, an educator, and a proponent of revolutionary and creative Afrocentric thought. Importantly, he was a relevant figure in the Black arts movement in Chicago. Donaldson was a founding member of OBAC (Organization of Black American Culture), and a founding member of AFRICOBRA (African Commune of Bad Relevant Artists), both in Chicago. At Northwestern University, he devised the unprecedented CONFABA (Conference on the Functional Aspects of Black Art), a landmark event that defined Black art in the canon of American art history. He was chair of the Department of Art and dean of the College of Fine Arts at Howard University, Washington, DC. In 1977, Donaldson was director of the North American Zone of FESTAC (Second World Black and African Festival of Arts and Culture), in Lagos, Nigeria. He served on the board of the National Center for Afro-American Artists and was vice president of the Barns Foundation. He has exhibited in museums and galleries worldwide, including the Brooklyn Museum, New York; Crystal Bridges Museum of American Art, Arkansas; the Broad, Los Angeles; Miami Museum of Contemporary Art, North Miami; Museum of Contemporary Art, Chicago; Hood Museum, Dartmouth College, New Hampshire; FESTAC, Theatre Gallery, Lagos, Nigeria; Tate Modern in London; and in AFRICOBRA *Nation Time* at the 2019 Venice Biennale. His work is in the collections of major museums, nationally and internationally.

Jae Jarrell. Education: School of the Art Institute of Chicago; advanced graduate studies in art, Howard University, Washington, DC; textile design, Parson New School of Art, New York, New York; magna cum laude, and on the Dean's List, Howard University, BFA; Bowling Green State University, Bowling Green, Ohio.

Jae was born Elaine Annette Johnson in 1935 in Cleveland, Ohio, to Roscoe Hamlin and Adelyn Koiner Johnson. Her father was a chauffeur for a private girl's school and for the affluent. Her mother was a housewife who had an interest in collecting antiques, fine china, glassware, and vintage clothes. Jae was born into a bloodline of tailors, inherited from her grandfather Robert S. Koiner. She is the youngest in a family of five, three boys and two girls. Her early interest in art, from second to twelfth grade, was in music. At age eleven she played in a piano quartet. She changed instruments from piano to string bass and performed in Patrick Henry Junior High and Glenville High School orchestras. She also played string bass in the All City Symphony Orchestra at age eighteen at Masonic Hall in Cleveland, Ohio. In Chicago, she owned Jae of Hyde Park, a one-of-a-kind boutique for women, which included mailorder service; Male Bag, men's clothing; and Tadpole Togs, a boutique for toddlers. She was a founding member of AFRICOBRA. Jae was chair and director of Creative Modern Dress and Fashion for FESTAC, in Lagos, Nigeria. In Athens, Georgia, she designed educational wood toys for Tadpole Industries, which later expanded to Tadpole Toys and Hobby Center, a company created by her and her husband, Wadsworth. Jae taught art in private schools: at Athens Academy, Athens, Georgia, and at the Lovett School, Atlanta. In Atlanta, Jae owned Say Cheese Bakery and worked in Jae Jarrell Studio Workshop–Fashion Design. In New York City, she owned Jae Jarrell Vintage Menswear and Collectibles in Tribeca, which also carried period furniture. Her clients were fashionable men interested in period furniture and fashions, and she supplied period fashions for the theater and movie industry. Jae has exhibited in museums and galleries nationally and internationally, including the Brooklyn Museum, New York; Cleveland Museum, Ohio; Crystal Bridges Museum of American Art, Arkansas; the Broad, Los Angeles; Miami Museum of Contemporary, North Miami; Museum of Contemporary Art, Chicago; Hood Museum, Dartmouth College, New Hampshire; Smart Museum of Art, Chicago; FESTAC, City Hall, Lagos, Nigeria; Tate Modern in London; and in AFRICOBRA *Nation Time*, at the 2019 Venice Biennale. Her work is in the collections of major museums, nationally and internationally.

Barbara Jones-Hogu. Education: Illinois Institute of Design and Technology, Chicago, MS; School of the Art institute of Chicago, BFA; Howard University, Washington, DC, BA.

Barbara Jean Jones was born in Chicago, Illinois, in 1938 to William and Thelma Louise Jackson Jones. Her father owned an ice company along with his brothers. Her mother was a keypunch operator, and later a tax examiner. Barbara was oldest in a family of two, one girl and one boy. Her introduction and influence in art derived from comic books. She devised a language of art influenced by the cartoon font. As a young girl her allowance was one dollar per week, and she spent it all on comic books. She entered Saturday classes at the School of the Art Institute of Chicago at an early age, and students mentioned that her art resembled cartoons. In graduate school and beyond, Barbara extensively explored the serigraphy process and carved her signature in that medium. She was a member of OBAC and painted the Theater section on the *Wall of Respect*. She was also a founding member of AFRICOBRA. She was an early proponent of including politics in her art. Barbara addressed racism and the dilemma of African Americans in the United States. She was an educator in public schools in Chicago and in Washington, DC, as well as at the School of the Art Institute of Chicago, Northeastern Illinois University, and Malcolm X College in Chicago. Barbara has exhibited in museums and galleries nationally and internationally, including Brooklyn Museum, New York; Crystal Bridges Museum of American Art, Arkansas; the Broad, Los Angeles; Miami Museum of Contemporary Art, North Miami; Museum of Contemporary Art, Chicago; Hood Museum, Dartmouth College, New Hampshire; Tate Modern in London; and in AFRICOBRA *Nation Time*, at the 2019 Venice Biennale. Her work is in major museum collections, nationally and internationally.

Wadsworth Aikens Jarrell. Education: Howard University, Washington, DC, MFA; School of the Art Institute of Chicago, diploma; Ray Vogue School of Art, Chicago.

Wadsworth Aikens Jarrell was born in 1929 in Albany, Georgia, to Solomon Marcus and Tabitha Aikens Jarrell. His father owned a business, S. M. Jarrell Furniture Shop. Jarrell's father was a furniture maker, a finisher, an upholsterer, and an antique dealer. His mother was a housewife, a tailor, and a quilt maker. Wadsworth is the youngest of a family of six, four boys and two girls. His parents purchased twenty-eight acres of rural land five miles outside the city of Athens, Georgia. There, his father and oldest brother, Venus Alvin, built the family eight-room home. Wadsworth's interest in art derived from drawing scenes, the latest cars, and creating his own comic strip. In grammar school, he made scenes for plays and experimented with watercolor. He continued making art in high school. After high school he was drafted into the US Army, where he continued making art as company artist. In Chicago, he was a member of OBAC and painted the Rhythm and Blues section on the *Wall of Respect*. Additionally, he was a founding member of AFRICOBRA. Jarrell exhibited work and participated in FESTAC, in 1977, in Lagos, Nigeria. He was a professor of art at Howard University, Washington, DC; the University of Georgia in Athens; and Spelman College in Atlanta. He has exhibited extensively in national and international museums and galleries and is the recipient of important commissions and awards. He has exhibited at the Brooklyn Museum, New York; Detroit Institute of Art, Detroit; Crystal Bridges Museum of American Art, Arkansas; the Broad, Los Angeles; Cleveland Museum of Art, Ohio; Philadelphia Museum of Art, Pennsylvania; Museum of Contemporary Art, Chicago; FESTAC, Theatre Gallery, Lagos, Nigeria; Miami Museum of Contemporary Art, North Miami; the Tate Modern in London; and in AFRICOBRA *Nation Time*, at the 2019 Venice Biennale. His art is in the collections of numerous major museums, libraries, educational institutions, and corporations.

Gerald Williams. Education: Chicago State University, BA; Howard University, Washington, DC, MFA.

Gerald Williams was born in 1941 in Chicago, Illinois, to Abner and Alleane Williams. His father worked at US Steel Corporation as first helper, which is the final step in the quality-control process in making steel. He was the first African American to hold that position. Gerald's mother was a housewife who was active in community affairs: president of the PTA, on the board of directors of TWO (The Woodlawn Organization), and active in church affairs. Gerald was the eighth born in a family of twelve. He was the first male member in his family to finish high school, and the first family member to finish college. He grew up in Woodlawn in a neighborhood where Gwendolyn Brooks lived across the street from the family house, and he and Emmett Till attended the same grammar school. He took a circuitous route to becoming an artist. As a business major at Roosevelt University, he spent considerable time at the Art Institute of Chicago Galleries and saw a Gauguin retrospective exhibition that motivated him to draw and paint. He took formal evening art classes at the School of the Art Institute of Chicago, and art classes under Seymour Rosofsky at Chicago City College. His sister Jean was an amateur painter who also influenced him. In the US Air Force in Okinawa, Gerald was allowed to use a storage building for a studio. He became a founding member of AFRICOBRA in 1968 in Chicago. His work was exhibited, and he was a participant in FESTAC in 1977, in Lagos, Nigeria. He taught in public schools in Chicago and in Washington, DC. He joined the Peace Corps and worked at the Jacaranda School for the Mentally Handicapped in Nairobi, Kenya. He worked in Japan for five years as arts and crafts director, as well as in Italy and in the Portuguese Azores. Gerald has exhibited in museums and galleries nationally and internationally, including Brooklyn Museum, New York; Crystal Bridges Museum of American Art, Arkansas; Museum of Contemporary Art, Chicago; the Broad, Los Angeles; Smart Museum of Art, Chicago; Miami Museum of Contemporary Art, North Miami; FESTAC, Theatre Gallery, Lagos, Nigeria; Tate Modern in London; and in AFRICOBRA *Nation Time*, at the 2019 Venice Biennale. His work is in major museum collections nationally and internationally.

Napoleon Jones-Henderson. Education: American Artists and Student Center at Sorbonne in Paris, France; School of the Art Institute of Chicago, BFA; Northern Illinois University, Dekalb, BA; Mount Royal School of Art, Baltimore, Maryland, MFA.

Napoleon Jones-Henderson was born in 1944 in Chicago, Illinois, to Louis and Maxine Washington Henderson. His father was in and out of the veteran's hospital, suffering from a condition contracted in World War II. Today, it would be diagnosed as PTSD (post-traumatic stress disorder). His mother was a loving stay-at-home mom. Napoleon was the oldest in a family of twelve, seven boys and five girls. At a young age his interest was in art. In grammar school he was chosen to make backgrounds for school plays and other events. In Carver High School he was exposed to art in exhibitions at the South Side Community Art Center and had the opportunity to meet established visual and performing artists. Additionally, in high school, his teacher Helen Joyner was very influential in guiding his career in weaving. Napoleon became a member of African Cobra in 1969. He was the recipient of a traveling fellowship from the School of the Art Institute of Chicago, and he exhibited his work and participated in FESTAC, in Lagos, Nigeria. He was a professor of art in Malcolm X College in Chicago; Massachusetts College of Art and Emerson College, both in Boston, Massachusetts; and Benedict College in Columbia, South Carolina. Napoleon has been an artist-in-residence and has numerous commissions in the New England area and in the state of Florida. Napoleon has exhibited nationally and internationally in the Logan Center, Chicago; DuSable Museum of African American History, Chicago; the Studio Museum in Harlem, New York; Museum of the National Center of Afro-American Artists, Boston; Langston Hughes Center for Visual and Performing Arts, Buffalo, New York; New York State Museum, Albany, New York; Everson Museum of Art, Syracuse, New York; Miami Contemporary Museum of Art, North Miami; and in AFRICOBRA *Nation Time* at the 2019 Venice Biennale. His work is in the collections of major museums, nationally and internationally.

Nelson Stevens. Education: advertising design, Mohawk Valley Technical Institute, Utica, New York, AAS; University of Ohio, Athens, BFA; Kent State University, Kent, Ohio, MFA.

Nelson Stevens was born in 1938 to Nelson Lowell and Dorothy Edwards Stevens. His father was born in Rochester, New York, and his mother was born in Harlem, New York. His parents met while attending a dance at the Savoy Ballroom in Harlem, dancing to the music of the famous Chick Webb band. His father was a refrigerator repairman, and his mother was a telephone operator. Nelson is the oldest in a family of two, one boy and one girl. He taught in the Cleveland public school system and as a professor of art in Northern Illinois University, Dekalb, and at the University of Massachusetts at Amherst. He became a member of African Cobra in 1969. He exhibited his work and participated in FESTAC, in Lagos, Nigeria. As a professor of art at the University of Massachusetts, he directed thirty murals and created the Centennial Mural at Tuskegee College in Tuskegee, Alabama. At the University of Massachusetts, Nelson was director of *Drum* magazine and created an annual calendar containing art of twelve artists, entitled *In Service of the Lord*. Nelson has exhibited nationally and internationally, in Brooklyn Museum, New York; Crystal Bridges Museum of American Art, Arkansas; Studio Museum in Harlem, New York; Museum of Contemporary Art, Chicago; the Broad, Los Angeles; Miami Museum of Contemporary Art, North Miami; FESTAC, Theatre Gallery, Lagos, Nigeria; Tate Modern in London; and in AFRICOBRA *Nation Time* at the 2019 Venice Biennale. His work is in major museum collections.

Carolyn Mims Lawrence. Education: University of Texas, Austin, BFA; Illinois Institute of Design and Technology, Chicago, MS.

Carolyn Mims Lawrence was born in 1940 in Prairie View, Texas, to Alfred Joseph and Elizabeth Elaine Mims. She grew up in Houston, Texas. Carolyn was born into a family of educators as the oldest of three girls. Her father was a professor of engineering at Texas Southern University in Houston, and he also played piano in a jazz quartet in college. Her mother taught art in the public school system in Texas. Art and music had a prominent presence in their household. Her mother's sister Lenora Louise Backer played piano in a jazz group in Chicago in the 1950s. In 1967, Carolyn joined OBAC and painted the Dance section on the *Wall of Respect*. Carolyn joined African Cobra in 1969. She is a retired educator that taught in public schools in Indiana and in Chicago. At Kenwood Academy in Chicago, she was chair of the Art Department. She exhibited extensively with AFRICOBRA, and in 2008, one of her silkscreen prints, *Uphold Your Men*, sold at a premium price in Swan Auctions in New York. Carolyn has exhibited nationally and internationally, including in the Brooklyn Museum, New York; Crystal Bridges Museum of American Art, Arkansas; Museum of Contemporary Art, Chicago; the Broad, Los Angeles; the Smart Museum of Art, Chicago; Miami Museum of Contemporary Art, North Miami; and the Tate Modern in London. Her work is in major museum collections.

Sherman Beck. Education: Loyola University, Chicago; School of the Art Institute of Chicago; University of Illinois, Chicago, BFA.

Sherman Beck was born in Chicago, Illinois, to Owens and Lenora Beck. His father worked for the US Post Office driving a semitrailer mail truck. His mother was basically a housewife but worked as a nurse's aide and part time as a real estate agent. He was the second born into a family of three, two boys and one girl. He was the recipient of a one-year scholarship to Loyola University. Sherman was drafted into the US Army, and after his discharge, he entered the University of Illinois at Circle Campus in Chicago, majoring in studio art. He became a member of African Cobra in 1970. Beck was an educator teaching in the public school system in Chicago, mainly Dunbar High School. While performing his teaching duties, he was a freelance artist, illustrating in magazines, Afro-American publishing, *Ebony Jr.*, and *Black World.* He regularly exhibits his art in galleries and museums. He has exhibited nationally, including at the Studio Museum in Harlem, New York; Museum of the National Center for Afro-American Artists, Boston; Smart Museum, Chicago, DuSable Museum of African American History, Chicago, and Miami Museum of Contemporary Art, North Miami.

Omar Lama. Education: Kennedy King College, Chicago, Chicago State University.

Omar Lama was born John Porter in 1942 in Halls, Tennessee, to Robert and Hattie Porter. His father worked in factories, played blues guitar, and worked as a sign painter. His mother was a domestic worker. Omar was the second born in a family of three, two girls and one boy. His interest in art came from his father, who in addition to sign painting made drawings and paintings. As a youngster he enrolled in the Famous Artists correspondence course. At age thirteen, he won a scholarship in art for juniors from the Chicago Boys Club to the School of Art Institute of Chicago. He joined African Cobra in 1970. Lama illustrated books for Haki Madhubuti at Third World Press, and for books at Broadside Press in Detroit, Michigan. He has exhibited nationally at the Studio Museum in Harlem, New York; the National Center of Afro-American Artists, Boston; DuSable Museum of African American History, Chicago; Smart Museum, Chicago; and Miami Museum of Contemporary Art, North Miami.

Howard Raymond Mallory Jr. Education: Illinois Institute of Design and Technology, Chicago; School of the Art Institute of Chicago; Western Texas College, Snyder.

Howard Mallory Jr. was born in 1930 in Chicago, Illinois, to Howard Raymond, and Marketta Mallory. His father was an electrician, and his mother graduated with a law degree from John Marshall Law School in Chicago. Mallory was the oldest of two boys. He was an educator as a sculptor and ceramist. He taught ceramics for the City of Chicago, at the Parkway Community House, and at the Field House in Washington Park. He became a member of AFRICOBRA in 1971. Mallory was active as an exhibitor in exhibitions with AFRICOBRA for four years, and in museums, galleries, and venues in the Chicago area and in adjoining states, Indiana, Wisconsin, and Iowa. After the loss of his eyesight, his sculpture soared to the heights. His work then embodied the power and attitude of African sculpture. The masks and walking canes he created captured the spirituality of the Dogon of Mali in West Africa. He created an outdoor installation entitled *The Freedom Train.* Mallory has exhibited nationally at the Studio Museum in Harlem, New York; the National Center of Afro-American Artists, Boston; Brooklyn Museum, New York; and the Smart Museum of Art, Chicago. His work is in the collections of major museums.

Franklin Smith. Education: University of Illinois, Champlain, BFA; Howard University, Washington, DC, MFA.

Frank Smith was born in 1939 in Chicago, Illinois, to Warren and Dorothea Smith. He was born into a musical and artistic family. Both sides of the family contained musicians and visual artists. His father was born into a family of thirteen, and they all were musicians. Frank's mother's cousin Quinella Watson Hathaway was among the first African Americans to attend the School of the Art Institute of Chicago. His mother's cousin Alonzo Watson was a soldier in the Abraham Lincoln Brigade in the Spanish American War and was also a visual artist. Frank is the youngest and was born into a family of two, both boys. His brother, Warren Jr., is a highly celebrated drummer, who played in MBoom, directed by the late consummate drummer Max Roach. Frank was an educator as well. He taught in the Chicago and New York public school systems, and he was a professor of art for many years at Howard University in Washington, DC. He became a member of AFRICOBRA in 1972. In 1977, he participated and exhibited in FESTAC, in Lagos, Nigeria. He was the recipient of the artist-in-residence at Western High School from the DC Commission on the Arts. He has exhibited extensively in museums and galleries nationally and internationally, and he has won awards for numerous commissions in Washington, DC, and surrounding counties. Frank has exhibited at the Studio Museum in Harlem, New York; the National Center of Afro-American Artists, Boston; Brooklyn Museum, New York; Smart Museum, Chicago; DuSable Museum of African American History, Chicago; and at FESTAC, Theatre Gallery, Lagos, Nigeria. His work is in the collections of major museums.

Berry, Edwin, 26
Biggers, John, 49, 124
Bilbo, Theodore G., 112
Billy Wright Band, 21
Birmingham, Alabama, 51
black (color) in Black art, 84
Black aesthetic, aesthetics, 17, 206, 236;
 COBRA/AFRICOBRA and, 102, 133,
 159, 171, 197, 207; creation of, 90;
 defining, 242; Donaldson and, 41, 91–
 107, 114; era of, 204; human values as
 foundation for, 124; paradigm for, 4.
 See also aesthetic, aesthetics: African
 American and Black
Black American renaissance, 37–38
Black art and culture, 14, 38, 41, 73,
 88, 96, 124, 243; AFRICOBRA and,
 197; blackness of, 123; defining, 242;
 Donaldson on, 47–48, 53; exhibits of,
 203; history of, 124
Black artists, xxi, 73, 74, 84, 96, 111–12,
 121; acceptable art and, 92; Black
 memorabilia and, 85; in Chicago,
 30, 77; CONFABA and, xxiii, 124; in
 mainstream galleries and museums,
 207; new Black aesthetic and, 41;
 in 1960s, 52; OBAC workshop of, 53;
 protest art and, 236
Black Arts movement, 1, 37, 39, 237;
 Malcolm X and, 30; origins of, 53;
 Wall of Respect and, 59
Black Belt (Chicago), 55
Blackburn, Darlene, 36, 122; portrayed
 on *Wall of Respect*, 60
Black consciousness, 28, 29, 59, 168,
 169, 188, 241
Black ethnicity in art of Black artists,
 42–43
Black Experience, Black artists and, 92
Black Expo (Amphitheater, Chicago):
 AFRICOBRA exhibits in, 153, 159, 163,
 205
Black Family: COBRA's first exhibition
 and, 110; strong image of, 100–104.
 See also family and family unity
Black Family (Wadsworth Jarrell, 1968),
 104, *106f*

Black image, 100
"Black is Beautiful," 10, 52, 92, 102,
 116, 181, 241; in Wadsworth Jarrell's
 Revolutionary, 204
Black memorabilia, 84–85, 134
Black men, negative images of, 101
Black Muslims, 30; self-reliance
 philosophy of, 42
Black Nationalism, 60; OBAC and,
 52–53; *Wall of Respect* and, 51
Blackness, 186; in AFRICOBRA II, 202–3;
 of Black art, 123; colors of, 132; as
 elegant, 42; *Wall of Respect* and, 74
Black Panther Party for Self-Defense,
 99; Newton and, 75, 107, 168;
 in Wadsworth Jarrell's *Liberation
 Soldiers*, 229
Black people: AFRICOBRA art and,
 202–3; as American citizens, 7;
 in Chicago, 19–39; as colorful
 people, 97; encoded lifestyle of, 12;
 humanism of, xvii; interiority of, 12;
 lifestyles of, xviii; Mallory on, 229;
 political awareness of, 110; resolve of,
 83; self-pride of, 10; television and,
 107; values of, 89
"Black Power," 71, 92, 118, 242
Black Power movement, 37, 39, 60,
 168, 188; AFRICOBRA and, xxi–xxii,
 179, 237; artists and, xxii; pro-Black
 revolutionary art movement and, 1;
 Wall of Respect and, 51
Black pride, 104, 212; cultural, 49; *Wall
 of Respect* and, 67
Black Pride (WGN program), 104
Black Prince (Wadsworth Jarrell), xxi,
 xxii, 202
Black Repertory Theater (Harlem): at
 AFRICOBRA I opening, 53, 135–36
Black Repertory Theater (St. Louis), 38
Black revolution, 5, 37, 193, 206; *Wall
 of Respect* and, 51. *See also* revolution,
 revolutionaries
Blacks, as term, 2, 241
Black Sensibility, 92
Black Stone Rangers gang, 109, 110
Black studies, 29, 38, 109, 242

Cohen, Mickey, 66

Cohran, Phil, 36, *50f, 51f,* 111

COINTELPRO (Counterintelligence Program) of FBI, 65–66

Colbert, Herbert, 58

Cole, Kevin: as AFRICOBRA member, 240

Coleman, Floyd, 39, 87, 123, 242

Coleman, Ornette, 5, 81, 87; portrayed on *Wall of Respect,* 59

collage, 4, 15, *103f,* 210, 229

Collard, Allan, 111

collectives: AFRICOBRA as artists', 237; characteristics of, 86; creation of Black artists', 42, 47, 48, 97

collectivism, 27

color, colors, xvii, 4, 16, 83, 97–98; AFRICOBRA and, 121, 130; aggressive use of, 110; Donaldson and, 193, 212; in Howard's *From These Roots,* 229, 235; in Lawrence's *Legacy,* 228; open, xvii, 82; in Stevens's works, 188; vivid, 3, 16, 82; in Wadsworth Jarrell's *Liberation Soldiers,* 210. *See also* Cool Ade colors

Coltrane, John "Trane," 47, 87, 102; portrayed on *Wall of Respect,* 60

Columbia College (Chicago), 77, 243

Columbian Exposition (1893), 75–76

communist ideology, 29

community: African American, 134; Black control of own, 110; murals and, 49; *Wall of Respect* and, 58, 67, 68, 69, 70–71

Compared to What: I Am Better Than Those Motherfuckers and They Know It (Wadsworth Jarrell, 1969), 114, *115f,* 116

CONFABA (Conference on the Functional Aspects of Black Art), 121, 122–26; Donaldson and, xxii–xxiii, 244; participants in, 123

Conference on the Functional Aspects of Black Art. *See* CONFABA

conjure men, 14

Cool Ade colors, 107, 204, 241; AFRICOBRA II walls painted in, 197;

as COBRA/AFRICOBRA principle, xvii, 98, 101, 130, 132; Donaldson and, 157, 204; at Studio Museum, 135, 177; Wadsworth Jarrell and, 116, 186, 205, 229; Williams and, 97–98, 217

co-option of African American culture, 13

Cornell University, 109

Cortor, Eldzier, 30

Count Basie Band, 20

Cowans, Adger: as AFRICOBRA member, 240

Cowans, William, 10

Cowherd, Darryl, 52; photography of, 60, 61

Crosby, Israel, 112

Crudup, Arthur "Big Boy," 112

cubists, 28, 89

Cullen, Countee, 30

cultural pride: AFRICOBRA and, xxii

Cunningham, Lucile, 64

Dahomey, 222

Daley, Richard, 52, 70

Daley Plaza (Chicago), 93

Dameron, Tadd, 21

dance: African, xviii; African American, 33; in Chicago, 20, 21, 36; tap, 111; in *Wall of Respect,* 64

Daniels, Bill, 36

Daniels, Mary, 36

Darlene Blackburn Dance Troupe, 36

Darrow, Clarence, 76

dashiki, 102

Davis, Angela, 157, 217; painted by Wadsworth Jarrell, 181, 201, 203, 206

Davis, Gene, 93–94

Davis, Miles, 21, 47; portrayed on *Wall of Respect,* 59

Davis, Ossie, 201; eulogizes Malcolm X, 30, 32, 186; portrayed on *Wall of Respect,* 60

Davis, Sammy, Jr., 20

DeCarava, Roy, 135

decolonization, 193

Dee, Ruby: portrayed on *Wall of Respect,* 60

Presley, Elvis, 112

Price, Leontyne, 97

printmaking, printmakers: COBRA/
AFRICOBRA and, 99, 119, 164, *165f,
166f, 167f, 177;* grant funding for,
92; Stovall as, 172; Wadsworth Jarrell
as, 15

prints of COBRA/AFRICOBRA artwork,
100, 172, 174, 176–77

programmatic, as AFRICOBRA principle,
xviii, 127

propaganda, 212–13

protests and marches, 89; for African
American equality, 51; in Chicago,
32, 52

publicity, for *AFRICOBRA I,* 129

Pyatt, Okoe, 153

Raby, Al, 109

race and ethnicity: purity of, 216; racial
inequality and, 26; racial nationalism
and, 237

racism: artistic commentary on,
83–84; in Chicago, 19, 25, 33; COBRA
members' experiences of, 88;
Donaldson on, 48; epithets and, 25–
26; overt, 99; racial discrimination
and, 52; racial slurs and, 25–26;
racial stereotypes and, 84–85, 101;
in radio, 112; segregation and, 19, 25,
26, 30, 99

Rackley, Alex, 168

radio, 112; at Howard University, 197,
201

Rahman, Abdul, 153

Rainbow Sign Gallery, 172

Rainey, Ma (Gertrude Pridgett), 116

RAM (Revolutionary Action Movement),
99

Rand, Sally, 21

Rawls, Lou, 60

Ray Vogue School of Art: Wadsworth
Jarrell attends, 24

Reagon, Bernice, 123

realism, as COBRA principle, 87

Redding, Otis, 202

Reed, Jimmy, 21

Reid, Edsel, 123

Reid, Opie, 76

Reid, Shirley Woodson, 123

religion: on *Wall of Respect,* 60, 64

reparations, 7

repetition, in African art, 93

resistance: of African Americans
against injustice, 27–28; AFRICOBRA
and, xxii; Black artists and, 52; of
Black slaves, 101–2, 259n8

revolution, revolutionaries, 36; COBRA
members and, 101, 113; Donaldson
on, 97, 118, 159; grants and, 92; as
terms, 51; Wadsworth Jarrell as, xxi,
30, 32; *Wall of Respect* and, 74

revolutionary art: COBRA and, 80;
Donaldson on, 41; movement for,
75, 97

Revolutionary Suit (Bullet Belt Suit) (Jae
Jarrell, 1970), xxii, 136, *144f,* 163–64,
181, 203

Revolutionary (Wadsworth Jarrell, 1971),
xxii, 213; reviews of, 202–4, 206;
Richard and, 202–4

rhythm, 216; in African aesthetics, 133;
AFRICOBRA and, 17; complexity of,
241; in paintings, 83

rhythm and blues: on *Wall of Respect,*
60, 61, 64, 65, 68

Richard, Paul, on AFRICOBRA art,
201–4, 205, 212–13

Richards, Josephus, 123

Ricks, George, 52

Rickson, Gary, 244

Riley, Bridget: op art of, 3, *4f*

riots, 51; in Chicago, *35f,* 117; civil
rights, 30; after King's assassination,
75; race, 33, 117

Rivers, Conrad Kent, 52

Roach, Max, 21; portrayed on *Wall of
Respect,* 59

Roberts, Malkia, 123, 125

Robinson, Bill, 111

Robinson, Smokey: portrayed on *Wall of
Respect,* 60

Rochester, New York: AFRICOBRA
exhibit in, 205

"Soul," 92
South Africa, South Africans, 6, 118,
    228
South Carolina, 13
southern United States: Black culture
    of, 14; COBRA members from, 14;
    migration of African Americans
    from, 27; spirituality and magic in,
    13–14
South Pacific, aesthetics of, 213
South Side Community Art Center
    (Chicago), 209–10
South Side of Chicago, 20, 168; riots in,
    33, 117
space: intuitive, 5, 98; metaphysical, 12;
    negative, xix
Spellman, A. B., 123
Spelman College: Wadsworth Jarrell
    teaches at, 14
spirituality and occultism, African
    American, 13–14
sports: on *Wall of Respect*, 59, 61, 65
Spriggs, Edward, *44f*, 180, 207;
    AFRICOBRA and, 16–17, 129–30, 171,
    197, 205, 236; AFRICOBRA II and, 177,
    179; as director of Studio Museum,
    129, 135, 244
State Museum of New York (Albany),
    AFRICOBRA exhibit at, 205
statesmen: on *Wall of Respect*, 61,
    68–69
Steinberg, Leo, 8
Stennis, John C., 112
Stevens, Nelson, xxii, 172, 174, 204,
    207, 244; AFRICOBRA I and, *131f*,
    136; AFRICOBRA II and, 188, *190–91f*;
    AFRICOBRA III and, 211, 216–17; *After
    She Removed Her Street Disguise*
    (1973), 216, 217, *220f*; biography of,
    267–68; in Boston, 243–44; *The
    Brother Who Knows* (1969), 119, *120f*,
    121; COBRA/AFRICOBRA and, 121,
    132, 240; CONFABA and, 123, 125; *A
    Different Kind of Man* (1970), 136,
    145f; on Donaldson, 43; *Jihad*, 136;
    lives in Massachusetts, 212; *Nina*
    (1972), 188, *191f*; *Oneness* (1972), 213,
    214f, 216; as professor at Northern
    Illinois University, 205; *Spirit Sister*
    (1971), 180, 188, 190; students of,
    159; *Together*, 216–17; *Trilogy: From
    Assimilation to Identity* (1970), 132,
    136, *146–47f*; *Uhuru* (1971), 216, *221f*;
    Unite, 188; *Wholy*, 188
Sticks and Stones (Donaldson's shop),
    43
Stout, Renee: as AFRICOBRA member,
    240
Stovall, Lou, 172
Stubblefield, John, 111
Studio Museum (Harlem), 16, *44f*,
    128, 244; AFRICOBRA artists at,
    135; AFRICOBRA I at, 127, 129;
    AFRICOBRA II at, 171, 177
style, confluence of, 15–16
Sullivan, Louis, 76
Sullivan, Maxine, 48
Sunbeam Corporation, 207
Sun Ra, 81
superiority of Black blues musicians,
    116–17
Supremes, the 58
Swahili, 153
swastika, 84
Sweden, 15
swing music, 112
symbolism, symbols: in art, 84; of *Wall
    of Respect*, 70–74
symmetry, free: as AFRICOBRA
    principle, xviii, 5, 127
Syracuse, New York: AFRICOBRA exhibit
    in, 205

tapestries by Napoleon Henderson, 137,
    188, 192, *195f*, 223
Taylor, Ann, 123
Teer, Barbara Ann, 38, 124
television: AFRICOBRA II on, 204–5;
    COBRA on, 104, 107; *Like It Is* on,
    65–66; *Outlaw Gangsters* on, 66
Tennessee State University, 89
Texas, 38
theater: on *Wall of Respect*, 60, 61
Third World Press, 38